HSBA Handbook on Ship Finance

Orestis Schinas • Carsten Grau • Max Johns
Editors

HSBA Handbook on Ship Finance

Springer

Editors
Orestis Schinas
Hamburg School of Business Administration
Hamburg
Germany

Carsten Grau
L2C
Hamburg
Germany

Max Johns
German Shipowners' Association
Hamburg
Germany

ISBN 978-3-662-43409-3 ISBN 978-3-662-43410-9 (eBook)
DOI 10.1007/978-3-662-43410-9
Springer Heidelberg New York Dordrecht London

Library of Congress Control Number: 2014955654

Printed on acid-free paper

Springer is part of Springer Science+Business Media (www.springer.com)

To our daughters...

Foreword

In Hamburg, an economy without shipping is unthinkable. Port and shipping companies as well as the numerous businesses that provide shipping-related services form one of the central pillars on which the business location of Hamburg is based. In addition, Hamburg is one of the world's leading financial hubs for ship finance, though the excellent prospects up until 2008 have deteriorated somewhat in the wake of the shipping crisis. This crisis on the shipping markets and the huge uncertainties in the field of ship finance demonstrate the vulnerability of the maritime industry and the need to come up with new ideas and concepts to overcome these challenges. The high level of local demand combined with many years of experience creates a solid foundation for this important industry. The maritime finance environment is currently characterized by tighter regulatory requirements, limited lending, and unsettled investors. The once-common adequate supply of credit for the shipping industry no longer applies. As a result, in future we will need to tap alternative sources of capital and different investors for the maritime industry. Taking the most recent developments into account, this book, *HSBA Handbook on Ship Finance*, presents ideas and practical solutions to meet the current and future requirements placed on the maritime finance industry. The renowned authors are geared both to academia and to decision-makers in industry, thus making a special contribution to the exchange of theoretical and practical knowledge.

I wish you stimulating reading.

Hamburg, Germany
November 2014

Hans-Jörg Schmidt-Trenz

Preface

This book aims to present fresh ideas and concepts to the maritime and ship financing community. It is not a textbook or a collection of papers that reflect pure academic views but an anthology of viewpoints of experts and a compilation of solutions employed by decision-makers and specialists in order to tackle complicated market and financial conditions. The topics and subjects considered demonstrate also the innovative character of this effort.

This book is not solely written for graduate students; it aims to address some of the needs of professionals who deal daily with the riddles and the puzzles of financing ships either as lenders or as borrowers or as advisors. To this respect, the reader must have a good understanding of the fundamentals before reading these texts, as some of the topics might be considered as "advanced". The editors strived to collect contributions that balance the academic interests and the professional needs and reflect the recent developments, as all contributions are submitted in late 2012 until mid-2013. The editorial team believes a book like this should not distinguish too strongly between those readers working in the industry and those pursuing academic goals because ship finance is a multidisciplinary and complex subject often driven by the practicalities of the markets. There is a vital interchange of ideas and concepts between the praxis and the theory that advances the state of the art in this field. Ship finance is still a relatively new field and very little literature exists. Theory and practice is far from settled, it evolves very dynamically.

In view also of the above, the editorial team and the authors endeavored to discuss the development and the breakthroughs of the sector in stand-alone contributions, instead of recycling or refining fundamentals and information provided, exhaustively and in a stricter, more scientific way in other textbooks. As a result, the reader can approach the topic of his or her interest without necessarily reading all other chapters or parts of this book. Nevertheless, the editors consider that the readers could gain more when reading the whole part, i.e. a collection of relevant contributions, rather than limiting their attentiveness to a single text.

This book consists of six distinct parts. The first part revisits some of the fundamentals of conventional ship financing. Lemper and Tasto provide an analysis of the market cycles and offer some insights on demystifying the statistics and signals of the market. Then Schinas and Kewitsch summarize the key concept on risk management and of financial assessment of ship loans. This part concludes with the contribution of Scholl and Otto, who thoroughly analyze the loan agreements from a legal point of view.

The second part of this book focuses on equity financing. Johns and Sturm provide a thorough analysis of the KG system that dominated the German market for many years and is currently under revision if not under opprobrium, due to the oversupply and low (if not negative) returns of recent investments. Markwardt and Schröder complete this subject with their contribution on the KG, focusing on the recent Alternative Investment Fund Managers Directive (AIFMD) as well as its impact on private equity companies. This part could not be completed without the contribution of von Oldershausen on the Norwegian KS system, an equity structure scheme similar but not identical to the German KG model. Anagnostara and Sigalas provide interesting insight and views on this issue presenting the case of Seanergy divulging also an approach of capping foreign capital markets; Krutemaier's contribution on the case of HCI offers additionally an understanding of equity financing from a German perspective.

The third part focuses on the issue of pricing of assets. Myer presents concisely the Long Term Asset Value (LTAV), a Hamburg ship evaluation standard, which takes into account not only the present value but also the discounted value of expected future revenues. On the other hand, Mietzner presents a very innovative approach, the Qualitative Adjusted and Audited Algebraic Estimation on the basis of Last Done (QAAELD) that takes into account the age, the current market asset valuations among other parameters. Both approaches attract the interest not only of academics but also of practitioners, as their application can affect the balance sheet of both lenders and borrowers, and impact the expectations and the endurance of the market, especially when freight-rates are weak.

The fourth part of the book is devoted on the institutional framework and its impact on ship finance. Alexandropoulou is presenting the framework of ship finance in Greece, a country with well-established and mature conditions for maritime ventures. On the other hand, Atamer is presenting the new Turkish legal framework, which uncovers and enlightens on the intention of the Turkish administration to facilitate more maritime ventures in the future. This part concludes with the analysis of Haase on the double tax treaties and the practical problems related to the OECD Model Convention.

The fifth part compiles current approaches to commonly faced problems, such as restructuring, risk management as well as alternative ways to manage and finance tonnage. Experts share their experiences and provide solutions and ideas that may trigger innovative thinking and unprecedented approaches in ship finance. Clausius examines and provides insights into the leasing structures; examples and interesting data demystify the complex leasing schemes. Papachristidis and Papachristidis outline the benefits of shipping pools, present model schemes, and convey experiences and knowledge gained from past projects. Lammerskötter discusses the challenges of restructuring through the outstanding example of the CSAV. Miller, Cassels, Craig, Hale, Höth, Kroll, Lowe, Miller, Schöne and Ward outline the tools for financial risk management with a focus on the container markets in their extended work that is also full with examples and information for hands-on practitioners. This chapter concludes with the analysis of Nijoe on Islamic finance, a source of finance that could bridge some of the gaps in many maritime ventures.

The last part of this book focuses on services closely related to ship finance. Bornozis explores and analyzes the issue of investor relations and its role in effective corporate communications, a topic of crucial importance for public companies or for ventures that involve regulated investments. Finally, von Ruffin-Zisiadis outlines the role and the services of newbuilding brokers.

The impressive list of international and Hamburg-based experts and contributors, as well as their expertise, promises and assures thought-provoking contributions and a transfer of knowledge and expertise from the industry. The book shall stimulate discussions among peers and partners, in academia and in the offices around the world that are engaged in ship finance. Feedback from the readers to the editors is highly encouraged.

As editors, we can only wish to the reader to enjoy reading this book, to professionals to consider some of the messages and experiences conveyed, and to the academic community, both to students and lecturers, to learn from the experiences gained at the first lines of the front!

Hamburg, Germany
November 2014

Orestis Schinas
Max Johns
Carsten Grau

Contents

Part V Challenges and Advances

List of Contributors and Editors

Vera Alexandropoulou Law Firm, Lawyer and Solicitor, Piraeus, Greece

Christina Anagnostara Seanergy Maritime Holdings Corp., Glyfada, Athens, Greece

Kerim Atamer Department of Maritime and Insurance Law, Istanbul University, Law School, Beyazit, Istanbul, Turkey

Nicolas Bornozis Capital Link Inc., New York, NY, USA

John Cassels Field Fisher Waterhouse LLP, London, UK

Philip Clausius Transport Capital Pte. Ltd., Singapore, Singapore

Ashley W. Craig Venable LLP, Washington, DC, USA

Carsten Grau L2C, Hamburg, Germany

Florian Haase Rödl & Partner, Hamburg, Germany

Tyler Hale Venable LLP, Washington, DC, USA

Andreas Höth TPW Todt & Partner GmbH & Co. KG, Hamburg, Germany

Max Johns German Shipowners' Association, Hamburg, Germany

Sebastian Kewitsch NAVES Corporate Finance GmbH, Hamburg, Germany

Carrie A. Kroll Venable LLP, Washington, DC, USA

Jan Willem Krutemeier Hammonia Reederei, Hamburg, Germany

Dirk Lammerskötter HSH Nordbank AG, Hamburg, Germany

Burkhard Lemper Institute of Shipping Economics and Logistics (ISL), Bremen, Germany

Elizabeth K. Lowe Venable LLP, Washington, DC, USA

Karsten Markwardt MPC Münchmeyer Petersen Capital AG, Hamburg, Germany

Daniel Mayr PwC, Frankfurt am Main, Germany

Andreas Mietzner Continental Chartering GmbH & Co. KG, Hamburg, Germany

Edward Miller Field Fisher Waterhouse LLP, London, UK

Kai Miller HSH Nordbank AG, Hamburg, Germany

Joseph Nijoe Stephenson Harwood Middle East LLP, Dubai, UAE

Stefan Otto Commerzbank AG, Hamburg, Germany

Basil Ph. Papachristidis Hellespont Ship Management GmbH & Co. KG, Hamburg, Germany

Phrixos B. Papachristidis Hellespont Ship Management GmbH & Co. KG, Hamburg, Germany

Orestis Schinas Hamburg School of Business Administration (HSBA), Hamburg, Germany

Thilo Scholl Commerzbank AG, Hamburg, Germany

Swen Schöne Field Fisher Waterhouse LLP, Hamburg, Germany

Axel Scroeder MPC Münchmeyer Petersen Capital AG, Hamburg, Germany

Christos Sigalas Seanergy Maritime Holdings Corp., Glyfada, Athens, Greece

Christoph Sturm Deutsche Seewert GmbH & Co. KG, Hamburg, Germany

Michael Tasto Institute of Shipping Economics and Logistics (ISL), Bremen, Germany

Christian von Oldershausen Deutsche Seewert GmbH & Co. KG, Hamburg, Germany

Leandros von Ruffin-Zisiadis W.J. Hinneberg, Hamburg, Germany

Richard Ward ICAP Shipping Ltd., London, UK

List of Figures

Part I
Introduction to Ship Financing

Chapter 1
Demand and Supply of Maritime Transport Services: Analysis of Market Cycles

Burkhard Lemper and Michael Tasto

Abstract In their contribution, authors Lemper and Tasto review the evolution of the supply and demand side of the major shipping markets since the beginning of the new millennium. The dry bulk, liquid bulk, and container shipping markets are reviewed in detail and special regard is paid to interesting market developments and limitations of forecasts during the year of the global recession 2009. For this year, the industry forecasts are matched against the effective outcome. Based on the experience of the authors, selected tips are presented on how to analyze shipping markets with the help of statistics and the concepts of inter- and intracompetition of analyzing shipping markets are touched briefly. The contribution ends with a review of the different types of shipping cycles and the lessons learned from the last boom period (2002–2008).

1.1 The Demand and Supply Side of Shipping Markets

Among economists, it is considered a common wisdom that shipping markets are the markets where the classic "pig-cycles" can be observed and analyzed par excellence since not only the supply side and the demand side are relatively well-documented, but also the market results (the freight rates or time charter rates). It is common understanding that the demand side of the markets is represented by the need for freight transport, whereas the supply side consists of the ships that deliver the commodities.

Both sides meet on the freight market, where the service "transport" is exchanged most commonly against US$. Stopford (2009) lists five elements influencing the development of either one of the sides of this market (see Fig. 1.1).

B. Lemper (✉) • M. Tasto
Institute of Shipping Economics and Logistics (ISL), Universitätsallee 11-13, 28359 Bremen, Germany
e-mail: lemper@isl.org; tasto@isl.org

O. Schinas et al. (eds.), *HSBA Handbook on Ship Finance*,
DOI 10.1007/978-3-662-43410-9_1, © Springer-Verlag Berlin Heidelberg 2015

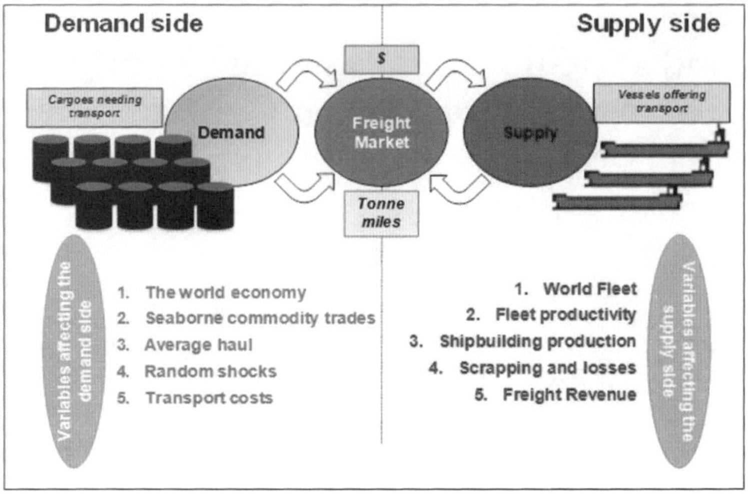

Fig. 1.1 Supply and demand side of a shipping market. *Source*: Lemper/Tasto based on Stopford (2009)

1.1.1 The Demand Side

The seaborne transport of commodities is regularly documented in statistical publications of leading brokers, NGOs or research institutes. Quite often though, these statistics are based on estimates as most publications reporting on international trade flows do not worry about the volume of goods transported as much as about their value. Therefore, the figures published on global seaborne transport volumes sometimes differ significantly from source to source and are adjusted several times. According to Stopford (2009), the development of the demand side is affected by:

(a) **The world economy**, as a higher (or lower) economic output regularly requires a higher (or lower) input of resources and also generates more (or less) merchandise available for foreign trade. Hence, both the business cycle as well as the trade development cycle (nations going through a period of transition from a traditional society to a society of mass consumption and, hence, develop different consumption/production patterns of raw materials or merchandise) have a major impact on the demand for seaborne commodity transport.
(b) **Seaborne commodity trades**, which may be subject to seasonal cycles in the short run (examples can be found in the crude oil, grain, or container trade) and which on may evolve in the long run, resulting from:

- changing industrial demands
- changing transport policies
- depletion or discovery of resources
- relocation of processing plants.

(c) **Average haul and ton miles**, being the more precise measurement of the demand side than the pure information about the volume of shipped goods as the distance over which the commodities are transported can vary widely and often demand peaks (resulting in a higher volume) have to be satisfied using more distant suppliers (generating an even larger impact on the ton miles).
(d) **Random shocks like**, wars, economic downturns, natural disasters, which can intensify the impact of seasonal or economic cycles or mess with the average haul...
(e) **Transport costs**, as the general theory of maritime trade suggests that trade takes place if a commodity can be bought more cheaply in a different country, the ever declining cost of transport (resulting from the economies of scale) in itself has helped to boost maritime trade (Stopford 2009, pp. 140–149).

1.1.2 The Supply Side

The supply side of the markets is represented by the ships that carry the cargoes. The information about the historical development of the fleet is quite accurately documented in the leading fleet registers, for example, the Clarksons Register or the databases of IHS Fairplay. The future development of the fleet can in the short term be deviated from the orderbook of the yards and assumptions on likely scrapping activity although the financial crisis of 2008/2009 has shown that cancellation, slippage, or conversion of orders can play a major role in the short run. According to Stopford (2009), the supply side is affected by:

(a) **The world merchant fleet**, contracting and expanding in cyclical movements of up to 20 years, and bringing about new ship types and designs eventually while phasing out older designs or vessel types.
(b) **The fleet productivity**, which may vary depending on the use of the vessel. The effective transport capacity each vessel can provide during a given period of time is a function of the speed of the vessel, the time the vessel is caught up in the cargo handling procedures as well as the regular or non-regular maintenance. All these elements can change over time with investment in handling technology or changing demand patterns of the ship buyers. Additionally, the time spent ballasting or pursuing cargo contracts also limits the trading capacity of the vessel. A Clarkson study of the time use of VLCCs, for example, suggests that on average, VLCCs spend no more than 135 days per year on sea voyages with a cargo in the tanks. Lastly, the utilization of the vessels in terms of physical tonnage capacity used may also vary.
(c) **The shipbuilding production**, being a cyclical industry, where a time span between the placement of the order and the actual delivery of the vessel can range up to 4 years.
(d) **Scrapping and losses**, which are the counterpart to the shipbuilding production by reducing the fleet capacity. While age is the primary factor driving the

demolition of the vessels, there are other factors like the market prospects, scrap prices, financial situation of the owners, etc. which play a role in the decision whether to scrap a vessel or not.

(e) **The freight revenue**, being probably the most important element driving the supply side. In the long run, there seems to be an evident correlation between the earnings of a fleet segment and the amount of investment that is taking place in this particular market. In the short run, the supply-side reacts to higher freight revenues by speeding up the operation and thus delivering more trading capacity (Stopford 2009, pp. 151–160).

There are quite a few approaches to categorize shipping markets and it can be done by both loading categories, ship type designs, commodities, or even the way, the markets are organized (Biebig et al. 2008, p. 138).

From the viewpoint of a maritime economist aiming to analyze a shipping market, the most interesting perspective though would be to look at the competitive environment of a certain type of vessel. This analysis has become more complicated or easier in the second half of the past century – depending on one's perspective.

Before the 1950s, the majority of seaborne trade would be transported on liner or tramp vessels of often equivalent sizes and designs and, hence, the tonnage could generally be switched between trades. The system worked well but was labor-intensive and because of the increasing labor costs, the shippers of industry raw materials sought to benefit more strongly from the economies of scale that the larger, more specialized vessels had to offer. Resulting from this as well as from the introduction of the container, the highly specialized shipping markets we are facing today have evolved. Those shipping markets offer individual vessel designs, charterers, and port equipment (Stopford 2009).

As these modern vessel types are basically no longer interchangeable like they used to be around the 1950s, analyzing the market of a certain type of vessel has become more easy because regularly only a few commodities need to be considered on the demand side (in case of very large oil or natural gas carriers as little as one commodity). Yet, as will be discussed in Sect. 1.1.3.5, some overlapping in the demand and supply of selected shipping markets appears to exist.

1.1.3 World Seaborne Trade and Merchant Fleet Development

Whilst some figures related to 2011 are still estimated and revisions of cargo handling statistics are a regular phenomenon in the runner-up year, it seems that the total amount of cargo trade has reached a volume of 9.1 bn tons and is headed for the 10 bn ton milestone in the near future.

As slightly more than 70 % of the entire seaborne trade (see Fig. 1.2) are raw materials or energy sources (see Table 1.1), it becomes clear why on average the seaborne trade has been growing in line with the output of the world economy over the last 20 years (see Fig. 1.3). Depending on the commodities, periodically special

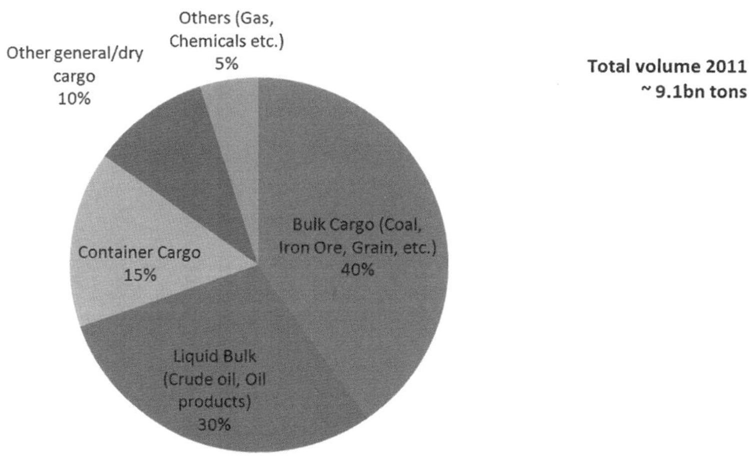

Fig. 1.2 Total seaborne trade by major loading categories. *Source*: ISL 2012 based on Clarksons Research

preconditions will lead to surprisingly high or low growth rates, as we will see in the following subchapters, which take a closer look at the major shipping markets and highlight the most important developments of the recent years.

1.1.3.1 Dry Bulk Shipping Markets

Stopford (2009) defines bulk commodities as cargoes which are carried in bulk carriers. Their common denominators are that they travel in large quantities and their physical attributes allow for easy (automated) handling. The alternative suggested definition is that they are commodities, which can be poured, tipped or pumped into the hold of a ship.

According to figures from Clarksons Research in the year 2011, roughly 3.6 bn tons have been transported on the dry bulk shipping markets. The volume comprises of the major bulks: iron ore, coal, and grain as well as bauxite/alumina and phosphate rock.[1] These commodities travel in large parcels and account for two-thirds of the entire trade volume. The remaining third of the dry bulk trade is composed of a broad mixture of agricultural products, forest products, steel products as well as non-ferrous metal ores or scrap but also cement or fertilizers. These commodities typically are required in smaller quantities by the importing industries and typically show a higher value per ton.

Until the beginning of the new millennium, the demand-growth on the dry bulk shipping markets was fairly static and mostly reliant on the steam coal trade.

[1] The latter two are sometimes found excluded from the "major bulks" and grouped with the "minor bulks" instead.

Table 1.1 Different approaches of categorizing shipping markets

Loading categories	Dry bulk		Liquid bulk			General	
Commodity group	Major bulks	Neo-bulk/ minor-bulk	Liquefied gas	Oil/oil products	Chemicals	Conventional	Container
Commodity (selection)	Iron ore, coal, grain	Bauxit, phosphate rock, fertilizer, oilseeds, steel, timber, non-iron metals and ores, sugar, salt, cement, …	LPG (liquefied petroleum gas), LNG (liquefied natural gas)	Crude oil, petroleum, diesel, gasoline, koresene, …	Vegetable and animal oils and fats, organ. and anorgan. chemicals, foodstuffs	Sawn wood, cars, project cargo, rail cars, steel coils, cellulose, reefer cargo, …	Other manufactured and semi-manufactured goods, foodstuffs, consumer and investments goods, all theoretically containerisable goods
Trading area	World-wide			…	Coastal shipping		
Availability	Prompt tonnage			…	Forward contracts		
Ship type	Bulker; tanker (gas, oil, oil products, chemicals, …); general cargo (container, multipurpose, heavy lift, …)						

Source: Lemper/Tasto based on Biebig et al. (2008)

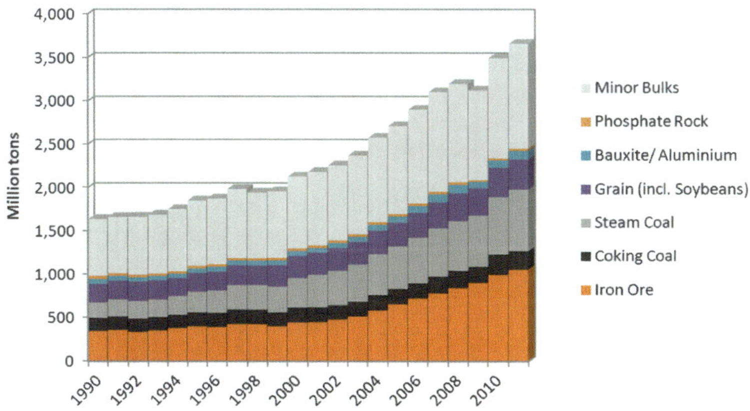

Fig. 1.3 Development of seaborne trade in dry bulk commodities 1990–2011. *Source*: ISL 2012 based on Clarksons Research 2011 = preliminary estimates

This changed radically around 2002/2003, when China, already back then the largest producer of steel, massively increased its volume of iron ore imports at a pace that was underestimated by the largest parts of industry observes.

Between 2003 and 2008, the demand impact from the Chinese imports of iron ore has been the central topic around the development of freight and time charter rates. Although investment in new vessels accelerated around 2003 already, the Chinese hunger for raw materials kept exceeding the forecasts and when vessels were queuing up in congested ports (affecting the supply side by reducing the "fleet productivity") and the Australian suppliers could not keep up with the Chinese demand growth and Brazilian suppliers stepped in happily (affecting the demand side by increasing the "average haul"), the markets have seen never before reached earnings as well as never before seen investments in new tonnage.

According to figures from IHS Fairplay, this unprecedented ordering boom has led to the dry bulk fleet surpassing the tanker fleet as the largest segment of the entire world merchant fleet, reaching a capacity of 602 M dwt early in 2012. The capacity growth of 17.1 % in 2010 and 14.8 % in 2011, respectively, has even surpassed the long term average capacity growth of the rapidly expanding container fleet, which grew by 11.5 % over the last 20 years (see Fig. 1.4).

Whilst having been notoriously undersupplied with tonnage during the years 2003–2007 and throughout most of 2008 (until the start of the global recession), the supply-demand-balance on the dry bulk shipping markets has developed in favor of the shippers in recent years, leaving shipping investors with relatively poor earrings and – resulting from the still filled orderbook early in 2012 only with medium-term hopes for a sustained recovery.

During periods of fundamentally oversupplied markets, it is not uncommon for freight rates to edge up sharply, as tonnage on the spot markets may be tight occasionally, resulting from unforeseen demand spikes (see Fig. 1.5). This has

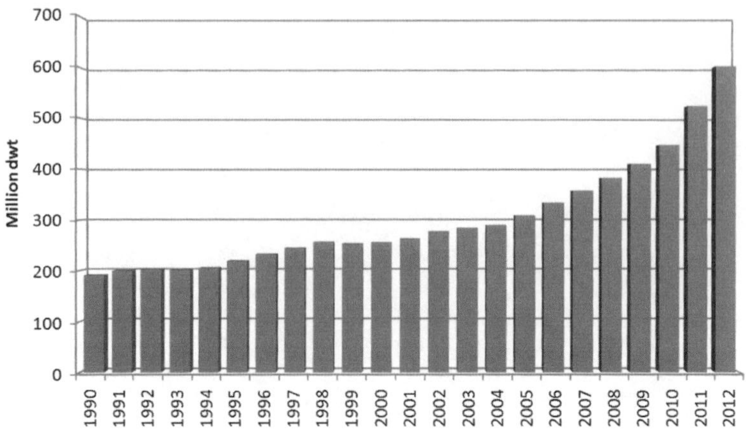

Fig. 1.4 Development of the Dry Bulk Fleet 1990–2012 (start of period). *Source*: ISL 2012 base on IHS Fairplay

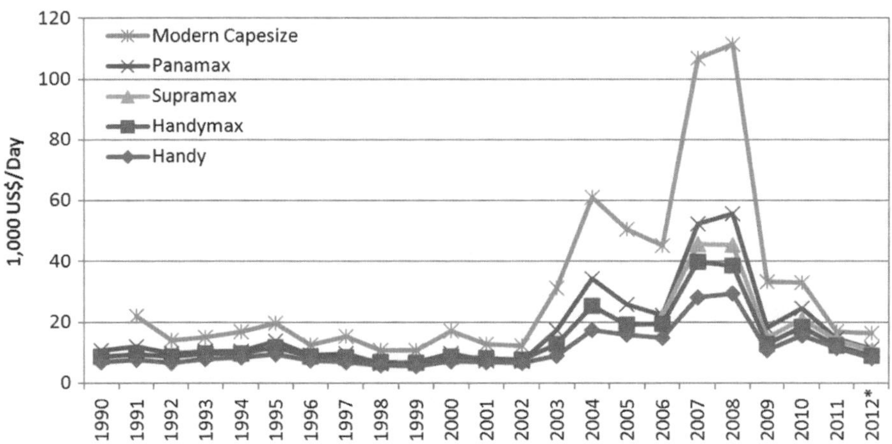

Fig. 1.5 Development of 1 year time charter rates for different bulk carriers 1990–2012 (period averages). (*Asterisk*) January until begin of March. *Source*: ISL 2012 based on Clarksons Research Shipping Review and Outlook 2012 (Clarksons Research 2012)

been observable, for example, late in 2011, when Chinese steel-mills stockpiled large amounts of iron ore, sending the Baltic Dry Index and especially capsize earnings to relatively high levels but having only a modest impact on the longer-term time charter earnings, which incorporate the future expectations of the market participants – the latter ones being quite bearish recently.

Although the longer lasting 1 year time-charter rates regularly smoothen out the volatility of the spot-market, time charter rates are quite volatile too. In the case of bulk shipping time charter-rates though, the volatility of the nineties is dwarfed by the scaling required by the 2007 and 2008 spike in earnings.

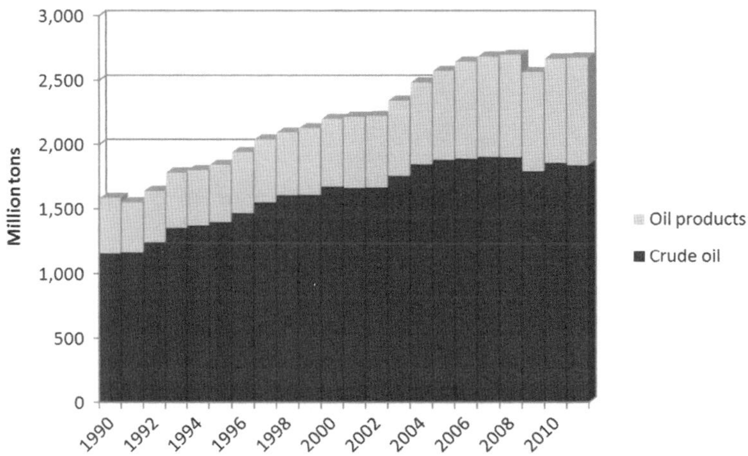

Fig. 1.6 Development of seaborne trade in oil and oil products 1990–2011. *Source*: ISL 2012 based on Clarksons Research 2011 = preliminary estimates

1.1.3.2 Liquid Bulk: "The Tanker Markets"

When brokers or market reports discuss "the tanker markets", they are typically just referring to two particular trades, one being crude oil, one being the oil products trade. Whilst it is true that chemicals and liquefied petroleum gasses or liquefied natural gas or even juices, wine, or beer may travel in vessels referred to as 'tankers', these latter vessels are operating in a different and segmented market with virtually zero overlap.[2]

After initially having been transported only as refined products, the crude oil transport soared in the 1950s, 1960s, and early in the 1970s. After the 1970s recession and oil price shock, the seaborne crude oil trade fell sharply but has recovered since then and stands—with some distance to the iron ore trade left—as the largest individual commodity being shipped in bulk. For the year 2011, Clarksons Research estimated the crude oil trade volume to be 1.84 bn tons. The estimate for the oil products trade at the same time was about 1 bn tons smaller and stood at 837 m tons (see Fig. 1.6).

Early in 2012, the capacity of "the tanker fleet" has surpassed the "half-a-billion-milestone", the relatively rapid expansion that becomes noticeable around the year 2004 is only partly attributable to the increased demand dynamics of the emerging Asian economies (see Fig. 1.7). Partly, the modern, double-hull tonnage had been

[2]*Note*: this is not entirely true as chemical tankers are well-equipped to carry oil products and will do so to fill the holds on an otherwise underutilized voyage or during repositioning to a different trading area.

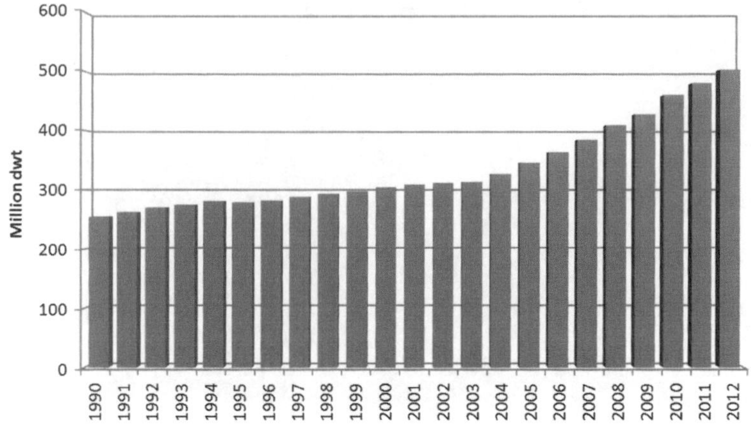

Fig. 1.7 Development of the tanker fleet (oil, oil products and chemical tankers) 1990–2012 (start of period). *Source*: ISL 2012 base on IHS Fairplay

ordered in advance of the phase out of the older single hull vessels, which was due in 2010.[3]

Looking at the development of time charter markets for large crude oil tankers in the years 2008 and 2009 leaves the reader puzzling. Based on the fundamental dynamics (an economic downturn, colliding with an ongoing fleet expansion), a more massive downturn in earnings would have been expected. Yet, especially around the end of 2008, large crude carriers earned surprisingly strong rates on the spot markets (see Fig. 1.8).

Although the fleet expansion later on was clearly driven by the positive earnings situation, earnings during the boom years were not as strong as in the dry bulk sector. Hence, the advance ordering has certainly contributed to smoothen the market peak of the tanker markets. As a result, compared to the dry bulker markets, the tanker markets are equipped with a slightly more optimistic outlook for the medium term early in 2012—albeit from low levels.

The often made reference to the shipping markets being "perfect" markets, however, is related to the perfect competitive behavior of the tanker shipping industry (Glen et al. 2006, p. 270). This degree of competitiveness cannot be found in every shipping market though.

1.1.3.3 Container Shipping Markets

The clockwork-like double digit growth of the container shipping markets was fuelled by the globalization of trade flows as well as the containerization of the

[3]For selected single-hull-tankers, using a condition assessment could prolong the life-span as far as 2015.

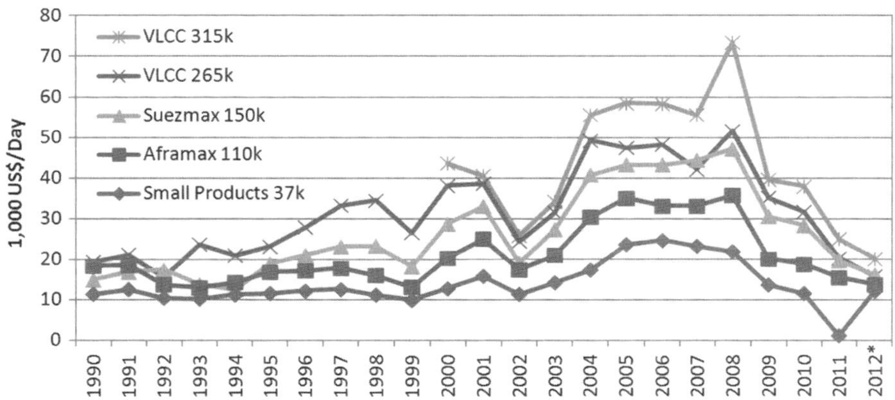

Fig. 1.8 Development of 1 year time charter rates for different tanker vessels 1990–2012 (period averages). (*Asterisk*) January until begin of March. *Source*: ISL 2012 based on Clarksons Research Shipping Review and Outlook 2012

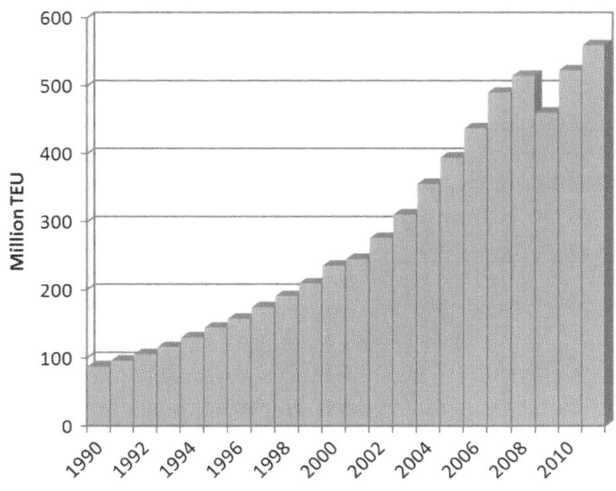

Fig. 1.9 Development of world container handling 1990–2011. *Source*: ISL 2012

already existing general cargo flows (see Fig. 1.9). Whilst most industry observers expect both these demand drivers to lose momentum eventually, they still expect the container traffic to grow super proportionally in relation to the global GDP. Whilst historically, there have been only few opportunities to "mis-invest" in an industry with a regularly reappearing demand growth, the sharp economic downturn of 2008/2009 has set back the long term growth path of the demand side by approximately 3 years.

Measuring the container trade itself is a complicated task since it is not a reported item in official statistics and the assessments of industry observers show large

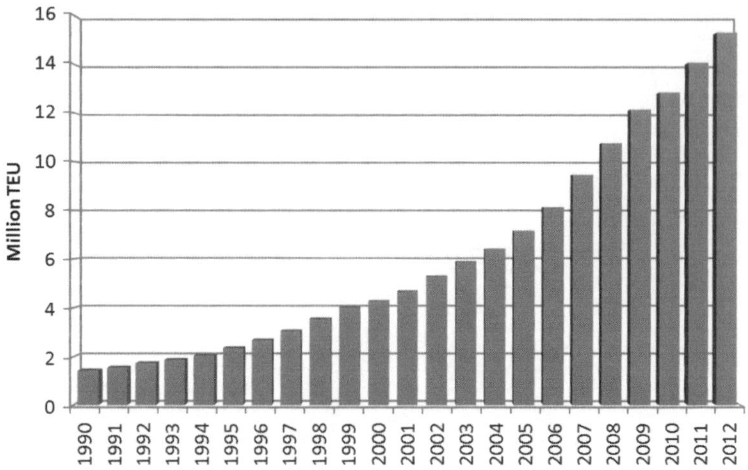

Fig. 1.10 Development of fully cellular container fleet 1990–2012 (start of period). *Source*: ISL 2012 base on IHS Fairplay

differences. Hence, the handling volumes of containers, which are more precisely traceable are usually used as an indicator for the demand side of the markets (Dörn et al. 2012, pp. 14–16).[4]

According to preliminary estimates, world container handling grew by 7 % in 2011, reaching a new all-time high of ~560 M TEU. Taking into account that at least in the industrialized economies everything that may reasonably be transported in a container is nowadays being carried in such steel boxes as well as that the soaring market penetration of Chinese manufactures around 2002–2005 are both losing steam/gradually wearing of, the age of double-digit growth rates on a worldwide level may well be over for container shipping. Yet, ISL forecasts that the billion-TEU-milestone is likely to be reached around the year 2020 which reflects an expected average annual growth rate of around 6.5 % for the coming decade.

Early in 2012, the fully cellular fleet has reached a nominal capacity of 15.6 M TEU (see Fig. 1.10), spread among 5,000 units of different size classes, with the largest regular units in service having slots for as much as 15,500 standard-boxes and a handful of even bigger vessels currently on order.[5] Unlike the more matured dry and liquid bulk fleets, the containership fleet is still evolving in its dimensions. Whilst there are numerous historic miss-assessments about the final limit of this evolution process, the market currently seems to settle for vessels of 14,000 TEU and the larger units are being eyed somewhat cautiously. With a length of little less

[4]Recent research suggests that an index tracking the monthly handling volumes of containers provides some fair amount of insight into the health and state of the world economy and thus forms a "leading indicator".

[5]The Maersk EEE-Series of vessels reportedly will be able to carry 18,000 TEU.

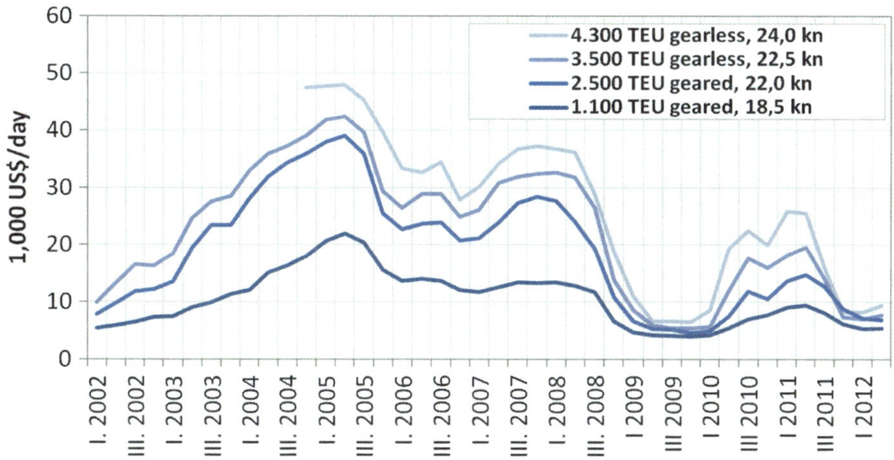

Fig. 1.11 Development of 1 year time charter rates for container ship sizes 2002–2012 (period averages). (Asterisk) II 2012 only April. *Source*: ISL 2012 based on Howe Robinson

than 400 m, a width of 23 boxes across (about 59 m), and a draught of up to 16 m, their deployment options remain strongly limited in the short run.

One result of this ongoing evolution of ship sizes, as well as the organization in liner shipping form, is that the time charter markets are as of 2012 only regularly documented for vessels from ~500 TEU to the panamax segment (~4.400 TEU). The larger vessels came into service only during the last 10–15 years and, hence, are regularly still tied up in their initial charter contracts. Periodically, one of the larger units appears on the markets as the large operators sometimes charter out their tonnage to other operators. Yet, these transactions are still not common enough to allow for the creation of monthly time series. This is likely to change in the near future though. The fleet growth in terms of numbers is currently taking place almost exclusively in the size classes above 4,000 TEU, increasing the "market volume" of the larger units and the vessels of 5,000+ TEU are starting to appear more regularly on the charter markets.

Coming from a somewhat discouraged sentiment surrounding the burst of the dot-com bubble and the terrorist attacks in 2001, the container shipping markets have been taken by surprise by the impact of China's ascension to the WTO. The strong trade growth fuelled the charter markets, peaking in 2005. Until early in 2008, the markets remained in positive territory. Although the fleet growth was catching up with the demand side, the ever increasing fuel costs and record high bunker prices of the years 2007 and 2008 made "slowsteaming" an economic viable strategy (see Fig. 1.11). Thus, part of the newly built tonnage could be absorbed in the markets without increasing the fleet effective transport capacity. Put precisely, the fleet productivity (supply side) was shrinking but freight and charter markets remained relatively stable despite over-proportionate fleet growth.

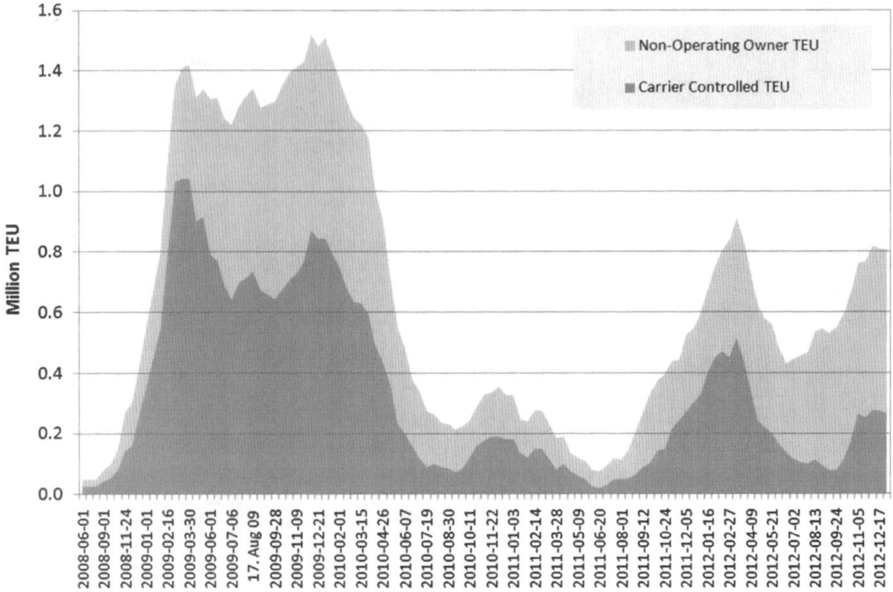

Fig. 1.12 Development of idle container vessels capacity 2008–2012. *Source*: ISL based on Alphaliner

When trade volumes fell strongly late in 2008 and early in 2009, accompanied by the trough in the inventory cycle and the regular seasonal downturn of the container shipping markets, a strong fleet growth collided with a before unseen decline of the demand side. Within a very short time, container ships with an aggregate capacity close to 1.6 M TEU have been reported as inactive and have pushed the time charter markets into a long-lasting trough. The increase in rates in 2010 came as surprising as the strong recovery of the demand side. Yet, it proved to be short-lived (see Fig. 1.12).

1.1.3.4 Other Specialized Shipping Markets

Next to the major shipping markets of dry-bulk, liquid bulk, and container shipping, various smaller market segments with individual ship designs and only limited overlap exist. The most important ones are the markets of:

- **Liquefied gas transportation**. It should be pointed out that the individual commodities and vessel designs, as well as the parcel sizes and typical ship sizes, differ strongly from each other in this sector, as do the demand and supply mechanisms of the commodities (see Fig. 1.13).
- **The chemicals trade** consists of a wide mixture of sophisticated cargoes, which mostly travel in small parcels, consequently, two-thirds of all chemical tanker

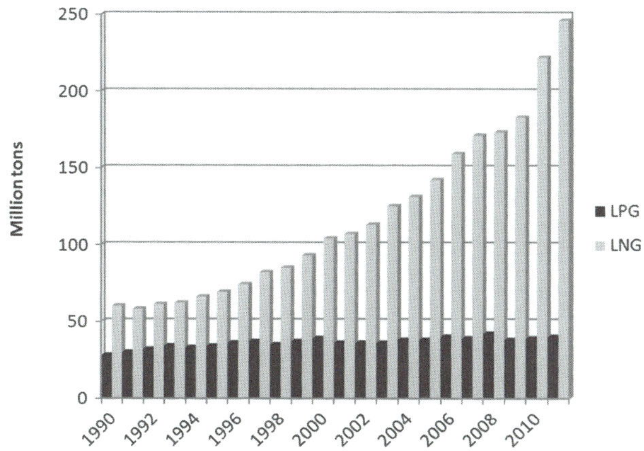

Fig. 1.13 Development of seaborne trade in liquefied gases 1990–2011. *Source*: ISL 2012 based on Clarksons Research 2011 = preliminary estimates

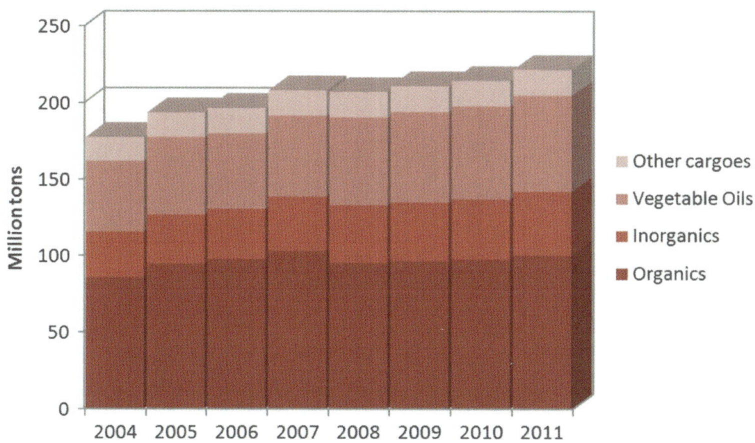

Fig. 1.14 Development of seaborne trade in chemicals 1990–2011. *Source*: ISL 2012 based on Drewry Shipping 2010/2011 = preliminary/forecast

vessels do not exceed a capacity of 20,000 dwt, whilst having several individual holds (tanks) for cargoes, ranked in grade by their hazardous potential (see Fig. 1.14).

- **The car/vehicle trade** is mainly done with specialized vessels (PCC = pure car carrier or PCTC = pure car truck carrier), which are especially designed for this purpose. They are constructed as more or less huge multi-storey car park with capacities up to 8,000 vehicles. In most cases, these vessels are sailing on relatively fixed routes and in addition in some cases there also exists a regional feeder network like, e.g. from the northwest European ports to the Baltic. This market—except for the 2009 crisis—is steadily growing and expected to continue on a moderate growth path.

- **The reefer trade**, being somewhat of a declining phenomenon, whilst for many years the persistent belief was that for a large part of the refrigerated commodities, containerization is not an option, the reefer fleet is currently declining whilst the reefer-container fleet is constantly growing. In several ports the removal of installations for handling of e.g. bananas as typical cargo for reefer vessels has already started.
- **The general/project cargo trade**. The general cargo trade has experienced a bit of a renaissance despite the unstoppable success of the container shipping markets, which have transferred the liner connections between the major trading partners. Whilst general cargo liner trades have become a niche business, the general cargo spot market has benefited strongly from the growth of project cargo shipments. This sector of the shipping markets is particularly hard to gauge or quantify. Often, residuals of the foreign trade statistic ("miscellaneous cargoes") are being transported and—as comes with the definition of "project"—this transport is being carried out on an irregular base. A (non exclusive) list of typical industries, demanding theses shipping services includes not only the mining industry, power plants, wind energy, railways, pipelines, offshore industries, the metal processing/producing industries but also chemical or high tech industries.

1.1.3.5 Spillover Effects: Intra-Competition of Shipping Markets

The modern merchant fleet is divided into clearly distinguishable vessel designs, which cater to a particular type of shipping demand. Additionally, major shipping markets are typically disaggregated by size and each vessel is involved in the transportation of certain commodities. Yet, there is possible competition from the adjacent segments within the fleet, as the tonnage is generally substitutable, particularly in the bulk shipping markets where the spot demand for a vessel size may occasionally outweigh the spot supply by so much that the freight rates justify using larger vessels (with a resulting deadfreight) or two (or even more) shipments using smaller vessels.

Consequently, positive as well as negative shocks from one sector of the fleet are passed on to the other sectors. Alizadeh and Nomikos (2002) looked into this phenomenon and found that shocks stemming from the larger vessel sizes tend to have a higher impact on the market, resulting from the larger capacity of those vessels combined with their inflexibility in terms of trading possibilities. This intra-competition of vessels goes a long way in explaining why the peaks and troughs of certain vessels sizes are mirrored by the adjacent segments. When, for example, capesize-tonnage is in such short supply that shippers start employing two panamax units, this additional unusual panamax-demand is driving the rates up for panamax bulkers as well. Correspondingly, if the spot-rates for the large capesize-vessels are low, they place a lid on the rate-levels, which the smaller panamax-bulkers could potentially reach (see Fig. 1.15).

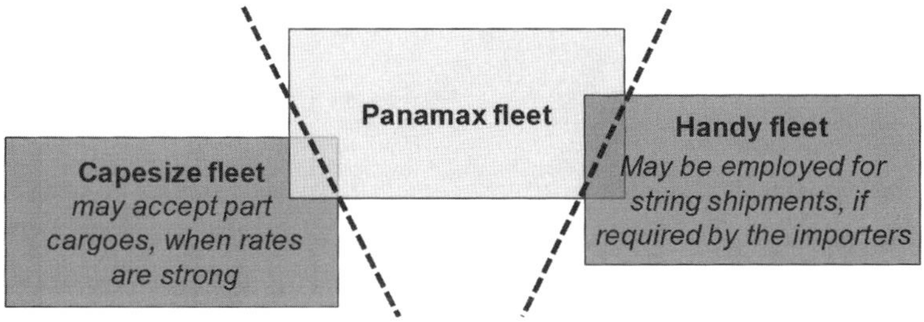

Fig. 1.15 Illustration of the intra-competition of the bulk shipping markets. *Source*: ISL based on Alizadeh and Nomikos (2002) (pp. 243ff.)

1.1.3.6 Spillover Effects: Inter-Competition of Shipping Markets

On top of the **intra**-competition there is also a certain amount of **inter**-competition from different vessel types, which may be employed in the same trades. Products tankers, for example, may be used for crude oil transport, but because the cleaning of the holds after the crude oil transport is quite expensive and likely to wear down the coating and the products fleet has higher capital and operation costs, it is seldom done (read: when the price is right). Similarly, the chemical tanker fleet will often accept product cargoes to avoid dead freights or to subsidize the repositioning to a different trading area.

An example where competition from two shipping markets seems to be given are the multi-purpose vessels. These are typically general cargo vessels with holds that are box-shaped without cell-guides. Hence, they can transport bulk cargoes, containers, or large project cargoes.

Figure 1.16 illustrates how the time charter rates for multi-purpose vessels have been affected by the all-time highs of the container shipping markets (around 2005) as well as the sky-high earning of the dry-bulk shipping markets (2007, 2008).

1.1.4 How to Interpret and Work with Shipping Statistics

Whilst shipping markets appear to be very transparent and well-equipped with sufficient data for analysis, one should bear in mind that ultimately, all statistics are created by humans and human beings are prone to errors. Hence, irrational jumps in time series should always be taken with a pinch of salt and questioned. Another item which is often discussed alongside the IAME-conferences (International Association of Maritime Economists) is the degree to which statistics may be regularly estimated by brokers in the absence of real data. Whilst it is beyond doubt that those closest to the market are most qualified to provide an educated guess to where a market could be at a given point of time, one should not fall into the trap of taking every quoted rate or price for face value, as they often reflect discounted

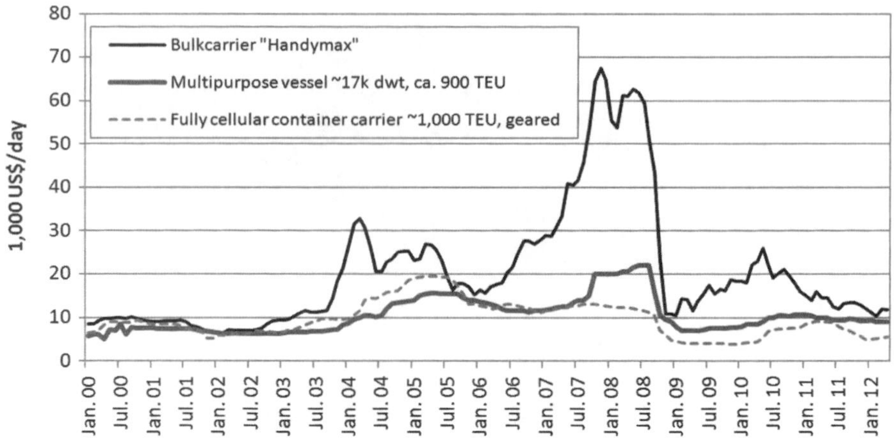

Fig. 1.16 Illustration of the inter-competition on the multi-purpose markets. *Source*: ISL 2012 based on Fearnleys and Clarksons Research

values of neighboring size classes or comparable vessel ages. Also, statistics should always be interpreted against the background of knowledge and experience. During the 2009 recession, for example, the sale and purchase market practically collapsed as the ideas of buyers and sellers differed too fundamentally to form a sound market base. During this time, some brokers rightfully stopped reporting second-hand-prices as there were only limited sales taking place to back those figures, yet others continued and even those brokers who temporarily abandoned the coverage of selected vessels nowadays report second-hand values for tonnage for the months early in 2009.

Another example showing the need for the right reading and interpretation can be found in the "statistics" on global container handling volumes. Several analysts are publishing figures on handling volumes of container ports, but figures often/usually differ.

1.1.4.1 Different Sources Reporting the Same Item Will Seldom Match

Worldwide Container Handling 2007 according to different sources:

- ISL: "490,6 Mil. TEU"
- Drewry: "496,6 Mil. TEU"
- Clarkson: "472 Mil. TEU"

Every analyst team has to make the best of what is statistically available to them and some ports, which may respond to the questionnaires of team A, may not cooperate with team B and vice versa. Hence, to some extent, the data needs to be estimated. All handling volumes of containers of ports, tracked in ISLs port-data-base, regularly add up to ~85 % of all container trade ISL presumes to exist. The remaining volumes are expected to be "lost" in small ports, which mostly do not release statistics or which simply don't report the amount of boxes handled, but release only general information about "general cargo tons".

1.1.4.2 Different Release Dates Will Lead to Slightly Differing Numbers

Whilst providing this article, most, but by no means all ports have reported "final" handling statistics for their seaborne trade. Yet, those ports that did not report "final" statistics for 2011 at least provided preliminary estimates. Earlier in 2012, the share of preliminary estimates was even higher. Depending on the time of report, the assessment of the reported item will change. Depending on the reported subject, these changes may go back several years. For example, the assessments of the past growth rates of the world economy are often re-adjusted after as much as 2–3 years. The changes become smaller, as more time has passed, but they still are common.

1.1.4.3 Different Time Series of the Same Source Often Won't Match

This is a result of a combination of both previous elements in play. As time series for seaborne trade volumes often have to be enhanced with estimates, changes to the way these estimates are made will then lead to changes in the total volume of trade being reported. To estimate the market growth rates correctly, the new methodology then would have to be applied to the previous year as well. Whilst the current growth rate then should be reflected decently, the growth rate of the year $t-1$ versus the year $t-2$ would be distorted. Hence, market reporters often correct a couple of years in the historic time series to provide a more accurate total volume for "today" as well as a more accurate historic development of growth rates. However, at some point, the methodology is skipped, leading to irrational jumps in the historic time series from one market report to the next one.

1.1.4.4 Beware of Different Use of Vocabulary or Units

When talking about the ports of the Hamburg-Le Havre Range, the term "transhipment" regularly only means one thing: containers which are arriving in the port by sea-going vessels and which are leaving the port again by seagoing vessels. In other parts of Europe, "transhipment" may very well also relate to all forms of transit cargoes, which arrived in or leave the port by land. Another example would be the port of New York, which reports monthly TEU handling volumes but those related only to laden containers.

Some market reports will quote both growth rates for transported tons and ton-mile demand. While the latter is certainly the more accurate measure, it is harder to compile and may differ from the growth of the total trade.

1.1.4.5 Time Series Regarding Particular Vessel Sizes Will Evolve Around "the Market"

The bulk shipping markets are more matured in the evolution of different vessel sizes compared to the still young container shipping fleet. Yet, the individual size classes of the bulk carrier fleet keep evolving. An example are the modern "supramax" – designs, which can have a capacity of to 55,000 dwt and which have evolved from the previous "handymax" vessels. Similarly, "typical capesize" – bulkers first used to have a capacity of around 150,000 dwt, then edged up to 170,000 dwt and – in line with the latest ordering trends and deliveries – are likely to evolve further in the near future. When the focus of a market changes, reported time series will often be abandoned, or merged with the new "standard"-vessel sizes. This will often be found in the explanatory notes related to the time-series provided by market reporters and should be taken into consideration when analyzing the time-series over longer periods.

The lesson to be learned from all of the above points certainly is: "be very careful when blending different time series when analyzing data". If it cannot be avoided, the merging of the series should be properly documented to allow the reader to understand how gaps or irrational jumps in the data have been treated.

1.1.5 Forecasting Challenges and Limitations

> Although this may seem a discouraging way to introduce a discussion of forecasting techniques, at least we are getting off on the right foot by accepting that our forecasts will often be wrong. (Stopford 2009).

Forecasting charter rates is a bit of a black art because it involves the precise prediction of a market result. However, analyzing the development trends of the demand and supply side allows for some general insights into which directions the markets are likely headed. Yet, there is always the chance that the market participants behave or things turn out differently than expected. Some interesting examples for this will be discussed in the following subsections. It is generally accepted among maritime economists that the growth of the demand side of shipping markets is **mainly** driven by the development of the economic activity. As far as raw materials are considered, elements like depletion of existing resources or discovery of new resources do play a role, yet in the short run, the simple formula applies "a higher economic output requires a greater input of raw materials". The question how this relationship is exactly defined depends on a few elements. First, technological

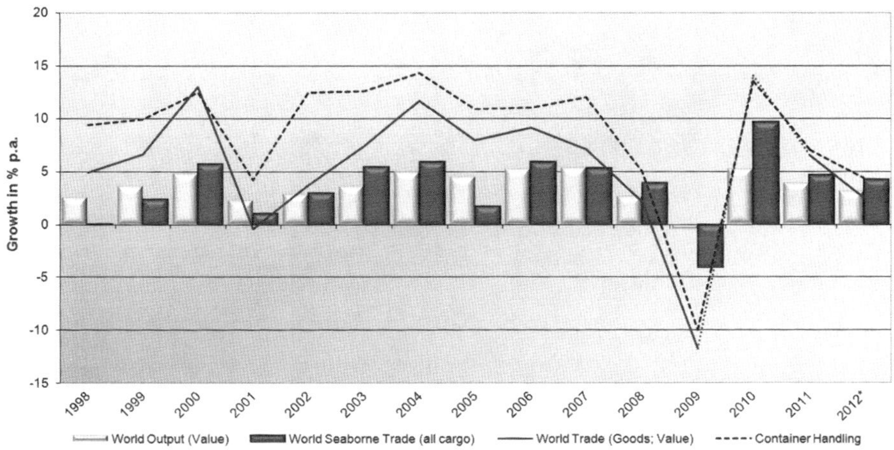

Fig. 1.17 Annual growth of world GDP, word trade, world seaborne trade and world container ports throughput (1998–2012). (*Asterisk*) Estimate/forecast. *Sources*: IMFOECD-Economic Outlook, ISL estimates 2012

innovations regularly allow for a greater economic output to be realized with fewer resources. Second, according to the trade-development-cycle (Stopford 2009, pp. 407–411), as economies mature, the economic growth shifts away from the resource intensive sectors to a higher importance of services.

This well-established relationship between the growth of shipping demand and the growth of economic activity goes a long way in explaining the great attention paid by the maritime industry to the forecasts of economic growth in both the developing and the developed economies.

The developments of the supply side on the other hand side can – in a normal market environment – be deducted relatively precisely from the age structure of a certain fleet of vessel as well as the orderbook for that particular market segment.

However, the global recession has produced some unforeseeable irregular developments on both the demand as well as the supply side (see Fig. 1.17).

1.1.5.1 The Crisis of the Container Shipping Industry in 2009: Forecasts and Outcomes

The global recession of the year 2009 has managed to turn established ratios of the container shipping demand upside down. Starting in autumn 2008, container trade volumes first grew slower and then declined rapidly as the regular seasonal downturn of container shipping demand and the trough in the inventory cycle were taking their toll. Around the turning of the year 2008/2009, the worldwide monthly container handling volumes were down by as much as 16 % compared to the volumes 12 months ago (see Fig. 1.18). Combine that with an industry that was used to and

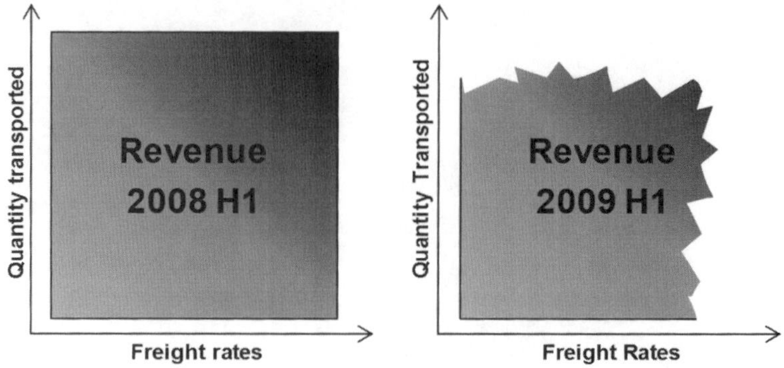

Fig. 1.18 Illustration of the impact of the global recession during 2009 H1 on the freight revenue of the liner shipping industry

expecting enduring double-digit growth rates and which has been ordering tonnage not only in anticipation of that market growth, but also in anticipation of market share gains and all of the sudden the container shipping markets have been hit by something often referred to as "the perfect storm".

In panic, the liner shipping companies tried to fill their new vessels fighting for the quickly dwindling box trade volumes with low freight rates. Consequently, their revenue came under pressure from two dimensions. The number of transported containers declined, while at the same time the revenue per box was shrinking fast to unprofitable levels. At the same time, the cost structure of a liner service operation is relatively static, as the ships are deployed on routes and have to be operated in order not to scare away the remaining customers. The cumulated losses of liner industry have been estimated to be US$20 bn in 2009.[6]

From a point of view early in 2009, the fundamental outlook for the near future of the container shipping markets was a grim one: the capacity of the units reported as "inactive" was soaring rapidly, reaching close to 1.4 M TEU early in 2009, the forecasts of both economic activity and world trade had undergone one downwards adjustment after the other and the container fleet was set to expand at a pace unseen before as a result of the ordering boom of the previous years (see Fig. 1.19).

Consequently, most industry observers predicted a strong further increase of inactive vessels, as the oversupply was a given reality and according to the forecast demand and supply fundamentals the gap between supply and demand was set to widen during the rest of 2009 as well as 2010.

Strangely enough, the total amount of inactive capacity never ever made it far beyond the 1.5 M TEU mark and actually declined relatively quickly in 2010. What had happened? The industry had somewhat overcompensated and in expectation of a very poor year 2010 postponed large parts of the newbuilding deliveries as well as

[6]See also Lloyd's List, March 3rd, 2010.

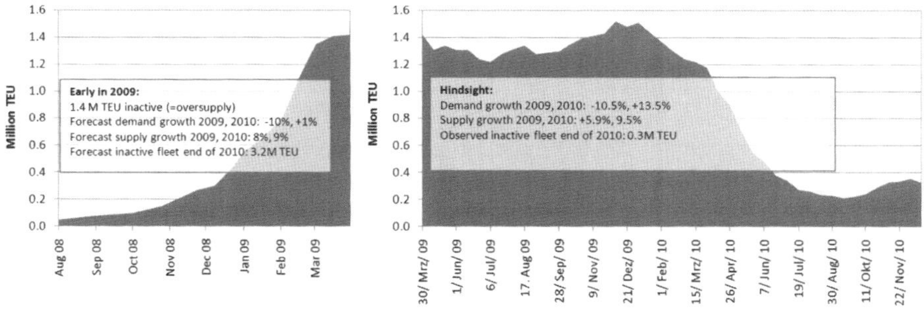

Fig. 1.19 Build-up of inactive units—forecast from a 2009 point of view and actual development. (*Left*) *Source*: Inactive fleet statistics based on Alphaliner, supply/demand forecast: ISL 2009 (base case). (*Right*) *Source*: Inactive fleet statistics based on Alphaliner, supply/demand based on IHS Fairplay/ISL

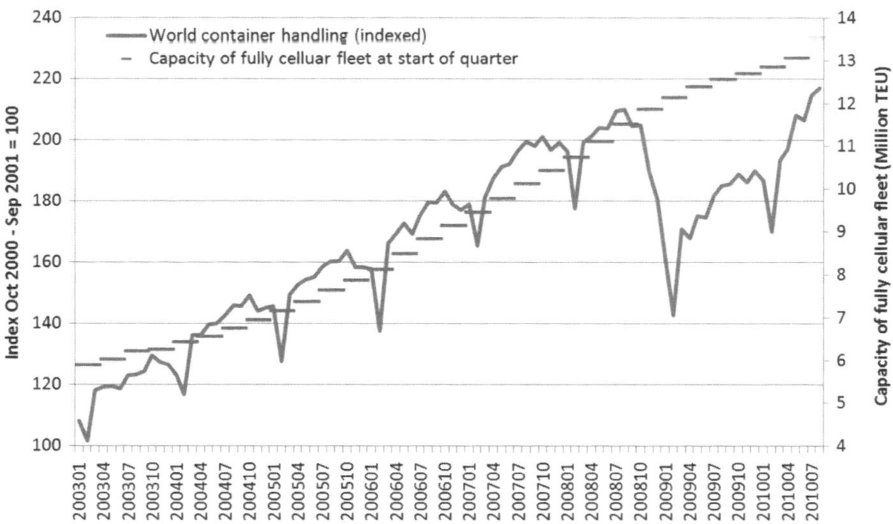

Fig. 1.20 Development of supply and demand on container shipping markets 2003–2010. *Source*: ISL 2010 based on ISL Monthly Container Port Monitor, IHS Fairplay

scrapped a high volume of older units. Additionally, the slowsteaming, which was introduced around 2005/2006 when fuel prices started to increase, was applied on a massive scale, thus reducing the effective fleet productivity. In addition, all of a sudden, when the world economy recovered vividly from the sharp downturn, so did the container trade growing by 13.5 % in 2010. Consequently, instead of further increasing the inactive tonnage remained almost stable during 2009 and already early 2010, the supply-demand gap started to close rapidly with the effect of a fast reduction of idle capacity and increasing charter rates (see Fig. 1.20).

A result, unimaginable from within the gloomy months early in 2009. Within a few weeks, tonnage actually became scarce, freight rates edged up sharply and some companies which had been fighting for survival in 2009 posted record earnings in 2010. The impact of the slowsteaming on the total market balance becomes understandable when the supply and demand side (indexed) are joined together in a diagram. In the summer of 2010, freight rates were high and the idle units mostly back in service. Yet, it was too early to get excited as the supply side was set to grow in 2011 and 2012 partly due to postponed deliveries, partly due to newly placed contracts while the demand side was bound to lose steam in 2011, as much of the growth of 2010 was attributable to the recovery and the comparison to the weak volumes of 2011.[7]

1.1.5.2 The Crisis of the Dry Bulk Shipping Industry in 2009: Forecasts and Outcomes

The earnings of the dry bulk shipping markets in 2007 and 2008 have been unparalleled yet. Whilst it became evident that a bubble was building up on the markets, the ever soaring Chinese commodity demand kept tonnage tight and ports congested (reducing the fleet productivity). Also, more distant suppliers had to step in (increasing the average haul) and driving the freight markets – and as an almost directly related result, the investments in new vessels to heights never seen before.

When late in 2008, the global economic bubble burst and the world industrial production went into a sharp decline, the general industry consensus was that this party was over for good. At the beginning of 2009, the dry bulk fleet was looking at annual capacity growth rates in excess of 15 % and demand was expected to decline by 4 % in 2009 and recover only gradually in 2010. Around that time capesize-bulk carriers who in the peak of 2008 could fetch spot-earnings of up to US$250,000/day on the Brasil–China Route, dwindled down quickly and owners (sometimes admittedly with large and comfortable cash reserves) had to settle for spot earnings as low as US$1,000/day.

The more exciting and almost “disturbing” was that early in 2010, suddenly the freight markets started to improve as is represented by the Baltic Dry Index, which is effectively a blend of the spot earnings on a number of defined routes and vessels sizes (which each have their own sub-indices).

The initial response of market observers asked to explain this increase early in 2010 was to shrug and trace the development back to a market which had been extremely tight before the economic downturn and that it would not be uncommon to experience short-lived spikes in such an environment since the doom (represented by the 72 % strong orderbook) was only set to hit the waters in the years to come.

[7]Resulting from these developments, both freight and charter rates were quite week late in 2011, after the liner shipping companies had initially in 2011 fought for market shares at the expense of freight rate revenue.

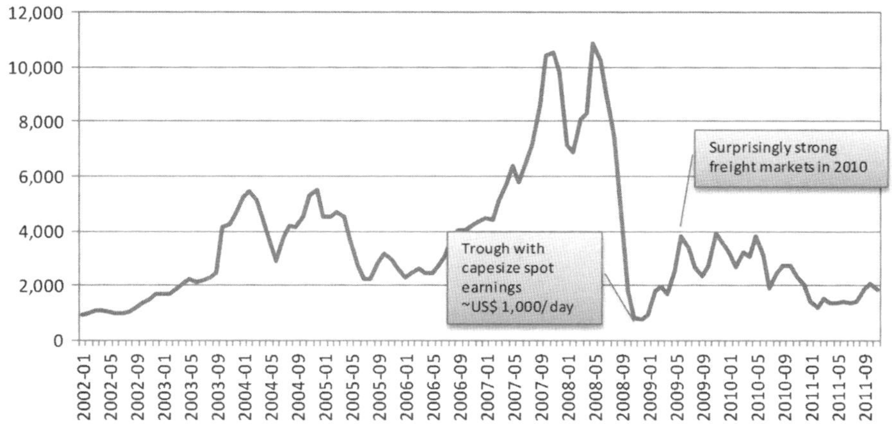

Fig. 1.21 Development of the Baltic Dry Index 2002–2011. *Source*: ISL 2012 based on Baltic Exchange

It was not before April/May until it finally became evident what was really driving the markets. According to figures from Clarkson Research, the Chinese imports of iron ore (which accounted for 52 % of all seaborne iron ore trade in 2008 already) were skyrocketing once more, increased by an unbelievable 41 % in the year of the biggest post-war-economic downturn, turning around the fortunes of the dry-bulk market on its own. With hindsight, this development became understandable:

Generally speaking, trade is a function of the prices of a commodity in the domestic country, the foreign country and the tariffs and freight (Stopford 2009, p. 16). In 2008, both the freight for shipping iron ore to China as well as the international commodity prices had reached historical heights. Yet, China reached a new all-time high of iron ore imports in that year. When in 2009, both the freight rates as well as the commodity prices fell sharply, the price of imported iron ore was almost halved from the point of view of the Chinese steel mills.

Whilst China thus saved the dry bulk markets in the short run, the fundamental problems of a too large orderbook remained and when the delivery of new bulk tonnage finally soared during 2010 and 2011, the earnings finally came under the expected pressure (see Fig. 1.21). Early in 2012, the dry bulk shipping markets are likely going through the trough of this "mega-cycle".

1.1.5.3 The Crisis of the Tanker Shipping Industry in 2009: Forecasts and Outcomes

Crisis? What crisis? Late in 2008, very large crude carriers (VLCC's) were doing quite fine on both the spot and time-charter markets. According to figures from Fearnleys research, modern VLCC tonnage could still fetch 1-year time charter contracts valued at around US$50,000/day late in 2008, which is a very acceptable

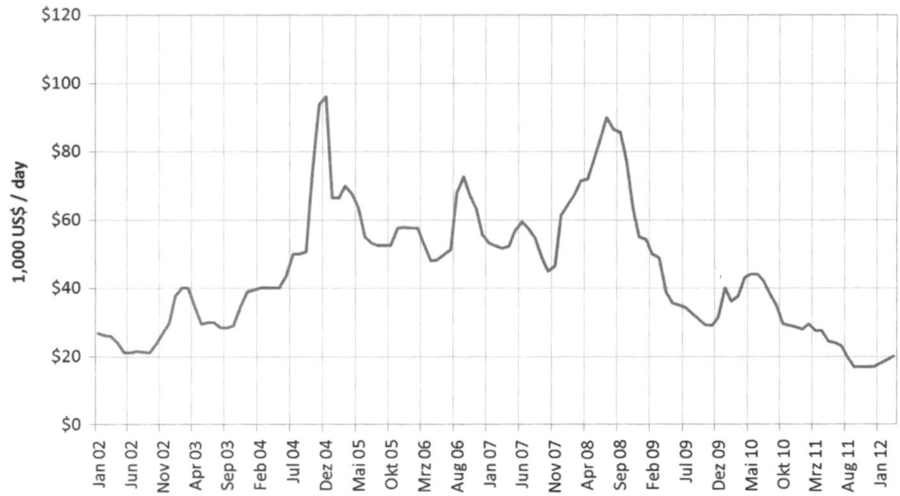

Fig. 1.22 Development of 1-year time charter rates for Very Large Crude Carriers (VLCCs) 2002–2012. *Source*: ISL 2012 based on Fearnleys

level for ship-owners (see Fig. 1.22). Yet, it is offsetting for shipping market analysts, as the fleet (the supply side) has been growing at an accelerated pace throughout the years from 2003-2008 and was set for further dynamic expansion in 2009 and 2010, whilst the crude oil demand, being centered in the industrialized economies, was expected to decline sharply in line with the economic downturn.

A couple of special developments have been taking place at the end of 2008—early in 2009 which have affected the supply and demand side of the tanker markets beyond what can be seen from the pure fleet and trading volume statistics.

First, piracy increased sharply in the Gulf of Aden around the year 2008. As a result, a lot of tanker operators chose to avoid the passage through the Suez Canal and instead opted for a routing around the Cape of Good Hope. Thus, the average haul of the commodities was artificially increased, leading to a higher demand for ton-miles.

Second, a number of the older single-hull units of the fleet were already earmarked for timely scrapping. When suddenly earnings on the dry bulk shipping markets spiked, some of the tanker owners took a different strategy and decided to convert their tankers into dry bulkers. This conversion is hardly ever economically viable and probably adds to underline the extreme nature of the dry bulk earnings of those years. Consequently, the supply side of the market was reduced.

The third and fourth element can be traced back to the falling oil prices. Before the collapse of Lehman Brothers, which became a synonym for the start of the global recession in 2008, crude oil had become increasingly expensive, passing the US$130/bbl mark around mid of 2008. When crude oil prices fell sharply in the following months,

- The largest consumers started to import additional volumes to fill up their reserves, generating an additional demand
- Speculative traders bought huge quantities of the energy resource, expecting to be benefiting from a recovery in prices. They then chartered VLCCs to store away the oil for the time being. According to Lloyds Shipping Economist, early in 2009 between 50 and 70 units of the roughly 530 strong fleet of VLCCs have been tied up in these kind of storage contracts, cutting into the fleet productivity and, hence, reducing the supply side.

Lastly, a fifth element came into play here which is disguised in the combination of the fleet statistics, the trading volume and the charter rates. Early in 2010, Clarksons Research published an analysis of the number of spot voyages, which the older single-hull tankers have been conducting per year.[8] According to this research, this figure peaked in the strong markets of 2004 at close to seven fixtures per ship, but has been declining ever since, as sufficient modern tonnage came into the markets and was more sought for by the charterers. By the year 2009, the average number of fixtures/year for the older single-hull tankers had reportedly fallen as low as 2.5. Hence, the development of the total tanker fleet in comparison to the total seaborne trade can be misleading here, as the total tanker fleet also contained a stock of less-desirable single-hull tankers, whereas the time-charter rates portrayed for example by brokers like Fearnleys generally refer to the more modern double-hull vessels. Favoring the more modern vessels is inarguably a political decision carried by the shippers of the cargoes and, hence, an element of the demand side.

Like on the container shipping and dry bulk shipping markets, it was foreseeable that these special developments could not out-run the market fundamentals forever and the tanker markets are early in 2012 also considered to be going through the trough of their own cycle.

1.2 Analysis of the Market Cycles

Shipping always has been and always will be a cyclical industry. Stopford (2009) found evidence of shipping cycles dating back more than 260 years.

1.2.1 Different Types of Shipping Cycles

Generally, the analysis of Stopford (2009, pp. 95–97) suggests three types of trade cycles:

[8]See: http://www.clarksons.net/markets/feature_display.asp?section=&news_id=29828&title=Mysterious+Tanker+Disappearing+Trick+%96+We+Reveal+All.

- **Seasonal cycles**

  These are regularly reoccurring annual upswings and downturns of shipping demand. In an otherwise balanced market, these cycles may have a noticeable impact on the freight markets Examples include:

  – The summer peak season in container shipping, which results from the stockbuilding in the western economies in summer/autumn and is reinforced by the Chinese new year holidays at the beginning of the year. As a result of the Chinese ascend to the workbench of the world, the Chinese Lunar Holiday has an impact on port handling volumes worldwide, which can also be seen in the monthly container port statistics of the Institute of Shipping Economics and Logistics (ISL)[9]
  – The higher crude oil demand of the western hemisphere resulting in stocking up movements before the winter
  – The timing of the grain harvests
  – The harvests of fresh fruits (relevant for the reefer trade)

- **Short cycles**

  These are the classic shipping cycles which have four identifiable stages:

  – A trough
  – A recovery
  – A peak
  – A collapse

  Each of these stages has some clearly identifiable characteristics (Stopford 2009, p. 98) and together they coordinate supply and demand in the shipping market. Examining these cycles on the dry cargo freight markets between the years 1741 and 2007, Stopford found 22 cycles with average peaks of roughly 4 years and average troughs of 7 years.

- **Long shipping cycles**

  which "are driven by technical, economic or regional change" (Stopford 2009, p. 98). These long lasting economic cycles have been examined by Kondratieff and Schumpeter. Whilst of economic relevance, their impact on the shipping markets is hard to quantify as is their individual state.

1.2.2 Lessons Learned from the Various Cycles

The short term shipping cycles are an unavoidable reality of the markets and are unlikely to be overcome, as the supply side can only react to changes of the demand side with a time-lag for it takes time before the new ships can be delivered in

---

[9]See also ISL Monthly Container Port Monitor. This regularly reoccurring demand fluctuation can be recognized in Fig. 1.20 of this chapter.

strong markets or older units are finally being removed from the markets in weak times. Generally, "Freight cycle peaks and troughs are produced by the inelastic demand curve moving along the supply curve" (Stopford 2009, p. 173). Sadly for the analysts, Stopford found out that no cycles ever resemble each other and that the variance in the length of the peaks and troughs is quite noticeable.

1.2.3 Lessons Learned in the Last Boom Period (2002–2008)

One feature of the previous mega-cycle[10] certainly was the increasing dependency on one new key-player in the shipping markets. The People's Republic of China is the most important exporter of containerized merchandise, the most important importer of dry bulk cargoes and has surpassed Japan as Asia's leading importer of crude oil. Whereas in the container shipping market, much depends on the demand of the consumer-powerhouses in northeast Europe, China has already demonstrated that its demand swings can turn around the fortunes on the dry bulk shipping markets in extremely short times. The (shortlived) spike that can be seen in the Baltic Dry Index diagram late in 2011 is an example of such a demand spike by Chinese iron ore stockbuilding. As soon, as this cyclical demand levelled off, early in 2012, the BDI hit a new all-time-low.

Another particular development in the collapse of this cycle was the increasing unreliability of forecasts in the face of the severe economic downturn. Within just 8 months time, the assessment of the increase of the global economic output was slashed from a robust 3.9 % growth, suggesting a vivid increase in seaborne trade volumes, to a global recession of −1.4 %, suggesting an only limited growth respectively a decline in the development of seaborne trade (see Fig. 1.23).

Furthermore, the vessel deliveries of the years 2009, 2010, and 2011 suggest that the orderbook has partly lost its high degree of reliability in the short run. Whilst for bulk carriers, it became clear that the yards would not be physically able to construct the massive contracted volumes on time,[11] the genuinely foreseen box-ship deliveries for the year 2009, which seemed more feasible have been postponed on a massive scale.[12]

[10]In line with the definition of the stages of a cycle, the current trough experienced on all three of the major shipping markets is considered to be the beginning of the next cycle. Ordering activity is declining, scrap volumes are high and while trade volumes are growing, the seed for a recovery is sown.

[11]New records were met in the delivery of dry bulkers continuously though and in 2011, the total volume of delivered dry bulk tonnage exceeded the tonnage volume of all merchant vessels delivered in 2007 according to databases from IHS Fairplay.

[12]According to the IHS Fairplay orderbook database as of autumn 2008, a total of 468 vessels with a capacity of slightly more than 1.8 M TEU was earmarked to go into service in 2009. In Hindsight, only 265 of those units with a capacity of close to 1.1 M TEU were actually delivered.

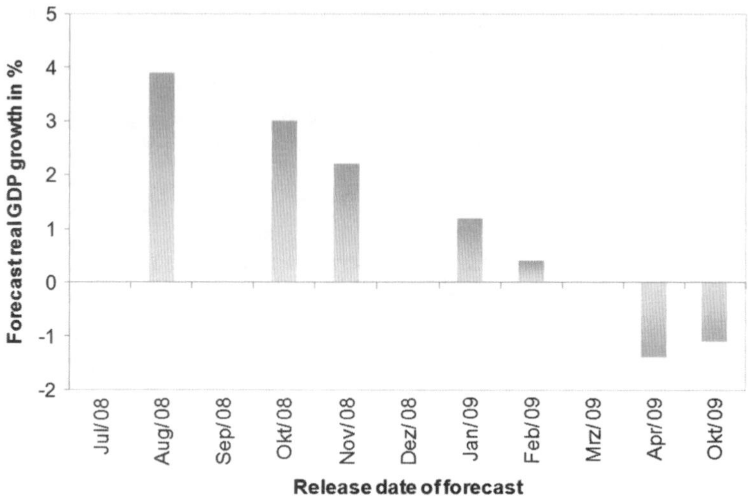

Fig. 1.23 Evolution of forecast world GDP growth for the year 2009. *Source*: ISL based on IMF World Economic Outlook (various issues)

If anything, the crisis has left the ship finance industry as well as shipping investors more risk-aware and the banks are requiring higher degrees of private equity to be willing to grant finance for new vessels.

References

Alizadeh AH, Nomikos NK (2002) The dry bulk shipping market. In: The handbook of maritime economics and business. Informa, London

Biebig P, Althof W, Wagener N (2008) Seeverkehrswirtschaft. Oldenbourg, München

Clarksons Research (2012) Shipping Review and Outlook Spring 2012. Clarkson Research Services Limited, London

Dörn W, Maatsch S (2012) Containerumschlag-Index als Frühindikator für den Welthandel. Schifffahrt & Häfen, August 2012, No. 8

Glen D, Martin B (2006) The tanker market: current structure and economic analysis. In: The handbook of maritime economics and business. Informa Law, London

Stopford M (2009) Maritime economics. Routledge, Abingdon

Chapter 2
Loans and Risk Management Considerations

Orestis Schinas and Sebastian Kewitsch

Abstract This chapter aims to outline the considerations associated to the financial decisions related to loans and the related risk management approaches. The first section presents the elementary calculations related to loan calculations and the impact of the decision-variables. The basic financial criteria for projects are also briefly presented and sensitivity analysis on the basis of numerical examples set forth the effect of the selected assumptions. The second section analyses the key risks and presents the ways commonly mitigated in the ship loan policies.

2.1 Introduction

All shipping projects are based on ideas, facts, expectations, and financial data. The attractiveness of a project depends on its terms and assumptions as well as on the expected results. A promising project might easily allure investors and financiers even in periods where the markets are weak or funds are scarce. The accuracy of the data provided as well as the rationality of the assumptions determine the quality of the business plan. Therefore, it is crucial to present all parameters validly and transparently in the plan, and test key assumptions by selecting various scenarios and performing a sensitivity analysis, thus highlighting the possible limits between success and failure.

O. Schinas (✉)
Hamburg School of Business Administration (HSBA), Alter Wall 38, 20457 Hamburg, Germany
e-mail: Orestis.Schinas@hsba.de

S. Kewitsch
NAVES Corporate Finance GmbH, Domstraße 17, 20095 Hamburg, Germany
e-mail: sebastian.kewitsch@naves-finance.com

O. Schinas et al. (eds.), *HSBA Handbook on Ship Finance*,
DOI 10.1007/978-3-662-43410-9_2,

Modern risk management of shipping projects demands a holistic approach and the initial financing of the ship (or of the fleet) reflects the views of both lenders and borrowers or of the investors when equity financing prevails. Therefore, this chapter aims to briefly outline the loan calculations and to discuss the risk management considerations reflected in business plans and agreements.

The reader can in the first section of this chapter review the basic modeling of a typical loan scheme and examine the impact of the key parameters and assumption. A review of simple loan calculations highlights the importance of duration and interest as well as their impact on the installment. Basic financial calculations, the setup of financial plans, the criteria and the use of spreadsheets are considered elementary knowledge. Simple cases are presented and examined using the commonly used criteria of Net Present Value (NPV), Internal Rate of Return (IRR), and Required Freight Rate (RFR); the impact of cost of capital, scrap value, tax, and depreciation is also discussed. The aim of the second section is to identify the main risks and outline the ways they are commonly mitigated in the policies and impact the financial planning and decision-making of the whole venture. Common lending risks, such as liquidity, interest, and counter-party risks are discussed as well as risks related to the industry and parameters than cannot be controlled, such as asset price fluctuations and regulatory changes are considered. A brief recapitulation concludes this chapter.

2.1.1 Reviewing Loan Calculations

All loan agreements feature a schedule of payments. The terms of the loan determine the necessary parameters, which are:

- the amount of the loan (principal): A (commonly in USD in shipping projects)
- the interest (yield): r (a percentage based on Libor and/or Euribor[1])
- the duration (tenor): N (commonly in years)
- the instalments: capital and interest outlays

From the financing perspective, the interest lies with the estimation of the instalment required to repay the capital and pay the interest. Repayment of capital is an issue of the loan agreement. Should the capital be repaid in equal instalments? Is there a grace period? Are the instalments and the interest linked to the outstanding loan? These are only some of the aspects that arise when discussing and negotiating the loan agreement. For simplicity, in the following example, it is assumed that the capital should be repaid in equal annual installments. It is easy to express the fixed amount of installments mathematically, given the A, r and N parameters.

[1] London Interbank Offered Rate (Libor) and Euro Interbank Offered Rate (Euribor) are the primary benchmarks for short-term interest rates. Libor is the estimated interbank borrowing interest rate of the British Bankers' Association (BBA). The Euribor is a daily reference rate based on the averaged interbank interest rates among Eurozone banks.

Assume that A_t is the amount of outstanding loan at the end of period t. In the first year, $A_0 = A$, and at the end of the loan period, $A_N = 0$. If B is the requested installment, then for every year $t = 0, 1 \ldots N$, the following relationship is derived:

$$B = (A_t - A_{t+1}) + rA_t \tag{2.1}$$

This implies that the installment is equal to the difference in outstanding capital between two consecutive years (A_t, A_{t+1}) and the interest payment rA_t. Equation (2.1) can be rewritten as $A_{t+1} = (r+1)A_t - B$, where $t = 0, 1 \ldots N$. This means that:

$$\begin{aligned}
A_1 &= (r+1)A - B \\
A_2 = (r+1)A_1 - B &= (r+1)^2 A - (r+1)B - B \\
A_3 = (r+1)A_2 - B = (r+1)^3 A &- (r+1)^2 B - (r+1)B - B \\
&\vdots \\
A_i = (r+1)A_{i-1} - B &= (r+1)^i A - \sum_{k=0}^{i-1} (r+1)^k B \\
&\vdots \\
A_N &= (r+1)^N A - \sum_{k=0}^{N-1} (r+1)^k B
\end{aligned} \tag{2.2}$$

But $A_N = 0$, therefore:

$$\begin{aligned}
A_N = (r+1)^N A - \sum_{k=0}^{N-1} (r+1)^k B = 0 \Rightarrow \\
B = \frac{(r+1)^N A}{\sum_{k=0}^{N-1} (r+1)^k} \\
B = \frac{A_r}{1 - (\frac{1}{1+r})^N}
\end{aligned} \tag{2.3}$$

Spreadsheets can easily handle such calculations, enabling users to build powerful models and plans. Equation (2.3) suggests that the higher the interest, the higher the installment B and the longer the duration N of the loan, the closer B is to the interest payment—i.e. $B = A_r$, when. Furthermore, one can quickly calculate the expected payments, given A, r and N. Thus, in the numerical example where

Table 2.1 Instalment: interest vs. duration of the loan

	4 %	5 %	6 %	7 %	8 %	9 %	10 %
4	6,887,251	7,050,296	7,214,787	7,380,703	7,548,020	7,716,717	7,886,770
5	5,615,678	5,774,370	5,934,910	6,097,267	6,261,411	6,427,311	6,594,937
6	4,769,048	4,925,437	5,084,066	5,244,895	5,407,885	5,572,995	5,740,185
7	4,165,240	4,320,495	4,478,375	4,638,830	4,801,810	4,967,263	5,135,137
8	3,713,196	3,868,045	4,025,899	4,186,694	4,350,369	4,516,859	4,686,100
9	3,362,325	3,517,252	3,675,556	3,837,162	4,001,993	4,169,970	4,341,013
10	3,082,274	3,237,614	3,396,699	3,559,438	3,725,737	3,895,502	4,068,635

Table 2.2 Difference from the original instalment: interest vs. duration of the loan

	4 %	5 %	6 %	7 %	8 %	9 %	10 %
4	64.5 %	68.4 %	72.3 %	76.3 %	80.3 %	84.3 %	88.4 %
5	34.1 %	37.9 %	41.8 %	45.6 %	49.6 %	53.5 %	57.5 %
6	13.9 %	17.6 %	21.4 %	25.3 %	29.2 %	33.1 %	37.1 %
7	−0.5 %	3.2 %	7.0 %	10.8 %	14.7 %	18.6 %	22.7 %
8	−11.3 %	−7.6 %	−3.8 %	0.0 %	3.9 %	7.9 %	11.9 %
9	−19.7 %	−16.0 %	−12.2 %	−8.3 %	−4.4 %	−0.4 %	3.7 %
10	−26.4 %	−22.7 %	−18.9 %	−15.0 %	−11.0 %	−7.0 %	−2.8 %

$A =$ US\$25 m, $r = 7\,\%$ and $N \rightarrow \infty$ years, the instalment $B =$ US\$4,186,694 is derived. Tables 2.1 and 2.2 indicate the sensitivity of the instalment over various years of duration and interest rates as well as the extent of difference from the given original case.

Borrowers and lenders often agree on terms such as interest payment on the outstanding capital, negotiate a balloon or a bullet loan,[2] or decide on a grace period where no capital repayment is expected. Based on the following example, the differences in financing costs are clearly exposed in Tables 2.3 (outstanding capital), 2.4 (repayment with a grace period of 2 years) and 2.5 (bullet payment). In all these tables, the difference Diff. indicates the difference from the fixed interest payment of the first case. Table 2.6 summarises the cost of financing, i.e. the cumulative interest payment; it is clear that the bullet payment and the grace period schedule are the most expensive to borrowers. The substantially lower interest payments at the beginning of the loan period are compensated with substantially higher payments at the end. This could also raise concerns regarding the repayment capabilities of the borrowers; therefore, lenders might opt for a more conservative approach to the payment schedule. A counterargument that supports lower CapEx through a grace period scheme or a similar one at the early stages of the project

[2]A balloon payment is one where the capital repayments are not equal, but gradually increase towards the end of the agreed duration; a bullet payment is one where the capital is repaid at the end.

Table 2.3 Interest payment on the outstanding capital

	Outstanding capital	Interest	Capital	Installment	Diff.
1	25,000,000	1,750,000	3,125,000	4,875,000	16.4 %
2	21,875,000	1,531,250	3,125,000	4,656,250	11.2 %
3	18,750,000	1,312,500	3,125,000	4,437,500	6.0 %
4	15,625,000	1,093,750	3,125,000	4,218,750	0.8 %
5	12,500,000	875,000	3,125,000	4,000,000	−4.5 %
6	9,375,000	656,250	3,125,000	3,781,250	−9.7 %
7	6,250,000	437,500	3,125,000	3,562,500	−14.9 %
8	3,125,000	218,750	3,125,000	3,343,750	−20.1 %

Table 2.4 Interest payment on the outstanding capital (grace period of 2 years granted)

	Outstanding capital	Interest	Capital	Instalment	Diff.
1	25,000,000	1,750,000	0	1,750,000	−58.2 %
2	25,000,000	1,750,000	0	1,750,000	−58.2 %
3	25,000,000	1,750,000	4,166,667	5,916,667	41.3 %
4	20,833,333	1,458,333	4,166,667	5,625,000	34.4 %
5	16,666,667	1,166,667	4,166,667	5,333,333	27.4 %
6	12,500,000	875,000	4,166,667	5,041,667	20.4 %
7	8,333,333	583,333	4,166,667	4,750,000	13.5 %
8	4,166,667	291,667	4,166,667	4,458,333	6.5 %

Table 2.5 Bullet payment

	Outstanding capital	Interest	Capital	Instalment	Diff.
1	25,000,000	1,750,000	0	1,750,000	−58.2 %
2	25,000,000	1,750,000	0	1,750,000	−58.2 %
3	25,000,000	1,750,000	0	1,750,000	−58.2 %
4	25,000,000	1,750,000	0	1,750,000	−58.2 %
5	25,000,000	1,750,000	0	1,750,000	−58.2 %
6	25,000,000	1,750,000	0	1,750,000	−58.2 %
7	25,000,000	1,750,000	0	1,750,000	−58.2 %
8	25,000,000	1,750,000	25,000,000	26,750,000	538.9 %

Table 2.6 Comparison of the cost of financing

Method	Interest	Diff.
Fixed	8,493,552	7.9 %
On the outstanding	7,875,000	0.0 %
Grace of 2 years	9,625,000	22.2 %
Bullet	14,000,000	77.8 %

suggests the reduced financial burden at the beginning, when liquidity is often at stake.

The loan calculations are similar to many amortisation financial schemes and provide the basis for the estimation of capital expenses (CapEx).

2.1.2 *Financial Viability Criteria*

2.1.2.1 The NPV and IRR Criteria

Given the schedule of the loan, it is possible to proceed to more complicated calculations related to the project. In shipping projects, the NPV, RFR, and IRR criteria are considered more frequently. The NPV and the IRR are directly interrelated, while the NPV and the RFR are also conceptually intertwined.

The NPV calculations result in a discounted stream of annual profits or losses using the following formula:

$$\text{NPV} = \sum_{t=1}^{N} \frac{(\text{Revenues} - \text{Expenses})_t}{(r+1)^t} \tag{2.4}$$

where r is the discount rate—in most cases, this discount rate equals the opportunity cost of capital or reveals the expected rate of return on an investment in financial markets with similar risk—and N is the duration of the project. Given the maritime business environment, the revenues are commonly proceeds from a time charter (T/C), contract of affreightment or income from employment, e.g. from the spot market. On the other hand, capital (CapEx) and operating (OpEx) expenses as well as expenses related to voyages (VoyEx) should be taken into account, given the employment and operational pattern. If the outcome of the NPV calculation is positive, then this is a potentially lucrative project that should be financed. On the basis of formula (2.4), the IRR is estimated when NPV0 and the discount rate r is approximated numerically. Microsoft *Excel*^{TM} supports functions for all these calculations. NPV is not a widely accepted criterion in shipping, as it is sensitive to the discount rate r, and the IRR criterion is potentially risky, as the formula might have multiple roots within a given space. Thus, both NPV and IRR criteria should be used cautiously. The IRR criterion neglects the size and risk characteristics of the investment, while the NPV is sensitive to the discount rate r, which, sometimes, is either fluctuating or not necessarily known.

2.1.2.2 Required Freight Rate

The RFR criterion is a variation of the NPV formula and is calculated based on a given ship (asset). This criterion determines the economic feasibility of a project at its early design stages, indicating the minimum required freight that sets NPV = 0, thereby indicating the point of indifference of the investor. Expected freight rates higher than the RFR deem the project profitable. Given formula 2.4, the RFR formula is expressed as:

$$\text{NPV} = \sum_{t=1}^{N} \frac{F * X_t - C_t}{(r+1)^t} = 0 \tag{2.5}$$

where:

- X_t is the expected payload in year t
- C_t is the expected total cost in year t (all costs included)
- r is the discount factor
- F is the freight

When $F = F*$, then NPV $= 0$, so $F*$ is the minimum required freight rate. The application of the RFR is illustrated in the following example, where the following conditions of a mini-bulker project are considered:

1. Purchase Price: US$4.5 m (in year 0)
2. Expected Life of the Project (operational horizon): 10 years
3. Remaining Value of the Asset: US$0.3 m (in year 10)
4. Annual Operating Expenses: US$0.8 m
5. Annual payload: 120,000 tons
6. Linear Depreciation in 10 years
7. Cost of Capital: 10 %

$$\text{NPV} = 0 \Rightarrow -4.5 * 10^6 + F * 120 * 10^3 \sum_{r=1}^{10} \frac{1}{(1+0.1)^t} + \frac{0.3 * 10^6}{(1+0.1)^10}$$
$$-0.8 * 10^6 \sum_{r=1}^{20} \frac{1}{(1+0.1)^t} = 0 \tag{2.6}$$

Equation (2.6) can be solved numerically, and the final result is F = US$11.03/ton, which implies that any freight rate over and above the lower limit of US$11.03/ton leads to positive results. As in the case of NPV and IRR, RFR is not a flawless criterion. The size of the investment is "neglected", as previously. In reality, this criterion favours large and relatively slow ships that inherently offer a low unit cost of transport. It is also a static criterion because freight markets fluctuate. Yet, the counterargument is that it offers a benchmarking level.

2.1.3 Concluding Remarks

All the criteria aim to estimate the present value of future streams, and the impact of financing, such as CapEx, is predominant. A bullet payment implies that a lender receives in the current year, capital of value X at a price of $\frac{X}{(1+r)^t}$ in the year t of maturity. This may be compensated with higher interest throughout the loan period. The option of equal capital repayments could lead to more affordable instalments B. Yet, the total cost of financing might be higher than that of other loan schedules (see Table 2.6). This endless discussion depends on the loan terms and the outcome of negotiations between lenders and borrowers. Both sides are aware of the simple mechanics of the cost of capital.

In general, the weighted average cost of capital (WACC) is considered in the NPV, IRR, and RFR formulas, reflecting gearing and expected returns on equity (ROE). This is also a key benchmark, as capital with a higher cost (say a loan with an interest $r >$ WACC) decreases the value of the NPV (the financial attractiveness of the project), reduces the IRR and increases the RFR; therefore, the lower the cost of capital, the more attractive the investment. Generally, a loan (debt) magnifies the financial results when $r <$ WACC ceteris paribus.

Another point of interest is the depreciation and tax schemes. Depreciation is not an outlay of cash per se; however, it determines the taxable income. So, the higher the depreciation in a fiscal year, the lesser is the expected taxable income, all other parameters remaining equal. Therefore, depreciation schemes might decide whether an investment is attractive. Lastly, most jurisdictions have a tonnage tax scheme i.e. a taxation scheme dependent on the size, type and age of the asset so that tax can be a fixed annual outlay.

2.2 Analysing a Simple Case

The following example[3] can help the reader understand the risks and hidden assumptions related to the financial plan of a maritime venture. Assume the following case:

- The purchase price of the new building is US$35 m and a loan of US$20 m is provided. The duration of the loan is eight fiscal years and the interest is 7.5 %. A fixed capital and interest instalment [see Eq. 2.3] is expected from the beginning of the project (say fiscal year 0, when the ship is under construction). Equity returns are omitted.
- The operating expenses (OpEx) are estimated at US$7,500/day in the first year of operation (say fiscal year 1) and with an expected escalation rate of 2.5 %.
- Employment is secured for the first five fiscal years with a time charter agreement of US$21,000/day. In a fiscal year, 330 days of normal operation are estimated. The operation days are reduced to 300 in the fifth and tenth fiscal years due to the statutory special surveys and required dry docking. It is also estimated that a time-charter agreement of US$18,000/day should be expected between the sixth and tenth fiscal years.
- At this moment of the project, the ship is expected to be sold and transferred to new owners at a minimum price of US$5 m at the end of the fiscal year 10, as there is a policy of operating only relatively young tonnage.

[3]All figures are absolutely fictitious and considered here only for the needs of comprehensive reading.

Given the above scenario, one can easily draft the spreadsheet and calculate the NPV and IRR of the project, where B=US\$3,415,540 is the annuity, i.e. the annual cost of financing (capital and installment):

$$\mathrm{NPV} = \sum_{t=1}^{N} \frac{(\mathrm{Revenues} - \mathrm{Expenses})_t}{(r+1)^t} = +\frac{5*10^6}{(r+1)^{10}} + \sum_{t=1}^{5} \frac{\mathrm{TC}}{(r+1)^t} + \sum_{t=6}^{10} \frac{\mathrm{TC_{est}}}{(r+1)^t} - \sum_{t=0}^{7} \frac{B}{(r+1)^t} - \sum_{t=1}^{10} \frac{\mathrm{OPEX}_t * (1+2.5\,\%)^{t-1}}{(r+1)^t} \tag{2.7}$$

Considering $r = 12\,\%$ as WACC and by substituting the appropriate values, the NPV is estimated as NPV ≈US\$2.9 m. Hence, this project scenario is a lucrative one. Based on formula (2.7), one could perform a sensitivity analysis and check the influence of the assumptions:

- If the operating days are reduced by 10 % ceteris paribus, then the NPV is negative (≈US\$0.4 m). This implies that the efficiency of the technical managers should be sufficiently high and the ship should avoid off-hire situations.
- If the OpEx are increased at a ratio higher than the expected 2.5 % per annum, then the attractiveness of the project is decreasing. Assume a growth rate of 4 % per annum ceteris paribus, and the NPV is US\$2.0 m. This result implies the requirement for strict cost control and monitoring of all expenses.
- Should the interest of the loan be higher, say 10 %, then the NPV would decrease to approximately US\$1.1 m. At higher levels of cost of financing, the project could be considered as indifferent, and the negotiation limits could be outlined.
- Assume that the market conditions deteriorate steadily, thus making the expectation of US\$18,000/day time charter after the fifth fiscal year unrealistic. Then it is possible to approximate the minimum value of circa US\$13,550/day, where NPV → 0, thereby indicating the financial viability limits.

The discounted cumulative profits of the last fiscal year imply a return of 6.5 % over the total value of US\$35 m of the asset or 14.8 % over the loan amount. In many cases, the level of returns is also a benchmark for the further consideration of the project. On exploring the previous case further, no time-charter agreement backing this project is assumed. The owners might follow a speculative strategy and offer this ship in the spot market. This implies two more sets of risks:

1. the fluctuation of the spot market rates, and
2. the fluctuation of bunker prices, which comprise the highest part of the expenses.

To explore these risks, assume the previous case, but with a different employment pattern:

- A spot rate of US\$33,000/day is estimated.
- Almost 220 days per year at sea and 110 days at port are considered. In the fifth and tenth fiscal years, the days at sea are reduced to 190 due to the obligatory dry docking, while the days at port remain 110.

- A consumption pattern of 25 tons/day HFO at sea and 2 tons/day at port is estimated at an average price of US$700/ton of bunkers and an annual price increase of 3 %.

Given the above data, the adjusted NPV formula [Eq. (2.7)] yields US$2.4 m and the sensitivity analysis suggests:

- Should the assumption of US$33,000/day did not materialise and only a lower market rate is possible, say US$30,000/day, then the NPV is negative and the project should be rejected.
- Should the average price of bunkers be higher, say US$800/ton (i.e. 14 % higher), then the NPV is also negative.
- Should the consumption of bunkers be higher, say 28 tons/day, then the NPV is also negative.

The returns are affected by changes in the parameters of the project and the financing.

2.3 Risk Management

In the previous section, only numerical considerations were presented, and the impact of various assumptions was explored. In reality, not all parameters and assumptions can be quantified and objectively considered in a formula. Real world is complex and there is no perfect financial or technical model, so there are many considerations left to be taken into account, in more qualitative form.

In the business jargon, the 5C summarise the main set of risks to considered, namely: Collateral, Capital, Conditions, Character, and Capacity. Capacity refers to the ability of the owners to repay the loan and generally to honour the financial obligations undertaken. Collateral is directly related to the capacity as it refers to securities of all forms that can be provided to the banks or the investors. Capital in this context represents the involvement of the owners in the venture by risking and contributing own funds. Character is a subjective judgement made by the bankers and the investors about the perspective client. It is a matter of trust among the parties involved. Finally, under conditions there are twofold approaches: one can assume the global economic climate and the specific conditions in the maritime industry, such as freight rate levels, offered tonnage, etc. or the conditions of the intended loan or business plan.

This pattern of analysis is extremely helpful and highlights the part of "art" vis-á-vis the part of "science" of modern financing. Apparently, this approach might be considered scientifically "näve" as there are no crisp rules and criteria that can determine the preference among projects or their distinct financial structures. Nevertheless, this analysis has a rational and reflects experience gained over the years.

Unquestionably, a shipping venture is exposed to a number of different risks. There are risks related to operations and technical performance, financial developments or conditions, as well as regulatory developments are only some that impact the overall expected or actual performance of the project and impacts at some extend the standing of the ship owners, of borrowers and of the investors. Ship finance practitioners have adopted risk management strategies, either as a response to an aftermath, such as of numerous loans that are not honoured, or due to compliance needs, such as Basel III Requirements, or as a trend and recommended set of best practices, the so-called "lessons learned". Risks associated with the project per se, are called *specific*, while risks associated with industry are regarded as*systematic*.

2.3.1 Project-Related Lending Risks

Given the previous cases, the financial plan reveals some risks that borrowers and lenders should consider, discuss and mitigate jointly if possible. These risks can be briefly summarised as follows.

2.3.1.1 Credit and Counter-Party Risk

Is the risk associated with breach of obligations or commitments assumed towards any kind of creditor? Counter-party risk is related to selecting inappropriate counter parties for conducting business (counter parties that are unlikely to honour their obligations and commitments towards the company) and/or relying on a single counter party for doing business. This can be mitigated only by asking for credit ranking and establishing risk assessment and monitoring procedures. Such risks commonly include the following:

- A probability of counter parties not honouring their financial obligations (i.e. charterers) also exists. This probability could be limited by enabling agreements with only first-class charterers and carrying out internal assessments of counter parties prior to any engagement.
- There is also a probability of potential decline in the vessel's market value, which may lead to a default in loan agreements. Policies and written instructions regarding heavy amortisation of loans and loan covenants could be considered as mitigation policies by both lenders and borrowers.

2.3.1.2 Financial Risks

Financial risk is related to volatility in foreign exchange rates and to the movement of interest rates. Various risk approaches mitigate, transfer or accept the associated risks. A typical issue with foreign exchange rates is that all revenues generated are in USD but a significant portion of companies' expenses are incurred in other currencies, such as the Yen or the Euro. Monitoring the fluctuation of USD against other currencies as well as foreign exchange exposure and a potential adoption of hedging policies are expected.

2.3.1.3 Interest Rate Risk

A potential significant increase in the cost of money will burden the company's financing expenses, thereby negatively affecting financial results. In practice, borrowers and lenders can only monitor the cost of funding and, when necessary, agree on corrective measures (i.e. hedging policies).

2.3.1.4 Freight Rate Risks

The fluctuation of freight rates and the cyclical nature of the industry may lead to volatile changes in revenues and vessel values, which may adversely affect the company's earnings and financial standing.

2.3.1.5 Fuel Prices

Under voyage-charter agreements where the ship owner has to pay for voyage expenses, rising bunker fuel prices can reduce earnings significantly and make voyages unprofitable. This is prevalent when vessels are employed in the spot market due to a strategic option or speculation.

2.3.1.6 Vessel (Asset) Values

The market value of vessels may fluctuate significantly. Losses may occur when the vessels have to be sold or due to the writing down of the vessels' carrying value. Such losses reduce the company's earnings and profit margins while raising tax and depreciation concerns.

Although the above risk elements are discussed extensively in the academic and business literature, many project teams fail to manage them efficiently. In order to avoid troubled situations, banks usually draft a policy, i.e. a set of general criteria that refer to terms and conditions of employment and projections. Although it is impossible to generalise these criteria, the following points are present in most lending policies:

- There are age limits for the ships (assets) to be financed, say 15 years for a cargo ship and 20 years for a passenger ferry.

- There is a limit to the financing provided, say the bank is willing to finance only 60 % of the purchase price or fair market value, whichever is lower.
- The loan agreement includes conditions relating the outstanding loan and the market value of the ship, say a clause standing that the market value of the mortgaged asset should exceed the outstanding loan by a minimum of 20 %. If this is not the case, then lenders should ask for additional securities as collateral.
- The maximum loan duration should not exceed a specific limit, say 10 years from the loan disbursement.
- The terms and the expected return from the ship loan should be in accordance with the general risk management rules of the bank.
- The bank should approve the ship insurances and relevant agreements or limits (e.g. the deductibles.)
- The bank could perform credit checking regularly on charterers (and owners) in case of long-term charter agreements.
- The bank might ask for cash flow projections of the owner's fleet, not only of the ship under discussion, and perform various liquidity checks' or draft relevant clauses.
- The bank might ask for securities, such as:

  1. First preferred mortgage on the ship under discussion, and possibly first or second mortgage on other ships of the owner's fleet (cross-collateral structures)
  2. Assignments of insurance
  3. Assignments of freight
  4. Guarantees (personal and/or corporate)

All the above provisos aim to safeguard the interests of lenders and they also reflect the risk management strategy of the lending portfolio of the bank and the options available for marketing. Most of them are also explicitly stated in the loan agreements, as binding terms for both parties. Nevertheless, the risks related to price-fluctuations and other non-controlled parameters cannot be considered in loan agreements; therefore, more sophisticated and company-wide risk management strategies are required. The quality of the risk management plan of the ship owners could be contemplated as an element determining the "capacity" and "character" of the borrower.

2.3.2 *Industry-Related Risks*

An investment in the company involves a significant degree of risk for both equity investors and debt providers, as the decision to support a shipping project financially involves capturing capital and restraining liquidity for a relatively long period. There is no assurance that the company's objectives will be achieved or that there will be any return of capital. Potential investors and lending institutions should carefully consider all of the information set forth in the loan agreement, including the following risk factors, and consult professional advisors before deciding to invest in the company. The company's business, results of operations, financial condition and prospects could be adversely affected if any of these risks occur. Consequently, the value or price of the shares could decline and investors could lose all or part of their investment. The risks described below are not exhaustive and may not be the only risks. The order in which the risks are presented does not reflect the likelihood of their occurrence nor the magnitude or significance of the individual risks. The value or price of the shares could fall if any of these risks were to materialise, in which case investors could lose all or part of their investment. The risks involved indicate that investment in the company is suitable only for those persons or entities that can bear the economic risk of the investment, understand the high degree of risk involved, believe that the investment suits their investment objectives and financial needs, and have no need for liquidity of investment. Should any non-professional investor invest in shares of the company, it is advisable that only part of the sum that such an investor intends for long-term investment should be invested herein.

The risks described below can occur in combination with each other, which may intensify the material adverse effects on the company's business, financial conditions and results of operations.

2.3.2.1 Risks Relating to the Shipping Industry

- **Cyclicality of the Markets**

  The company is exposed to cyclical fluctuations of the shipping industry through its charters, which result in the volatility of sales, profitability and vessel values. The company's portfolio may comprise both long-term and short-term charters (including voyage charters) of vessels as well as pool employment. Since its charters would be affected by cyclical fluctuations in the relevant shipping industry segment, the company would be affected indirectly. The shipping industry is subject to cyclical fluctuations primarily due to changes in the supply of and demand for different shipping capacities, which result in the volatility of sales, profitability and vessel values. The demand for vessels and charter rates themselves are influenced by global and regional economic conditions, developments in international trade, changes in seaborne and other transportation patterns, weather patterns, climate changes, armed conflicts, canal closures, bunker prices, foreign exchange fluctuations, embargoes and strikes, among other factors. Furthermore, there can be no assurance that an unexpected increase in the number of vessels on order and/or delivered will not occur. Many of the factors influencing the supply of and demand for shipping capacity are outside the company's control, and the nature, timing and degree of changes in industry conditions are unpredictable. Decreases in the demand for shipping services or increases in the supply of capacity could lead to significantly lower charter rates, which could have a material adverse effect on the company's business, financial condition and results of operations. The same applies if at the end of the charter period or upon early termination of a charter as per the charterer's termination right, the company finds no new employment or only employment at low rates for the vessel.

The company's results of operations may be affected by increases in the operating expenses of owned vessels. Under time charters, the charterer bears all voyage expenses, including the cost of bunkers, as well as canal and port charges. The ship manager is responsible for the operation and management of each vessel on behalf of the company, including crewing, repairs and maintenance, periodic dry docking and insurance. The costs are borne by the owner of the vessel. The ship manager provides these services to the company pursuant to the individual ship management agreements and acts as an agent for the company. The ship manager receives a ship management fee for services rendered based on market practice and standard market terms. In case the ship's management is executed by a related party of investment advisors, the maximum fee for technical and commercial management of the vessels will be around 3–4 % of the gross charter. In addition to payment for these services, the company will—except for bareboat charter contracts—pay the operating expenses and dry-docking expenditures for the vessels. Furthermore, the company will reimburse the ship manager for actual costs incurred in respect of certain other operating costs. Any changes in the operating expenses for the company's vessels will affect the results of operations. In addition, factors beyond the company's control, such as developments relating to market premiums for insurance, increase in material cost and/or crew labour cost or change in regulations or laws may cause the operating costs of the company's vessels to increase.

- **Off-Hire and Docking Periods**

  In case of off hire and dry dockings, the company receives no charter hire but has to bear all costs incurred during the period. Under the company's charter and pool agreements, when a vessel is off hire or not available for service, the charterer or pool manager would generally not be required to pay the company the charter hire. The company would have to cover all costs during such off-hire and possible repositioning, including the cost of bunkers. A vessel will be considered to be off-hire if there is an occurrence preventing the full working of the vessel due to, among other factors, operational deficiencies, dry docking for repairs, maintenance or inspection, equipment breakdowns, delays due to accidents, crew strikes and boycotts, certain vessel detentions or similar problems, the company's failure to maintain the vessel in compliance with its specifications and contractual standards or failure to provide the required crew. At least every 5 years, a vessel needs to be dry-docked for an average of 8 days to undergo major repairs, subject to the size, type, condition and age of the vessel.

- **Performance and Credit Risks**

  The company faces the performance and credit risks of the charterers under the charter agreements. The company's income is primarily derived from the charter income of vessels. Thus, the company is dependent on the charterers' due performance of their respective obligations under the charter agreements. A default or delay by a charterer in the payment of the charter income, or failure by a charterer to perform other obligations under a charter, including re-delivery of the vessels in the conditions specified under the charter, could result in a loss of income or additional costs for the company; therefore, it could have a material adverse effect on the financial performance of the company.

- **Asset Price Fluctuations**

  The company is exposed to trends inherent in the shipping industry. In general, vessel values experience a degree of volatility. The fair market value of the company's vessels can be expected to fluctuate depending on the economic and market conditions affecting the shipping industry as well as on competition from other shipping companies in a largely fragmented market, from different types and sizes of vessels and from other modes of transportation. In addition, the value of aging vessels is expected to decline. These factors affect the value of the company's portfolio at the termination of the charter contracts or earlier, at the time of sale of a vessel. Changes in the value of a vessel could also have significant effects on loan agreements, including on value maintenance clauses, i.e. higher borrowing costs or even termination of a loan. This could have a material adverse effect on the financial performance of the company.

- **Size of Fleet and Delivery Dates of New Buildings**

  The size of fleet affects both revenue potential and cost structure of the company. The percentage of new ships as well as the newbuilding program shape also the capital requirements at large. As the company's revenues will be generated through spot (including voyage charters) and medium- to long-term charters as well as income from the employment of vessels within pools, the company's financial results will be largely affected by the size of the company's fleet and the delivery dates of its vessels. Generally, the larger the number of available ships, the higher the chances for implementing an effective physical hedging strategy that keeps the total revenue of the fleet at desirable levels. In practice, some ships are under long-term time charters, while other under medium-term time ones, and the rest of the tonnage seeks short-term employment, e.g. in the spot market. The revenues from the time-chartered ships might subsidy ships of the fleet faced with high capital expenditures, such as dry-docking and repairs, or ships that do not earn enough to cover their own expenses. This is a strategy, many tonnage operators follow, due to the inherent economies of scale and ability of moving cash from various cost- and profit-centers, e.g. from the ships of the fleet.

  Considering the mix of existing ships and ships in the order book, any deviation from the contracted delivery dates of new buildings will significantly affect the operating results either due to postponed availability of cash flows, reduction in charter rates or even full cancellation of the charter contracts. For this reason, the company intends only to sign shipbuilding contracts with experienced, high-quality, reputable yards with a proven track record of delivering vessels in time, and negotiate stringent clauses that decrease the contractual value. Nevertheless, the delivery of newbuildings is often delayed.

- **Inadequate Insurance Coverage**
  The operation of an ocean-going vessel carries inherent risks. These risks include but are not limited to the possibility of marine disasters, war, terrorism or piracy, political action in various countries, environmental accidents, cargo and property losses or damage, business interruptions caused by mechanical failure, human error as well as by labour strikes, port closings, boycotts or adverse weather conditions. Any of the above or any other unforeseen circumstances or events could increase the costs of the investment structure, lower its revenues or ultimately result in a total loss without any compensation. The involvement of the company's vessels in an environmental disaster may also handicap the company's reputation and have a material adverse effect on the company's business, results of operations or financial condition. Due to the structure of the company holding vessels in separate investment structures, liability is usually limited to the equity investment of the company in each individual investment structure. Nevertheless, the company might be liable beyond the initial equity investment if a risk is not adequately insured. Despite the insurance coverage, risks may arise against which the investment structure or even the company is not adequately insured or is unable to insure itself. For example, a catastrophic oil spill or gas explosion could exceed the insurance coverage of the investment structure and the company, and could have a material adverse effect on its operations. In addition, the company may in future be unable to procure adequate insurance coverage on terms and conditions comparable to those that the company is currently expecting to realise. If it is an insurable event at all, the company expects to be protected against business interruption risks only from the 15th day off hire up to a certain limit. Thus, the investment structure will have to bear any commercial costs arising during or after the period not covered by the insurance. Furthermore, business interruptions like labour strikes, e.g. by the stevedores, could be substantial enough to cause a material adverse effect on the company's earnings and financial condition. The investment structure is also exposed to liability in the event that cargo is delivered without being presented with an original bill of lading. Although a counter indemnity from the charterer is generally required to mitigate such a liability, recovery of indemnified amounts from the charterer may not be possible. Such risks are not covered by protection and indemnity insurance in the shipping industry. In addition, the company cannot ensure that any particular insurance claim will be awarded or paid. New and stricter environmental regulations have led to higher costs for insurance covering environmental damage or pollution, and new regulations could lead to other increases or even make this type of insurance unavailable. Even if the company's insurance coverage is adequate to cover losses, the company may not be able to obtain a replacement ship in time in the event of a loss. The company may also be subject to calls or premiums in amounts based not only on the company's own claim records but also the claim records of all other members of the protection and indemnity associations through which the company obtains insurance coverage for tort liability. The company's payment of these calls could

result in significant expenses to the company, which would reduce profits or even cause losses.

- **Regulatory Changes and Associated Costs of Compliance**
  The shipping industry is extensively regulated. The company's operations could be affected by the substantial and evolving environmental protection laws and other regulations in the form of numerous international conventions, national, state and local laws, and national and international regulations in force in the jurisdictions where the vessels operate as well as in the country or countries where such vessels are registered. Compliance with such laws and regulations may entail significant expenses, including expenses for ship design modifications and changes in operating procedures. The ship manager may also incur, on behalf of the company, substantial costs in order to comply with existing and future environmental, health and human safety requirements, including obligations relating to air exhaust emissions, maintenance and inspection, development and implementation of emergency procedures and insurance coverage. These costs could have a material adverse effect on the company's financial condition and results of operations. The operating certificates and licenses for the vessels are renewed periodically during each vessel's required annual survey. However, government regulation of vessels, particularly in the areas of safety and environmental impact may change in the future and require the ship manager to incur, on behalf of the company, significant capital expenditure on the vessels in its portfolio to ensure compliance under a charter agreement. In addition, the company is required by various governmental bodies to obtain the permits and licenses required for the operation of its vessels. These permits may become costly or impossible to obtain or renew. Vessels in the company's portfolio have to operate within the rules, international conventions and regulations adopted by the International Maritime Organization (IMO) as well as the environmental protection laws, health and safety regulations and various marine protection laws in each of the jurisdictions where the company's vessels operate. Since the IMO's International Management Code for the Safe Operation of Ships and Pollution Prevention (ISM Code) became effective in 1998, shipping companies and individual vessels are required to establish safety systems and have them certified by standardisation bodies. In complying with IMO regulations and other regulations that may be adopted, the ship manager may be required to incur, on behalf of the company, additional costs in meeting new maintenance and inspection requirements, in developing contingency arrangements for potential contamination by vessels and in obtaining insurance coverage. Since such conventions, laws and regulations are often revised, the company is unable to predict the long-term costs of compliance. The adoption of additional laws and regulations could limit the ship manager's ability to do business and could have a material adverse effect on the business, financial position and results, business operations of the company, and distributions to shareholders.
- **Operations in Various Jurisdictions**
  The company is expected to own and operate vessels through various investment structures. Each investment structure is governed by its organisational

documents as well as the jurisdiction under which the investment structure is organised. The rights of the shareholders, the responsibilities of the governing bodies and the corporate governance standards of these investment structures may differ depending on the jurisdiction. Some jurisdictions may provide less protection to the interests of the shareholders than do other jurisdictions. Thus, pursuing claims and enforcing rights as well as judgments for the investment structures may be more difficult than with an investment structure that operates within a single jurisdiction. Additionally, insolvency procedures may be treated very differently depending on the relevant jurisdiction. Furthermore, the investment structures may be affected by political, legal, economic and other changes in the jurisdiction of their organisation and their operation.

- **Political and Work Economy Related Risks**
  The vessels call at ports in various countries around the world, including in emerging markets. Hence, the company's business is subject to the political, economic and social conditions of the countries where these ports are located. For example, the company will be exposed to the risks of political unrest, war and economic and other forms of instability, such as natural disasters, epidemics, widespread transmission of communicable or infectious diseases, acts of God, terrorist attacks and other events beyond its control, which may adversely affect local economies, infrastructures and livelihoods. These events could disrupt the business of the company's customers and lead to seisure of or damage to the customers' assets. They could also make it difficult for the company to protect its assets, including by enforcing its rights, in these jurisdictions. These events could also cause the partial or complete closure of particular ports and sea passages, such as the Suez or Panama Canal, thereby potentially resulting in higher costs, vessel delays and cancellations of some lines. Furthermore, these events could lead to reductions in, or in the growth rate of, world trade, which could reduce demand for vessels and/or services. The political, economic or social conditions in any of these countries may affect the business and financial conditions of the company's customers. This may affect the creditworthiness of the customers and increase the risk of default on the charterers, which would adversely impact the ability of the company's customers to pay a charter income under the charter agreements for the vessels. Consequently, this would affect the stability of income flow to the company and its ability to expand its business.

2.3.2.2 Risks Related to the Company

- **Risks Associated with other Investments**
  The company may invest in other companies or in other investment vehicles using similar investment strategies while domiciled in jurisdictions where these vehicles are not subject to control by a supervisory authority affording investor protection. Consequently, shareholders of these vehicles cannot benefit from the protection ensured by such a supervisory authority. Furthermore, investment by the company in other companies or in other investment vehicles may result in a

duplication of certain costs and expenses that will be charged to the company, i.e. setting up, filing and domicile-related costs, subscription or redemption fees, management fees, custodian bank fees, auditing and other related costs. For shareholders, the accumulation of these costs may lead to higher expenses than would have been charged to the company if the latter had invested directly in the underlying assets.

- **Debt Financing**

  As already outlined in Sect. 2.3.1, use of debt will expose the company to risks associated with debt financing in general, including the risk that the company's cash flows will be insufficient to meet principal and interest payments as required by the loan agreements as well as the risk of not being able to refinance at all or at unfavourable terms and conditions compared to the existing debt. If the company engages in debt agreements with variable or floating interest rate payments, it will be exposed to fluctuations in the underlying interest rate markets, thereby leading to higher debt service on higher market interest rates that adversely affect the company. In future, the company may engage in transactions to limit its exposure to rising interest rates, as it deems appropriate and cost effective. These transactions could expose the company to the risk that counter parties to such transactions may not perform, thereby causing adverse effects on the company associated with increases in market interest rates. The above-described effects related to debt may increase with the overall level of debt.

- **Management Team**

  The company's ability to compete successfully and implement its business strategy will depend significantly on the ability of the board of directors, the investment committee and the investment advisors to identify and consummate suitable investments, to assist in improving the operating performance of investment structures, and to dispose of and exit investments at a profit. The loss of services of the company's key management and its inability to hire and retain other qualified key personnel could have a material adverse effect on the company's business, financial condition and results of operations.

- **Exchange Rate Fluctuation**

  Fluctuations in exchange rates between the USD and the relevant local currencies, costs of conversion, hedging arrangements (if any are used) and exchange control regulations will directly affect the value of the company's investments and the ultimate rate of return realised by the shareholders.

- **Financial Hedging Risks**

  The company may use hedging instruments such as interest rate swaps and forward freight agreements. The use of hedging strategies is not an assurance that their use will achieve the intended result, that adequate hedging arrangements will be available to the company on an economically viable basis, or that the company will engage in hedging strategies when available. Furthermore, hedging instruments may limit the company's ability to benefit either partially or fully from the increase in the value of an investment above a certain level. While such hedging transactions may reduce certain risks, such transactions themselves may entail certain other risks, including, but not limited to, counter-party credit risk and market liquidity risk. In addition, if judgments made with respect to future stock prices, exchange rates, market conditions or trends are not correct, hedging strategies could result in losses to the company.

- **Conflicts of Interest**
  Conflicts of interest may occur relating to the company and its service providers who are engaged in businesses and have interests other than that of managing, distributing and otherwise providing services to the company. These activities and interests include potential multiple advisory, transactional, financial and other interests in securities and instruments that may be purchased or sold by the company, or in other investment vehicles used in purchasing or selling such securities and instruments.
- **Indemnity Risks**
  The company is exposed to risks in connection with indemnification obligations in favour of its management. The company will indemnify members of the board of directors, the investment committee, the investment advisors, and their respective directors, officers, employees, agents, advisors, partners, members, affiliates and personnel against claims, liabilities, damages, costs and expenses, including legal fees, judgments and amounts paid in settlement incurred by them through their activities on behalf of the company or the investors. No such person will be liable to the company or any investor for any act or omission (including any error in judgment in making an investment decision) in the absence of gross negligence or wilful misconduct (as finally determined in a court, arbitration, or administrative proceeding) by the person. Investors will not be individually obligated with respect to such indemnification beyond the extent of their commitments.
- **Investments Through Subsidiaries Bear Structural Risks**
  Investments may be made in investment structures through wholly or jointly owned subsidiaries under certain circumstances; in most cases, the aim is to minimise tax exposure, to facilitate future sales of investment structures, or to facilitate an initial offering of stock of the holding company on an international stock exchange. These subsidiaries may have different depositaries, administrators and auditors than the company or no such depositaries, administrators, or auditors. Therefore, the interposition of these subsidiaries entails additional risks that would not have been incurred had the investments been made directly. Such risks could have material adverse effects on the company's business, financial condition and results of operations.

All above risk elements should be taken into account when formulating the risk management strategy of the ship owning and managing company, and at a tactical level be reflected in the Enterprise Risk Management (ERM) system, i.e. a given management approach of identifiable risks and objectives that outlines also the necessary actions. In many cases, an ERM system might be required by regulators, such as the well-known Sarbanes-Oxley Act (SOX), with the official name "Public Company Accounting Reform and Investor Protection Act" or "Corporate and Auditing Accountability and Responsibility Act", that should be in place for all listed companies in the USA. An effective and efficient risk management system ensures access to financial sources, and especially to equity markets. At the same time, it is required by the traditional lenders such a system to be in place, as the challenges of short-term liquidity and long-term capital investment are coupled, and no tonnage owner or operator afford the luxury to ignore the risks of the industry of the projects.

2.4 Concluding Remarks

The understanding and the negotiation over the basic loan terms as well as the accuracy of the risk planning of a project and the thorough examination of all related parameters and assumptions are of paramount importance for both lenders and borrowers. The financial plans of maritime projects are not too complicated and are based on elementary calculations. Discounted cash flows and streams are taken into consideration and typical financial criteria, such as the NPV, the IRR and the more branch-specific RFR, are estimated and support decisions, despite their inherent flaws.

The terms of financing largely determine the financial viability of the project. The calculations can be conducted easily with the help of spreadsheets. Since the basic mathematical formulation is not difficult, fast and accurate results can be achieved manually as well. The development of scenarios and the analysis of sensitivity of the key assumptions also determine the boundary conditions of the financial attractiveness of the project, thereby indicating the upper and lower limits to be considered by borrowers and lenders.

Even an accurate financial planning is not enough to secure a feasible and successful project. Thorough risk assessment strategies and policies should be drafted. These must reflect either as specific clauses in the loan agreement or as general rules for the bank's lending policy, such as the challenge of addressing industry-related risks effectively. The lending policy reflects the wider risk management concepts and philosophy of the bank and might also determine the relative position of the bank vis-á-vis competitors. The additional clauses in the loan agreement reflect the riskiness and attractiveness of the project and safeguard the interests of the lenders. Even then, the interests of both parties cannot be secured against the volatility of the markets and trust. Goodwill, thorough preparation, and seamless communication among all involved parties are expected to address potential risks in due time and effectively. Lastly, the more transparent the relationship among all partners and the more effective the corporate governance of all involved parties, the better managed are all related risks. Transparency, efficient corporate governance and pro-activeness are essential elements for a smooth relationship between lenders and borrowers.

Chapter 3
Legal Treatment of Ship Finance Loans: Analysis of the Ship Loan Contract

Stefan Otto and Thilo Scholl

Abstract This chapter is an introduction to and overview of ship financing and its proper documentation. Ship owners will have a constant need to raise money to support their activities. Their financial needs will have to be predominantly covered by taking recourse to the financial markets. The most common form of finance is to borrow money from a bank. The chapter is intended to give an analysis of the loan agreement, which encloses the terms and conditions under which the ship finance is being advanced. The structure of the loan agreement is orientated on the term sheet agreed between the parties. After a short introduction to the term sheet as legal basis for the loan agreement, the article deals with the structure of the loan agreement and the typical clauses of a loan agreement such as Definitions, Purpose of the Loan, Conditions precedent, Interest, Fees, Representations and Warranties, Covenants, Securities, Events of Default, Changes to the Lenders, as well as Law and Jurisdiction.

3.1 A Banker's View on Shipping

3.1.1 Credit Crisis: The Effect of the Recession

Since 2011, the recovery of the world economy has faced a number of headwinds which have put downward pressures on shipping demand. A weak recovery in the US, sovereign dept crisis and a slowdown in emerging markets have seen world GDP growing by just above 3 % p.a. in 2012 and 2013 according to IMF. The fund expects growth to improve going forward but remain below 4 % p.a. over the 2014–2016 period.

S. Otto (✉) • T. Scholl
Commerzbank AG, Domstraße 18, 20095 Hamburg, Germany
e-mail: stefan.otto@commerzbank.com; thilo.scholl@commerzbank.com

O. Schinas et al. (eds.), *HSBA Handbook on Ship Finance*,
DOI 10.1007/978-3-662-43410-9_3,

Owing to the crisis, the ocean transport demand decreased significantly. Freight and charter rates in the context of container trade dropped substantially. Besides, the market values for container vessels decreased noticeably. Ongoing market pressure and liner companies' fight for market share led to first consolidation efforts in the form of alliances among liner companies and associations among charter companies. From today's perspective, it seems clear that this trend is by far not terminated. Except for the larger container vessels, charter rates in the container segment continue on operating cost levels. Charter rates for bulker and tankers improved towards the end of 2013 but earings are still below breakeven levels in many segments.

Due to the unfavorable conditions and the uncertainties surrounding the financial markets and the seaborne trade, the ship finance banks in Germany were very selective in its new loan business in the last years. The activities of the banks were almost limited to drawdowns under existing loan commitments and the necessary restructuring of existing exposure. The German KG model did not turn out to be crisis-resistant. However, the model is not dead, but it will require a new setup with a larger equity cushion and viable risk control. In case of new financings, the banks are likely to demand equity of at least 30–40 % upfront and will refuse to pre-finance equity because weak capital position of fund initiators caused shifting of fundraising risk toward the banks. Likewise, the banks will favor financings with corporate structure and abstain from financing single purpose vehicles without the possibility to shift the risk to the parent company.

3.1.2 Outlook on Shipping Markets

The global economic outlook for the next 2 years is precarious and influenced by a number of factors. The growth in the United States, Europe, and China is expected to be moderate or even lower than in previous years. Continuing weak charter markets for container vessels, bulk carriers, and tankers are anticipated for the second half of 2014. Exempted from this development are offshore activities, cruise vessels, and LNG tankers, which are enjoying continued strong growth.

3.2 Commonly Used Structures

Ship owners will have a constant need to raise money to support their activities. Only few ship purchases are paid by cash generated from the ship owner's own resources. Therefore, the financial needs of the ship owners will have to be predominantly covered by taking recourse to the financial markets. The three main groups of sources in the financial markets are debt finance, equity finance, and mezzanine finance.

3.2.1 Debt Provision: Syndicated, Bilateral, and Club Transactions

The most common form of finance is to borrow money from a bank. Due to global shifts caused by deterioration of the market value of ships and charter rates, debt financing has become more and more difficult as ship financing banks nowadays are very reluctant to borrow money under these circumstances and have even decided to withdraw completely or in part from this market.

In the past, most of the loans have been conducted on a bilateral basis meaning that the relationship has been established between a borrower and one bank. Because of the high amounts involved and to split the risk, syndicated loans have become more frequent. By selling part of the loan commitment, banks can actively manage their own portfolio to reduce risk. However, this form of finance might be disadvantageous as syndicates are difficult to control and, in the context of restructuring or workout, bring to bear other views and interests. Likewise, syndication is not always beneficial for the borrower as it often does not have much influence where the ultimate lender may be domiciled.

In case of larger transactions, for example, a fleet purchase or placing orders for new buildings "club" deals are still a favored form of finance among ship financing banks. In a club deal, usually a small number of banks combine together to finance a given project collectively. This form of finance allows the participating bank to voice its opinion and to exercise more influence in the structuring and negotiating process.

3.2.2 Equity Contribution: Shares, Private Placements, or Private Equity

In finance, equity is the residual claim or interest of the most junior class of investors in assets after all liabilities are paid. In case of bankruptcy, all the secured creditors are paid against proceeds from assets. Afterwards, a series of creditors, ranked in priority sequence, have the next right on the residual proceeds. Ownership equity is the last or residual claim assets, paid only after all other creditors are paid. Therefore, ownership equity is also known as risk capital or liable capital.

In the past, equity finance for shipping was raised in most cases from retained earnings from vessel operation and retained profit on ship sales. Although there have been various efforts to attract equity from outside the shipping industry, these sources remain the principal source of shipping finance equity to this day (Russel 2006, p. 34).

For private and limited companies, the most common form of ownership is evidenced by the public offering of shares to the general public. Through this process, a private company transforms into a public company. Although the issuance of shares offers many advantages, there are also significant disadvantages. Among these are the costs associated with the process, and the requirement to disclose certain information that could prove helpful to competitors. Listing of shipping shares on the stock exchanges have not been, generally, a successful means of raising funds for shipping companies in the past. The reasons for this are to be found in the structure and the ownership profile of many shipping companies, which are still family owned and where the owners do not want to relinquish full control.

Private placement is a funding round of securities which are sold not through a public offering, but rather through a private offering, mostly to a small number of chosen investors. Investors in this type of finance are seeking capital growth through participation in the continued strength of a project. They rely on a strong operating management, a successful performance record, good asset quality, a positive trend in cash follow, or earning potential. As shipping is perceived as a cyclical industry, investors have shown restraint to participate in a shipping project as there has always been a preference for minimizing dependence on non-cyclical activities.

The German KG model was established to raise private equity as a specific form of finance for projects. With a view to raising funds, initiators set up single-purpose companies and placed the equity among individuals as private investors. The single-purpose companies are organized in the legal form of a German limited partnership (*Kommanditgesellschaft*). The structure of the KG is comprised of one general partner and one or several limited partners. To limit the overall exposure to the raised equity, a limited company (*Gesellschaft mit beschränkter Haftung*) serves as a general partner of a German KG. The risk for private investors as limited partners of the KG is limited to the amount of their single investment. In proportion to their equity stake, each private investor participates in the profit and loss of the KG (Bartsch 2012).

3.2.3 Mezzanine Finance

Mezzanine finance is a generic term that covers a broad spectrum of financing between equity and senior debt (Brauner et al. 2006, p. 76). This form of debt is subordinated to the senior debt and is only repaid after all senior obligations have been satisfied. As a result, mezzanine capital is often a more expensive financing source for a company than senior debt. In return for the higher risk involved, the lender will demand a significantly higher interest margin and will often receive some form of equity kicker, which might include the right to take an equity stake in the borrowing company at a future date (Russel 2006, pp. 34ff.). However, investors are very careful as they want to avoid a consolidation of the ship-owning company.

3.3 Analysis of the Loan Agreement

A loan agreement encloses the terms and conditions under which ship finance is advanced. The structure of a loan agreement is based on the term sheet agreed between the parties. Due to time constraints, the commercial side often tends to neglect the importance of a proper documentation and in particular, the term sheet. The term sheet provides a basis for the relationship between the lender and borrower, and is therefore a key factor in the forthcoming negotiations of the structure and contents of the loan agreement between the parties. Although it is difficult to generalize about the form of the loan agreement as each bank and law firm has its own way of drafting documents, most of the documentations will try to approach the LMA standard. This standard is governed by English law. In the past, efforts have been undertaken to establish a standard under German law (Wand 2005, pp. 1932ff., 1969ff.). The result was a remarkable framework of legal provisions for commercial borrowing (*gewerbliche Kreditvergabe*). However, the documentary praxis in shipping finance adopts the LMA standard, which is adjusted to German law by a working group consisting of representatives of the major German banks and a number of Frankfurt-based law firms. The main objective of the working group is to align the LMA English documents to the requirements of German law and banking practice (LMA 2012). In praxis, the major problem in the potential use of the LMA German documents is that the LMA adaptation does not take into consideration Sections 305–310 of the German Civil Code (*Bürgerliches Gesetzbuch*) relating to general business terms, in consequence of which specific provisions thereof may remain unenforceable. Even legal experts tend to make the qualification that they do not express an opinion as to whether the loan agreement constitutes general terms and conditions.

3.3.1 Term Sheet

The term sheet (see Table 3.1) provides a legal basis for the loan agreement to be concluded between the parties. It contains the intention of the lender to offer a finance facility to a borrower following certain qualifications. The term sheet sets out the essential structure of the facility and some specific terms and conditions which will be contained in the loan documentation. Both under English and German law, the term sheet is seen as a document with binding character during the negotiation and completion of the loan agreement and security documents (Brauner et al. 2006, pp. 78ff.).

It is advisable that the term sheet contains an expiry date, after which the offer of the lender becomes invalid. In addition, in situations where the structure is constantly changing, it should include a provision that the current term sheet supersedes and replaces prior term sheets.

If the term sheet is utilized only for indicative purposes, it should outline that the information is only indicative and subject to documentation to be agreed on with the lender, to the consent of the competent credit body of the lender and, if applicable, to the syndicate. The lender might also want to include the presumption that no substantial adverse changes have occurred at the time of the signing of the documentation.

Table 3.1 Post-delivery financing (sample for a term sheet)

Purpose	Re-financing of the pre-delivery loan and the financing of the delivery installment.
Loan amount	[Currency, amount]
Currency	Currency [if applicable: leading currency is [currency]. [Optional, in conjunction with leading currency, but to be used restrictively:]
Drawdown	In one sum upon [delivery] [takeover] of the ship subject to fulfillment of the disbursement conditions laid down in the loan agreement, but no later than [date].
Term	[number] years, beginning with [delivery] [takeover] of the ship [if applicable: until [date] at the latest].
Repayment	In [number] [semi-annual/quarterly installments] [if applicable: and one final installment/balloon amounting to [currency, amount]], beginning [3] [6] months after [delivery] [takeover].
Extraordinary repayments	Extraordinary repayments are possible at the end of an interest period [if applicable: equivalent to an amount of [currency, amount] or a multiple thereof] and must be notified to the lender [number] banking days beforehand. Extraordinary repayments will be appropriated to the repayment installments last due and result either in a shortening of the term of the loan, or in a reduction of the balloon/final installment and may not be drawn down again.
Margin	[x] % p.a. [If applicable: The margin initially applies for a period of [x] [months/years] and must be renegotiated afterwards.]
Interest rate	LIBOR/EURIBOR plus margin plus funding fee.
Funding fee	[x] % p.a. This markup serves to compensate for the accruing funding costs and will be negotiated for the following interest period each time. [If applicable: This markup initially applies for a period of [x] [months/years] and must be renegotiated afterwards.]
Interest period	3, 6, or 12 months; other interest periods as agreed upon with the lender.
Calculation of interest	Interest will be calculated on the basis of the Euro market interest computation method (365/360 days).
Commitment fee	[x] % p.a. in terms of the loan amount promised in principle but not used as from the acceptance of the binding commitment in principle, due, and payable quarterly in arrears.
Securities	Typical of this type of transaction, but not necessarily limited to: • [Alternative 1 (German law):] Abstract promise to pay the debt amounting to [130] % of the maximum loan amount plus 15 % p.a. for interest and costs, backed by a first ranking ship mortgage under German law in the same amount on the ship to be financed including a submission to execution clause with regard to a partial amount payable last of 10 % of the amount of the ship mortgage. • [Alternative 2 (international law):] First ranking ship mortgage under [select international law] [e.g. Liberia, Panama, and Cyprus] law amounting to [130] % of the maximum loan amount plus 15 % p.a. for interest and costs on the ship to be financed. [If applicable: [The abstract promise to pay the debt also secures the Lender's claims arising from [name type of the further loan/s].]

(continued)

Table 3.1 continued

	• [Open and confirmed] assignment of the borrower's rights and claims in connection with the construction and sales contract regarding the ship. • Open and confirmed assignment of the rights and claims by the assured/co-assured arising from the agreed insurances on the ship. • [Open and confirmed] assignment of all rights and claims arising from the charter parties including subcharters, any pooling agreements/pool revenue, freight revenue as well as other revenue connected with the ship operation. • [If applicable:] Open and confirmed assignment of the rights and claims arising from a charter guarantee (from an address to be agreed upon with the Facility Agreement) to underpin the value of the charter party.] [if applicable, further additional securities]
Covenants	Typical of this type of transaction, but not necessarily limited to: • Increased cost clause [for foreign financing (particularly with respect to the rules pursuant to Basel-II)]. • Loan to value ratio up to a maximum of [70 %] of the respective value of the ship • [If applicable: [105] % currency clause (in the event of infringement reduction to 100 % or provision of additional collateral).] • [If applicable: For the portion of the loan used in [currency], corresponding exchange and interest hedging transactions must be entered into no later than 4 weeks before the announcement of distributions to enable distributions by [date]. • Construction supervision to be arranged in consultation with the facility agent and lender [both quantitatively and qualitatively] • [If applicable: Quarterly construction progress reports and certificates issued by the classification society regarding the respective construction stages, which must be presented to the facility agent. Moreover, the facility agent is entitled to have the construction progress of the ship under construction verified by an expert agreeable to the Facility Agent. • Generally accepted market transfer clause • Market disruption clause
[If applicable] Financial covenants	Typical of this type of transaction, but not necessarily limited to: • Equity ratio at least [30] % [or at least [currency, amount]]. • [If applicable: No withdrawals by the partners and no distributions to the partners without the facility agent's prior consent if the loan servicing is not ensured and/or the partnership's equity ratio is <[30] %. • No withdrawals by the partners and no distributions to the partners without the facility agent's prior consent if the equity ratio is <[30] %. • Minimum liquidity amounting to [currency/amount]. Ratio of net financial liabilities to EBITDA at the most [3.5 to 1].

3.3.2 *Loan Agreement*

The loan agreement contains the terms and conditions under which the financing is advanced. The post delivery financing will be carried out by a term loan by which the lender will lend the ship-owner a fixed amount repayable over an agreed period of time. In general, the loan will be paid out to the borrower in one drawing and will be repayable in equal installments over the duration of the term (Russel 2006, p. 16). The length of the term will be between four and 12 years. In the following, the loan agreement provisions of particular significance will be described in greater detail. Most loan agreements will contain a similar structure, although arranged or subdivided differently.

1. **Definitions and Interpretation**
   The loan agreement starts with the clauses, which define a wide range of terms used within the document. Most of these definitions are relatively standard in any form of loan agreement.
2. **Purpose of the Loan**
   According to paragraph 4.3.2. of the Circular as to the Minimum Requirement for Credit Operations (*Mindestanforderungen für das Kreditgeschäft*) issued by the German Federal Financial Supervisory Authority (*Bundesanstalt für Finanzdienstleistungsaufsicht*), the bank has to supervise if the contractual obligations have been fulfilled by the borrower. In particular, the bank has to check whether the loan has been utilized according to the purpose agreed between the parties (Wand 2005, p. 1937). In general, the post-delivery loan is to be used for the re-financing of the pre-delivery loan and the financing of the delivery installment.
3. **Conditions Precedent of Utilization**
   The obligation of the lender to make any disbursement under the post-delivery loan is subject to the receipt of a large amount of information and a large number of documents to be made available in form and substance satisfactory to the lender. These include, inter alia, the following:

   - Delivery of the drawdown notice
   - Complete set of corporate documents regarding each of the relevant parties
   - Execution and delivery of the loan documents, especially the loan agreement and the security documents
   - Delivery to the lender of all delivery documents
   - Copies of the classification certificates regarding hull and machinery issued by the classification society acceptable to the lender
   - Evidence in writing and confirmation or report of an insurance broker, in form and substance satisfactory to the lender
   - No event of default having occurred (in particular, no material adverse change in the financial situation of any of the relevant parties)
   - No breach of the loan to value undertaking

- Evidence reasonably acceptable to the lender that the financing of the total investment cost is secured in full
- If requested by the lender, confirmation in the form of legal opinions confirming, inter alia, the validity and enforceability of the loan documents governed by such laws, in each case in form and substance reasonably acceptable to the lender

4. **Repayment and Prepayment**
   Loan repayments can be negotiated in many different forms, although in the most common form the loan is available to the borrower in one drawing only and is repayable in equal installments throughout the period of the facility. Most loan agreements are accompanied by a repayment schedule allowing for regular installments. The most common form will be found in equal principal installments.
   The clause also contains voluntary prepayment rights as well as a mandatory prepayment obligation, including break cost indemnities and any required notice period. It is customary that the prepayment of a facility is permitted in whole or in part without penalty usually on any rollover date, provided a reasonable (usually five business days) notice is given. In case the vessel becomes a total loss, the borrower has the obligation to prepay the outstanding loan to the lender in full.
5. **Interest**
   This clause sets out the mechanics for fixing the interest rate and paying interest on the loan. The obligation shall accrue from the respective date of disbursement until the date of repayment of the loan to the lender. The terms for which the loan is outstanding shall be divided into successive interest periods, for example, for 1, 2, 3, or 6 months, or any other interest period agreed upon between the borrower and the lender. In most cases, the interest rate applicable to the loan shall be the rate per annum which is the aggregate of the initial margin plus Libor or Euribor. Normally, the initial margin will be fixed for an initial period until, for example, the fourth or fifth year of the date of disbursement. The borrower and the lender undertake to enter into negotiations and agree in good faith prior to the end of the initial period which new margin shall be applicable for one or more subsequent periods until the repayment date.
6. **Fees**
   This section sets out the fees that are payable by the borrower to the lender-in particular, a coordination fee (*Bearbeitungsgebühr*). If the lender wishes to syndicate or grant sub-participation in the loan, they might wish to take a turn on the fees rather than simply pass on a proportion of the fees to the participants. In this case, details of the fees are set forth in a separate fee letter. However, the borrower's contractual obligation to pay the fees remains in the loan agreement.
7. **Representations and Warranties**
   The representations and warranties are a declaration from the borrower that all measures and conditions are current for the first time with the signing of the loan documentation. They will be repeated several times throughout the lifetime

of the loan agreement (Russel 2006, p. 25; Welter 2011, p. 4044). The loan agreement features a combination of actual repetition and deemed repetition of those representations (LMA 2012, pp. 3ff.). Each utilization request envisages an actual repetition of the representations and warranties.

The representations and warranties of the post-delivery loan is comparable to the standard established for a normal corporate term loan, for example, as to the borrowers corporate status, powers and authority, effective charge over the vessel, all governmental or other official approvals, consents, licenses, registrations or authorizations, absence of any litigation or insolvency proceedings before any court, the information provided by the borrower to be true, complete and accurate and that the loan documents constitute the legal, valid and binding obligations of the borrower, which will be enforceable against the borrower in accordance with their respective terms.

8. **Covenants**

The loan agreement also includes covenants relating to the borrower as well as to the vessel. The covenants relating to the borrower may be divided into positive and negative covenants stating the actions the borrower should take and those they should not (Russel 2006, p. 26; Welter 2011, p. 4044).

The positive covenants encompasses the responsibilities of the borrower to comply with the terms and conditions of their financial and other obligations, to register the vessel in a ship register reasonably acceptable to the lender and to fly a flag, which has been approved by the lender, to provide all necessary information required by the lender and to promptly disclose to the lender any event of default. One of the most important responsibilities of the borrower is to ensure that the value of the vessel always exceeds a certain percentage of the loan outstanding. The clause provides for a mechanism for assessing the value of the vessel on the basis of a sale on arms length as between a willing seller and a willing buyer without taking into account the charter or any other engagement concerning the vessel. All attempts in the recent past to implement a valuation taking also into account the charter were for obvious reasons unsuccessful as only the realizable market value gives the lender the certainty as to sufficient collateralization.

Characteristic of the negative covenants is, inter alia, not to encumber its assets with liens, not to sell, transfer or otherwise dispose of the vessel, not enter into (and thereafter amend and terminate) any agreement relating to the operation, employment or chartering of the vessel without the prior written consent of the lender, to pay dividends and not to change its ownership.

The covenants relating to the vessel contain, inter alia, the obligation of the borrower to insure the vessel on or before delivery and to keep the vessel insured throughout the term of the loan until repayment of the outstanding indebtedness against each and any risk, which are customarily insured against by a prudent and respectable ship owner (in particular, insurance against fire, marine, and other usual hull and machinery risks, insurance against war risk, protection and indemnity insurance, loss of hire insurance and mortgagee's interest, additional perils insurance, etc.).

9. **Securities**
   The borrower undertakes to execute and to grant to the lender collateral as security for the loan together with accrued interest and each and any other monies now due or to become due hereunder, under the security documents and the parallel debt (Russel 2006, pp. 30ff.).
   Insofar as the realizable value of the securities exceeds, permanently and not just temporarily, the claim to be secured by more than 10 %, such excessive part of the security may have to be released upon request of the borrower. According to a decision by the Federal Court of Justice (*Bundesgerichtshof*), this will not affect the validity or enforceability of the remaining security.
   The following are the principal types of security for which a lender will look in a post-delivery financing. It should be added that this list is by no means exhaustive.

   (a) **Mortgage**
   In case of the registration of a German mortgage the borrower undertakes to register a first priority mortgage over the vessel with the register in favor of the lender securing an abstract acknowledgement of debt (*abstraktes Schuldversprechen*) in an equal amount plus fifteen per cent interest and submission to immediate forced execution in rem and a personal submission to immediate forced execution by the borrower, in each case in the amount of ten per cent of the abstract acknowledgement of debt.
   The ship mortgage is junior to possible maritime liens arising under German law (*Schiffsgläubigerrechte*) and/or under foreign law which—albeit not registered—ranks prior to the lien created by a German ship mortgage and which pursuant to Section 754 German Commercial Code include wages of the crew, port and pilot fees, tort claims for damages inflicted to persons or goods in connection of the operation of the vessel, salvage claims and claims relating to general average and claims of social security authorities against the relevant owner of the vessel.
   (b) **Earnings Assignment**
   The borrower undertakes to execute a deed of first priority assignment in respect of all rights, benefits, claims and interests relating to the operation of the vessel, including without limitation, under and pursuant to the charter with notice to and acknowledgement by the charterer and any other charter agreement, or other contract for the employment of the vessel.
   (c) **Insurance Assignment**
   Furthermore, the borrower, the manager and the bareboat charterer execute a first priority assignment of the insurances with notice of such assignment (for attachment by way of endorsement to the respective insurance policy) to and acknowledged by the insurers or respective insurance brokers.
   (d) **Personal or Parent Company Guarantee**
   In the time of volatile charter rates the lenders are not longer willing to accede anymore to borrower's request to dispense with personal or parent

company guarantees, as without them the lenders lose any recourse to those behind the ship owning company (Russel 2006, p. 3).

(e) **Pledge of Shares**

The lender might want to get hands on the borrowing company itself. In this case, he might ask the borrower to agree to a pledge of shares. As such, the lender can have direct influence over the activities of the company. Most lenders have been very reluctant to use their rights under the pledge as it is not clear what level of influence might be viewed by the German courts as making the lender a de facto shareholder. According to the Federal Court of Justice (*Bundesgerichtshof*), a lender can be treated like a shareholder if the pledge of shares in combination with other agreements grants the lender rights similar to the rights of a shareholder like the voting rights and other decisions, which require the previous consent of the lender. This leads to the result that, in case of an insolvency of the borrower, any loan is treated as shareholder loan pursuant to Section 39 para 1 no. 5 of the German Code of Insolvency. Under such circumstances, the lender will rank behind other creditors of the borrower.

The list is not exhaustive and might also include the assignment of the building contract, a charge over or pledge of the shares of the borrower and a pledge over a cash deposit and/or earnings and retention account.

10. **Events of Default**

Most loan agreements will contain a list of events of defaults, which will entitle the lender to declare the outstanding balance of the loan, accrued interest, and any other sums due and payable under the loan agreement. Typical events of default contained in a post-delivery loan will be the failure to repay the loan or to pay interest, but also others including material misrepresentation, breach of covenant, material adverse change, insolvency of the borrower, or if the ship becomes a total loss.

11. **Changes to the Lenders**

For the purpose of re-financing, relief of equity or risk diversification, the lender may transfer its commitment under the loan or part thereof to a third party. The transfer may be done, inter alia, by way of assignment, sale, and transfer by the lender of its commitment, credit derivatives, or granting sub-participations (Wand 2005, pp. 1977ff.). The assumption by the new lender of the contractual position of an existing lender will be executed, either partially or as a whole, by a transfer certificate whereby the existing lender will assign all his rights and transfer all his obligations to the new lender.

The two principal methods available to the lender to "sell" a loan are assignment and assumption of contract (LMA 2012, p. 5). In case of an assignment of receivables, any obligations owed by the existing lender remain with the existing lender since obligations cannot be assigned. In contrast to an assignment through an assumption of contract, it is possible to also transfer obligations. It should be pointed out that assumption of contract needs the consent of the borrower as obligor. According to the German law version of the LMA recommended form of Primary Documents, the consent of all parties is granted in advance on the condition that the procedure set out in the loan agreement is complied with. The assumption of contract itself is facilitated by the execution of a transfer certificate.

12. **Law and Jurisdiction**
    The clause contains the agreement of the parties to German governing law (likewise English law) and the borrower's submission to the jurisdiction of the German courts (likewise English courts). The choice of German law to govern any contractual obligations arising out of or in connection with the documentation will be recognized and upheld by a German court.

3.3.3 Closing of a Transaction

Once an agreement is reached about the documentation and the parties are ready to proceed with the transaction, a closing is arranged. Prior to, or simultaneous with, the disbursement of any funds, all the security documents need to be completed and all the conditions precedent need to be met, or at least, in progress to the lender's satisfaction. However, owing to the complexity of the transaction, this is not always easily achievable. The lender is required to have their mortgage recorded and the owner requires clean and unencumbered title to be in a position to give the mortgage. And as if that were not enough the yard requires safe receipt of the delivery installment. This is very much a "chicken and egg" situation, which can only be solved by experienced lawyers and direct involvement of the register.

References

Bartsch G (2012) The German KG model. In: Finance & investment briefing. Watson Farley & Williams, Hamburg

Brauner A, Illingworth P (2006) Shipping finance. Stephenson Harwood

Loan Market Association (2012) Supplemental Users Guide the German law version of the LMA recommended form for Primary Documents (Update February)

Russel M (2006) Shipping finance. Stephenson Harwood, London

Wand L (2005) Musterdarlehensvertrag für gewerbliche Kreditvergaben. Wertpapier-Mittelungen, Frankfurt

Welter R (2011) Bankrechtshandbuch. Schimansky/Bunte/Lwowski, Munich

Part II
Equity Financing

Chapter 4
The German KG System

Max Johns and Christoph Sturm

Abstract The German "KG System" is an almost unique national model to finance ships. It has been one of the cornerstones of the resurgence of the German merchant fleet after World War II. Germany counts today the largest container shipping fleet in the world. The vehicle to finance this remarkable growth has been the KG. The article investigates the historical emergence of the model, its various incarnations and practical applications, especially in conjunction with different tax models. Particular focus is put on the combination with the tonnage tax. The article further investigates the fund-vehicles that commonly used the combination of KG and tonnage tax, describes the participants and finally gives an outlook on the prospects of the model.

4.1 KG as Incorporation

The German "KG System[1]" has been a subject of both envy and mockery. As an almost unique national model for financing ships, it has been one of the cornerstones of the resurgence of the German merchant fleet. In a very few years, German shipowners and private investors have built up the largest container shipping fleet in the world. The vehicle for financing this remarkable growth has been the KG system.

---

[1]This is also referred to as KG-model or simply KG, which have the same meaning.

M. Johns (✉)
German Shipowners' Association, Burchardstr. 24, 20354 Hamburg, Germany
e-mail: johns@reederverband.de

C. Sturm
Deutsche Seewert GmbH & Co. KG, Atlantic Haus, Bernhard-Nocht-Strasse 113, 20359 Hamburg, Germany
e-mail: c.sturm@seewert.de

O. Schinas et al. (eds.), *HSBA Handbook on Ship Finance*,
DOI 10.1007/978-3-662-43410-9_4, © Springer-Verlag Berlin Heidelberg 2015

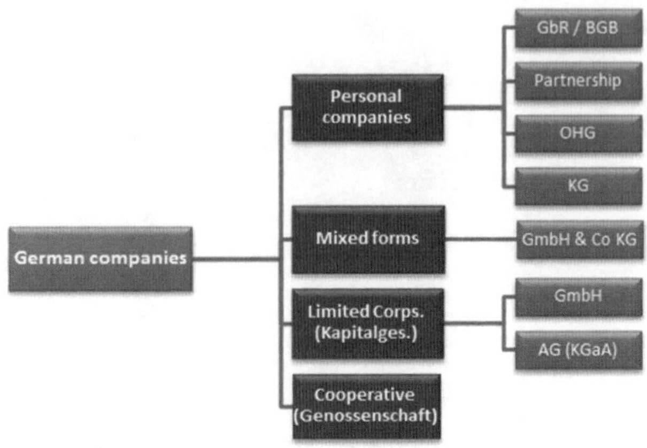

Fig. 4.1 Schematic view of different ways in which companies can be incorporated in Germany

The German "KG System" has been so named with good reason: it is a system that goes beyond the sheer legal incorporation of a single purpose company (SPC). The acronym "KG" stands for Kommanditgesellschaft, one of the possible forms of incorporation in Germany with which the country has been familiar throughout the twentieth century (see Fig. 4.1). The "system" refers to a range of reincarnations of the German tax laws, which made investments in ships and less in shipping as such attractive throughout the decades since the 1950s. The KG system was the catalyst for ship-owners, and manages to attract capital injections from outside the industry itself.

With its merchant fleet practically reduced to zero, Germany's ship-owners struggled after World War II to restart their businesses. Capital was scarce and limitations imposed by the Allied Forces narrowed the scope of possibilities. The first few ship orders in the 1950s were placed by entrepreneurial owners, sometimes relying on their own financial resources, but often in partnership with some close associates. The centuries-old system of "Parten" seemed ready for a revival. Associates who grouped together to acquire a ship were strictly entrepreneurs, rarely mixing with institutional investors.

When German merchants started to take a financial interest in owning ships on a wider scale, dating back to the eighteenth century, they had formed a small group of individuals or companies who built or bought a ship. They had to bear all costs and responsibilities of acquiring and operating the vessels directly and, likewise, were the direct beneficiaries of the operating results. Bank finance and other forms of financial resources were not available, wherefore the group had to put up on their own all the monies required to buy, equip, and staff a merchant vessel. They also had to have sufficient expertise in actual shipping matters.

It was not uncommon that the largest or sole shareholder in the ship acted as the master at sea. He/she also often represented the cargo interests and was in charge of negotiating and concluding the sale of the cargo at the port of destination.

A modernized form of Partenreederei survived until 2013,[2] though only on a comparatively small scale. In this simple form of ship ownership, each individual stakeholder fully participates in the results of the venture according to his/her share in the company. The downsides of this type of ship ownership include the high capital requirements of the individual participant and that each shareholder ("Partenreeder") is subject to unlimited liability for the corporate debt, albeit only for the quota corresponding to his share of the total.

The rare examples were chosen by institutional investors and cash-rich individuals during the second half of the previous century, by then often supported by ship-financing banks, which could rely on the financial strength of the individuals or companies behind the owning company.

In this more modern form of the Partenreederei, the stakeholders usually entrusted a professional ship manager to deal with all practical aspects of shipping operations, including chartering. Usually the stakeholders in the modern Partenreederei were no longer identical with the cargo owners. The genuine interest of investors of a Partenreederei was still to simply derive profits from trading.

However, the provision of unlimited liability limited the number of able or interested parties. The traditional system of Parten was an inappropriate model for the mainstream shipping company of the twentieth century in Germany as it could strictly encompass only a single ship. Modern transport, booming trade and the division of labor between continents necessitated larger ships and fleets and thus entailed demands for capital, which asked for new sources of equity and entirely new structures. While the stock market had been tested at the end of the nineteenth century by some shipping companies, German investors remained skeptical of those public markets. The "KG-System" provided the appropriate answer and attracted the needed capital.

4.2 Historic Start with "ABC"

The original idea of attracting a larger group of private investors from outside classical shipping circles was brought to Germany by an outsider. Axel Bitsch-Christensen, often referred to as "ABC", came from Denmark to set up a company in Hamburg.[3] When he moved to start his own passenger liner company in Hamburg, the Hamburg Atlantic Line, he planned to build on the historic success of Hapag and Norddeutscher Lloyd. These two were the leading liner companies before the two World Wars, providing the backbone of transatlantic passenger travel. He acquired

[2]With the changes to the German Commercial Code *Handelsgesetzbuch* that came into force on 25 April 2013, the incorporation of a Partenreederei has ceased to exist. Those that had been incorporated before can continue based on grandfather clause.

[3]He came in 1952 from Denmark.

the "Hanseatic[4]" in 1958 and planned for an even larger second ship in the early 1960s. With the German economy gaining momentum, the "Hanseatic" was nicknamed the "Traumschiff des Wirtschaftswunders", epitomizing the rapid ascent of the German economy after World War II. Being unable to finance the second ship, planned "Hamburg", out of the cash flow all by himself, he issued a prospectus for possible investors. The target group was a narrow focus group of previous passengers, typically wealthy individuals who had appreciated the amenities of a similar asset. Bitsch-Christensen was successful in raising a staggering DM 30 m from 212 private investors.

However, unfortunate timing resulted in disaster. In 1966, the "Hanseatic" was ruined by a devastating fire in the port of New York. A fluctuating dollar made the bunker very expensive and personnel costs skyrocketed by 70 % in only 4 years. Finally, ABC had underestimated the effects of airplanes on transatlantic travel: Neither business nor leisure travelers remained loyal to ocean travel, abandoning ships for planes. It was little relief to the investors that the bankrupt ship was sold as "Maxim Gorky" to the USSR and played a key role in the movie Juggernaut, which starred Omar Sharif and Anthony Hopkins, and later played host to the Bush-Gorbachev summit in late 1989 in Maltese waters.[5] Apart from the inexperienced private investors, high-profile investors such as Reemtsma, Körber and the state government of Hamburg also incurred significant losses on their investments and guarantees provided to support the project.

Though the first project failed, a long-lasting idea was born: The German shipping industry should from now on collect a large share of the equity it needed from private investors to play a pivotal role in world shipping. The typical vehicle should become the legal form of a Kommanditgesellschaftthus the nickname "KG-model". While the basic legal structure remained steady well into the second decade of the new millennium, the motivation of the investors changed, as was mirrored in the legislation that was adapted. From a purely tax-driven scheme to support the local ship-building industry, it morphed through a phase of massive tax breaks into the local application of tonnage tax to become the major equity source for the German ship-owners.

From the 1960s onwards, the German government decided to cut down on direct help for ship-owners and shipyards, and devised numerous tax-relief schemes. Basically, private investors were encouraged to put their money into ships to gain massive write-offs. Colloquially, this scheme attracted a group of "Zahnwälte" a mix of dentists and lawyers, seeking intelligent ways to reduce their tax burden.

To attract investors from outside the industry, the investors needed to be shielded from unlimited liabilities. The Kommanditgesellschaft as a personal company needed to be amalgamated with the advantages of a Limited company, the GmbH.

---

[4]The 30,000 GT passenger ship had already had a colorful history as "Empress of Scotland", "Empress of Japan", and "Scotland", when it was sold in 1958. It could accommodate almost 1,350 passengers. The usual route for the Hamburg Atlantic Line led from Cuxhaven to New York.

[5]The two leaders discussed the fall of the Berlin wall at this summit.

The 1970s saw the breakthrough of single-purpose companies using a "GmbH & Co KG" structure to shield themselves from the risk and limit the exposure of investors. Wealthy individuals could be attracted due to the unusual tax breaks. Tax deductions were allowed on unlimited losses, making the gain on the tax side often higher than on the profit of the ship operations themselves.

The newly developing, so-called grey financial market attracted a new breed of intermediaries who liaised between ship-owners and potential investors.[6] The well-meant tax incentives created a situation in which the highest loss of a ship in operation could prove most attractive for the loss-seeking investors, who tried to balance high gains in other fields. In certain cases, tax losses exceeding 400 % of the individual investment were declared. These substantial losses were accumulated through a combination of high-leverage bank financing, individual equity financing, accelerated depreciation schemes, and a variety of tax-efficient cost items and fees applied during the early phase of the investment.

However, an important prerequisite for any German ship-owning structure was that the tax authorities had to be convinced that the venture would genuinely aim at making an overall profit. Therefore, the investment plan had to provide for any initial losses to be ultimately set off by profits from trading and disposing of the asset at the end of the investment cycle. Failing that, the entire venture was in jeopardy, set to be viewed as an intentional loss-making structure by the financial authorities. The competent authorities always considered the presumption that some expenses or losses were not eligible for the tax-benefit, and there was a number of cases where the ship investment failed the test resulting in actual, but not tax-effective, losses.[7]

Nevertheless, this new concept proved highly successful, and consequently, specialist syndicators ("Emissionshäuser") accordingly started to offer products to a wider range of investors. Since the profitability of the product was of lesser importance to investors, it was possible to create and charge a variety of upfront fees for putting together the shipping project and raising the equity. The usually front-heavy investment schemes allowed equity brokers to be employed to raise equity from end users. However, the fee-driven nature of this revised investment scheme increased the distance between the actual investor and the investment asset.

The legislators tried to stop the over-optimistic tax incentives and reduced them in the 1980s, as the tax-driven nature of the scheme drove the system to absurd heights: it helped to attract investors with a minimum interest in profitable ships. Shipping projects were supposed to attract investors because of the profitability, not for their loss-making capabilities.

In the late 1990s, the overreaching tax advantages were reduced. Finally, in 1998–99, the tax system was overhauled and fundamentally changed. Following the

---

[6] Serious early movers in the new market were companies like DIVAG (1968), Conti (1970) and Norddeutsche Vermögen (1975) or Hansa Treuhand (1983).

[7] It should be noted in this context that whilst usually the term "tax loss" is used to describe the effects of this type of investment, it would be more appropriate to call this scheme "tax deferral," as subsequent to the initial losses, taxable profits were to be generated by the ship-owning company.

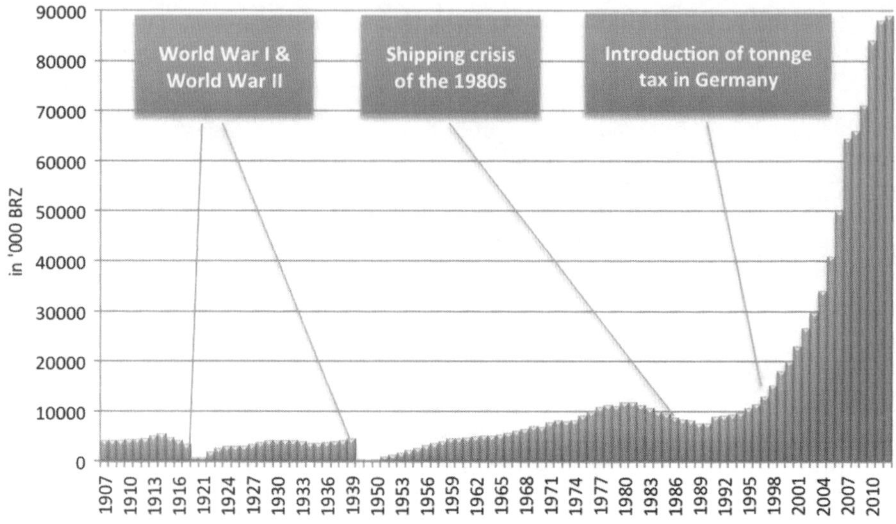

Fig. 4.2 German merchant fleet in gross tonnage. Clearly visible is the almost exponential growth rate after the introduction of tonnage tax in 1999. Other factors like China's entry into the World Trade Organization (WTO) helped emphasize the effect. Significant drops in tonnage occurred at the end of both World Wars, and during the severe shipping crisis in the 1980s. *Source*: VDR

example of other European maritime nations, Germany introduced the tonnage tax. Finally, in 1999, the introduction of the tonnage tax saw the continuous application of the KG-system. Loss-making was no more an option as investors needed a profitable project to be on the upside of the tonnage tax. In 1999, the Pauschale Gewinnermittlung, commonly known as the German tonnage tax, was implemented with the aim of eliminating tax efficient losses from ship investments. However, in return, investors could enjoy the benefit of having profits from the investment being taxed based only on the physical size of the shipping asset. As this nominal tax was limited and well-defined, usually between 1 and 3 % of the expected income from trading, profits from ship investments were often perceived as "tax-free".

This change in taxation deprived investors from continuing to be able to reduce their tax bill, yet it gave ship investments through the KG scheme a unique position in comparison to other standard means of investment like public stocks, real estate or cash deposits, which were all still liable to standard normal taxation.

While a significant number of doomsayers expected the German fleet to be driven out of the country as a result of the change in taxation laws and operating profitably out of Germany did not seem possible any longer, the opposite materialized: the German merchant fleet has increased almost tenfold in the first two decades of the tonnage tax (see Fig. 4.2). Investors came in droves and enabled German owners to build the largest container fleet in the world.

The combination of a Kommanditgesellschaft (with a shielding GmbH) as a legal form plus the application of the tonnage tax enabled a high number of investors to

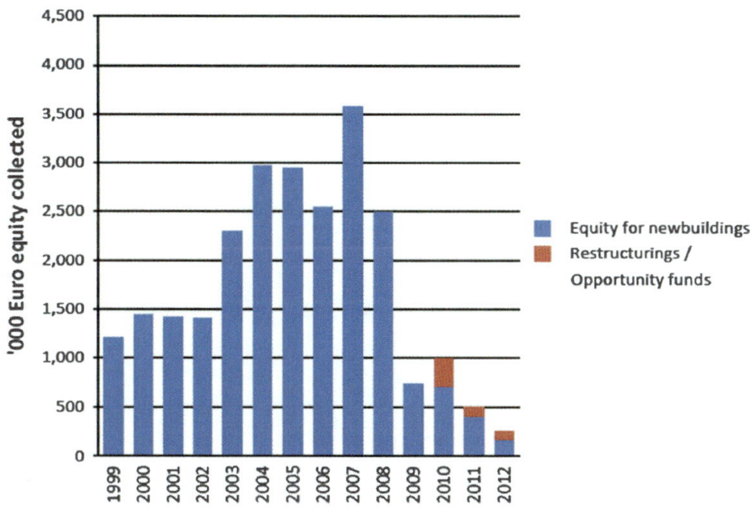

Fig. 4.3 The equity collected from investors through Emission Houses since the introduction of tonnage tax. Since 2010, a sizeable amount was collected from restructurings or opportunity funds. *Source*: VGF

participate in a single ship. The exact structure used in the boom in the first decade of the new millennium is further described below. A large number of investors, estimated to be upward of 500,000, was attracted to the shipping industry. In the year 2007 alone, some €3.5 billion went into the equity side of ship orders (see Fig. 4.3). Altogether, investments from the private side since the mid-1990s added up to some €30 bn.

The Kommanditgesellschaft, as a type of incorporation, consists of one or more partners (Kommanditisten), who may be persons or companies. Their internal liability for the KG debts is limited to the nominal value of their individual share of the KG's registered capital (Kommanditkapital) and their third party liability is limited to the amounts listed in the German corporate registry (Haftkapital). It is not uncommon to limit the third party liability to only 10 % of the internal liability.

In addition to that, at least one other partner being a Komplementär is needed, who again may be a person or company and whose liability for the KG debt is by definition unlimited. There are no legal minimum requirements for paid-up capital within a KG structure.

To avoid unlimited liability for corporate debt to the Komplementär as well, the typical corporate structure for German ship-owning entities and other closed end funds often features a company acting as general partner or Komplementär, rather than a person. To that end, a Gesellschaft mit beschränkter Haftung, or "GmbH," which is a limited liability corporation company, is chosen, which, by default, is able to limit its liability to its share of paid-up capital. The minimum requirement under German GmbH law is a paid-up capital of EUR 25,000. To limit liability even further, it is permissible since 2008 to have an "Unternehmergesellschaft (haftungsbeschränkt)" as a general partner, which is a small GmbH aimed at small start-up companies with a minimum paid-up capital of EUR 1 only.

The result of these liability limitation options is a ring-fenced structure, requiring very little upfront cash equity tailor-made for a single purpose investment.

When a GmbH is acting as a general partner to KG, the correct legal term to be used is "GmbH & Co. KG", thus indicating to the public that all partners in the corporate structure enjoy a limitation to their individual liability. Hence, when market participants mention the phrase "KG finance" or "KG owners", they actually refer to a corporate structure only, which is not only common in ship-owning entities, but is widely used for other types of businesses throughout Germany.

Together with the change in tax rules in 1999, the investor base interested in investing in the expanding market of closed-end shipping funds broadened as well. No longer were ship investments a domain of the wealthy segment of Germany's population; even individuals with below-average incomes thought it attractive to invest.

4.3 Forms of Funds

4.3.1 Single-Ship-Fund

The original fund was constructed to invest in a single asset. It has remained the predominant form of investment vehicle in the KG market.

4.3.2 Savings Fund

As of the mid 2000s, some special funds based on continuous monthly equity collections rather than front-end equity investments were set up to raise equity for ship investments from individuals, who had only limited free cash available for investing every month. It was marketed similar to a savings plan.

4.3.3 Fleet Fund (Flottenfonds)

To cater to the strong increase in demand for ship investments, syndicators started to put together groups of ships within the same funds (Flottenfonds[8]), usually using a holding structure, owning several single-purpose ship-owning entities. Whilst in

[8]The "Flottenfonds" refers to a fleet of two or more ships.

the beginning, these funds commonly comprised ships of identical age and make, later on different types and sizes of ships were grouped together. In doing so, the syndicators purported to reduce the comparatively higher risk of investing in just one particular shipping market by entering, for e.g., tankers, dry bulk carriers and container vessels into one investment fund.

4.3.4 *Fund-of-Funds (Dachfonds)*

This vehicle had been copied from other fund markets. The umbrella fund invests only in other funds, not directly into ships.

4.3.5 *Opportunity Funds*

This type of fund had been motivated by the financial and shipping crisis and was conceived for the first time in 2009. It had the goal of collecting money from investors either for additional required equity in existing funds or as a possible way of buying up financially distressed tonnage. Commonly blind-pool structures were chosen i.e. at the time of fund-raising, the actual target assets were described, but not identified.

4.4 Participants

A typical modern KG company may feature the following participants to be able to finance one or several assets.

4.4.1 *Ship-Owner/Ship Manager*

The ship-owner even though this terminology may be confusing in the KG-world or ship manager, often having both functions, aims to expand his/her fleet or replace existing tonnage. He/she is either unable or unwilling to provide all equity necessary to obtain full finance to acquire or order ships. In his/her function as ship manager, he/she often takes care of the full technical and commercial management, including accounting, of the vessels in his/her fleet. In addition to that, the ship-owner/manager, in most cases, provides the corporate management of the ship-owning entities as well, which in itself creates a conflict of interest. However, the ship-owner/manager regularly takes a share in the ship-owning entity that is often comparatively small. Importantly, the ship-owner/ship manager is in most cases the initiator of the project.

4.4.2 Ship Financing Bank

The bank provides the third party finance based on shipping projects, usually between 50 % and, in former boom markets, occasionally up to 90 % of the vessel acquisition cost. Most KG-model ships were financed in the place by German shipping banks. A special feature of the German ship financing banks was, past tense intended, to pre-finance the cost of building a ship, the equity, and sometimes even the cost of raising equity, bringing the German banks' exposure often in excess of 100 % of the ship acquisition cost and ship value. In lieu of security, the bank got a first preferred mortgage on the asset and an assignment of all earnings and insurance proceeds. Where pre-financing of equity or other cost was involved, additional securities like placement guarantees were demanded by the bank. However, the bank did not intend to take an equity stake in the KG company.

4.4.3 Syndicator/Emission House

The syndicator is entrusted with the task of raising equity in the German market.[9] The syndicator produces the offering memorandum to the investment market and either directly, or through equity brokers, collects equity from investors. Frequently, they have to provide placement guarantees to the ship financing banks in cases where investors are sought only after the ship acquisition has taken place. Often the syndicator, in addition to taking a small share in the ship-owning company, owns a controlling share in the ship-owner/manager, the corporate management company (Komplementär) and/or the trustee, which leads to various conflicts of interest at different levels of the structure.

4.4.4 Trustee

Representing the interests of the shareholders, the task of the trustee is to act for and on behalf of the shareholders of a ship-owning KG. By definition, the trustee should be in every respect independent from the syndicator, which, however, frequently is not the case. Taking a small share in the ship-owning company is common for the

---

[9]Some of the more prominent syndicators are Conti, HCI, MPC, Lloyd Fonds, König & Cie. and Nordcapital.

trustee. Often he/she acts as full representative of the investors towards the other participants in the ship-owning company ("Treuhandkommanditist").

4.4.5 Equity Broker

The equity broker directly acquires equity from individual investors. They either operate alone, or as part of an equity broking pool. In certain cases, they provide equity placement guarantees toward the syndicator or the ship-financing bank. The equity broker may or may not take a share in the ship-owning company.

4.4.6 Advisory Board

In many cases, an advisory board is formed from within a ship-owning KG structure, with the task of advising and controlling the management of the KG company. More often than not, the advisory board comprises those equity brokers who raised the largest part of the equity. The advisory board is elected by the KG shareholders during the annual shareholders' meetings. Its term is normally for fixed periods of between 1 and 4 years. The advisory board usually cannot overrule the management's decisions. However, the board is entitled to be given access to all documentation and information pertaining to the KG structure. Members of the advisory board commonly are shareholders of the KG company. However, in most cases, there is no general requirement to that effect. Quite often, the trustee is entitled to having an own representative present during advisory board meetings, but does not participate in resolutions taken by the board. Frequently the Komplementär has the right to nominate one of its own persons to the advisory board.

4.4.7 Ancillary Service Providers

Further participants in modern shipping KG ventures include legal advisors on contracts, memoranda of agreement, articles of association and bank documentation, auditors to verify the offering memorandum and later to oversee the investment process, tax advisors to safeguard a tax-efficient structure, and public notaries to file the various kinds of inaugural and statutory corporate documentation. None of them usually takes a share in the ship-owning structure.

4.4.8 Investor

The investor aims to invest in an asset-backed venture and expects security from the asset plus above average net proceeds from the investment. Depending on the details of the setup of the ship-owning company, the investor may take an indirect share in the ship-owning company then represented by the trustee acting as "Treuhandkommanditist", which would grant a certain level of anonymity as the investor in this case will not be recorded in the corporate registry. Or he/she would take a direct share in the KG company and be listed in the corporate registry. Given the multitude of service providers involved in the KG structure, the investor has few other tasks to look after than signing the KG documentation, effecting the payment of his share, and often issuing a power of attorney to the trustee, enabling the latter to effect the registration (and later changes to the same and/or deregistration) of the investor to and from the corporate registry.

It has been fashionable at times for investors to leverage their own equity by financing their KG share through specialized banks, often being able to achieve a rather high leverage of up to 90 %. In doing so, investors would be able to leverage an already highly leveraged investment even further.

4.5 Strategic Approach and Key Features

Contrary to the majority of other leading ship-owning nations, the modern German KG system for ship investment is not primarily directed at deriving profits from asset play, but rather at generating steady cash flows from operating the assets, preferably under time charter contracts. KG funds were not set up for fast action on the market but for a long, steady, and predictable investment period (see Table 4.1).

The steady nature of the investment projects equally led to a relatively illiquid second-hand market for KG shares. If investors needed or wanted to divest (in the typical cases of inheritance, divorce or change of investment allocation[10]) this could prove difficult. Several Emission Houses thus offered secondary market platforms for their own investors. Meanwhile, public platforms have also gained traction.

As described above, the "KG-System" became a formula for success in 1999, when the tonnage tax was introduced in Germany. Today, these two components are being considered two sides of the same coin, which has resulted in the historical boom—the fleet expansion in the country—ever since. For the sake of completeness, the tonnage tax component is briefly described below.

---

[10]This could also comprise profit realization or tax optimization.

Table 4.1 Key advantages and disadvantages of investing in modern German KG shipping funds

Advantages	Disadvantages
For investors	
Investment possibilities starting from € 10,000 and lower	There are usually little or no financial reserves available to structure it, making it vulnerable in times of crisis
No own shipping expertise necessary for investor	Low level of transparency
Vehicle for realizing high-volume transactions for syndicators with little or no own equity	Comparatively high cost of equity acquisition
Comparatively high leverage financing possible without additional securities outside of the investment target	Syndicators have no own transportation requirements
Detailed and all-encompassing contractual paperwork	Multiple conflicts of interest among key organs of the funds
Favorable tax environment: ROI + tonnage tax usually brought better returns than other closed-end funds	Little or no influence on corporate and ship management for investors, particularly disadvantageous in times of crisis
For ship-owners	
Investment with long-term horizon	Limited possibilities for asset play
Commercial control of the vessel(s)	Numerous and varying shareholders for every ship
Growth opportunities beyond the base of ship-owner's equity	Country-specific model
No cross-collateralization	
Transfer of financial risk to investors while retaining his/her position as "ship-owner"	Moral obligation to contribute disproportionately in the rescue of distressed assets

4.6 Tonnage Tax

When tonnage tax was introduced through §5a of the German income tax law, the lawmakers had two major goals in mind: first, it was to draw a line under the various forms of subventions, tax-breaks and tax-schemes that had supported shipping since 1949. Secondly, it was to harmonize German tax laws with international and particularly European taxation. As the EU has set out clear guidelines about the applicability of tonnage tax regimes in member-states, the framework was closely defined. Thus, tonnage tax has become the standard way of taxation in the maritime European countries. After Greece, the Netherlands and Norway led the field with the introduction in 1996, followed by Germany (1999), the UK (2000), Denmark, Spain, Ireland, Belgium and France (all 2002), Lithuania (2006), Poland and Slovenia (2009), Cyprus (2010) and Finland (2011).

Despite its nomenclature, tonnage tax is not a tax as such. It is a way of determining the individual taxation of people and entities that fall under income tax. In other terms: it defines the amount that is being taxed with the normal tax rate. The tax rate is not changed, only the amount of income is alternatively defined.

The basis of the taxation—and this is the anomaly—is not based on the profit from operations of the ship but rather on the tonnage of the asset. The principle being, that the taxation basis is set relatively low, but remains unchanged for 10 years. No matter if the ship makes a profit or accrues losses, the tax on the constantly defined "income" is always due. Tax deductions for losses are no longer possible. Therefore, in years with positive income, the rule is rather advantageous for the investors in shipping KGs, as was the case until 2008. In years of negative income, the fiscal benefit can become very large, as steady taxes are due despite losses, as was the case for many ships since 2009.[11] In colloquial terms, the tonnage tax is as some kind of "flat-rate-tax", a bet for the investor that more years are positive than negative while the ship operates under tonnage tax.

When introducing tonnage tax, the lawmakers also had in mind that the net fiscal effect should be positive[12] while the scheme was also supposed to have a measurable positive impact on the maritime cluster. Thus, some conditions apply for any ship to be able to come under tonnage tax:

- The company head office needs to be in Germany,
- It applies only to merchant vessels in international trade (including tugs and some research ships)
- The ship needs to be in the German ship registry for at least 183 days per year
- The employer function for the ships officers needs to be carried out from Germany
- Once attributed, the tonnage tax is binding for 10 years

The tonnage tax applies also to some collateral business under very narrow guidelines.

Calculation of Tonnage Tax

The practical calculation of the tonnage tax is almost identical to most other European countries. An illustrative example assumes an investor with a share of € 100,000 in a fictitious capsize bulker named "Paula". The investor has an income tax rate of 35 %.

The basis for the calculation is the net tonnage (NRZ) of the ship. The "Paula" has a gross tonnage of 175,000 GT. This translates to a net tonnage[13] of 58,083 NRZ. The total equity investment in "Paula" is € 20,300,000.

The calculation of the applicable tax base (per day) is done in four steps, taxing the smaller tonnage heavier than the larger tonnage, as per Table 4.2.

[11]However, the historical returns for ships under the KG-system have been positive for more than 94 % of the projects from 2000 until 2011, with an average capital growth of 11.3 %.

[12]The latest study conducted by the government from 2006 showed in that year alone a fiscal net benefit from shipping of € 167 million even in booming years for the industry. The net benefit has been much larger since the downturn.

[13]Nettoraumzahl or NRZ.

Table 4.2 Current tonnage tax levels in Germany

NRZ	Euro/100 NRZ	Taxable profit (in Euro)
100–1,000	0.92	9.20
1,000–10,000	0.69	62.10
10,000–25,000	0.46	69.00
>25,000	0.23	76.09
Total		216.39

Assuming that the ship has been in the German register for the full year, this defines the flat profit as 365 × 216.39 = €78,982.68 p.a. This flat rate does not depend on the days the ship was in operation. For the investor with a share of 100,000 from 20,300,000 (or a little less than half of a percent), this defines a taxable income of €389,077 in respect to the investment. With the assumed tax rate of 35 %, the tax due—independent of the income situation of the ship—is €136,18. The effective tax rate is typically below 5 %.

4.7 Outlook

At the time of writing, the KG model for German ship financing is subject to severe challenges. A number of single-purpose ship-owning companies have filed for insolvency. The combination of the worldwide financial crisis, the shipping crisis, and the delivery of the ships ordered during the boom times between 2003 and 2008 have resulted in a vast oversupply of tonnage, which will take years for the markets to digest.

Whether the German ship finance model through KGs as such will survive this perfect storm remains an open question. Most market participants expect at least an extended drought in German private equity and supply of bank finance to the shipping industry. When eventually the equity markets will turn their attention back to shipping, private investment through KGs is unlikely to take up its role as the dominant source of equity for the German shipping industry.

However, it is important to note that the KG as a structural setup—in tandem with the tonnage tax—is not in question. They are both on a reliable and comparable basis. The tonnage tax has proven to be of benefit to the government. What may change is the type of investors who feel comfortable about using the system for the allocation of investments and the size of their investments.

Chapter 5
Equity Capital Market in Shipping

Karsten Markwardt and Axel Schroeder

Abstract In general, the placement of new equity in shipping falls under the scope of the Alternative Investment Fund Managers Directive ("AIFMD"). The article describes the essentials of the AIFMD, its purpose and scope, the regulatory requirements it contains and, in particular, its provisions regarding the valuation of funds and the appointment of a depositary to ensure the proper monitoring of cash flows. In Germany, the AIFMD has been implemented through the enactment of the Investment Code ("Kapitalanlagegesetzbuch"—hereinafter "Code"). The article describes the purpose and the scope of the Code in relation to shipping funds structured as limited partnerships. The different types of AIFs and their requirements as stipulated in the Code are explained. Institutional investors and their needs are classified with reference to the AIFMD and the Code. The article concludes by considering those structures where institutional investors prefer to invest their equity with a focus on private equity investments.

5.1 Introduction

German partnerships structured as limited partnerships ("Kommanditgesellschaft") own the world's largest fleet of container vessels.[1] The investors in those partnerships are mostly retail investors with partnership interests worth, on average,

[1]Source: IHS Fairplay, status: 31.12.2011, latest update: 1 August 2012, cf. http://www.reederverband.de/daten-und-fakten/2012/internationalemarktposition.html: German partnerships own 1,793 container vessels with a total capacity of 5,021,000 TEU (20-foot equivalent unit) equivalent to 32.9 % of all container vessels.

K. Markwardt (✉) • A. Schroeder
MPC Münchmeyer Petersen Capital AG, Palmaille 71, 22767 Hamburg, Germany
e-mail: k.markwardt@mpc-capital.com; a.schroeder@mpc-capital.com

O. Schinas et al. (eds.), *HSBA Handbook on Ship Finance*,
DOI 10.1007/978-3-662-43410-9_5,

between EUR 25,000 and EUR 35,000.[2] Investments are made either directly or indirectly through a trustee. The recent financial and shipping crises have essentially caused placement of equity in partnerships with retail investors to collapse. Shipping investors in general and retail investors in particular have suffered bitter losses. As a consequence, almost no additional equity was placed with retail investors for investment in new vessels in 2012 and 2013.[3] Retail investors are not expected to be ready to invest in the shipping market again at any time in the near future. On the other hand, institutional investors are seeking to benefit from the crash in the shipping market by investing now to participate in higher yields when the market recovers. The structures used by institutional investors are diverse.

On 22 July 2013, the Alternative Investment Fund Managers Directive (AIFMD) entered into force. The Directive regulates alternative investment funds within the European Union which, prior to its enactment, were unregulated. The AIFMD contains provisions on portfolio, risk and liquidity management. Fund managers have to comply with these requirements, which means that they have to provide minimum initial capital, an independent valuation of the managed assets on an annual basis and appoint a depositary to supervise the use of liquidity in compliance with the fund's investment policy. However, the AIFMD covers the structuring of the fund only partially and is silent on certain points. For example, the AIFMD does not lay down any conditions with regard to the marketing of AIFs other than to restrict marketing to institutional investors.[4] However, Member States are given discretion as to whether to allow marketing of AIFs to retail investors. In Germany, the AIFMD has mainly been implemented through the enactment of the Investment Code ("Kapitalanlagegesetzbuch"—hereinafter the "Code"), which replaced the Investment Act ("Investmentgesetz").[5] The Code not only implements the AIFMD, but also supplements it in relation to the marketing of AIFs to retail investors by stipulating further requirements regarding their structure and the placement of equity.

It is our intention in this article to present a concise overview of a new and rather complex area of the law, while focusing on German legal requirements as a result of the AIFMD. We begin by exploring the regulatory framework set down in the AIFMD for the European Union (section 5.2) before turning to deal with the implementation of the AIFMD in Germany through the Code and its effect on the placement of equity with retail investors in shipping (section 5.3). The importance of the term investment fund ("Investmentvermögen") is discussed as are the different types of investors. Both of these issues are important when considering whether the placement of shipping funds with institutional investors will be subject to special requirements in the future. After analyzing the different classes of investors, we

---

[2]Source: http://www.sachwerteverband.de/statistik/branchenzahlen.html.

[3]Source: http://www.sachwerteverband.de/statistik/branchenzahlen.html.

[4]Member States may allow marketing to retail investors, cf. Art. 43 AIFMD.

[5]The AIFMD has been implemented by the Act Implementing the Directive 2011/61/EU on Alternative Investment Fund Managers ("AIFM Umsetzungsgesetz") consisting mainly of the Investment Code ("Code").

take a look at the investment structures used by institutional investors. It will be shown that the range of potential structures is relatively diverse as compared with the structures used under what is known as the "limited partnership model" (section 5.4).

5.2 General Principles of the AIFMD

5.2.1 Purpose and Scope of the AIFMD

The AIFMD aims to establish a framework to cover the potential risks which can arise from the activities of funds managers and to ensure the effective monitoring of those risks by the competent authorities within the European Union. Originally, it was intended to restrict the application of the AIFMD to managers of hedge or private equity funds. However, the AIFMD's scope of application now covers the management of all fund structures which were not regulated in the past. Nevertheless, the scope of the AIFMD is limited to entities whose regular business is managing AIFs regardless of whether the AIF is of an open-ended or a closed-ended type, whatever the legal form of the AIF, and whether or not the AIF is listed. In addition, the AIFMD is limited in scope to entities managing AIFs which raise capital from investors with the aim of investing the capital for the investors' benefit in accordance with a defined investment policy. Investment undertakings, such as family office vehicles which invest the private wealth of investors without raising external capital, are not considered to be AIFs according to the AIFMD. Fund managers who already managed AIFs before 22 July 2013 and which do not make any additional investments after 22 July 2013 do not fall under the scope of the AIFMD and are allowed to continue such management without authorization under the AIFMD.

5.2.2 Regulatory Requirements

According to the AIFMD, the management of AIFs is subject to authorization granted by the competent authority (in Germany, this authority is the Federal Financial Supervisory Authority—"BaFin"). No authorization is required (a) for fund managers whose managed assets, including any assets acquired through use of leverage, in total do not exceed a threshold of EUR 100 million or (b) if the managed assets do not exceed a threshold of EUR 500 million where the portfolios of AIFs consist of AIFs that are unleveraged and have no redemption rights. Those small funds are only subject to registration with the competent authority and must keep it informed of their activities.

AIFs can be managed either internally or externally by third parties. Where the managing partner manages the assets (in Germany, this is in most cases the general partner "Komplementär"), this amounts to internal management. External management exists where a third party manages the assets under the terms of a management contract ("Fremdverwaltungsvertrag").

For the sake of simplicity, the regulatory requirements under the AIFMD may be classified in three groups:

1. The requirements for authorization
2. The rules for ongoing operation, in particular, appointment of an independent depositary and valuation of the AIF's assets according to a proper and independent valuation procedure (cf. section 5.2.3.)
3. Obligations regarding transparency and information (cf. section 5.2.4.)

The persons who effectively conduct the business of the AIFM must be of a sufficiently good repute and be sufficiently experienced. In addition, the shareholders must be suitable. Where an AIFM is appointed as the external manager of an AIF, the AIFM must have an initial capital of at least EUR 125,000.00. If, on the other hand, the AIF is managed internally, the initial capital must amount to EUR 300,000.00. The capital must in general be increased where the value of the AIF portfolios managed by the AIFM exceeds EUR 250 million. The additional amount must be equal to 0.02 % of the amount by which the value of the portfolios of the AIFM exceeds EUR 250 million but the required total amount of the capital must not exceed EUR 10 million. Moreover, the AIFM must either have additional own funds which are appropriate to cover potential liability risks or hold professional indemnity insurance against liability for damages arising from professional negligence. The initial capital, including own funds, must be invested in liquid assets readily convertible to cash in the short term and must not include speculative positions.

Certain requirements are placed on the way fund managers operate their businesses. In general, AIFMs must take all reasonable steps to avoid conflicts of interest and, when they cannot be avoided, to identify, manage and monitor and, where applicable, disclose those conflicts of interest to prevent the AIFM from adversely affecting the interests of the AIFs and their investors and to ensure that the AIF investors are fairly treated. The system of remuneration of the senior management and any employees whose professional activities have a material impact on the risk profiles of the AIFMs or the AIFs they manage (risk takers) must be consistent with effective risk management and must not encourage risk-taking which is inconsistent with the risk profiles of the AIFs. AIFMs are required to separate functionally and hierarchically the functions of risk management from the operating units, including the functions of portfolio management. Risk management also includes the implementation of an appropriate, documented and regularly updated due diligence process when investing on behalf of the AIF. Risk management also entails ensuring that risk is monitored on an ongoing basis, including through the use of appropriate stress testing procedures, especially with regard to the maximum level of leverage employed on behalf of each managed AIF. Furthermore, AIFMs have to provide an appropriate liquidity management system by adopting procedures enabling them to monitor the liquidity risk of the AIF and conduct stress tests on a regular basis. The core tasks of AIFMs are portfolio and risk management. If AIFMs wish to delegate these tasks to third parties, those persons have to be authorized or registered as asset managers, and they are subject to the supervision of the competent authority.

5.2.3 *Specifically: Valuation and Depositary*

The AIFMD requires assets under management to be valued regularly, i.e. at least once a year according to a proper and independent procedure. The valuation must be performed either by an external valuer or the AIFM itself, provided that the valuation task is functionally independent from the portfolio management and the remuneration policy and other measures ensure that conflicts of interest are mitigated. There is a duty to inform investors of these valuations and calculations. The AIFM is responsible for the proper valuation of AIF assets and can be held liable by the AIF and its investors regardless of the fact that an external valuer conducted the valuation.

The AIFM must appoint an independent depositary to ensure that the AIF's cash flows are properly monitored, and that all of the AIF's cash is properly booked in cash accounts. Moreover, as far as assets other than financial instruments are concerned, the AIFM has a duty to verify and record the AIF's ownership of such assets. The depositary itself is subject to regulation and ongoing supervision. In addition, Member States may allow that in relation to AIFs which have no redemption rights exercisable during the period of 5 years from the date of the initial investments and which generally do not invest in assets that must be held in custody, the depositary may be an entity that carries out depositary functions as part of its professional activities in respect of which such entity is subject to mandatory professional registration (e.g. auditors, tax consultants or lawyers).

5.2.4 *Transparency Requirements*

The AIFMD provides for extensive information obligations. Before deciding to invest in an AIF, AIFMs are required to make available to investors a description of the AIF's investment strategy, a description of the types of assets where the AIF may invest, the techniques it may employ and all associated risks, the circumstances where the AIF may use leverage, the maximum leverage, a description of potential conflicts of interest, a description of any delegation of functions to third parties, a description of the AIF's valuation procedures, the identity of the depositary, a description of the AIF's liquidity and risk management and all fees, charges and expenses and the maximum amounts which have to be borne by the investors directly or indirectly as well as the latest net asset value of the AIF. The AIFM is obliged to make available an annual report for each financial year not later than 6 months following the end of the financial year, to both the competent authorities and on request to the investors. The annual report must at least contain, inter alia, the balance sheet, an income and expenditure account, a report on the activities, any material changes, and the total amount of remuneration for the financial year. The AIFM must regularly report to the competent authorities of its home Member State regarding the liquidity and risk management systems as well as certain facts and numbers, and also respond to any further requests of the competent authority.

5.2.5 EU Passport, Non-EU AIFs/AIFMs

Once a fund manager has been granted authorization by the relevant competent authority within the European Union ("EU AIFM"), the authorization is also valid in other Member States ("EU passport"), i.e. AIFs located in Member States other than the home Member State can be managed by the AIFM, either directly or through a branch. An EU AIFM is generally also authorized to manage AIFs which are not domiciled within the European Union, and entitled to market them to institutional investors inside the European Union. On the other hand, a non-EU AIFM requires authorization granted by a competent authority within the EU if it intends to manage AIFs domiciled in the EU.

5.3 Implementation of the AIFMD in Germany Through the Investment Code ("Code")

5.3.1 Purpose and Scope of the Code

The AIFMD has been substantially transposed into German law by the Investment Code ("Code"). Therefore, the aspects of the AIFMD described above also apply under the Code. The Code modifies the marketing regime in respect of retail investors. Its scope of application is broadly defined so that any structure that can be considered an investment fund (Investmentvermögen) is deemed to be governed by the Code. For the purposes of the application of the Code, the definition of the respective investment fund is relevant. The Code seeks to ensure that all fund structures are regulated. However, companies conducting business operations which do not have as their sole purpose the financing of investments in shipping and the raising of equity in this connection are not subject to the Code.

In Germany, where business is conducted by shipping funds structured as limited partnerships, the funds always bear an entrepreneurial risk. If companies conduct their own business operations, they do not fall within the ambit of the Code. The

BaFin recently issued an interpretive letter that elaborates the meaning of the term "investment fund" under the Code. The BaFin clarified that in any case a company which owns a ship and charters it out to a charter company under the terms of a time charter contract will be considered to be conducting a business operation and will not be subject to the Code. Under a time charter contract, the vessel is hired for a specific length of time. The owner still manages the vessel, organizes the crew and ensures that the vessel is ready for operation. The charterer gives directions for the deployment of the vessel. The owner is responsible for nautical affairs and gives instructions to the captain of the vessel.

The situation is different where the owner enters into a bareboat charter contract instead of a time charter contract. In the case of a bareboat charter, the owner charters out the vessel but is not responsible for its readiness for operation. The charterer assumes responsibility for hiring the crew and maintaining the ship during the period of the charter, i.e. bears the legal responsibilities of an owner. However, bareboat charter contracts are relatively rare due to the fact that ship owners only qualify for application of the tonnage tax (sentence 2 of §5a(2) of the German Income Tax Act) if they conclude time charter contracts.

Moreover, the assessment of whether a company is conducting its own business operations or is an investment fund will be different depending on whether the company uses a one-tier or two-tier structure. In the latter case, investors invest in a holding company whose sole purpose is to hold partnership interests in subsidiaries that own and manage vessels. The holding company is not regarded as conducting business operations and is therefore subject to the Code.

By way of conclusion, it can be said that it will continue to be possible to use the German one-tier limited partnership model without falling within the ambit of the Code. Regulation of fund management is minimal in these cases. However, marketing of investments to investors is regulated by the Capital Investment Act ("Vermögensanlagengesetz"), which makes it mandatory for issuers to provide potential investors with a prospectus approved by the BaFin. The Capital Investment Act also imposes obligations regarding annual reporting. It only permits the marketing of investments to sales agents that have an authorization either under the German Banking Act ("Kreditwesengesetz", §32 KWG) or under the Industrial Code ("Gewerbeordnung", §34 and §35 GewO). The Capital Investment Act does not apply to the sale of limited partnership interests if either

1. No more than 20 interests are offered,
2. The total amount of all interests does not exceed € 100,000.00, or
3. Each investor has to invest a minimum amount of € 200,000.00

5.3.2 *Public AIFs and Special AIFs*

Under the AIFMD, the marketing of AIFs to institutional investors is allowed and Member States are granted a discretion as to whether they wish to allow marketing to private investors. The Code generally allows the marketing of interests in AIFs to private investors, but imposes additional requirements in respect of the design of these AIFs so as to provide private investors with greater protection against AIFs which are exposed to higher risks. Moreover, the Code provides supplementary requirements for the marketing of those funds and the de minimis rule (100/500 million euros) does not apply.

Although the Code applies to both closed-ended and open-ended funds, it attaches different legal consequences to each of them. In the case of AIFs that are open-ended funds, investors are entitled to redeem their shares at least once a year. Other AIFs without such a right of redemption are considered to be closed-end funds.

In the area of closed-end funds, the Code distinguishes between public AIFs and special AIFs, depending on the type of investor who is permitted to invest in the AIFs. Public AIFs may allow all types of investors, including private investors. Special AIFs are restricted to semi-professional and professional investors. The Code defines "private investors" as investors who are neither professional nor semi-professional investors. The different types of investors are described in greater depth under section 5.4.1 below.

The Code sets forth detailed requirements for the structure of AIFs and their marketing to protect private investors. Public AIFs may only invest in certain types of assets which are specified in the Code. These assets are, in particular, physical assets. Vessels are also included in the group of assets which are considered to be appropriate. Derivatives transactions may only be pursued if this is necessary to protect the AIF's assets against impairment. Moreover, assets may only be subjected to currency risks if the value of the assets exposed to these risks does not exceed 30 % of the value of all of the AIF's assets. Investments in physical assets must be based on a valuation according to which the physical asset is acquired for a price which does not materially exceed its identified value. AIFs must comply with the principle of risk diversification. However, the Code makes an exception from the principle of risk diversification if the AIF is invested in physical assets and the private investors fulfill certain requirements. They are required to invest a minimum amount of EUR 20,000.00. The requirements placed on semi-professional investors in this case also apply to private investors save for the investment amount. Public AIFs may be leveraged up to a maximum of 60 % of the value of their assets. Details regarding the encumbrance of assets must be outlined in the AIF's investment policy. Furthermore, the maximum leverage is subject to approval from the depositary. Finally, the Code requires the prospectus to include any information relevant for an investment decision, i.e. information on risk exposure.

Unlike in the case of public AIFs, the Code imposes further requirements on special AIFs in relation to their investment policy and the existence of adequate leverage.

5.4 Institutional Investors

5.4.1 *Classification of Institutional Investors*

5.4.1.1 Definitions According to the AIFMD and the Code

On the basis of the MiFID, the AIFMD defines professional investors as banks, investment firms and other financial institutions supervised by competent authorities, insurance companies, UCITS, national or regional governments and large companies that fulfill two of the following three conditions:

1. Balance sheet total of EUR 20 million
2. Net revenues of EUR 40 million
3. Equity in the amount of EUR 2 million

Moreover, investors may make a written request to be treated as professional investors provided that they have received detailed advice regarding potential risk exposure and have agreed to assume same in an agreement separate from the investment contract.

Under the AIFMD, a private investor is any investor who is not considered to be a professional investor. The Code defines so-called "semi-professional investors" who are permitted to invest in special AIFs if they fulfill the conditions necessary to qualify as semi-professional. They must invest a minimum of EUR 200,000.00 and undergo a process where they declare that they have the necessary expertise for investments in special AIFs and are aware of their potential risk exposure.

The Code makes provision for an additional type of investor in the case of public AIFs which are not subject to risk diversification rules. These investors are expected to fulfill all of the conditions relevant to semi-professional investors except the minimum investment amount for them is not EUR 200,000.00 but EUR 20,000.00.

5.4.1.2 Potential Institutional Investors

As potential institutional investors for investments in shipping, one may consider pension funds, insurance companies, family offices, wealth managers and finally private equity companies ("PE companies"). The return assumptions of those investor groups vary significantly. Whereas pension funds and insurance companies expect a ROI in the range of 3–7 % p.a., PE companies expect a ROI of at least 10 % p.a. Insurance companies and pension funds are not yet very experienced in shipping investments. In particular, the regulatory requirements under the German Supervision Insurance Act ("Versicherungsaufsichtsgesetz") make it difficult for insurance companies to invest in shipping because they are restricted to investments which can provide a regular cash flow and which may be redeemed or disposed of at any time. PE companies have a higher risk regarding their investments. The following section deals in detail with the investment strategy of PE companies.

5.4.2 *Structures*

5.4.2.1 Objectives

PE companies see the shipping market as a risky business due to the volatility of charter rates and the prices which can be achieved in the secondary market for vessels. PE companies have a strong interest in exiting from their investments within a time period of 3–7 years. Current market conditions mean that an IPO is not a reliable exit strategy. On the other hand, the sale of the vessels on the secondary market can be a promising scenario because vessel prices are at an all-time low. PE companies are largely unwilling to accept the soft cost rates paid in the retail investors market. They are even reluctant to bear the expenses of external advisors incurred during the structuring of projects and try to charge these expenses to the companies where they plan to invest. This may in turn cause problems under the applicable corporate law. Investments have to be structured differently depending on the objectives pursued by the PE companies, for example in ships through the secondary market or in new buildings, the acquisition of loan receivables significantly below their nominal value or the contribution of equity to distressed funds. However, investment by PE companies may be conditional on the willingness of banks to waive a significant part of their outstanding loans or banks agreeing to a part of their loans being subordinated to the fresh money invested by the PE companies (junior tranche). Finally, PE companies may also be interested in investing in the established players in the shipping market and seek to participate not just in the recovery of vessel values but also in other areas such as vessel management.

5.4.2.2 Private Equity Structures

PE companies prefer to invest in companies which conduct their own business operations, hence PE structures are generally not considered to be AIFs. Moreover, the assets where PE companies hold a stake may not be separated from the other fund assets. However, if companies approach investors themselves to raise capital, they will be considered AIFs. In this case, they are subject to both the AIFMD and the Code. Furthermore, PE companies are subject to supervision if they seek to acquire a majority share in or otherwise gain control of unlisted companies.

PE structures are generally not driven by a desire to obtain the advantages of tonnage taxation. Therefore, the companies they invest in do not have to be domiciled in Germany to be subject to tonnage taxation.

PE structures exhibit the following characteristics: They prefer not to invest in companies already listed on the stock exchange. Their shareholders generally enter into a shareholders' agreement which usually covers the following five topics:

1. The shareholders agree on the investment amount to be contributed by the PE company and the percentage of the PE company's shareholding.

2. The shareholders agree on the establishment of a supervisory board and grant the PE company the right to appoint one supervisory board member. Furthermore, the shareholders' agreement normally includes corporate governance rules, in particular a catalogue of business transactions which are subject to the prior consent of the shareholders or the supervisory board.
3. The fund company undertakes to deliver information regarding, inter alia, its financial, equity, P&L and cash situation to the PE company on a regular basis.
4. Shareholders may only transfer their interests with the prior consent of all of the other shareholders. This consent is often conditional upon compliance with procedures regarding specific rights of the PE company. It is common for PE companies to have a right of first refusal. This is a contractual right that gives the PE company the option of entering into a business transaction with another shareholder on specified terms before the other shareholder is entitled to enter into a transaction on the same terms with a third party. Another right which is fairly standard in such shareholders' agreements is a tag-along right. This right ensures that if the majority shareholder sells his stake, the PE company will be entitled to join the deal and sell its stake on the same terms and conditions as the majority shareholder. Finally, PE companies often wish to have a drag-along right included. The purpose of a drag-along right is to ensure that if the PE company sells its stake, the minority shareholders will be forced to join the deal on the same terms and conditions. Whereas a tag-along right serves to protect a PE company in a situation where it is not the majority shareholder, a drag-along right protects it where it is the majority shareholder.
5. Finally, shareholders' agreements also make provision for different exit strategies either via an IPO or a trade sale, i.e. the sale of all of the company's shares to a third party, which is often a competitor.

5.4.2.3 AIFs

The fact that AIFMs are supervised by the competent authority may facilitate the placement of equity with institutional investors. Regulation is likely to increase investor confidence, especially in the case of investors in highly regulated industries, because they have the assurance that the AIFM's investment policy has been approved by the authorities and is therefore binding. The existence of an excellent track record resulting from compliance with regulatory requirements may provide insurance companies with the reliability they seek. A further way of encouraging insurance companies to invest in AIFs could be the grant of a put option which ensures the desired cash flows. However, as insurance companies expect to generate reliable cash-flow from day 1, it can be assumed that it will only be possible to attract a greater investment volume from this group of investors after the shipping market has made a sustainable recovery.

5.5 Conclusion

The traditional German limited partnership model no longer plays the decisive role in relation to the placement of new equity in shipping that it did in the past. It is also unlikely to do so in the near future. The Code has implemented the AIFMD in Germany in such a manner that it does not apply to most traditional, shipping-related limited partnership structures. Under the Code, a company is not subject to regulation if it runs an operational business. The BaFin assumes that this is the case if the company charters out vessels on the basis of time charter contracts.

Nevertheless, it may be worth considering structures that are subject to regulation, e.g. those companies which do not run an operational business because they are invested in companies owning vessels. Retail investors may perceive regulation under the AIFMD and the Code and the supervising role of the BaFin as positive changes. In fact, the requirements under the Code ensure public AIFs' risk exposure is lower than in the case of the limited partnership model. The risks resulting from, inter alia, high leverage (maximum 60 % of the value of all assets) or currency risks (maximum 30 % of the value of all assets) are limited. Moreover, public AIFs have to comply with the principle of risk diversification unless the retail investors fulfill further requirements regarding minimum investment volume and have adequate experience with regard to the risks to which public AIFs are exposed.

In addition, institutional investors which are themselves subject to significant regulation probably prefer it if investments in AIFs are subject to regulation. In contrast, PE companies are interested in simple and cost-efficient structures to maximize their return on investment. Therefore, they are looking for stakes in companies with certain rights attached such as the right to receive information, control rights over the management and exit scenarios.

However, PE companies can, if at all, only be an interim solution as a source of equity in the current distressed market. It is also unlikely that funding from insurance companies, pension funds or family offices will close the gap in equity financing. Based on long-term considerations, the question is whether the limited partnership model can be reactivated to supply the finance desperately needed for shipping activities.

Chapter 6
Other Equity Markets for Shipping

Christian von Oldershausen

Abstract The Norwegian Market proves to be an attractive source of equity for the international shipping industry, mobilizing substantial amounts of equity. The most common Norwegian private equity investment structures are: Limited partnership (Kommandittselskap, "KS"), Silent partnership (Indre selskap, "IS"), Limited liability company (Aksjeselskaper, "AS"), General partnership (Anvarlig selskap, "ANS"). Recently the Silent partnerships, generally known as ISs, have become the most popular investment vehicle replacing the formerly widely used KSs as ISs are very flexible and tax efficient. A Norwegian Silent partnership is not liable to pay taxes. The silent partners are taxable to their relevant share of a calculated taxable income/loss and net worth according to the tax rules of their domicile. This makes the silent partnership structure attractive for non-Norwegian investors as they are not taxed in Norway whereas Norwegian investors are taxed according to ordinary Norwegian taxation.

6.1 Norway and its Limited Partnership Structures

The Norwegian Market has also proven to be an attractive source of equity for the international shipping industry, appealing to both Norwegian residents and foreign investors. Similar to the German KG structure, the Norwegian market has been able to mobilize substantial amounts of equity due to a certain affinity of investors for the domestic shipping and offshore sector.

C. von Oldershausen (✉)
Deutsche Seewert GmbH & Co. KG, 10. OG, Atlantic Haus, Berhard-Nocht-Str. 113, 20359 Hamburg, Germany
e-mail: c.oldershausen@seewert.de

O. Schinas et al. (eds.), *HSBA Handbook on Ship Finance*,
DOI 10.1007/978-3-662-43410-9_6, © Springer-Verlag Berlin Heidelberg 2015

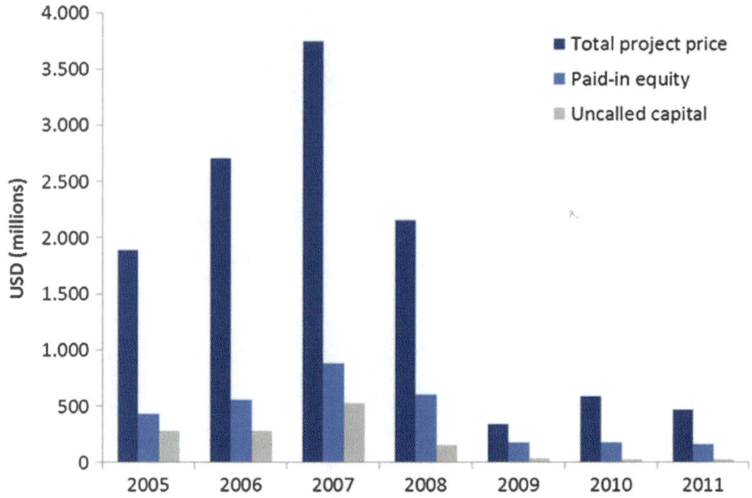

Fig. 6.1 Total project capital invested in Norwegian market (balance is primarily senior debt, however in some cases supplemented by a sellers' credit)

6.1.1 Norwegian Market for Private Equity Investment

Norwegian limited partnerships, generally known as KSs, have been in use since the 1970s and are most commonly used for investments in shipping and commercial property. For shipping, the glory days of the KS were in the late 1980s when several loopholes in the Norwegian tax system allowed for substantial deductions on an individual's tax return as a result of hyper-accelerated depreciation schedules. A similar development could be seen in Germany well into the early years of the new Millennium. Since then, the tax laws have been changed and the latest tax reform in 1996, which addressed the taxation of shipping companies, removed all but a few tax advantages for investors in the KS structure. Nevertheless, a substantial amount of capital has been raised in the heydays of the latest shipping boom culminating in 2007. During the last couple of years, Silent Partnerships, generally known as ISs, have become the most popular investment vehicle replacing the KSs, as they are very flexible and tax-efficient also for investors outside Norway (see Fig. 6.1).

There is a definite advantage by using a specialist underwriter for a shipping KS/IS to secure a liquid second-hand market of the KS stakes. There are a few specialized underwriters of a shipping KS/IS of this type in Norway (see Fig. 6.2).

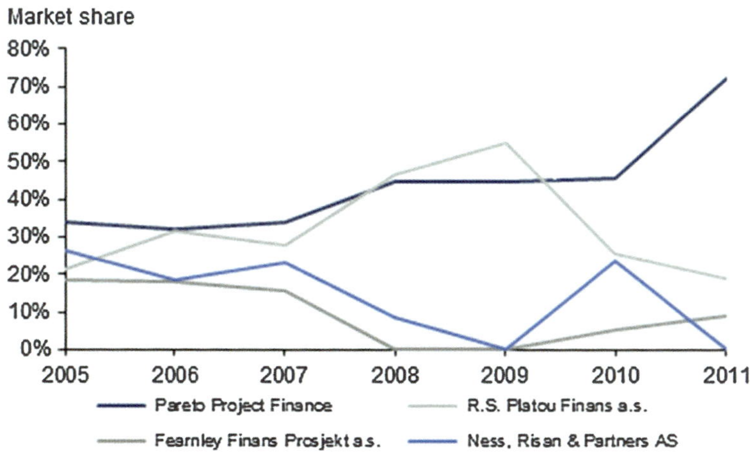

Fig. 6.2 Market shares of different Norwegian corporate finance service providers in shipping

6.2 Types of Structures

The most common Norwegian legal structures used as vehicles for private equity investments are:

- Limited partnership (Kommandittselskap, "KS")"
- Silent partnership (Indre selskap, "IS")
- Limited liability company (Aksjeselskaper, "AS")
- General partnership (Anvarlig selskap, "ANS")

The silent partnership has the most similarities with an offshore limited partnership and has become the predominant Norwegian legal structure. Both limited partnerships and silent partnerships are referred to as limited partnerships in this chapter which will not cover the AS structure.

6.2.1 Norwegian Limited Partnerships

The Norwegian limited partnership is governed by the Norwegian Partnership Act ("Selskapsloven") of 23 June 1985 No. 83 ("Partnership Act"). The Partnership Act differentiates between various partnerships such as (a) general partnerships with unlimited liability for all partners ("ANS"), (b) internal partnerships with limited liability for the silent partners ("IS"), and (c) limited liability partnerships with limited liability for the limited partners ("KS"). Limited partnerships are governed not only by the provisions of the Partnership Act but also by the provisions of the limited partnership agreement (the latter only to the extent that there is no conflict with mandatory provisions of the Partnership Act).

6.2.2 The Limited Partnership "KS"

To be considered a single-purpose limited partnership ("KS"), the KS must be established by two or more individuals or legal entities, which may be Norwegian residents or foreigners, and must consist of one general partner ("komplementar") and at least one or several partners with limited liability ("kommandittist"). The general partner must hold a minimum share of 10 % in the KS and has unlimited liability toward the company's creditors to the extent of their personal assets. The limited partners make their contribution to the capital of the company and their obligations are limited to each partner's share of the total committed capital of the KS. However, the limited partners hold a joint liability toward the KS if one of the other limited partners default on their obligations. A limited partnership does not require a minimum capital.

The primary company organ of the KS is the partnership meeting. The partners may choose not to elect a board of directors. In this case, the general partner will have powers and areas of responsibility similar to those of a board of directors. The general partner is always responsible for the supervision of the management of the day-to-day operations of the KS. Moreover, certain powers in principle belonging to the partnership meeting may be transferred to the general manager, depriving the partnership meeting of its right to instruct and set aside certain decisions made by the general partner.

It is required by the Partnership Act that the general partner provides at least 10 % of the committed capital of the KS and holds an interest in the KS similar to at least 10 % of its net assets and to share a part of at least 10 % of the deficits and profits of the KS. Each partner with limited liability must make a capital commitment of at least NOK 20,000 of which no less than 40 % must be paid within 2 years after its incorporation (the minimum amount of called and paid-in capital at the time of incorporation being 20 %). Provisions regarding payment of uncalled capital are left to be governed by the partnership agreement as the Partnership Act does not stipulate further requirements. It is usual that the partnership meeting or the general partner is given powers to demand payment of uncalled capital within a certain time limit. The KS's claim against its partners for uncalled capital may not be transferred to any other party or assigned to any party by way of security (e.g. to a lender providing financing to the KS). Forty percent of the total committed capital shall be "locked-in" capital, meaning that only equity in excess of that amount may be distributed to the partners as long as the KS remains in existence (see Fig. 6.3).

Even though a KS may be made subject to bankruptcy proceedings, the liability of the limited partners will always be limited to payment of their respective portion of the uncalled committed capital. Claims against such partners for payment of uncalled capital must be made by the KS itself (and/or its receiver) and may not be made directly by the KS's creditors.

The KS has been a popular way of organizing business ventures in Norway since the 1980s, especially within the shipping business. Apart from the obvious benefit

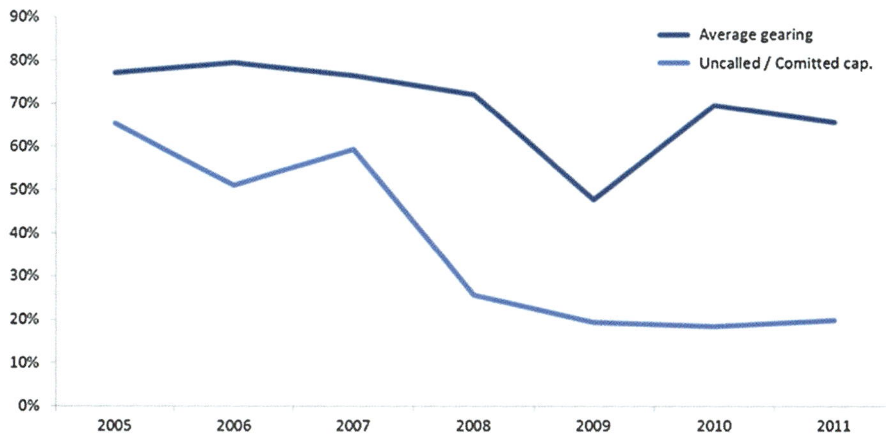

Fig. 6.3 A specialty of Norwegian KS financing is the so-called uncalled capital

of being liable up to a known limit (being the portion of the total partnership capital subscribed for) of the KS's legal liabilities connected to its business operations, there are certain tax advantages in owning assets through a KS. Partners with limited liability will, for tax purposes, be deemed to own a share in the asset(s) (for example, a vessel) directly corresponding to their ownership share in the KS and therefore, when filing their annual tax returns, be entitled to their corresponding share of the annual book value depreciation of the relevant asset(s). However, it should be noted that the tax advantages of owning assets through KSs have been reduced to some extent over the past few years as a result of the introduction of a new tax regime in Norway.

6.2.3 *The Silent Partnership "IS"*

A silent partnership is a special kind of partnership and as such is also governed by the Partnership Act. A silent partnership consists of a general partner and at least one silent partner ("stille deltaker"). The general partner has an unlimited liability for the partnership's obligations, whereas the silent partners have limited liability. The general partner may, and will normally be, a limited liability company ("AS").

In contrast to an ordinary partnership, the silent partnership does not publicly act or appear as a partnership toward contractual partners and other third parties. The silent partners cannot represent or commit the silent partnership in any way or form.

The general partner of the silent partnership carries out the business of the silent partnership. The general partner acts in its own name and assumes all rights and obligations toward third parties. Internally, between the general partner and the silent partners, the rights and obligations are normally divided according to a partnership agreement.

The legal basis of a silent partnership is laid down in a partnership agreement. There are no formal requirements that have to be met. Only a limited number of the statutory provisions of the Partnership Act apply to silent partnerships and as a result, the rights and obligations of the partners may have to be set out in greater detail in the partnership agreement of a silent partnership compared to other partnerships.

As opposed to a limited partnership, there are no specific requirements for the capital of a silent partnership. The silent partnership thus gives greater flexibility with regard to the calling of additional capital and the distribution of profits than a limited partnership.

According to the Partnership Act section 2–8 (2) silent partners may not be members of the partnership meeting. Thus, in a silent partnership with one general manager and several silent partners there is no partnership meeting as such. The silent partners may be given a right through meetings to instruct the general manager on certain matters. In addition, the silent partners may be given veto rights with respect to the operations of the partnership.

A silent partnership is not registered in the Norwegian Corporate Registry ("Foretaksregisteret"). The fact that the silent partnership is not registered in the Corporate Registry is attractive to investors wishing discretion regarding their investments.

A shareholders' agreement typically will contain important clauses stipulating the mechanism of triggering a sale or purchase of shares or a mandatory share offer should one partner become the owner of more than 75 % of the partnership shares in accordance with the Norwegian Securities Act 1997 ("Verdipapirhandelloven") section 1–4. 7.

A decision to increase the Partnership Capital may be made by the Partnership Meeting with the prior approval of at least 76 % of the votes cast at the Partnership Council.

6.2.4 *The Limited Liability Company "AS"*

This is the equivalent of a stock-based company where the owners cannot be held liable beyond each one's contribution to the company's stock capital. The private limited company must provide a minimum capital of 100.000 NOK. The shares of a Norwegian private limited company are registered and cannot be made public or transferred freely.

6.2.5 The General Partnership "ANS"

Norwegian partnerships are regulated by the Partnership Act and each partnership agreement. It can be established by two or more members who have the right to manage the company and are held responsible for the gains and profits of the company, and also the losses. All the partners are active, being general partners. Their liability is unlimited, the partners being liable to the company's debts and obligations. The general partnership does not require a minimum capital.

6.3 Taxation Aspects of Norwegian Limited Partnerships/Silent Partnerships

In general, there are no tax incentive schemes specifically aimed at encouraging investments in unlisted companies.

Typically, these structures are either tax transparent (taxed at the level of the investor) or taxed at the company level. The silent partnership structures are tax transparent, while the limited liability company is taxed at company level. However, this tax liability is generally mitigated by the exemption method. The exemption method applies to all corporate entity investors regardless of their tax residency and commonly exempts foreign investors from taxation in Norway. Under the exemption method, corporate investors in limited partnerships are not liable for tax in Norway on income from shares held by the limited partnership in companies that are tax resident within the European Economic Area (EEA).

A Norwegian limited partnership is considered to have a fixed place of business in Norway. Non-resident investors in a Norwegian limited partnership are normally considered to participate in a business in Norway, and are liable for taxation in Norway in the same way as an individual investor resident in Norway.

A Norwegian silent partnership is not liable to pay taxes (tax-transparent company). The investors (the silent partners) are taxable to their relevant share of a calculated taxable income/loss and net worth according to the tax rules of their domicile. This makes the silent partnership structure attractive for non-Norwegian investors as they are not taxed in Norway whereas Norwegian investors are taxed according to ordinary Norwegian taxation.

Currently, the tax rate in Norway for ordinary income is 28 % and the marginal assets tax rate ("Formueskatt") is 1.1 %. In Norway, the taxable loss allocated to the investors is limited to equity. The Norwegian personal investors are subject to tax (28 %) on dividends from the silent partnership. Total tax on income and dividends thus amounts to 48.16 %. Limited liability companies investing in a silent partnership are not subject to tax on dividends. The realization of shares is taxable for personal investors. Any loss will be subject to deductions in taxable income. For limited liability companies domiciled in Norway, realization of shares is covered by "Tax exemption model". This means that potential gains will be tax-exempt and

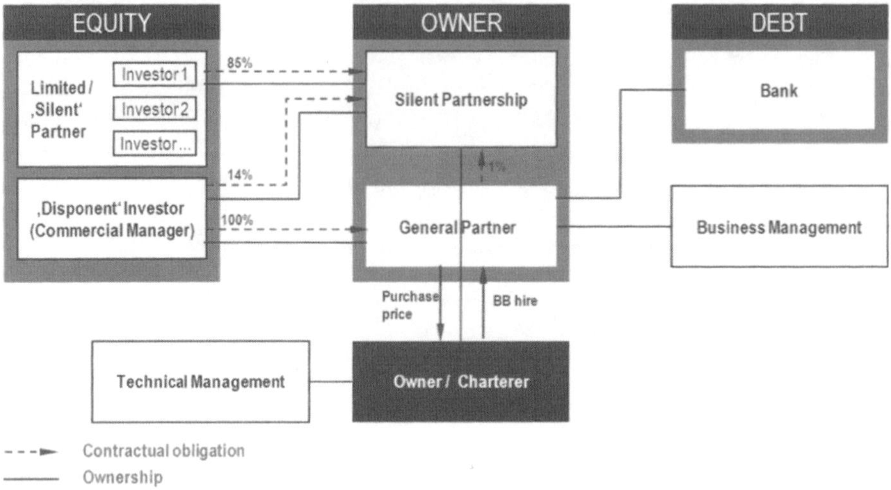

Fig. 6.4 Graphical representation of the structure of the transaction

potential losses will not be tax deductible. However, 3 % of the realization gains will be included in taxable income.

6.4 Example of a Typical Silent Partnership Transaction

The following example is an excerpt from the corresponding Pareto Finance AS Information Memorandum and outlines the acquisition and financing of two anchor handling tug supply vessels arranged by Pareto Project Finance AS, January 2012.[1]

Pareto Project Finance agreed with a Far East owner and certain of its subsidiaries the acquisition of two of the owner's Anchor Handling Tug Supply (AHTS) vessels by a special-purpose IS company for $64 m en bloc.

Post acquisition, the vessels were chartered to a company guaranteed by the owner on a 5-year "hell or high water" bareboat contract at a Bareboat rate of $11,000 per day per vessel. The owner will have the option to buy the vessels back at the end of the third, fourth, and fifth year at a price per vessel of $30.5 m, $29.7 m, and $28 m, respectively. If the purchase options are

(continued)

[1]Graphs and investment case courtesy of Pareto Project Finance AS, Dronning Maudsgate 3, P.O. Box 1396 Vika, 0114 Oslo, Norway.

exercised individually, it is the special-purpose company's choice to nominate the vessel.

Over the project's full 5-year lifetime, the average annual dividend is forecast at 15 % of the paid-in equity per year. Valuing the vessels at exit in year 5 at a level equivalent to the depreciated current charter-free market value, equity investors are expected to receive an internal rate of return (IRR) of 26 % per annum. 26 %-annual return is also expected if the owner exercises its option after year 5, while an exercise after years 3 and 4 yield an IRR of 29 and 28 %, respectively.

The vessels are of a high build quality and are suitable for operations in all major offshore fields across the world, including Brazil, Australia, and Asia, with the exception of harsh environments such as the North Sea.

The key investment highlights are summarized below:

- 5-year "hell and high water" bareboat charter to company guaranteed by the owner
- BB rate of $11,000 net/vessel/day
- Expected IRR of 26–29 % if call option is exercised/sale at depreciated values
- Expected annual dividends of 15 % (on average during BB period)
- Residual value equal to last 5-year low gives an IRR of 20 %
- Purchase price: $32 million per vessel-below charter-free market values of $33–36.5 million per vessel at the time of the transaction
- Seller's credit of $12.8 million en bloc as security for the bareboat contract, which implies a net purchase price about 25 % below values at the time of the transaction
- Charterer with diversified balance sheet, book equity of $1.4 billion (52 %) and $477 million in cash and time deposits as per March 31, 2011
- Bareboat contract no technical or market risk during charter party
- Residual value at $17.9 million per vessel gives money back, implying that values can drop by approximately 40 % from level at the time of the transaction
- Key financial data:
  - Project cost: US$66,400,000
  - Paid-in equity: US$11,600,000
  - Uncalled capital: US$6,000,000
  - Min subscription: 1 %: US$116,000
  - Uncalled capital per 1 %: US$60,000

The business manager for the IS single-purpose company is Pareto Business Management AS looking after the company's interests toward shareholders, preparing tax information for the participants and the company,

(continued)

preparing annual reports, organizing board meetings and general meetings, besides maintaining a secondary market for the shares. All secondary trading of shares in the IS will be handled through Pareto Business Management AS/the Equity Sales department of Pareto Project Finance AS. A graphical representation of the transaction structure is provided in Fig. 6.4.

Is it really an attractive investment? This type of a Norwegian limited partnership is more of a financial vehicle and the investment carries quantifiable risk factors. As we have seen in the example above, the acquisition and financing of two Anchor Handling Tug Supply Vessels are not very different from a sale-leaseback transaction. In this setup, a special-purpose company buys the vessel and charters it back on a bareboat charter to the seller. By having a long-term charter attached, the main risks to be evaluated from an investor's perspective are the residual value of the vessels and the ability of the owner/charterer to perform their obligations.

Chapter 7
Business Acquisitions as a Tool for Proactive Financial Management: The Case of Seanergy Maritime Holdings

Christina Anagnostara and Christos Sigalas

Abstract Seanergy, as a former SPAC company and owner of six vessels that were acquired at historical all-time high values in the dry bulk industry, had managed to sustain its operations amid a challenging market environment by implementing proactive financial management. The weak freight environment that followed just 3 months after the acquisition of the initial fleet, declared that Seanergy would not be able to serve its hefty financing obligations in the long run. The secured cash flows, which stemmed from the significant premium of the attached charter parties over prevailing market rates, provided a short term cushion. During that period, the Management of the Company decided that the only way to shield Seanergy against a future cash deficit and accounting losses was to add more vessels with a daily break even low enough to cover the high break even of the initial six vessels resulting from their high financing cost. The proactive business planning exercise, highlighted the fact that accretive business acquisitions can lead to a lower average break even for the Company as a whole. Therefore, Seanergy, had implemented its proactive financial management, by acquiring two businesses over the next 2 years. The combined impact of the two business acquisitions, apart from more than tripling the size of the fleet, also led to increased revenue, kept operating income positive and augmented cash flows. Seanergy's case, allows practicing managers in senior level financial positions to enrich their understanding about how business acquisitions can be used as a means of proactive financial management.

C. Anagnostara (✉) • C. Sigalas
Seanergy Maritime Holdings Corp., 1-3 Patriarchou Grigoriou Str. & 127, Vouliagmenis Ave., 16674 Glyfada, Athens, Greece
e-mail: ca@seanergy.gr; csigalas@seanergy.gr

O. Schinas et al. (eds.), *HSBA Handbook on Ship Finance*,
DOI 10.1007/978-3-662-43410-9_7,

7.1 Background Information

Seanergy Maritime was incorporated in August 2006 as a Special Purpose Acquisition Company (SPAC). SPACs, or the so-called shell or blank-check companies, do not have operations at the time of their inception and instead raise equity in the public markets with the intention of using the proceeds of their initial public offering (IPO) to acquire or merge with a company. If an acquisition is not concluded in a 2 years' time, then the funds are remitted back to the IPO's investors. SPACs usually raise blind pool funds, which are placed into a trust fund in the form of an escrow account for an unspecified business transaction, sometimes in a targeted industry. Seanergy Maritime was formed with the aim of acquiring companies or assets in the maritime shipping industry.

Seanergy Maritime consummated its IPO of shares in September 2007 raising total proceeds of $231 million on the American Stock Exchange (AMEX), presently known as NYSE Amex Equities and before March 2009 as NYSE Alternext U.S., which is the alternative market of the New York Stock Exchange. Each Seanergy Maritime SPAC unit was sold at $10 for one share of common stock and one warrant that could purchase one additional share at $6.5 per share until September 2011. Until early May 2008, Seanergy Maritime remained a development stage company with the main goal of identifying potential acquisition targets in shipping industry. The proceeds from the offering were kept in an interest bearing escrow account and the interest income for 2007 and 2008 was distributed to the IPO investors in the form of a dividend.

In May 2008, Seanergy Maritime reached an agreement to acquire six vessels from companies affiliated to the Restis family for a net price of $395.3 million. At the same time, entities affiliated to the Restis family acquired 9.62 % of Seanergy's share capital from the company's founding shareholders for $25 million. The vessels acquisition was financed partially by $149.1 million of IPO net proceeds after deducting the redemption of common shares valued at $63.7 million by shareholders that did not concur with the proposed transaction $218 million of bank debt and $28.2 million of convertible promissory note due in May 2010. In addition, the agreement included an EBITDA earn-out provision for the sellers of the vessels to receive up to 4,308,075 shares of Seanergy Maritime common stock subject to the company meeting an EBITDA target of $72 million in the 1-year period between October 1, 2008 and September 30, 2009. The target was achieved and the additional consideration was paid to the sellers of the vessels.

Upon completion of the transaction in August 2008, Seanergy Maritime acquired a fleet consisting of two Panamax, two Supramax, one Handymax, and one Handysize bulk vessels, with a carrying capacity of approximately 318 thousand DWT and an average age of 11 years. The acquired vessels came with 1 year time charter contracts with South African Marine Corporation, a chartering company affiliated to the major shareholder, at time charter daily gross rates of between $30 and $65 thousand. In September 2008, owing to the downturn in freight rates and vessels values, the market value of the vessels was $360.1 million or

Table 7.1 Dry Bulk companies listed on NASDAQ and NYSE

NASDAQ[a]		NYSE[a]	
Company	Date of IPO	Company	Date of IPO
Eagle Bulk Shipping	June 2005	Excel Maritime	February 1989
TBS International[b]	June 2005	Diana Shipping	March 2005
Freeseas	December 2005	Genco Shipping	July 2005
Star Bulk Carriers	December 2005	Paragon Shipping	August 2007
Seanergy Maritime	September 2007	Navios Maritime Partners	November 2007
Globus Maritime	June 2007	Safe Bulkers	May 2008
		Baltic Trading	March 2010

[a] In the event that some companies have listed their shares on the NASDAQ or on the NYSE after initially going public on a different exchange, the IPO date will not coincide with the listing date
[b] Delisted in 2012

$44.8 million lower compared to the agreed gross price in May 2008. The difference between the agreed and market value was recorded as goodwill from acquisitions in the Company's financial statements. From September 2008 through December 2008, significant disruptions took place in the credit markets that have affected many sectors of global economic activity, including the shipping industry. More specifically, since mid-August 2008, the charter rates in the dry bulk charter market have declined significantly and dry bulk vessel values have also decreased, both as a result of a slowdown in global economic activity and the significant deterioration in the availability of credit. In December of 2008, in light of the prevailing market conditions signalling a potential impairment, Seanergy Maritime decided to impair all of the goodwill recorded in the balance sheet along with $4.5 million of its vessels book value.

Following the completion of the acquisition and as the purpose of the blank-check company was fulfilled, Seanergy Maritime was dissolved in January 2009 and Seanergy Maritime Holdings emerged as its successor. Shareholders in Seanergy Maritime received one share in the new company in exchange for every share in the old company, and the shares commenced trading on the NASDAQ Stock Market in January, 2009. The NASDAQ was chosen as it had emerged as an important marketplace for raising equity capital for shipping companies since 2000. In particular, at least six pure-play dry bulk firms have floated their shares there. These, along with pure play dry bulk firms listed on NYSE, would bring the total to 13 (Table 7.1).

The agglomeration of dry bulk company listings in NASDAQ has to do with the increased transparency in financial reporting and strict corporate governance associated with a listing in the United States. At the same time, the reporting requirements for foreign stock issuers, such as shipping companies, allow flexibility which was particularly relevant in the case of Seanergy. High standards of corporate governance are considered crucial for all company stakeholders and a listing on NASDAQ acts as a testament of increased reporting transparency and accountability

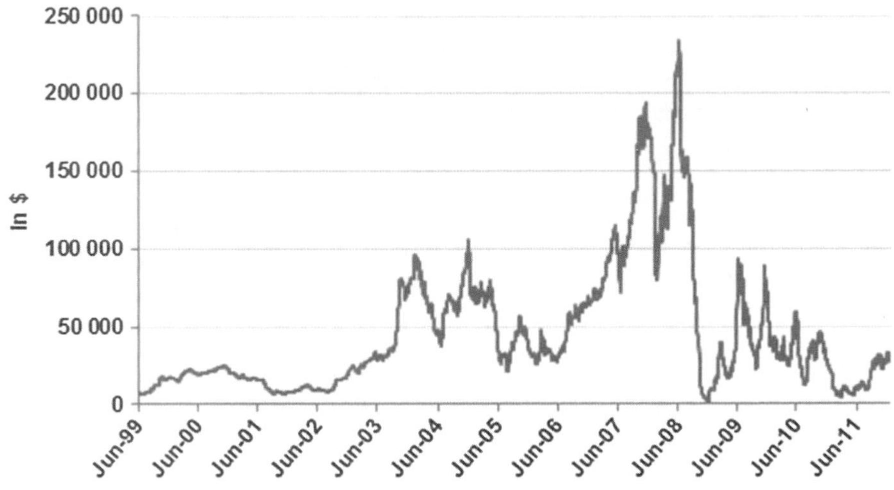

Fig. 7.1 The Baltic Capesize Index Time Charter Average

to investors. Furthermore, the high level of development in the financial services industry in the U.S. also makes it easier for ship-owners to contact lending institutions, investment banks, underwriters, and potential investors willing to subscribe to a share offering. Additionally, stock exchanges in the U.S. are the largest in terms of transaction volumes and attract a highly diversified investor base, as opposed to other bourses that lack the same international orientation. What is more important is that United States stock exchanges, such as the NASDAQ, enjoy increased liquidity and consequently lower transaction costs. This allows investors to trade in a company's stock and consequently results in a premium valuation compared to companies listed on less liquid exchanges. Another important reason for choosing the NASDAQ is the presence of an industry peer group that allows analysts to compare companies and provide stock valuations.

At the time of the six initial vessel acquisitions, the BDI index, which measures the cost of transporting dry bulk commodities across various routes, was close to its all-time high and so the vessels earned very high charter rates (see Figs. 7.1, 7.2, 7.3, and 7.4).

The above four graphs present the time series of average daily time charter rate paid for each of the four major types of dry bulk vessels. From the graphs, it can be seen that market rates for all vessel types peaked in May 2008. The healthy shipping market prevailing at the time enabled Seanergy to adopt a business model based on paying high dividends to shareholders out of internally generated cash flows. Besides, the relationship with the major shareholder and the options to purchase two additional vessels afforded the Company attractive growth prospects. Following the collapse of Lehman Brothers and the ensuing financial crisis, the BDI retreated by about 90 % compared to its previous peak and reached a low in December 2008. This prompted Seanergy's Management to suspend dividend payments from February

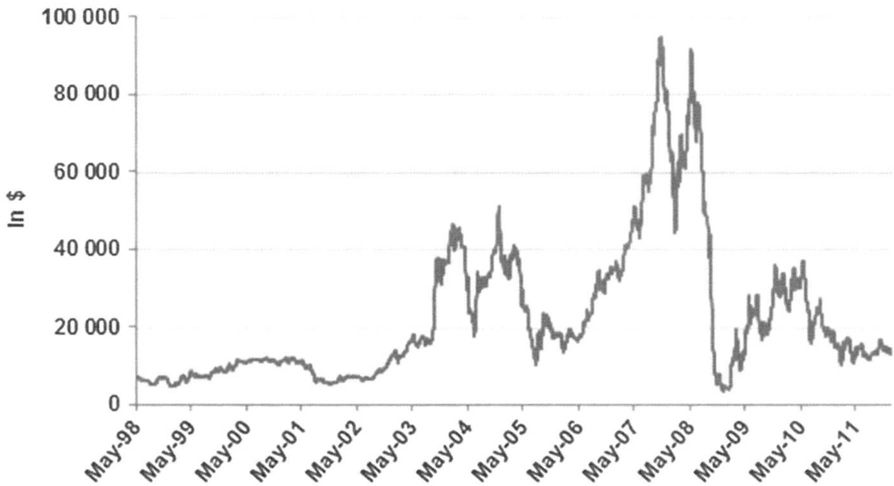

Fig. 7.2 The Baltic Panamax Index Time Charter Average

Fig. 7.3 The Baltic Supramax Index Time Charter Average

2009 onwards, with a view to conserving the company's cash during a volatile period. Furthermore, a waiver on the security margin covenant which is calculated as the ratio of fleet market value to net debt was obtained from Marfin Bank, as the precipitous fall in the dry bulk market caused a corresponding decrease in the market value of Seanergy's vessels. During this time, the aforementioned EBITDA earn-out clause in the purchase agreement of the vessels proved particularly useful as it provided the charterers with the incentive to continue to pay high charter rates for Seanergy vessels, whereas in the absence of that clause, it would clearly be in

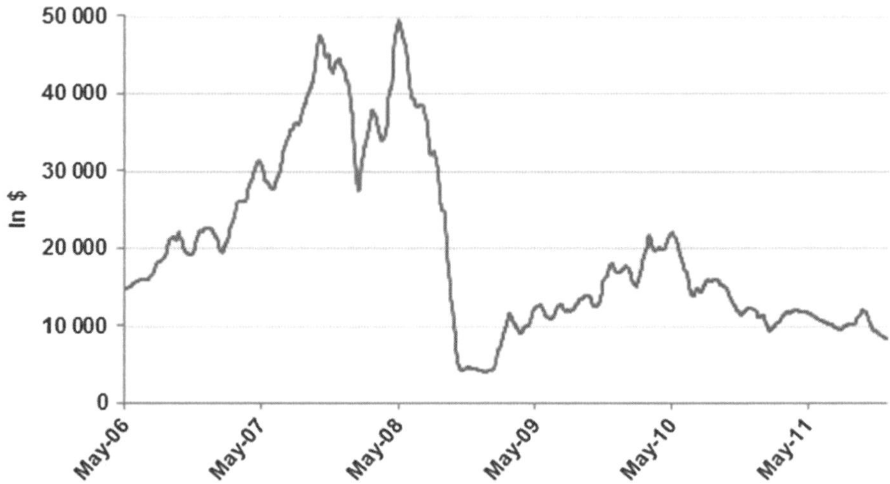

Fig. 7.4 The Baltic Handysize Index Time Charter Average

their interest to renegotiate the charters at considerably lower rates. In this way, Seanergy generated free cash flows throughout the term of the contracts.

As 2009 progressed, it became clear that Western economies had slipped into recession and that a complete economic meltdown had only been averted due to coordinated government stimulus aimed at increasing aggregate demand in the economy and the concurrent monetary easing undertaken by major central banks around the world. The negative impact on the dry bulk market was evident as charter rates in the market were substantially lower than what was seen in 2007 and 2008 for all vessel classes. Although Seanergy's charterers honoured their commitment to the previously signed charter agreements, redelivered vessels had to be chartered in the market at much lower rates. As Seanergy's vessels had been purchased at very high prices, the fall in market rates meant that covering expenses and repaying debt out of vessels cash flows had become unsustainable. Consequently, Seanergy had to plan its response to the ongoing crisis, both in shipping and in the financial markets. One possibility was to attempt to burn through existing cash for as long as vessels were to earn rates below what was required to break even. At the end of September 2009, cash in hand stood at around $64 million. However, the risks of such an approach would have been significant, as the Company would eventually run out of cash after a long stretch of unfavorable market rates. On the other hand, as future prospects in the shipping market were looking negative due to the massive influx of new vessels, there were opportunities to be found in acquiring vessels or shipping companies from financially distressed ship-owners at low prices. At the time, Seanergy was in a good position to capitalise on such opportunities mainly because of two reasons. Firstly, despite having purchased its fleet at what proved to be unfavourable price levels, it was a publicly listed company with the ability to obtain equity funding

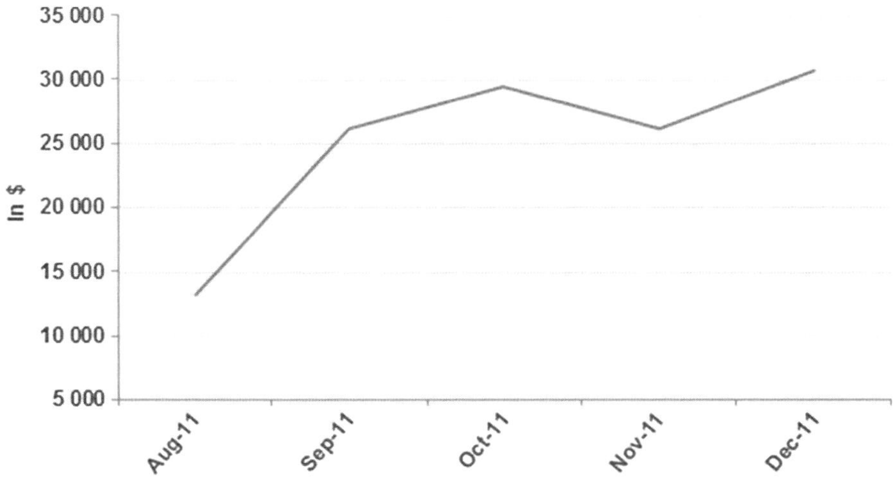

Fig. 7.5 The Baltic Capesize Index Time Charter Average (August 2011–December 2011)

in the market. Secondly, the affiliation with the major shareholder provided the Company with considerable advantages in terms of shipping industry connections, lenders' willingness to engage in negotiations and provide liquidity, as well as in finding opportunities to acquire distressed companies willing to sell their assets.

Seanergy's Management chose to take advantage of falling asset prices and engaged in the acquisition of a 50 % stake in Bulk Energy Transport (BET). At the time, BETs ownership was split equally between a company affiliated to the major shareholder and Constellation Bulk Energy, a subsidiary of Constellation Energy Group. At the time, BET suffered from high levels of debt relative to the falling value of its vessels and high economic uncertainty. Constellation was interested in divesting its stake in the shipping company and Seanergy took advantage of the opportunity by purchasing the 50 % for a nominal consideration of one dollar. The transaction was completed in August 2009 and as a result, Seanergy gained the control of a five vessels fleet that comprised one Panamax and four Capesizes. As a result, Seanergy controlled 11 vessels with a total capacity of one million DWT. The vessels were chartered to SAMC at profitable rates. It was an important milestone, as Seanergy acquired a controlling stake in a company for a relatively small cash outflow and initiated its exposure to the Capesize sector. This is particularly important because Capesize vessels are the primary means of transporting iron ore and the main driver of dry bulk shipping returns over the past years. As a result, it is a very volatile market where even a temporary shortage of ships can cause rates to rise dramatically. In this respect, it is indicative that since the beginning of August 2011, Capesize rates went from $9,300 per day to about $32,000 in December 2011, as can be seen in Fig. 7.5.

7.2 The Acquisition of BET

The acquisition of BET also marked an important milestone in terms of forming Seanergy's strategy of acquiring fleets at distressed prices, rather than opting for single, newly-built vessels. The Management's connections and wide network in the Capesize sector enabled Seanergy to enjoy superior commercial management and efficient operations. The acquisition of BET was accompanied by a debt restructuring that involved a $20-million prepayment of debt, which reduced the outstanding principle to $123 million from $143 million. At the same time, semi-annual instalments were reduced to $7.1 million from $8.3 million previously. Furthermore, temporary waivers to loan covenants were also obtained. After the expiration of the waiver period, the facility's covenants were temporarily amended, as the required ratio of equity to total capital fell to 17.5 % from 30 % previously and the ratio of the market value of ships to outstanding debt fell to 100 % from 125 % previously.

Following the acquisition of BET, Seanergy's capital structure was reinforced by the conversion into common shares of the promissory note that was issued to companies affiliated to the major shareholder. As a result, Seanergy reduced its outstanding debt without depleting its cash reserves. In the beginning of 2010, Seanergy took advantage of its position as a public company and engaged in a secondary sale of shares to obtain additional equity capital. In the beginning of February 2010, the contemplated share offering was priced at $1.2 per share and 20,833,333 shares were sold to the public, while the major shareholder purchased an additional 4,166,667 at the same price. On March 19, 2010, the underwriters exercised their option to obtain 1,985,000 shares to cover overallotments, which resulted in Seanergy achieving net proceeds of $28.1 million. The timing of the offering was particularly fortunate when considering the fact that shipping market sentiment deteriorated sharply in the months that followed making it hard to raise equity. Furthermore, there were a number of other advantages associated with it. Firstly, following the acquisition of BET, the capital structure of Seanergy was reinforced. Secondly, increasing cash levels allowed greater financial flexibility and ability to make acquisitions to capitalise on profitable opportunities. Lastly, the offering significantly diversified Seanergy's shareholder base, as the majority of shares were purchased by various investors. This was important in increasing the shares liquidity.

Following the strengthening of the company's balance sheet, Seanergy continued to look for accretive acquisition opportunities. In May 2010, Seanergy used the cash raised in the public share offering and purchased a 51 % stake in Maritime Capital Shipping (MCS), which is a Hong Kong-based owner of nine Handysize vessels. The price paid by Seanergy for the controlling stake was $33 million. In the aftermath of the transaction, Seanergy was in control of 20 vessels with a total carrying capacity of 1.3 million DWT. The acquisition of MCS increased Seanergy's exposure to the Handysize segment, where demand and supply fundamentals seem to be the most solid. In fact, it happens to be the case that at the time of the acquisition, more than 40 % of the global Handysize fleet was older than 20 years, while average annual fleet growth in terms of tonnage is in the 4–5 % range. Furthermore, Seanergy gained control of a fleet that was younger on average than the initial fleet and had high charter coverage with reputable counterparties, which greatly increased revenue generating potential, while also offered better access to the Asian shipping and financial markets through the office in Hong Kong.

At the time before the acquisition, the total debt of MCS stood at $166.9 million and comprised three different facilities, all with different lending institutions. $48 million was outstanding under the HSBC facility, $56.8 million under the UOB facility, and $62.1 million under the DVB facility. As MCS was in financial distress, a restructuring of debt was agreed with the purpose of making the company's debt burden manageable, given the weak market environment. The restructuring deal involved total debt prepayments of $28 million. For the HSBC, UOB, and DVB facilities, prepayments were equal to $7.6 million, $13.0[1] million, and $7.4 million respectively. The prepayments were accompanied by changes in the repayment profile of the loans as the instalments were modified to take account of the new debt outstanding of $138.9 million. Moreover, interest expense on the mezzanine tranche is capitalised, increasing the amount of the loan outstanding, instead of being payable at the end of each interest period. The mezzanine debt principle is to be repaid in whole concurrently with the final balloon instalments of the senior debt tranche.

The restructuring of the MCS debt was particularly important as the shipping market had entered a period of sustained weakness, during which daily rates earned were lower than before. As the debt agreements had been entered into amidst a favourable shipping market environment, it was clear that as generated cash flow would come under pressure, the servicing of the original repayment schedules would be unattainable. Consequently, the restructuring of the debt and the accompanying amendment of covenants and debt schedules proved important in making debt servicing viable. As a result, the prepayment and debt restructuring were mutually beneficial for Seanergy and its lenders by contributing to a sustainable capital structure. Seanergy, therefore, had the opportunity to generate a positive return on its investment in MCS, while the company's lenders reduced their exposure by receiving the prepayments. Furthermore, credit risk was reduced as the probability of default was smaller following the restructuring. Another important aspect of the restructuring is Seanergy's proactive stance toward the Company's lenders, in pursuing a prepayment and restructuring its liabilities in a timely manner, confirming the Company's sound financial planning and its status as being a counterparty of high credit quality. Moreover, as Seanergy is aiming to take advantage of opportunities to acquire vessels and grow its business, building a working relationship with multiple lending institutions had the capacity to prove useful in broadening Seanergy's future financing options.

---

[1]As far as the UOB facility is concerned, $9.25 million was repaid outright, while $13.8 million was transferred to a newly formed mezzanine tranche of which $3.8 million was prepaid.

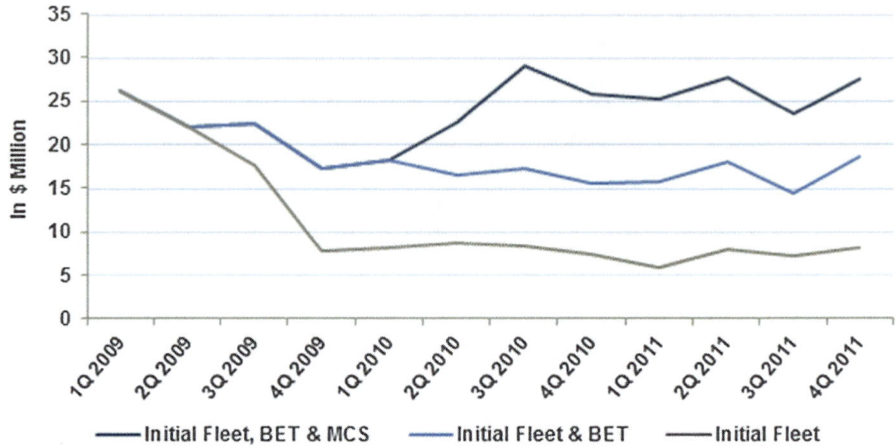

Fig. 7.6 Net revenue evolution due to business acquisitions

Since the end of the second quarter of 2010, Seanergy focused on the successful integration of its holdings in the companies it acquired. As part of this plan, it consolidated its ownership stakes by acquiring 49 % of MCS in the third quarter of 2010 and 50 % of BET in the fourth quarter of 2010. In total, it paid a consideration of $62 million to the sellers who were companies affiliated to the major shareholder, of which $10 million was paid in cash and the remaining consideration was in the form of shares issued at a 14 % premium to the market price prevailing at the time to avoid dilution of minority shareholders. With minimal cash outlays, Seanergy managed to gain full ownership of its fleet, which had more than tripled within a period of 2 years. Seanergy took advantage of the market turmoil to make accretive acquisitions that assisted in gaining growth, diversity, and profitability. What is important to mention here is the reorganisation of the Hong Kong office that took place in the second quarter of 2011, and is expected to contribute about $2 million each year in savings on general and administrative expenses.

As seen in Figs. 7.6 and 7.7, the proactive business acquisitions made by Seanergy in 2009 and 2010 have proved important in increasing revenue and keeping operating profitability within positive territory. This is especially important as the initial six vessels were acquired at high prices and are unprofitable in the current market environment. Supporting operational profitability through well-timed acquisitions with minimal cash outflows has provided a means for Seanergy to generate the cash flow necessary to meet future capital obligations. Furthermore, it assisted Seanergy to establish working relationships with various financial institutions as it has assumed the debt obligations of the two companies acquired. This took place through the loans attached to the vessels purchased in Seanergy's acquisitions. This is important in terms of managing liquidity and securing financing for future investment opportunities. As risks to global financial stability have risen markedly since the start of the Eurozone debt crisis, European banking institutions that have

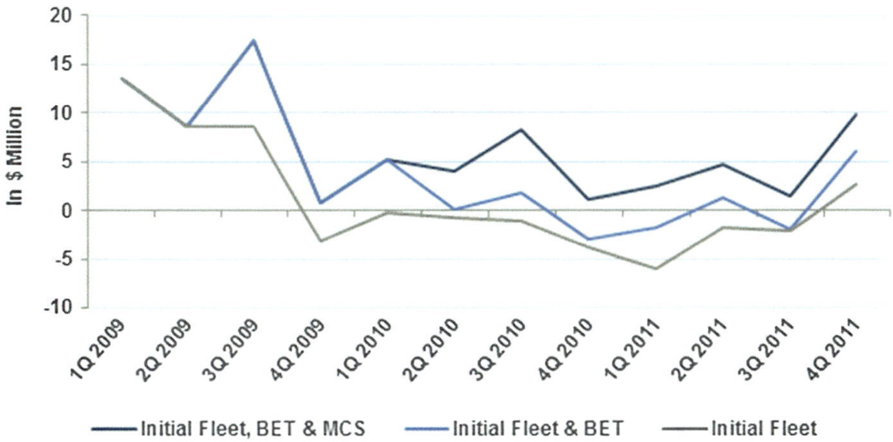

Fig. 7.7 Operating income evolution due to business acquisitions

in the past been traditional finance providers to the maritime shipping industry have found it more expensive to fund their operations. Besides, there is increased uncertainty about the ability of major European lenders to meet the new collateral rules and capital requirements set out as part of the Basel II and Basel III regulatory frameworks. Under these agreements, the risk weighting of corporate loans, including those made to shipping companies, has increased, requiring lenders to set aside more reserves for each loan made. At the same time, the total reserve requirements themselves have also been increased. As such rules fade in starting from 2013, banks will inevitably be required to set aside more equity capital, or dispose of parts of their loan portfolios, making it increasingly difficult for them to finance vessels. It is indicative that Societe Generale sold a large part of its shipping portfolio to Citi in 2012, while Commerzbank has elected to exit the shipping finance market altogether. These factors have made it increasingly difficult for ship-owners to finance vessel acquisitions or refinance existing loans. In light of these developments, one can appreciate the importance of forming relationships with multiple lenders in different locations to diversify a company's funding base. In this respect, the acquisition of MCS has benefited the Seanergy Group by making it somewhat easier to utilise Far Eastern finance providers.

7.3 Concluding Remarks

As a conclusion, it is worth mentioning that Seanergy, as a former SPAC company and owner of six vessels that were acquired at historical all-time high values in the dry bulk industry, had managed to sustain its operations amid a challenging market environment by implementing proactive financial management. The acquisition of the initial fleet at high market values prevailing at the time bequeathed Seanergy with increased financing costs that impacted cash flows. In addition, the weak freight environment that followed just 3 months after the acquisition of the initial fleet lowered the prospects of the Company. The secured cash flows, which stemmed from the significant premium of the attached charter parties over prevailing market rates, provided a short-term cushion. The Management of the Company decided that the only way to shield Seanergy against a future cash deficit and accounting losses was to add more vessels with a daily break even low enough to cover the high break even of the initial six vessels resulting from high financing costs. The proactive cash flow monitoring and business planning highlighted the fact that accretive business acquisitions can lead to a lower average break even for the Company as a whole. Bearing this in mind and capitalising on the major shareholders' extensive network in the shipping industry, Seanergy had managed to acquire BET for a nominal consideration. As part of proactive financial management, the debt restructuring of BET was essential for the success of the venture. Following the BET acquisition, Seanergy Group's cash flows and income statement were reinforced significantly. However, as market conditions remained week and volatile, it was imperative for Seanergy to proceed with further business acquisitions. Before doing so, the Management of the Company strengthened Seanergy's balance sheet by raising public equity in a secondary offering and by converting the promissory note, issued to partially finance the acquisition of the initial six vessel fleet, into shares. Both actions, part of proactive financial management, enabled Seanergy to proceed with the second acquisition. The acquisition of MCS, following its debt restructuring, reinforced Seanergy's cash flows and income statement even more, and maintained a positive operating income.

The combined impact of the two business acquisitions as a tool of proactive financial management was that apart from more than tripling the size of the fleet within a period of just 2 years, it led to increased revenue, kept operating income positive, and augmented cash flows.

It can be seen that in Seanergy's case, using acquisitions as a means of proactive financial management resulted in profitable expansion at attractive prices, while ensuring the continuity of the business during an unfavourable market environment.

Chapter 8
HCI Hammonia Shipping AG: A Case Study

Jan Willem Krutemeier

Abstract This article describes the Initial Public Offering (IPO) of a German ship-owning outfit (HCI Hammonia Shipping AG) in the German market and outlines its development over the first couple of years on the market, until August 2012. Directed mainly at institutional investors, the stock-listed company hit the market in an environment overwhelmingly dominated by the "KG-system" as most popular equity gathering method. However, the HCI Hammonia AG's business model is rooted in its home market as it owns container ships that are chartered out to container shipping lines. Against all odds, the company thrived even through the first years of the downturn.

8.1 Introduction

In Germany, raising equity for shipping projects has predominantly been carried out in the retail market, the so-called KG Market. Up to the late 1990s, tax shelter schemes dominated the market. These schemes facilitated the development of an industry cluster consisting of ship managers, issuing houses, distribution partners, and their respective service providers. With the significant reduction of tax relief through depreciation allowances and the introduction of the tonnage tax system in September 1998 investors put more focus on the profitability of the shipping projects. At the same time, the demand for capital in the shipping industry grew worldwide due to the increasing globalisation and, along with this, the growing world trade. This led internationally to a number of Initial Public Offerings ("IPOs") of asset management companies that aimed specifically at institutional investors. The peak for the time being was 2005 with 18 international IPOs of shipping companies, among others the IPO of Seaspan Corp at the New York Stock Exchange

J.W. Krutemeier (✉)
HAMMONIA Reederei, Elbchaussee 370, 22609 Hamburg, Germany
e-mail: krutemeier@hammonia-reederei.de

O. Schinas et al. (eds.), *HSBA Handbook on Ship Finance*,

DOI 10.1007/978-3-662-43410-9_8,

Table 8.1 Listed shipping companies

Company	Market segment	Date of IPO	Current market capitalization (in million euros)	Stock exchange
DryShips	Bulker	February 2005	936	NASDAQ
Diana Shipping	Bulker	March 2005	578	NYSE
Genco Shipping and Trading	Bulker	July 2005	163	NYSE
Seaspan Corporation	Container	August 2005	1,010	NYSE
Danaos	Container	October 2006	437	NYSE
First Ship Lease Trust	Misc.	March 2007	81	Singapore
Rickmers Maritime	Container	May 2007	88	Singapore
Paragon Shipping	Bulker	August 2007	30	NYSE
Seanergy Maritime Holdings Corp.	Bulker	September 07	24	NASDAQ
Global Ship Lease	Container	August 2008	159	NYSE
Costamare Inc.	Container	November 2010	881	NYSE

Source: Company websites: www.comdirect.de from August 2012

("NYSE") raising rd. ab. US$6 billion at that time. In Table 8.1 some examples of international IPO of shipping asset management companies are given.

Germany's KG market developed further, but remained tailored to the needs of retail investors. An explanatory approach for the absence of investment vehicles for institutional investors respectively investment vehicles at the German stock exchanges up to 2007 may be the ample success of the KG market which did not necessitate efforts of ship managers and issuing houses to accommodate the needs of institutional investors with tailor-made structures. Alone in the years from 1999 to 2007, the equity raised from retail investors increased from EUR 1 billion p.a. to about EUR 3 billion p.a.

The main obstacle for institutional investors to join a KG fund is the legal structure. Investment guidelines of banks, savings banks, and insurance companies generally require investments in publicly listed companies to ensure a daily price fixing and in addition a simplified exit option from the investment. In addition, private limited partnerships (*Kommanditgesellschaften*) do not fulfill the custody qualifications (*Depotfähigkeit*). Private limited partnerships are therefore for the most part not considered an eligible investment vehicle even though secondary markets for KG shares have been established.

In 2007 and 2008 three alternative shipping investment vehicles were publicly offered in the German market structured as public limited companies (*Aktiengesellschaft*) to tap into the market of institutional investors (Table 8.2).

The initiators were issuing houses and ship managers with the objective to also develop access to the capital markets to diversify funding sources and to safeguard future growth. In the following chapters an abstract based on the experiences gained in recent years shall be given with regard to one of those investment vehicles,

Table 8.2 Listed shipping companies in Germany

Company	Market segment	Date of IPO	Current market capitalization (in million euros)	Stock exchange
MARENAVE	Misc.	November 2006	69	Hamburg
HCI Hammonia Shipping AG	Container	November 2007	35	Hamburg
Vilmaris	Bulker	June 2009	30	Hamburg

Source: Company websites: www.comdirect.de from August 2012

the HCI Hammonia Shipping AG ("HHX"), paying particular consideration to its distinctive features and differences to the prevailing ship investment vehicles in Germany at that time.

8.2 Initial Public Offering

HSH Nordbank AG, Nord LB and HSC Hanseatische Sachwert Concept GmbH (a subsidiary of HCI Group) were entrusted with the placement of the shares. Preparations for the IPO of HHX started at the beginning of 2007. However, the presentation to potential investors commenced only in the middle of 2007. Target investors were especially banks, savings banks, pension funds, and insurance companies. A minimum subscription of EUR 550,000—i.e. 500 shares at EUR 1,100 each—was set deliberately to allow for a lean fund raising process. However, smaller amounts of shares could be ordered at the stock exchange. Some retail investors used that opportunity following the initial listing.

The marketing of the IPO was hampered by the fact that in August 2007 a rescue package had to be bundled to secure the solvency of IKB Deutsche Industriebank AG. At this KfW bore the brunt to avoid a chain reaction in the German banking market. This was the first forerunner of the transgression of the US subprime crisis to the German banking market and it led to respective disconcertment in the financial sector. However, the IPO of HHX could be completed successfully. The original target to raise € 130 million of equity was slightly surpassed with a final volume of € 150 million. Since the IPO, the shareholder structure has basically remained unaltered and is as of August 2012 (Fig. 8.1).

8.3 Company Structure

HHX is a management holding company in the legal form of a public limited company. Its shares are listed in the regulated market of Hanseatische Wertpapierbörse Hamburg (*Hamburg Stock Exchange*). It has also been listed by brokers in

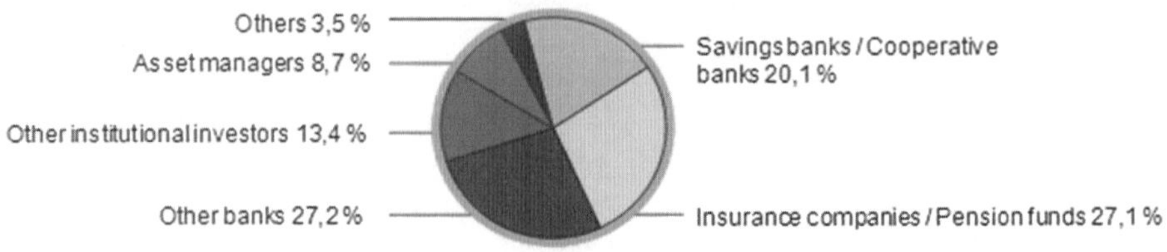

Fig. 8.1 Investors breakdown

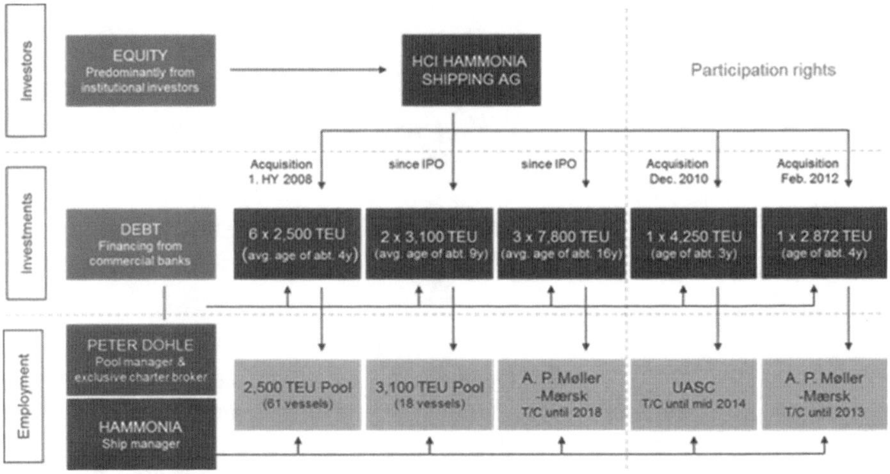

Fig. 8.2 Structure of the investment scheme

the regulated unofficial markets (Freiverkehr) at the stock exchanges in Frankfurt, Munich, and Stuttgart whereby a Designated Sponsor attends to the listing in the XETRA system. HHX holds interests in limited shipping partnerships with a limited liability company as general partner (GmbH & Co. KG). These limited shipping partnerships are in turn the owners of the respective vessels.

The current fleet of HCI Hammonia Shipping AG includes 13 container vessels. In addition to the previous eleven vessels of the 2,500, 3,100 and 7,800 TEU classes, a majority interest of 56 % in a 4,250 TEU vessel was acquired in December 2010 and a majority interest of 51 % in a 2,872 TEU vessel in February 2012. The chart (Fig. 8.2) shows the current organizational structure.

8.4 Business Model

The business concept of HHX is focused on the acquisition, operation, and sale of merchant ships. Market cycles shall be used to sell ships at high prices and replenish the fleet when prices are lower. HHX is merely an asset holder. The shipping companies of HHX provide the vessels' charterers with fully equipped, operational, and manned vessels.

8.4.1 *Focus on Container Shipping*

Through limited shipping partnerships, HHX operates a fleet of container ships. An expansion into other ship segments (e.g. bulk carriers) has been left open in the IPO prospectus. However, it has always been the concept of the management to focus on container shipping. While this takes away the possibility to diversify earnings over different shipping segments, the idea was to leave the decision whether to diversify (and if so, to which extent) to the investors as pure bulk carrier and pure tanker stock companies are available in the international stock markets. This is also a concession to institutional investors who carry out their own portfolio management. HHX's focus on container shipping is a distinctive feature to the other comparable investment vehicles in the German market.

8.4.2 *Involvement of the Initiators*

HHX has no own employees. All services are provided by means of outsourcing whereby HHX is a "true lean company". By using the resources and the skills of its initiators, HHX benefits from their market positions. The involvement of its initiators is an essential feature of the business model of HHX.

8.4.2.1 HAMMONIA Reederei GmbH & Co. KG

All vessels are commercially and technically managed by HAMMONIA Reederei GmbH & Co. KG ("HAMMONIA Reederei") which is a ship management company and project developer in international shipping. Originally founded by ship owner Peter Döhle Schiffahrts-KG ("PDS-KG") and issuing house HCI Capital AG in 2003, today HAMMONIA Reederei is a joint venture between three companies: Alongside PDS-KG and HCI Capital AG, GE Transportation Finance (part of General Electric Corp. US) joined as shareholder in 2008. HAMMONIA Reederei manages a range of vessels. Presently[1] the HAMMONIA Reederei fleet comprises 51 container vessels, 2 bulk carrier and also 15 multipurpose vessels. HAMMONIA Reederei provides HHX with a ship management of good reputation. In addition, they prepare in collaboration with the tax counsellor the quarterly reporting of

[1] That is at the time of writing August 2012.

the shipping companies based on the International Financial Reporting Standards ("IFRS"), a service which is deemed pivotal.

8.4.2.2 Peter Döhle Schiffahrts-KG

Being the exclusive broker, PDS-KG is in charge of the deployment of the HHX vessels, either in earnings pools or on a pure time charter basis. PDS-KG was founded in 1956 as an agent to ship owners ("Vertrauensmakler") to conduct commercial maritime services. PDS-KG acts not only as broker for its own and part-owned fleet but also on an exclusive basis to others such as HHX. Today the company manages the chartering for a modern fleet of around 400 container vessels, multipurpose vessels and bulk carriers. The market access of PDS-KG is a distinguishing factor for HHX.

8.4.2.3 HCI Capital AG

HCI Capital AG respectively its legal predecessor ("HCI") was founded in 1985 and has developed to be one of the leading issuing houses in the German market. As of August 2012 main shareholders of HCI are the Döhle Group (25.6 %), MPC Capital AG (25.6 %) and HSH Nordbank AG (19.9 %). A particular focus has always been on closed-end funds in the shipping segment: In total equity for more than 500 vessels, respectively more than EUR 4 billion has been raised over time. As a stock listed company, HCI is familiar with the respective regulative requirements. HCI provides commercial support for HHX being responsible for the coordination of the quarterly financial reporting, the organization of annual general meetings and supervisory board meetings, investor relationship management and compliance with legal regulations and corporate governance.

8.4.3 Concept of Employment

The vessels are chartered out on a long-term basis to liner trade companies with high credit ratings and/or proceeds are pooled with those of other owners' vessels of the same size to protect revenues against charterers' credit risk, fluctuating charter rates and the risk of a ship's discontinued operation. The pools are managed by PDS-KG (see above). The idea of this mix of employment is to diversify earnings of the fleet. The vessels with long-term charter employment do not allow for short to midterm upside potential. Their contribution to the overall return of the venture is limited. However, in a market downturn they stabilize the company's cash flow so that payment obligations of all vessels can be met. In contrast, the earnings of the vessels that are employed in earnings pools fluctuate with the development of the market. However, by means of a membership in a pool the earnings of the shipping

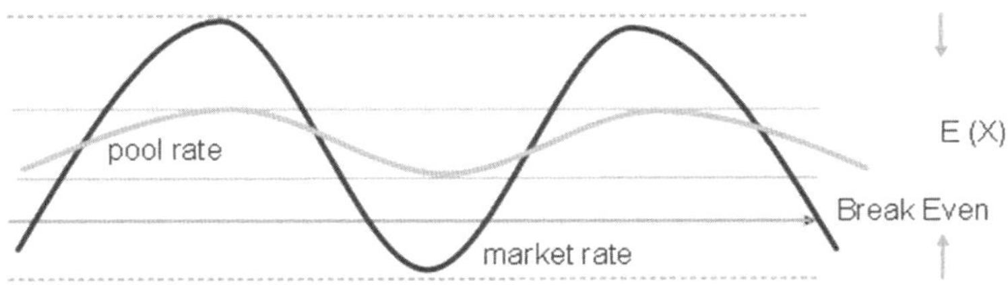

Fig. 8.3 Volatility mitigation scheme

companies that have chartered out their respective vessels only short term are also smoothed at least to a certain extent. The various charter contracts within a pool are entered in within different market phases and with different durations. As a result, market heights and depths are smoothed; the volatility is reduced whereby average earnings over time remain unchanged (see Fig. 8.3). The conservative employment concept of HHX allows for a higher degree of revenue stability in the fluctuating charter markets.

8.4.4 *Currency*

Revenues generated by the limited shipping companies through the operation of the vessels are denominated in US-Dollar. In addition, most of the shipping operating expenses (e.g. crew wages) are incurred in US-Dollar. However, a small part of the shipping operating expenses (roughly 30 %) is incurred in EUR, e.g. the wages for European officers and certain spare parts. Part of the EUR payment obligations are secured by forward exchange transactions. To minimise currency exchange risks the loans of the HHX fleet have been taken up in US-Dollar. Therefore, debt service (i.e. principal and interest payments) is effected in US Dollar as well. An exception is "Hammonia Pescara" with roughly 20 % Japanese Yen tranche respectively "Antofagasta" with a 50 % Japanese Yen tranche. The two majority participations were acquired at a time when the vessels had already been financed, delivered and were trading. Taken as whole, the HHX fleet is financed almost completely in the currency where the earnings are generated being the US Dollar. By contrast, KG funds and also other ship owners have often used partial refinancing in Japanese Yen and Swiss Franc to benefit from more favourable interest rates in these currencies. Not making use of such currency options is also a consideration towards the professional institutional investors who prefer to refrain from such speculation within an asset investment and to deal with it in separate currency products. There remains a currency mismatch with regard to potential dividends. However, this is an imminent risk of an investment in a US Dollar industry and it is not a risk related to the solvency of the company.

8.4.5 *Dividends*

The perpetual ambition of HHX is to disburse a dividend of about 6.5 % of the invested equity. However, the ability to pay a dividend depends on profitability, liquidity, capital requirements and business outlook as well as the general economic environment. Under German law, a resolution on a dividend payment and its distribution has to be based on a balance sheet profit recognised in the holding's individual financial statements prepared in accordance with the German Commercial Code ("HGB"). Profits and losses carried forward from previous years and withdrawals from respective allocations to the reserves have to be taken into account. This is an inherent difference to German partnerships (Personengesellschaften) that can effect payouts to their investors even if no HGB profit was made provided there is sufficient liquidity in the company.

8.5 Basic Income Tax Principles

8.5.1 *Level of the Shipping Partnerships*

In the year when the vessels were taken into service, HHX's limited shipping partnerships opted for the flat rate determination of profits according to Section 5a of the German Income Tax Act ("EStG"), the so-called tonnage tax (Sect. 4.6 in Chap. 4). As the shipping companies were set up as partnerships (Personengesellschaften), they are tax-transparent. The taxation takes place on the level of their shareholders, i.e. the holding company HHX.

Contrary to income tax regulations, the limited shipping partnerships are independent taxable entities and taxpayers as far as trade tax is concerned. The profit determined according to the tonnage tax scheme is regarded as trade earnings and is taxed respectively on a shipping company level [Sections 7 of the German Trade Tax Act ("GewStG")].

8.5.2 *Level of the Holding Company HHX*

Being a corporation, HHX is liable to pay tax on its whole income. Apart from the profit shares from the limited shipping partnerships, also interest income generated from liquid funds is subject to taxation. However, due to the business model the tax base on the level of HHX is predominantly determined according to the tonnage-based flat-rate method. Therefore, the specific advantages linked to the shipping companies' decision to opt for the tonnage tax regime are maintained on the level of the holding company HHX. The tax base determined in the manner described above is subject to corporate income tax of currently 15 % [§23.1 German Corporate Income Tax Act ("KStG")] plus a solidarity surcharge of 5.5 % of the assessed corporate income tax (§4 Solidaritätszuschlaggesetz 1995, "SolzG").

In addition, HHX is subject to trade tax. When calculating the relevant trade earnings, no trade tax is payable on the income from the investments in the limited shipping partnerships (Section 9 No. 2 GewStG) as the shipping partnerships have already been taxed with trade tax. Therefore, trade earnings on the level of the holding company are essentially the net interest income.

8.5.3 *Level of the HHX Retail Investors*

HHX has to retain withholding tax of 25 % (§43a (1) EStG) plus a solidarity surcharge of 5.5 % from the dividends distributed (§4 SolzG) to its shareholders and remits the amount withheld to the tax authority. For retail investors this effective taxation with a total rate of 26,375 % (plus, as the case may be, church tax) is a disadvantage in comparison to a conventional KG fund in the legal form of a private limited partnership which maintains the advantages of the tonnage tax regime even on the ultimate level of the investor.[2] A retail investor needs to balance this adverse effect against the amenities of a stock listed investment (e.g. the lower denomination and the at least in theory better liquidity of stocks).

Gains from the sale of shares that have been acquired after 31 December 2008 are fully taxable irrespective of the holding period. The tax rate is also 25 % plus 5.5 % solidarity surcharge (§20 (2) EStG; plus, as the case may be, church tax).

8.5.4 *Level of the HHX Institutional Investors*

According to Sections 1 and 4 KStG, the total income of insurance companies, banks, savings banks, large mutual insurance and pension fund associations and other German corporations is subject to corporate income tax. However, dividends are exempt from corporate income tax in accordance with Section 8b (1) KStG. This shall eliminate double taxation in case of multi-level shareholding structures. Section 8b (5) KStG specifies that 5 % of the income are non-deductible operating expense, which means that corporate income tax is payable on 5 % of the dividend income. As a result, 95 % of the dividend income is exempt from corporate income tax. If this tax exemption can be applied, the corporate income tax of 15 % (plus 5.5 % solidarity surcharge) will be charged on 5 % of the dividends paid out by

[2]For a comparison of tax rates, the taxation on the level of the holding company also needs to be taken into account; however, the taxable base is predominantly determined by the tonnage tax regime.

HHX, i.e. the effective tax rate on dividends is c. 0.8 %. The same applies to profits from the sale of shares (Section 8b (2) KStG). On the other hand, any losses resulting from the sale of shares are disregarded for tax purposes.

According to Section 8b (7) KStG, the aforementioned tax exemption does not apply if the shares are assigned to the trading book of a bank or financial services institution. Moreover, special regulations apply regarding the taxation of insurance companies.

Finally, corporates are obliged to pay trade tax. The dividends are fully taxed as trade earnings of the shareholder unless the shareholder holds more than 15 % of the share capital of HHX. However, gains from the sale of shares are only subject to trade tax based on the fictitious non-deductible operating expense of 5 %, irrespective of the size of the shareholding.

8.6 Corporate Governance and Compliance

The structure of governance and supervision implemented at HHX provides for a dual board system in accordance with German corporate law. The two members of the management board conduct the company's business with the objective of a sustainable increase in shareholder value. The supervisory board consists of three members who are elected by the shareholders at the annual general meeting. There are four scheduled supervisory board meetings per annum where the management board reports on the intended business strategy and other substantial concerns for the company. The supervisory board assumes monitoring and advisory functions. Among other things, it is responsible for the determination of the financial statements and for appointing and dismissing members of the management board. According to the statutes of HHX, certain decisions by the managing board require the prior consent by the supervisory board (e.g. acquisition, mortgaging, and sale of ships or investments in other companies).

The shareholders' meeting is held in Hamburg once a year. In particular, the following decisions are reserved for the shareholders' meeting:

- appointment of the supervisory board;
- appropriation of the net profit;
- discharge of members of the managing board and the supervisory board;
- appointment of the auditor;
- measures of raising capital and capital reduction and
- amendments to the statutes.

As a stock listed public company, HHX and its shareholders have to comply with various rules and regulations. A few examples are described in the following paragraphs.

8.6.1 *Financial Reporting*

As a publicly traded company, HHX is obliged to meet extended financial reporting requirements. Detailed information is provided in the form of annual reports and half-year interim reports. Those are based on the IFRS as required by section 315a German Commercial Code (HGB) and sections 37v to 37w German Securities Trading Act ("WpHG"). The company informs quarterly about developments via its interim financial statements (section 37x WpHG). HHX has to meet further reporting requirements such as notifications of the publication of financial statements and the publication of financial statements on the internet.

8.6.2 *German Corporate Governance Code*

The code comprises recommendations and suggestions for the management and supervision of German listed companies. It is based on nationally and internationally accepted standards of good and responsible corporate governance. HHX as well as any other company is under no duty to comply with the recommendations or suggestions of the code. However, according to section 161 of the German Stock Corporation Act, the managing board and the supervisory board of HHX have to publish a declaration of compliance (Entsprechenserklärung) on an annual basis stating that they have complied and continue to comply with the recommendations or stating which recommendations have not been and will not be applied. This declaration has to be made available to the shareholders on a permanent basis. Furthermore, HHX publishes a financial calendar according to the code.

8.6.3 *Risk Management System/Internal Monitoring System*

According to section 91 (2) of the German Stock Corporation Act ("AktG"), the managing board must ensure that an appropriate risk management system and an internal monitoring system are installed and operated within the Company so that developments that may jeopardise the continued existence of the company are identified at an early stage.

8.6.4 *Insider List (Insiderverzeichnis)*

Shareholders may not trade HHX shares by using insider information (section 14 WpHG). According to section 15b WpHG, HHX is obliged to keep a record of all persons who are employed by HHX or who act on behalf of HHX and who have access to insider information. This enables the supervisory authority to detect possible insiders in case of any suspicion of a breach of the rules. Furthermore, HHX is required to inform and educate these insiders regarding their responsibilities and legal consequences of respective breaches.

8.6.5 *Ad Hoc Disclosures*

In accordance with section 15 WpHG HHX is obliged to publish any insider information. The purpose is to ensure that other market participants have the same level of information and are therefore not disadvantaged. First the stock exchange management and the Bundesanstalt für Finanzdienstleistungsaufsicht ("BaFin") have to be notified. HHX uses the DGAP (Deutsche Gesellschaft für Ad-hoc-Publizität) to ensure that the announcement is released in the European Economic Area. Subsequently, HHX publishes the disclosure on its webpage. The Company Data Register (Unternehmensregister) is also notified to storage the disclosure.

8.6.6 *Directors' Dealings*

To enhance transparency, the members of the management and supervisory board as well as people closely related to them are required to notify dealings in HHX stocks both to HHX and the BaFin within five business days (section 15a WpHG). In turn, HHX has to publish the directors' dealings in a similar manner as the ad hoc disclosures.

8.6.7 *Voting Rights Announcements (Stimmrechtsmitteilungen)*

Under sections 21 and 25 WphG, shareholders of HHX are subject to certain reporting duties with respect to the size of their shareholding in HHX. If the voting rights of a shareholder reach, exceed or fall below certain thresholds (those being 3, 5, 10, 15, 20, 25, 30, 50 or 75 % of the overall voting rights), that shareholder must inform HHX as well as BaFin as soon as possible, but at least within four trading days of the fact that he has reached, exceeded or fallen below the respective threshold. He also has to report the new percentage of his voting rights. Following the receipt of such notification, HHX has to publish a respective report within three trading days, making its best efforts to ensure a Europe-wide circulation (section 26 WpHG).

8.6.8 *Takeover Bid*

If a shareholder's direct or indirect shareholding reaches or exceeds 30 % of HHX voting shares, that shareholder is obliged, under the German Securities Acquisition and Takeover Act ("WpÜG"), to publish this fact as well as the percentage of its voting rights. Unless an exemption is granted by BaFin, a statutory offer must then be submitted to all HHX shareholders at a price that must not be lower than the price paid by that shareholder during the last 6 months for any HHX shares. In any case, the price must not fall short of the weighted average share price during the last 3 months.

8.7 Development of the HHX Fleet

In preparation of the IPO, HHX respectively its shipping companies concluded purchase contracts for eight vessels, including two then 5 year old 3,100 TEU vessels built in Poland (MS "Saxonia" and MS "Westphalia") and six 2,500 TEU new buildings (MS "Hammonia Pomerenia", MS "Hammonia Bavaria", MS "Hammonia Holsatia", MS "Hammonia Massilia", MS "Hammonia Roma" and MS "Hammonia Teutonica"). One of the conditions precedent included in those purchase contracts was that the IPO of HHX would be accomplished successfully. Thereby, an important requirement, especially for institutional investors, could be met, i.e. there was a defined seed portfolio giving the investors transparency at an early stage of how the funds raised were going to be invested. The selling companies were owned by the initiators HAMMONIA Reederei and HCI. As the purchase contracts were subject to a successful IPO, the initiators took a short position during the preparation of the IPO and the actual IPO period to support a convincing business case. The six 2,500 TEU new buildings were consecutively delivered from the Chinese building yard between November 2007 and January 2009 whereby the HHX fleet grew continuously.

The vessels were partly debt-financed. Roughly, 70 % debt capital was raised in the form of ship mortgage loans. Parts of the loans for the 2,500 TEU new buildings were provided by The EXPORT-IMPORT BANK OF CHINA ("CEXIM") within the framework of a Commercial Interest Reference Rate financing ("CIRR"). The CIRR is determined by the OECD (Organisation for Economic Co-operation and Development) as a minimum interest rate for export financings supported by the governments of the OECD. A long-term interest rate such as CIRR mitigates the risk of changes in interest rates.

Accordingly, 30 % of the investment costs of the seed portfolio, roughly EUR 90 million, was financed through the net issuing proceeds from the IPO. Additional proceeds from the IPO of roughly EUR 55 million were at the disposal of the management for further investments, i.e. for the acquisition and the development of the ship portfolio. In April 2008, HHX succeeded to acquire three 7,800 TEU vessels, namely “Hammonia Fionia”, “Hammonia Dania” and “Hammonia Hafnia”, within the framework of a sale and charter back transaction. Contractual partner is the world’s largest container shipping company, AP Moeller Maersk. The sale and charter back structure provides a secure cash flow for at least 10 years from the time when the vessel was acquired. The intention of this purchase was to diversify the ship portfolio of HHX, in particular with regard to the employment. While the long-term charters do not allow for a profit participation in a market upturn, the function of these vessels is to stabilise the cash flow of HHX in a market downturn so that payment obligations of all vessels can be met. Retrospectively, this provident measure has proved to be prudent as shipping markets were negatively affected following the global economic downturn from autumn 2008 onwards.

In June 2010, the shareholders’ annual general meeting authorised the management to increase the company’s share capital via contributions in cash or in kind (authorised capital). Moreover, the shareholders approved the issuing of profit participation rights against contribution in cash or in kind in the total amount of up to EUR 75 million. In the amount of EUR 7.45 million, this authorisation was made use of in December 2010. These funds were used to finance the acquisition of the majority interest in a further shipping partnership which owns a modern 4,250 TEU container vessel (“Hammonia Pescara”) and which is chartered out to United Arab Shipping Company (UASC) until mid-2014. Along the lines of this deal structure HHX acquired a 51 % participation in a 2,800 TEU vessel, MS “Antofagasta” in February 2012. In this context, HHX issued further profit participation rights in the amount of EUR 5.8 million. With the successful issuance of the profit participation rights, HHX has proved to be regarded as acceptable corporate risk.

8.8 Economic Development of the Company

The main key financial figures are given in the table below. They illustrate the financial development of the company since the IPO in 2007 (Table 8.3).

At the beginning, the expansion of the fleet dominated the financial figures of the company. HHX took up its business operations at the end of November 2007, starting with three seagoing vessels. The fleet grew constantly during 2008 as the 2,500 TEU new buildings were subsequently delivered and put into service (the last two ships were delivered in January 2009), and finally the three 7,800 TEU vessels were acquired in April 2008.

From 2009 on the financial figures of HHX show impacts of the shipping crisis. The crisis had its origin in the financial market crisis, which had intensified significantly in mid-2008. In 2009, world trade reduced by 12 % compared to 2008. As the container vessel fleet was growing at the same time, charter rates slumped to the level of the operating expenses and sometimes even lower. Due to the conservative employment concept, revenues of HHX reduced disproportionately less. The earnings pools were able to soften the market downturn. On the one hand

Table 8.3 Key financial indicators

Age	2007	2008	2009	2010	2011
Revenues	1,592	46,712	62,254	62,647	67,804
Vessel operating results	863	32,471	42,639	40,929	41,696
Results from shipping operations	9,412	30,483	40,583	43,467	40,559
Earnings before interest and taxes (EBIT)	4,089	16,844	13,448	21,067	17,174
Consolidated net income/loss for the period	4,49	9,478	−2,753	4,834	−226
Total assets/total equity and liabilities	155,7	467,077	472,835	538, 421	541,790
Equity	151,133	153,216	151,122	163, 534	165,929

pool rates followed the charter rates only with a time lag, on the other hand the pool rates stayed significantly above the bottom prices in the charter market. As a measure of precaution, the profit and loss statement of 2009 contained impairments of EUR 4.9 million on assets and receivables that led to a negative overall result. However, EUR 1.6 million of these impairments could already be reversed in 2010 and HHX was once again operating in the black.

In 2011 revenues increased compared to the previous year. This is primarily due to the full consolidation of the "Hammonia Pescara" where HHX holds a 56 % stake since the year-end of 2010. In accordance with IFRS, the distributive share in profits of the minority interest in this partnership amounting to EUR 0.4 million is booked as interest expense even though these profits shares are not expenses from the point of view of the corporate group.

The significantly declined market environment is also reflected in the share price development. While the liquidity of the stock has always been low due to the marginal free float, the price fixings now include the higher risk that has to be applied to future expected cash flows. Therefore, the stock currently trades significantly under its book equity per share.

The graph (Fig. 8.4) shows an average correlation between the HHX share price and the ConTex, a charter rate index for container vessels, the coefficient of correlation being 0.5 in the given period as above.

This stands out as the vessels of HHX are not traded in the spot market but in stable long-term charter parties or in mitigating earnings pools. However, in a market crunch situation the risk that investors associate with HHX and the industry it operates in leads to an increased implicit discount factor for expected future cash flows. Notwithstanding that the pool concept reduces the volatility of the earnings; the development of the pool rates tends to follow the trend of the charter rates. By shifting the HHX share price development by 5 months the coefficient of correlation increases to 0.7 signifying a strong correlation.

It may be added that the share price of HHX has a strong correlation with some of its peers which pursue a similar business model such as Marenave in Germany which manages different ship types (coefficient of correlation of 0.9 in the given period)

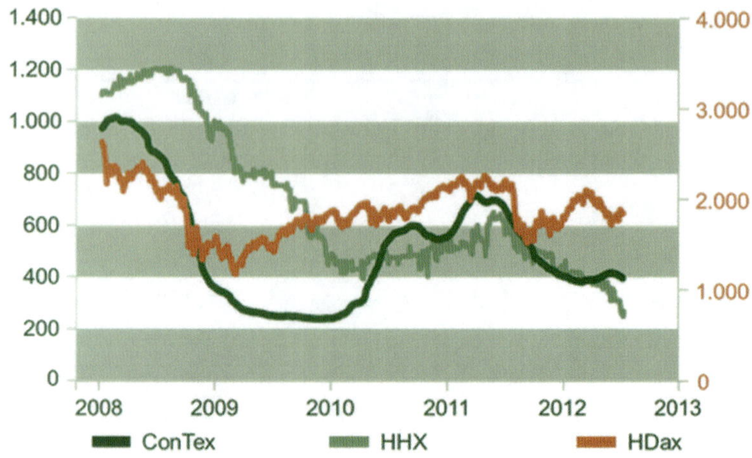

Fig. 8.4 Correlation of HHX vs. DAX and ConTex

and Danaos—a Greek container shipping company listed in New York (coefficient of correlation of 0.8). It also becomes apparent that HHX as well as the container charter market are only very weakly correlated with the overall stock market, the coefficient of correlation between HHX and the broad HDAX, the composite index of DAX, MDAX and TecDAX, being just 0.1. In contrast Daimler, as an example of the automotive industry, and Deutsche Bank, as an example of a financial institution, have coefficients of correlation in the same period of 0.9 respectively 0.7 with the HDAX. The fact that the supply/demand balance of container vessel tonnage can diverge from the overall economic situation and lead to significant time lag in the respective developments may explain this significant difference in the period under review.

In this context it should be pointed out that liner companies that charter in the vessels from tramp owners such as HHX have to be independently looked at. In a market upswing liner companies can earn healthy freight rates for the transport of containers while the charter rates they have to pay to the tramp owners may be still low. Then charter rates tend to follow freight rates with a time lag that may take longer in case of overcapacity of container vessel tonnage. Such overcapacities need to be reduced first before a normalised price mechanism between supply and demand can apply. A good example may be China Shipping Container Lines ("CSCL"), a pure container liner company, whose financial results are not distorted by the results of other non-related business areas. While the coefficient of correlation between HHX and CSCL in the period under consideration is −0.2 signifying a rather weak negative correlation, the coefficient of correlation between CSCL and the German overall market index HDAX is slightly above 0.6 showing a significant correlation.

8.9 Summary and Outlook

HHX was successfully placed at the Hamburg stock exchange in November 2007. Without really being given enough time to take up its operations and to build up additional reserves, the company had to cope with the aftermath of the worldwide financial market crisis from autumn 2008 on. The conservative employment concept stood the test. However, the financial figures could certainly not remain unaffected by the market development. Moreover, the increased risk that market participants factor in for the container shipping industry left its mark in the share price development, which is definitely unsatisfactory for the shareholders. The company has currently to cope with a long lasting shipping crisis and faces issues with regard to its ship financings such as required deferments of debt repayments and loan to value covenants. Mid- to long term the company is well-positioned to benefit from a market recovery while the question remains whether HHX may serve as model for future investment vehicles in the German shipping market.

A larger portion of free float shares to enhance the market liquidity is certainly recommendable as it could attract interest of institutional investors that require a certain degree of liquidity to consider an investment. Furthermore, to endorse a successful equity placement the interest of investors outside Germany needs to be drawn. This is necessary to find a critical mass of investment demand. Apart from that, a company structure such as HHX meets the preference of investors with regard to a diversified investment portfolio and even more the call of ship financing banks for corporate structures.

However, one cannot ignore that for a new vehicle the capital requirement for acquiring a seed fleet is considerable and that the currently prevailing risk aversion of investors and all the more of the financing banks may prevent IPOs in the near future. Nevertheless, after a market recovery the prospects could improve. With regard to the German market one needs to bear in mind that the equity raised in the classical KG Market is so immense it cannot be replaced in terms of volume by alternative investment vehicles such as HHX.

Part III
Asset Pricing

Chapter 9
Valuing Vessels

Daniel Mayr

Abstract For a long time, the valuation of vessels was a routine task based simply on the price of comparable vessels in recent transactions. However, since the beginning of the global financial and economic crisis in 2008, with vessel prices, if any observable, at record lows and market volatility at record highs, there has been a controversial discussion on whether the transaction price always represents the vessel's true value. As a result, valuation approaches based on earnings estimates are gaining increasing acceptance. A popular example of such an approach in the maritime industry is the Long Term Asset Value (LTAV) method. The LTAV method is based on a discounted cash flow (DCF) analysis, which is already commonly used and widely accepted for the valuation of businesses and long-lived assets. This chapter presents the basic principles of vessel valuations and places a special focus on the LTAV method. Particular attention is placed on the determination of reasonable valuation parameters as well as on the application possibilities of the LTAV method.

9.1 Introduction

For a long time, the valuation of vessels was a routine task. A vessel's value was derived simply from the price of a comparable vessel in a recent transaction (so-called market approach). However, since the beginning of the global financial and economic crisis in 2008, with vessel prices, if any observable, at record lows and market volatility at record highs, there has been a controversial discussion on whether the in the best case few observable transaction prices always represents the vessel's intrinsic value. To determine the value of a vessel in an environment of high volatility and uncertainty, valuation approaches based on earnings estimates are gaining increasing acceptance. A main advantage of these valuation approaches is

D. Mayr (✉)
PricewaterhouseCoopers AG, Friedrich-Ebert-Anlage 35-37, 60327 Frankfurt am Main, Germany
e-mail: daniel.mayr@de.pwc.com

O. Schinas et al. (eds.), *HSBA Handbook on Ship Finance*,
DOI 10.1007/978-3-662-43410-9_9, © Springer-Verlag Berlin Heidelberg 2015

that they are based on a long-term view, which is supposed to offset short-term market imperfections at least to a certain degree. A popular example of such an approach in the maritime industry is the Long Term Asset Value (LTAV) method, which was developed in 2009 by the Hamburg Shipbrokers' Association (*Vereinigung Hamburger Schiffsmakler und Schiffsagenten e.V., VHSS*) in cooperation with the accounting and consulting firm PricewaterhouseCoopers (PwC). The LTAV method is based on a discounted cash flow (DCF) analysis, which is already commonly used and widely accepted for the valuation of businesses and many long-lived assets (e.g. real estate, aircrafts, and power plants).

This chapter presents the basic principles of vessel valuations and places a special focus on the LTAV method. First, the most common reasons for vessel valuations, as well as the main different valuation approaches, are discussed. This is followed up with a discussion on the appropriateness of the market approach in the current market environment. Next, the main part of this chapter places particular attention to the LTAV method and its input parameters. Finally, typical, practical instances for using the LTAV method are described.

9.2 Reasons for Valuations and Valuation Approaches

9.2.1 Reasons for Valuations

There are several reasons why valuations of vessels are required. Vessel owners need vessel valuations for accounting (e.g. impairment test), planning (e.g. as a basis to decide on a potential capital increase) and controlling purposes. Potential buyers and sellers of vessels base their investment or divestment decisions on valuations. Shipbrokers use valuations when advising their clients in the course of transactions. Vessel valuations are also crucial for banks. Valuations determine lending decisions, borrower compliance with existing loan covenants, bank compliance with capital adequacy standards, and provisions for credit losses.

The demand for valuations rises especially in tough market conditions. As such, for example, the current shipping crisis has led to a consolidation within the market, which has resulted in an increased demand for valuations triggered by company law (e.g. valuations regarding ownership changes).

9.2.2 Valuation Approaches

Generally, the value of a vessel is based on the future financial benefits which both equity and debt investors can expect to receive as of the valuation date. The three widely accepted valuation approaches are the market approach, the income approach, and the cost approach. When markets are stable and market participants' assessment of future events are similar (low market volatility), all three valuation approaches usually provide comparable results for typical vessels. In contrast, if the course of future events seems to be highly uncertain, these approaches can provide a broad range of values and can be utilized as complementary methods for assessing the value from different points of view (e.g. going concern vs. liquidation scenario).

- **Market approach**
  According to the market approach (also known as the "last done", "mark-to-market", or "comparative valuation" approach), a vessel's value equals the market price of comparable vessels in recently completed arm's-length transactions between willing and knowledgeable buyers and sellers. To value a vessel using the market approach, a set of the most recently completed transactions of comparable vessels and the appertaining transaction prices must be identifiable. Comparability is based on four main factors: vessel type, size, age, and condition.[1] Additionally, immediacy is also a key issue: the need to sell quickly ("fire sale") normally results in a much lower price.
- **Income approach**
  Under the income approach, the value of the vessel is the present value of all future cash flows the vessel is expected to generate during the remaining economic useful life including its residual scrap value at maturity. While the income approach is the most theoretically rigorous approach available and is widely accepted as a proper approach for determining the value of assets including vessels, determining appropriate input parameters—particularly forecasts of charter rates—can be considered the most critical task. As the income approach requires a financial model with cash flow projections, it is also known as the mark-to-model approach.
- **(Replacement) Cost approach**
  According to the replacement cost approach, the vessel is valued based on how much it would cost to build a similar vessel in the same condition. The replacement cost of the vessel is adjusted for depreciation caused by physical deterioration and functional obsolescence. The replacement cost approach is mostly applicable to vessels with unique functionality or customized features (special vessels). Examples are maintenance, research, and floating museum vessels. The most obvious critique of this valuation method is that it does not consider the future cash-generating ability of the asset.

9.3 Equivalence of Value and Price

In fact, by far most people in the shipping business use some version of the market approach to value vessels. The central assumption underlying this approach is that the observable market prices reflect the fundamental or intrinsic value of

[1]Fixed charter agreements and other factors also affect prices. These include but are not limited to fuel consumption, classifications, type of the main engine, loading equipment (cranes and derricks), the shipyard where the vessel was built, and the location of the vessel at the time of sale.

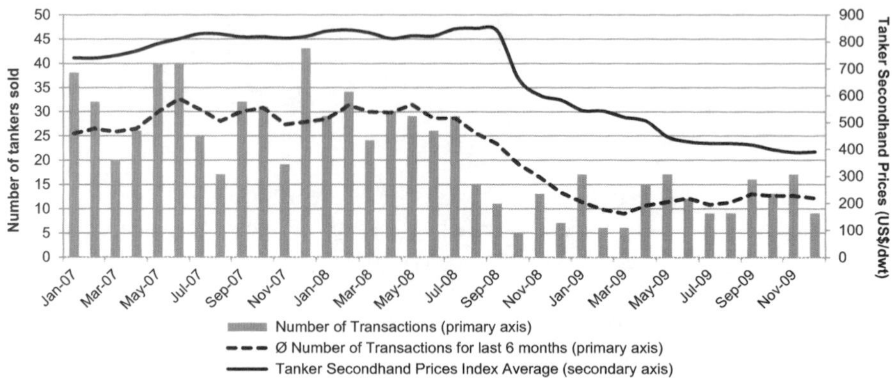

Fig. 9.1 Secondhand Prices and number of transactions for Tankers between January 2007 and December 2009. *Source*: Clarkson Research Services

the vessel. To use this as a reasonable assumption, various main conditions of the equivalence of value and price must be satisfied. There must be a sufficient number of recently completed arm's-length transactions with comparable vessels between willing and knowledgeable parties. The transactions must not include distressed or forced sales due to liquidity problems of vessel owners ("fire sale"), and credit must have been sufficiently and readily available to market participants. In addition, market participants should face low research and transaction costs within the transaction process. Finally, market participants should not be characterized by excessive optimism or pessimism (prudent investors).

An analysis of these prerequisites in light of the actual market conditions leads to the following results:

In consequence of the global financial and economic crisis, the number of accomplished vessel transactions decreased substantially. Moreover, these few vessel transactions are characterized to a large part by forced sales of ship owners with liquidity problems which resulted in a steep decline in the market prices (see Fig. 9.1).

In addition, loans granted by banks decreased substantially because of the financial crisis (see Fig. 9.2). Nowadays, to obtain a bank loan, additional collateral apart from the underlying vessel to be financed must often be provided. As vessels are financed largely than other assets with debt, particularly the shipping industry has suffered from the limited availability of bank loans.

The shipping market is also characterized by both excessive optimism and pessimism on the part of the market participants. This is expressed in the volatility of the vessel prices, freight rates, and the development of stock prices of shipping companies compared to the development of the economy and the stock market in general (see Fig. 9.3).

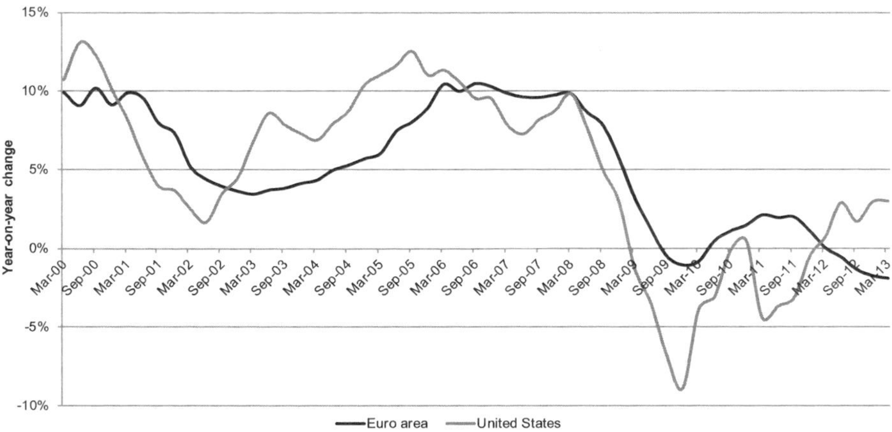

Fig. 9.2 Bank credit to the private non-financial sector. *Source*: Bank for International Settlements

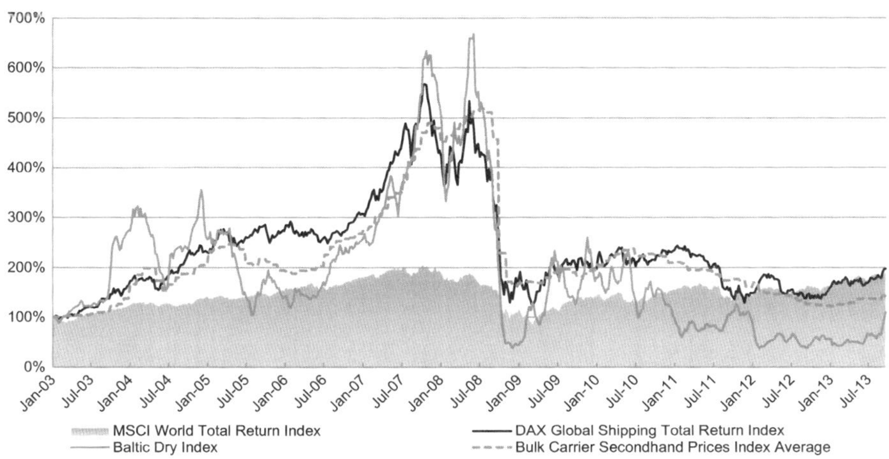

Fig. 9.3 Historical development of certain indices (indexed 1 January 2003). *Source*: Bloomberg, S&P Capital IQ, Clarkson Research Services

One reason for this high degree of volatility and the exaggerated market phases in the shipping markets is a delayed adjustment of the market supply to changes in the market demand, so-called pork cycles,[2] which intensifies the general price

[2]The pork cycle phenomenon for the shipping markets can be described as follows. In boom phases in the economy resulting from a strong demand in the market, high charter rates, as well as high secondhand prices, can be realized for vessels. Owing to the high profits which can be obtained, an increase in investments in new vessels occurs leading to an increased supply only with a delay due to the time for construction. As a result, there is normally an excess supply, especially if the market demand has decreased in the meanwhile. The consequences of this excess supply are substantially

fluctuations. Another reason is of structural nature: In the last market upswing attracted by tax advantages, favorable financing conditions (low credit margins) and prospects of high profits on the second-hand market the market participants showed excessive optimism with the result that more vessels than necessary were ordered with respect to the effective long-term market demand. Contrary to this, the market participants in the current shipping market trough are expressing excessive pessimism, leading to comparatively few loans and investments, despite expected strong future market demand. While the excessive optimism intensified the last market upswing, the resulting strong fleet growth in combination with the economic downturn in 2008/2009 have led to an excessive pessimism on the part of the market participants and a massive collapse of the market. However, both the scope of the upswing and the extent of the downswing do not reflect the realistic long-term market perspective.

Because of the shipping market environment market prices of comparable vessels are often distorted and the common market approach provides no reliable valuation results assuming a long-term going concern scenario. Instead, especially in phases of market disruption, valuation methods that are based on the long-term earnings potential of a vessel (income approach) are needed. This issue can be addressed by using the LTAV method; the general principles of this method are recorded in the Hamburg Ship Evaluation Standard (HSES).

9.4 The LTAV Method

9.4.1 Methodology

Considering only financial objectives, the value of a vessel is determined from the vessel's ability to generate financial surpluses for the suppliers of capital, both equity and debt. The determination of the LTAV, according to the HSES, is based on the DCF method and the concept of weighted average cost of capital (the so-called WACC approach[3]), which is widely recognized in theory and the valuation practice.

---

lower charter rates and a downturn in prices for vessels which lead to an investment backlog that affects the supply again with some delay. Additional scrapping of vessels increases the reduction in capacity and leads to a shortfall in supply during the next economic recovery. The described cycle then begins anew.

[3]In addition to the WACC method, there are two other recognized DCF methods for determining the asset value, the adjusted present value (APV) method, and the total cash flow (TCF) method. These differ especially in the definition of the underlying cash flows, how the tax benefits from debt are taken into account as well as in the underlying discount rate. All DCF methods lead to identical results in the case of consistent premises. Depending on the purpose of the valuation, the determination of the value of a stake in a single-vessel company exclusively from the point of view of the suppliers of equity capital can be relevant, instead of the valuation of the vessel as an asset from the point of view of the suppliers of equity and debt. In this case, the market value of debt

The LTAV of a vessel is derived accordingly by discounting the expected free cash flows (FCF_t) with the weighted average cost of capital (WACC):

$$\mathrm{LTAV} = \sum_{t=1}^{T} \frac{\mathrm{FCF}_t}{(1+\mathrm{WACC})^t} = \sum_{t=1}^{T} \frac{(C_t - \mathrm{OPEX}_t)}{(1+\mathrm{WACC})^t} + \frac{\mathrm{RV}_T}{(1+\mathrm{WACC})^T} \tag{9.1}$$

The free cash flows can be derived using the forecast charter revenues (C_t) less the expected costs for operating the vessel ($OPEX_t$), as well as a residual value (RV_T) at the end of the vessel's economic useful life.

9.4.2 *Determination of Free Cash Flows*

- **Charter revenues** (C_t)
  Assumptions about the daily future charter rates that can be earned for hiring out the vessel (gross charter rates), about the incurred management fees and freight commissions, as well as about the utilization rate (operating days per year) must be made to forecast the (net) charter revenues accurately.
  As the development of the free cash flows for the near future can normally be forecast with a higher degree of certainty than for later years, a detailed planning period of at least 3 years should be considered. Existing charter agreements should be taken into account when forecasting the charter revenues if the charterer has a reliable creditworthiness. If no charter agreement exists or if the vessel is to be valued for a specific purpose without consideration of an existing charter agreement, (time) charter rates that can currently be observed in the market are an appropriate starting point for forecasting the charter revenues for the detailed planning period. Shipbrokers (e.g. VHSS, Harper Petersen & Co.) as well as research companies (e.g. Clarkson Research Services) provide periodically (at least monthly) actual time charter rates or time charter equivalents for different charter periods (e.g. 1, 2, 3 and 5 year duration) for a wide range of vessel types. Based on the relationship between time charter rates with different durations it is possible to derive the market expectation of the future development of charter rates. In addition, market analyses with regard to the current fleet (volume and age profile) and the additional fleet capacity (order book) as an indicator for the expected market supply as well as market analyses with regard to the economic outlook as a proxy for the expected market demand support forecasts of charter rates for the detailed planning period. An analysis of

would have to be deducted from the LTAV. As an alternative, the market value of equity can also be determined directly by discounting the free cash flows belonging exclusively to the suppliers of equity capital (after deduction of interest and principal payments) using the cost of equity as the discount rate (so-called flow-to-equity [FTE] approach).

Charter Rates (US$/day)	Actual 2013	2014	Forecast 2015	2016	2017
Market-Implied Forecast (Clarkson)*	7,250	7,800	9,000	10,300	n/a
Research Forecast (MSI)	7,250	7,100	9,000	11,200	13,300

*based on charter contracts with different duration (1 year T/C: 7,250 US$/day, 3 year T/C: 8,400 US$/day)

Fig. 9.4 Charter rate forecast for a 1,700 TEU (geared) container vessel as of 30 June 2013

the difference of current freight rates and future freight rates (based on forward freight agreements) can also provide further indications for the future development of the charter rates in the near future. Finally, projections of future charter rates for the detailed planning period can be retrieved from research companies, e.g. Maritime Strategies International (MSI), Drewry Shipping Consultants, and Marsoft.

Figure 9.4 shows different charter rate forecasts for a geared 1,700 TEU (Twenty-foot, the T in TEU stands for Twenty-foot equivalent unit) container vessel.

Excursus: Sample market analysis: Market supply and market demand

To forecast charter rates for the detailed planning period, analyses of the current and expected market situations are important. Useful analyses should consider the fleet development (market supply) as well as the economic outlook (market demand).

Figures 9.5 and 9.6 summarize the deadweight capacity of the world cargo fleet and the volume of the order book (vessels ordered at shipyards) differentiated by main vessel types, as well as the expected increase of world trade volume, world oil demand and world GDP as of 30 June 2008 and 30 June 2013.

The analysis as of 30 June 2008 shows a substantial gap between the expected growth of market supply and market demand and thus an upcoming supply surplus. The ratio of the order book to the existing fleet less the expected scrapping rate (vessels older than 20 years as a percentage of the fleet) can be described as an indicator for the expected fleet growth. Assuming that the ordered vessels will be delivered over a period of approximately 2–3 years (up to the end of 2010), this indicator can be used as a proxy to estimate the growth of market supply up to the end of 2010. As of 30 June 2008, the projected fleet growth amounted to 43.3 % for container vessels, 32.2 % for oil tankers, and 35.2 % for bulk carriers. As opposed to this, the expected increase of world trade volume, world oil demand, and world GDP—good measures for the growth of future market demand—up to the end of

(continued)

2010 were projected to amount to 19.8, 3.7 and 8.6 % respectively. Because of the fact that from the perspective of 30 June 2008, the projected market supply growth significantly exceeded the expected market demand growth, an appraiser should have anticipated an upcoming overcapacity of vessels, leading to a significant decrease in the charter rates, as effectively seen in the last years.

Conducting the same analysis as of 30 June 2013 illustrates a substantial reduction in the gap between the projected market supply and demand growths. According to the ratio of the order book to the existing fleet and the expected scrapping rate the projected fleet growth up to the end of 2015 will amount to approximately 13.7 % for container vessels, 4.3 % for oil tankers, and 7.7 % for bulk carriers. Within the same timeframe and according to market analysts, the expected increase of world trade volume, world oil demand and world GDP will amount to approximately 13.2, 2.9 and 6.9 % respectively. In comparison to the situation in mid-2008 the gap between projected supply and demand is distinctly lower indicating no further deterioration in future charter rates. Nevertheless fleet growth is projected to remain slightly above the growth level of worldwide demand indicators for the next years. Due to this the excess capacity of vessels will probably persist. As a result, for the three vessel types—as of 30 June 2013—a continuation of the shipping crisis appears to be likely in the near future with the result that overall the charter rates will probably not improve significantly—albeit not deteriorating further—at least in the short run. The above analyses can be further broken down to the level of specific vessel size classes. For such more detailed analyses it is necessary to take into account interdependencies between different vessel size classes. Thus, for example, larger vessels are expected to replace smaller vessels on some trade routes due to economies of scale (so called "cascading" effect).

After the detailed planning period and given the cyclicality of the shipping markets with high volatility of charter rates (see Fig. 9.7), a reference to long-term historical average charter rates—at least over the last 10 years—is usually appropriate when forecasting the charter revenues far into the future. To offset extreme values it could be necessary to widen the timeframe or to select the median instead of the mean to measure the average. To verify if the assumption that history repeats itself is realistic, the specific attractiveness of the vessel in the market must be considered. For this purpose, the long-term historical average could be compared to the long-term charter rate forecasts of research companies.

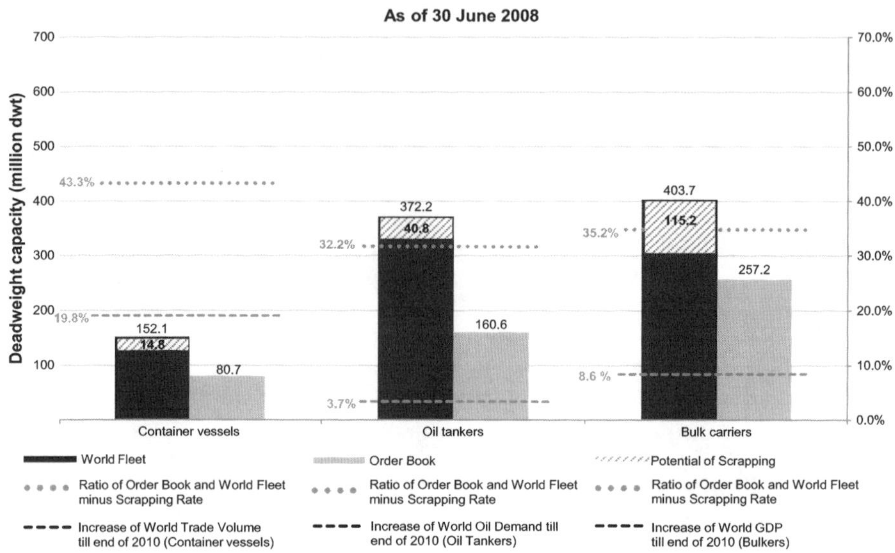

Fig. 9.5 Deadweight capacity of world cargo fleet and order book as of 30 June 2008. *Source*: Clarkson Research Services, The Economist Intelligence Unit, OPEC

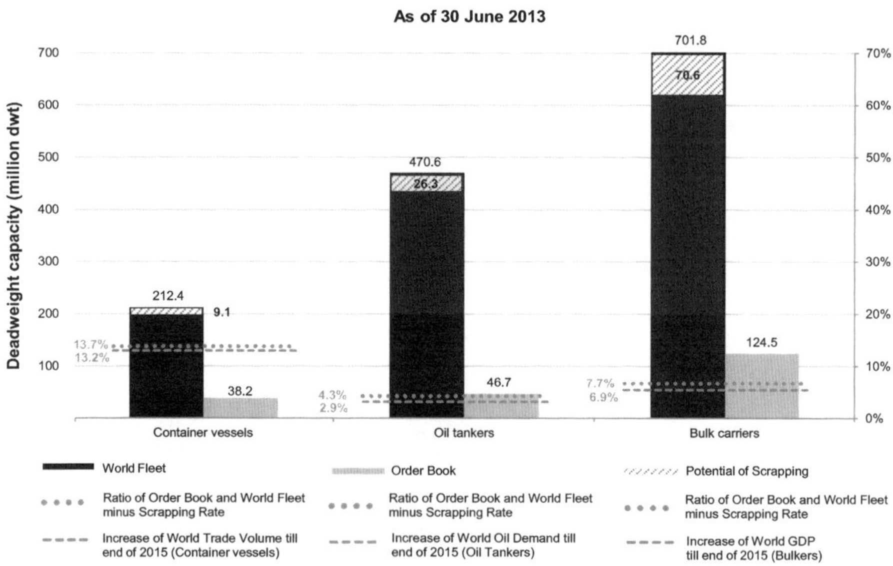

Fig. 9.6 Deadweight capacity of world cargo fleet and order book as of 30 June 2013. *Source*: Clarkson Research Services, The Economist Intelligence Unit, OPEC

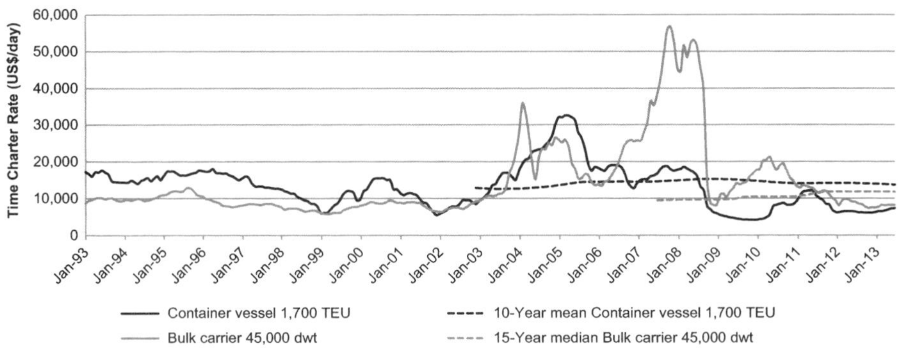

Fig. 9.7 Development of selected time charter rates (6–12 months; in $/day) between January 1993 and June 2013. *Source*: Clarkson Research Services

When forecasting the charter rates, expected increases in prices resulting from inflation should be considered to assure equivalency between the cash flow and the discount rate applied, as it is usually stated in nominal terms.[4]

Analyses of charter agreements show that compared to younger vessels older vessels often generate lower charter rates due to disadvantages in terms of efficiency (e.g. fuel consumption). This development should be reflected while forecasting charter rates. HSES recommends considering a discount when forecasting charter revenues for the periods when the vessel is older than 20 years. Experience shows that the charter rates for bulk carriers decreased by approximately 30 % and by approximately 15 % for container vessels and tankers.

Freight commissions and ship management fees are incurred when chartering. They usually amount between 1.25 and 5 % (freight commissions), respectively between 3 and 5 % (ship management fees) of the gross charter revenues.

For the estimation of the operating days of a vessel (utilization rate), a differentiation must be made between regular years of operations and years when the vessel is docked for renewing its class (normally every 5 years). In addition to the regular dry dock intervals, the forecast operating days must also take into account the other times when there is no operation (so-called off-hire times), for example, as a result of potential technical failures. HSES recommends 358 days of use in normal years and 343 days of use in class renewal years as a basis. Lower days of use might have to be taken into account due to expected additional off-hire times. The current shipping crisis has shown that due to excess capacity some vessels were not chartered and thus laid up. In such situations, a reduction of the usual utilization rate would have been reasonable.

- **Operating expenses** ($OPEX_t$)

  The operating expenses mainly include costs for personnel (e.g. crew wages and provisions), insurance, lubricants and other stores, spares, maintenance, repairs,

[4] As an alternative, an adjustment of the nominal discount rates to real discount rates is conceivable.

dockings and class renewals as well as for taxes. Payments for investments (e.g. due to environmental requirements) have to be considered as well under the operating expenses.
Due to increasing operating costs observed in the past and expected in the future, an orientation toward figures in the past when forecasting future operating costs is very questionable, contrary to the long-term forecast of charter revenues. Taking into account the current condition as well as the development of operating costs in previous years, the current operating costs should be used as a starting point for the forecast. Besides the current operating costs, the estimation in the detailed planning period should also consider expected new additional costs (e.g. investments due to environmental requirements). It must also be considered that the operating costs in class renewal years are higher by nature. For purposes of simplification, the costs for class renewals can be distributed on an annual basis. In a manner analogous to forecasting the future charter revenues, future cost increases resulting from inflation should also be taken into account while forecasting operating costs.

- **Residual value** (RV_T)
  To determine the residual value, reference to the scrap value at the end of the expected economic useful life (normally 20–25 years, Stopford 2009, p. 263) is appropriate. It is also important to take into account costs of disposal (e.g. commissions, costs of the voyage to the ship-breaking yard). When determining the scrap value, the light dis-placement weight of the vessel in (long) tons must be multiplied with the expected scrap price per (long) ton at the end of the economic useful life. As is the case with forecasting the future charter revenues and operating costs, the expected scrap value should also reflect price increases resulting from inflation.

9.4.3 Determination of the Discount Rate (WACC)

To value a vessel based on discounted cash flows, the expected free cash flows must be discounted to the valuation date using an appropriate discount rate. This rate is supposed to represent the required rate of return on an alternative investment which is equivalent to the investment in the respective vessel with regard to timing, risk, currency, and taxation of cash flows. As cash flows earned by vessels are usually denominated in USD, the discount rate should be determined as well based on US capital market data.

As the LTAV method is based on the free cash flows available for distribution among both, equity and debt suppliers of capital, the free cash flows must be discounted to the valuation date using a weighted average of required rates of return for the different sources of capital, equity, and debt. It is normally not necessary to take into account the benefit owing to the fact that interest on debt is a deductible expense for tax purposes because many important shipping nations have implemented a tonnage tax regime, where taxation is independent of the earned profits.[5] Thus, the expression of WACC is:

$$\begin{aligned} \text{WACC} = r_E \cdot \frac{E}{V} + r_D \cdot \frac{D}{V} \quad \text{where: } V &= E + D \\ r_E &= \text{Cost of Equity} \\ r_D &= \text{Cost of Debt} \\ E &= \text{Market Value of Equity} \\ D &= \text{Market Value of Debt} \end{aligned} \tag{9.2}$$

- **Cost of equity** (r_E)
  The Capital Asset Pricing Model (CAPM) is a widely accepted theory-based method for estimating the cost of equity (Sharpe 1964, pp. 425–442; Lintner 1965a, pp. 13–37; Lintner 1965b, pp. 587–615; Mossin 1966, pp. 768–783). The cost of equity can be broken down into a risk-free interest rate (r_f) and a risk premium required by the owners for the entrepreneurial risk incurred. The risk premium is derived by multiplying a general market risk premium (equity risk premium, ERP) with a specific risk factor, the so-called (equity) beta (β_E):

$$r_E = r_f + \text{ERP} \cdot \beta_E \tag{9.3}$$

  Based on the CAPM, there is a linear relationship between the required rate of equity return (cost of equity) and its systematic or non-diversifiable risk (expressed by the beta) (see Fig. 9.8).

  - **Risk-free interest rate**
    The risk-free interest rate represents the rate of return of an investment which can be earned without risk in the capital market. The risk-free nature relates to the risk in terms of currency, timing, and default (i.e. there is no uncertainty with regard to currency, the timing, and amount of the interest and principal payments).[6] As a completely risk-free investment in this narrow sense does not exist, reference to (quasi) risk-free investment alternatives such as government bonds having the highest possible credit rating is made as an approximation.[7]

[5]Contrary to the traditional profit-based business tax, the tax basis in the case of tonnage tax is based on the tonnage and, thus, the size of the vessel. In cases of a tax regime, where taxation is dependent on profits, the expression of WACC is WACC $= r_E \cdot E/V + r_D \cdot (1-t) \cdot D/V$, whereby t is the effective tax rate.

[6]This is different from the issue about the purchase power of the interest payments and accordingly how to deal with the risk of inflation. As the projected cash flows are normally based on nominal amounts, it is not problematic if the risk-free alternative investment is subject to a risk of inflation.

[7]A negligibly small default risk is normally assumed for developed industrial nations given the best ratings by rating agencies ("AAA" from Standard & Poor's and Fitch and "Aaa" from Moody's).

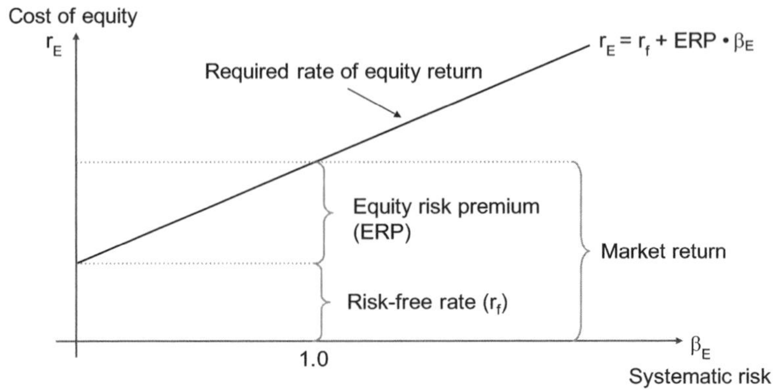

Fig. 9.8 Linear relationship between risk and return of the Capital Asset Pricing Model. *Source*: Sharpe (1964, p. 440)

Furthermore, the cash flows of the risk-free investment must be equivalent to the cash flows that are to be valued with regard to maturity to ensure identical risk exposure to changes in interest rates. In this context, preference is given to a set of zero bonds with corresponding terms to maturity. In practice, these zero bonds can only be found in the market occasionally, but interest rates of zero bonds can be mathematically derived from the observed yields to maturity for coupon-bearing bonds via an iterative procedure. A generally recognized method used by many central banks for estimating the continuous zero-coupon yield curve (term structure of interest rates) on the basis of observed yields to maturity for coupon-bearing bonds is the Nelson–Siegel–Svensson method (Nelson et al. 1985, 1987, pp. 473–489; Svensson 1994). Under this estimation method, the interest rate is defined as a variable depending on the residual maturity using the following exponential function (absolute term and various exponential terms with a total of six parameters):

$$i(m,\beta,\tau) = \beta_0 + \beta_1\left(\frac{1-e^{-\frac{m}{\tau_1}}}{\left(\frac{m}{\tau_1}\right)}\right) + \beta_2\left(\frac{1-e^{-\frac{m}{\tau_1}}}{\left(\frac{m}{\tau_1}\right)} - e^{-\frac{m}{\tau_1}}\right) + \beta_3\left(\frac{1-e^{-\frac{m}{\tau_2}}}{\left(\frac{m}{\tau_2}\right)} - e^{-\frac{m}{\tau_2}}\right) \quad (9.4)$$

In this equation, $i(m,\beta,\tau)$ refers to the interest rate for the residual maturity m in years as a function of the parameter vectors $\beta = [\beta_0, \beta_1, \beta_2, \beta_3]$ and $\tau = [\tau_1, \tau_2]$, which have to be estimated. These parameters are regularly estimated

To avoid a currency risk, the government bonds forming the basis of the risk-free interest rate must be in the same currency as the cash flows being valued.

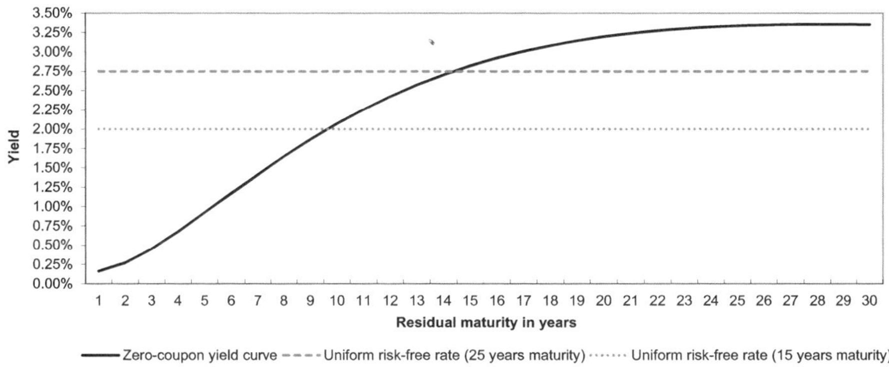

Fig. 9.9 Zero-coupon yield curve and uniform risk-free rates for different maturities as of 1 July 2013. *Source*: Federal Reserve, PwC Analysis

by various central banks[8] and published in historical sequence. If the identified interest rates for various residual maturities are illustrated in a graph, it is the zero-coupon yield curve.

Using data of the Federal Reserve the resulting interest rates are continuously compounding, while normally discrete annual interest rates are used for discounting in valuation practice. Therefore, the continuously compounding interest rates ($i_{\text{continuous}}$) must be converted to discrete interest rates (i_{discrete}) as follows:

$$i_{\text{discrete}} = e^{i_{\text{continuous}}} - 1 \tag{9.5}$$

To avoid errors in the approximation and to smooth short-term market fluctuations, reference is often made in valuation practice to average interest rates (e.g. over the last 3 months). For purposes of simplification, a uniform present value-equivalent interest rate is often determined. For example, given the yield curve parameters between April and June 2013, the following 3-month average zero-coupon yield curve and corresponding uniform risk-free rates depending on different terms to maturity result as of July 1, 2013 (see Fig. 9.9).

- **Equity risk premium (ERP)**

  The expected equity risk premium, which represents the difference between the expected return on an investment in the market portfolio[9] and the risk-free

[8]The individual parameters are determined by means of a non-linear optimization process under the criterion of minimizing the squared deviations between the estimated (theoretical) and the actually observed yields to maturity.

[9]The market portfolio theoretically consists of all risky assets including human capital, real estate, artworks, etc. and is therefore unobservable. In typical practice for valuation, the market portfolio is represented by a broad value weighted equity market index.

Table 9.1 Studies of the equity risk premium in the US

Estimation approach	Authors	Equity risk premium
Survey approach	Fernandez et al. (2012)	5.5 %
	Welch (2008)	5.0 % (geometric mean)
		5.7 % (arithmetic mean)
Historical equity risk premium	Dimson et al. (2012) 1900–2011	4.1 % (geometric mean)
		6.2 % (arithmetic mean)
	Ibbotson SBBI (2012) 1926–2011	4.7 % (geometric mean)
		6.6 % (arithmetic mean)
Implied equity risk premium	Damodaran (2012)	6.0 %

interest rate, can be determined based on *ex-post* or *ex-ante* estimates. *Ex-post*-based approaches use the average historical excess returns on investments in stocks compared to government bonds to estimate the expected equity risk premium. The calculation of the average returns is made by both arithmetic and geometric means. *Ex-ante* estimates, on the other hand, are estimates based on expected excess returns as of the valuation date. The expectations for the excess returns on investments in the market portfolio compared to government bonds are then determined based on surveys or inverted valuation models (implied equity risk premium).

Table 9.1 summarizes current empirical studies on the amount of the equity risk premium for the US capital market (Fernandez et al. 2012; Damodaran 2012; Dimson et al. 2012; Ibbotson SBBI 2012; Welch 2008).

According to these studies, the equity risk premium supposedly lies in a range of 4.0–7.0 %. Analyses indicate that in volatile market phases, the equity risk premium lies at the upper edge and in stable market phases, at the lower edge of such a range.

- **Beta** (β)

  The beta measures the asset's market or systematic risk, which, in theory, is the sensitivity of the asset's returns to the returns of the market portfolio. Concretely, beta equals the covariance of the asset's returns with the returns of the market portfolio divided by the market portfolio's variance of returns:

$$\beta_i = \frac{\mathrm{Cov}(r_i, r_m)}{\mathrm{Var}(r_m)} \tag{9.6}$$

  If beta is greater than one, the value of the asset reacts, on average, disproportionately high to market fluctuations. If beta is less than one, the change in value is, on average, disproportionately low.

  The beta for a specific vessel is estimated using an econometric process (ordinary least squares regression) on the basis of capital market data for peer group companies listed on the stock market with a market risk comparable to that of the vessel subject to valuation.

Besides determining peer group companies and a market index for representing the market portfolio, this requires determining the length of data period and the frequency of observations. A decision must be made between the statistically desirable longest time series as possible and the necessary consistency of the business activity for the peer group companies. Longer periods of time for analysis may lead to a reduction of potential errors in the estimation and to a narrower range of beta values in the course of time, but they cannot be applied if the risk of the analyzed companies has fundamentally changed. Therefore, in valuation practice, both 2-year betas based on weekly returns and 5-year betas based on monthly returns are applied.

As the betas of the listed peer group companies also include the risks resulting from their financial leverage (capital structure risk, financial risk), they must be adjusted to reflect the operating risks only (so-called process of unlevering). This adjustment is made by calculating the unlevered betas (β_E^U) using the observed raw betas (β_E) as a basis and taking into account the debt-to-equity ratio (D/E) of the respective peer group companies. Assuming that the debt of the peer group companies is subject to credit risk, the following expression is used in financial theory:

$$\beta_E^U = \frac{\beta_E + \beta_D \cdot \frac{D}{E}}{1 + \frac{D}{E}} \tag{9.7}$$

whereby debt beta (β_D) is defined as follows:

$$\beta_D = \frac{r_D - r_f}{\text{ERP}} \tag{9.8}$$

The unlevered betas of the peer group companies then reflect the isolated degree of the operating risk arising from the economics of the industry. The unlevered beta for a specific vessel is then the median or average peer group beta.

Subsequently, the unlevered beta must be adjusted for the expected future capital structure of the vessel subject to valuation (so-called process of relevering), according to the restructured formula above:

$$\beta_E = (\beta_E^U - \beta_D) \cdot (1 + \frac{D}{E}) \tag{9.9}$$

Due to the difficulty in determining the individual debt beta values for the peer group companies, debt beta is often assumed to be zero. If this assumption is made, it is important to use the same levering formula—with debt beta equals zero—for both the process of unlevering and relevering.

- **Cost of debt** (r_D)
  Ship financing is often based on agreements of variable interest rates linked to interbank interest rates (e.g. LIBOR) plus a credit risk premium (credit spread). As a result, interest rate swaps can be referred to as starting point when

determining the cost of debt. Interest rate swaps reflect the costs for hedging the risk of a change in interest rates by swapping the variable interest rate payment to a fixed interest rate payment for the corresponding term. The amount of the credit spread depends not only on the ability to realize the value of the vessel in the case of insolvency, but also on other influencing factors, e.g. the performance of the shipping company or the existence of long-term charters with creditworthy counter-parties.

- **Capital structure** (D/E)
  Vessels are normally financed with 50–70 % debt. The capital structure is generally only of subordinate relevance for the amount of the weighted average cost of capital, as a higher level of debt leads, on the one hand, to a higher beta and to an increased rate for the cost of equity accordingly, while, on the other hand, the relative weight of equity capital in the weighted average cost of capital-formula (E/V) is lower[10] (Modigliani et al. 1958, pp. 261–297; Modigliani et al. 1963, pp. 433–443).

9.4.4 *Suitability of the LTAV Method*

Especially, due to the existence of pork cycles and excessive optimism and pessimism on the part of the market participants, shipping markets are characterized by exaggerated and disrupted market phases. Market prices for vessels reflected in these phases are materially influenced by short-term transactions (e.g. fire sales) and show a high degree of volatility.

The LTAV method can offset these market inadequacies at least to a certain degree by focusing on the long-term earnings potential of a vessel and, thus, also represents a reliable basis in the decision-making process of long-term investors even in phases of market exuberances. The method assumes that the suppliers of capital are acting rationally in economic terms, implying that they will provide supplemental financing if the long-term prospects are positive (expectation of generating risk-adjusted returns on investment).

The LTAV method can be applied to value vessels regardless of the market conditions. Hence, it is a necessary supplement to approaches based on transaction prices, which can be applied for vessel valuation in functioning and stable markets only.

[10]In a perfectly efficient capital market, the value of a vessel is independent of its capital structure. In this case the discount rate (WACC) equals the unlevered cost of equity according to formula 9.3 with beta being the unlevered beta according to formula 9.7. In the case of valuations of vessels, the required postulate of a perfectly efficient capital market is often not violated by income taxes which are dependent on the financing due to the predominant taxation based on tonnage. However, other market imperfections exist also in the shipping markets.

LTAV Sample Calculation

Assumptions:

Vessel Type	Container vessel	
Size	1,700 TEU	
Age	10 years	
Light Displacement	8,000 long tons	
Economic Useful Life	25 years	
Valuation Date	June 30, 2013	
Operating Days	358	
Operating Days in Years with Dry Docking	343	No Dry Docking (class renewal) at the end of economic useful life due to scrapping of vessel
Gross Charter Rate 2013 per day (p.d.)	$7,250	Current 6-12 Month Timecharter Rate as at valuation date (Source: Clarksons Research Services)
Gross Charter Rate 2014 p.d.	$7,100	Charter Rate Forecast (Source: Maritime Strategies International)
Gross Charter Rate 2015 p.d.	$9,000	Charter Rate Forecast (Source: Maritime Strategies International)
Gross Charter Rate 2016 p.d.	$11,200	Charter Rate Forecast (Source: Maritime Strategies International)
Gross Charter Rate 2017 p.d.	$13,300	Charter Rate Forecast (Source: Maritime Strategies International)
Gross Charter Rate p.d. from 2018 onwards	$13,500	10-Year Historical Average Charter Rate (Source: Clarksons Research Services)
Age Discount	15%	Reduction in the Daily Gross Charter Rate for ships over 20 years old
Fees and Commissions	6.5%	Ship Management Fees and Freight Commissions as a percentage of Gross Charter Rate
Annual Operating Expenses in 2013	$2,290,000	Operating Expenses including Tonnage Tax; Assuming Dry Docking provisions are an annual expense
Inflation Rate per annum (p.a.)	2%	Affects the Charter Rate from 2019 onwards and Scrap Value
Expected increase in Operating Expenses p.a.	3%	From 2014 onwards
Scrap Price (per long ton) as at Valuation Date	$360	Considering disposal costs; Scrap Value = Light Displacement (in lt.) x Scrap Price (per lt.) x (1+Inflation Rate)^Years
Discount Rate (WACC)	7.3%	Considering timing, risk, currency, and taxation of cash flows

Year	Ship Age (Years)	Operating Days	Daily Gross Charter Rate	Age Discount	Charter Rate after Age Discount	Fees and Commissions	Daily Net Charter Revenue	Annual Net Charter Revenue	Annual Operating Expenses	Scrap Value	Free Cash Flow	WACC	Present Value Factor	Present Value
2013	10.5	172	$7,250		$7,250	6.5%	$6,779	$1,165,945	$1,145,000		$20,945	7.30%	0.9654	$20,220
2014	11.5	358	$7,100		$7,100	6.5%	$6,639	$2,376,583	$2,358,700		$17,883	7.30%	0.8997	$16,089
2015	12.5	358	$9,000		$9,000	6.5%	$8,415	$3,012,570	$2,429,461		$583,109	7.30%	0.8385	$488,934
2016	13.5	358	$11,200		$11,200	6.5%	$10,472	$3,748,976	$2,502,345		$1,246,631	7.30%	0.7814	$974,179
2017	14.5	358	$13,300		$13,300	6.5%	$12,436	$4,451,909	$2,577,415		$1,874,494	7.30%	0.7283	$1,365,165
2018	15.5	343	$13,500		$13,500	6.5%	$12,623	$4,329,518	$2,654,738		$1,674,780	7.30%	0.6787	$1,136,735
2019	16.5	358	$13,770		$13,770	6.5%	$12,875	$4,609,232	$2,734,380		$1,874,852	7.30%	0.6326	$1,185,957
2020	17.5	358	$14,045		$14,045	6.5%	$13,132	$4,701,417	$2,816,411		$1,885,006	7.30%	0.5895	$1,111,258
2021	18.5	358	$14,326		$14,326	6.5%	$13,395	$4,795,445	$2,900,903		$1,894,542	7.30%	0.5494	$1,040,894
2022	19.5	358	$14,613		$14,613	6.5%	$13,663	$4,891,354	$2,987,931		$1,903,423	7.30%	0.5120	$974,626
2023	20.5	343	$14,905	0.0% / 15.0%	$13,787	6.5%	$12,891	$4,421,627	$3,077,569		$1,344,058	7.30%	0.4772	$641,388
2024	21.5	358	$15,203	15.0%	$12,923	6.5%	$12,083	$4,325,620	$3,169,896		$1,155,724	7.30%	0.4447	$513,993
2025	22.5	358	$15,507	15.0%	$13,181	6.5%	$12,324	$4,412,132	$3,264,992		$1,147,140	7.30%	0.4145	$475,466
2026	23.5	358	$15,817	15.0%	$13,445	6.5%	$12,571	$4,500,375	$3,362,942		$1,137,433	7.30%	0.3863	$439,369
2027	24.5	358	$16,134	15.0%	$13,714	6.5%	$12,822	$4,590,383	$3,463,830		$1,126,552	7.30%	0.3600	$405,560
2028	25.0	179	$16,456	15.0%	$13,988	6.5%	$13,079	$2,341,095	$1,783,873	$3,876,101	$4,433,323	7.30%	0.3355	$1,487,420
													LTAV	$12,277,256

Fig. 9.10 LTAV sample calculation for a charter-free 10-year-old 1,700 TEU (geared) container vessel

9.4.5 Sample Calculation Using the LTAV Method

The LTAV method is illustrated based on a fictitious, charter-free 10-year-old 1,700 TEU (geared) container vessel with an expected total economic useful life of 25 years. The assumptions required for the valuation as well as the determination of the LTAV are summarized in Fig. 9.10.

9.5 Possibilities for Applying the LTAV Method

9.5.1 LTAV for Investment and Divestment Decisions

The LTAV method can be used in the investment and divestment decision-making processes. Attractive investment and divestment opportunities can be identified using a comparison of the values determined based on the LTAV method and the observed market prices. Vessel prices lower than the values determined by the LTAV method represent attractive buying opportunities for a potential investor (net present value of the investment > 0), while vessel prices above the corresponding LTAV indicate attractive selling prices.

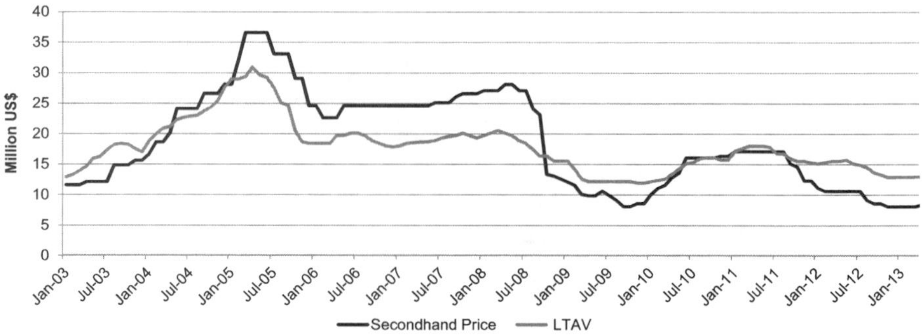

Fig. 9.11 Historical comparison of second-hand prices and theoretical LTAVs for a 10-year-old 1,700 TEU (geared) container vessel. *Source*: Clarkson Research Services, PwC Analysis

Actual market price > LTAV:	Implication for potential buyer:	Don't buy
	Implication for vessel owner:	Sell
Actual market price < LTAV:	Implication for potential buyer:	Buy
	Implication for vessel owner:	Don't sell

Figure 9.11 shows a comparison between historical market prices and theoretical values determined by the LTAV method for a 10-year-old 1,700 TEU (geared) container vessel.

Due to a more stable economic environment, the observed market prices for vessels more or less corresponded to their LTAVs from 2003 to 2004. A comparison with the LTAVs shows that higher market prices could be realized from 2005 up to mid-2008, indicating overpriced vessels. The transaction prices observed since the end of 2008 most of the time are substantially lower than the LTAVs, indicating bargain prices and corresponding high expected returns on investment.

Mispriced vessels can also be identified by comparing the internal rate of return (IRR) to the required rate of return (WACC). IRR works out the discount rate which gives a net present value (NPV) of zero. From an investor's point of view, the expected IRR can be determined by solving the following formula to IRR via an iterative procedure:

$$\text{NPV} = -\text{Actual market price} + \sum_{t=1}^{T} \frac{(C_t - \text{OPEX}_t)}{(1+\text{IRR})^t} + \frac{\text{RV}_T}{(1+\text{IRR})^T} = 0$$

$$\leftrightarrow \sum_{t=1}^{T} \frac{(C_t - \text{OPEX}_t)}{(1+\text{IRR})^t} + \frac{\text{RV}_T}{(1+\text{IRR})^T} = \text{Actual market price} \qquad (9.10)$$

If the expected IRR of the investment is higher than the risk-equivalent required rate of return (WACC), assets in the market are cheap, and the investment should be made. On the contrary, if the expected IRR of the investment is below the required risk-equivalent rate of return, assets in the market are expensive, and it should not be invested.

IRR < WACC:	Implication for potential buyer:	Don't buy
	Implication for vessel owner:	Sell
IRR > WACC:	Implication for potential buyer:	Buy
	Implication for vessel owner:	Don't sell

9.5.2 LTAV for Accounting Purposes of Vessel Owners

The LTAV method is suitable for accounting purposes, especially for impairment testing. The corresponding accounting standards of the company (e.g. US GAAP, German GAAP, International Financial Reporting Standards [IFRS], etc.) must be complied with. Consideration must be given to the fact that a central assumption in the LTAV method is the focus on the long-term earnings potential of the vessel which explicitly assumes a going concern scenario until the end of its economic useful life. In the case of a gone concern scenario, as a general rule, valuation methods based on the current market prices must be used.

According to IFRS, DCF models are accepted and commonly used for impairment testing of assets. IAS 36 (Impairment of Assets) seeks to ensure at each balance sheet date that the vessel's carrying amount is not higher than its recoverable amount, which is defined as the higher of the vessel's fair value less costs to sell and its value in use. The vessel's fair value is the amount obtainable from the sale in an arm's-length transaction between knowledgeable and willing parties. The vessel's value in use is the present value of the future cash flows expected to arise from its continuing use and from its disposal at the end of its economic useful life. As a result, this leads to a common usage of the LTAV method for accounting purposes according to IFRS.

Moreover, in other accounting and reporting standards (e.g. US GAAP, German GAAP, etc.), DCF models for the purpose of impairment testing are widely accepted.

9.5.3 LTAV for Accounting Purposes of Banks

Ship-financing banks can use the LTAV method with minor adjustments (especially the discount rate is often defined by accounting standards, e.g. the effective interest rate under IFRS according to IAS 39) to determine any need to adjust the book value of the loans receivable and to make provisions for credit losses. From a bank's perspective, the main question in the context of vessel financing is whether the expected free cash flows (the numerator in the LTAV calculation) earned by the vessel are sufficient to satisfy all payment obligations (interest and principal) including any possible additional obligations with regard to current account financing and deferrals.

In that context, the scheduled repayments of principal and the expected interest payments must be determined. Any shortfall in financing must bear interest separately and must be taken into account over the term of the financing.

If the free cash flows are not sufficient to cover all payments of interest and principal (including interest on deferred payments and any additionally required current account financing) until the end of the expected economic useful life of the vessel, the loan must be subject to allowances.

The amount of the provision for credit losses can be derived by discounting the remaining loan balance at the end of the vessel's economic useful life with the respective interest rate or by comparing the present value of the expected loan payments with the book value of the loan.

9.6 Concluding Summary

This chapter presents the basic principles of vessel valuations with a main focus on the LTAV method. In uncertain and volatile market conditions and under the assumption of a going concern scenario, vessels should be valued based on their long-term earnings potential and not on the basis of often-distorted transaction prices. The LTAV method is a appropriate method for such a income-oriented valuation approach. It is a necessary complement to the market approach for valuing vessels. The LTAV method is based on a discounted cash flow (DCF) analysis, which is already commonly used and widely accepted for the valuation of businesses and many long-lived assets (e.g. real estate, aircraft, power plants, etc.). Possibilities for applying the LTAV method are investment and divestment decisions, impairment tests for preparing financial statements, and the determination of provisions for credit losses at banks.

References

Damodaran A (2012) Equity risk premiums (ERP): determinants, estimation and implications - the 2012 edition. Stern Business School Working Paper. http://people.stern.nyu.edu/adamodar/pdfiles/papers/ERP2012.pdf

Dimson E, Marsh P, Staunton M (2012) Credit Suisse global investment return yearbook 2012

Fernandez P, Aguirreamalloa J, Corres L (2012) Market risk premium used in 82 countries in 2012: a survey with 7,192 answers. IESE Business School Working Paper. Available at SSRN: http://papers.ssrn.com/sol3/papers.cfm?abstract_id=2084213

Ibbotson SBBI (2012) Ibbotson SBBI 2012 valuation yearbook

Lintner J (1965a) The valuation of risk assets and the selection of risky investments in stock portfolios and capital budgets. Rev Econ Stat 47:13–47

Lintner J (1965b) Security prices, risk, and maximal gains from diversification. J Finance 20:587–615

Modigliani F, Miller M (1958) The cost of capital, corporation finance and the theory of investment. Am Econ Rev 48(3):261–297

Modigliani F, Miller M (1963) Corporate income taxes and the cost of capital: a correction. Am Econ Rev 53:433–443

Mossin J (1966) Equilibrium in a capital asset market. Econometrica 34:768–783

Nelson C, Siegel A (1985) Parsimonious modeling of yield curves for US Treasury bills. NBER Working Paper Series 1594

Nelson C, Siegel A (1987) Parsimonious modeling of yield curves. J Business 60(3):473–489

Sharpe W (1964) Capital asset prices: a theory of market equilibrium under conditions of risk. J Finance 19(3):425–442

Svensson L (1994) Estimating and interpreting forward interest rates: Sweden 1992–1994. IMF Working Paper 94/114

Stopford M (2009) Maritime Economics. 3rd edn.

Welch I (2008) The consensus estimate for the equity premium by Academic Financial Economists in December 2007. Available at SSRN: http://papers.ssrn.com/sol3/papers.cfm?abstract_id=1084918

Chapter 10
Developing a Dynamic Vessel Valuation Method Based on Real Market Transactions

Andreas Mietzner

Abstract This contribution develops a mathematical method (Qualitative Adjusted and Audited Algebraic Estimation based on "Last Done"—QAAELD) for the evaluation of the market values of oceangoing vessels. The dynamic approach is based on real market transactions, which are adjusted according to the weighted ratio of properties of the evaluated vessel and the sold comparison vessels. The method incorporates changes in market level as well as those in age-related attrition. It delivers robust results and offers an alternative to the common approaches of vessel valuation.

10.1 Introduction

In shipping, the vessel is the market participants' main asset and unlike in most other industries the main asset is traded on a secondhand market. This diminishes barriers to market entry (and exit) and enhances competitiveness. Several forces drive the asset price. While among others speculation and fleet development have some influence on the price, the secondhand price is mainly driven by charter and freight market developments. A vessel's market value is constantly changing due to the high volatility of shipping markets as well as age-related attrition. Therefore, it is important for those involved, e.g. ship owners or banks, to periodically assess the vessel's value. Whether one wants to compare a ship's book value with the current market value or know which amount could be realized on the current market, a decent and reliable valuation method is required.

So-called desktop valuation has been conducted by ship brokers since decades. However, in many cases valuation utilizes intuition and heuristics rather than a clearly defined valuation scheme. In most cases so far, vessel valuation has lacked

A. Mietzner (✉)
Continental Chartering GmbH & Co. KG, Ballindamm 17, 20095 Hamburg, Germany
e-mail: research@continental-chartering.de

O. Schinas et al. (eds.), *HSBA Handbook on Ship Finance*,
DOI 10.1007/978-3-662-43410-9_10, © Springer-Verlag Berlin Heidelberg 2015

a precise definition. To cope with this absence of precision we have created an in-house guideline for vessel valuation, which is based on real market transactions, incorporates market changes and considers changing market dynamics. First, it requires accurate market data gained by continuous market observation, recording, and filing. Secondly, a clearly defined manual of valuation to work with the data will ensure the robustness of the results and will allow for flexibility and dynamic market change.

10.2 Other Approaches of Vessel Valuation

Before presenting a new valuation approach, two commonly used approaches are briefly discussed. The most common approach is actually a bunch of vessel valuation heuristics, which can be subsumed under "ordinary desktop valuation". Ordinary desktop valuations are rather qualitative approaches that rely on the individual valuators expertise and his intuition. Usually, in such a scheme, the valuator considers historical data, market conditions, probable future earning potential and other relevant information to figure out the vessel's value. He may undertake certain calculations, but in the end the method remains qualitative and in most cases the result is represented as a black box. An advantage of this approach is that it is usually based on real market transactions and is conducted by people who are close to the market. Thus, it may deliver good results in a large number of cases. However, such a procedure relies on a broker's intuition and is therefore liable to failure due to its subjectivity.

Another approach is the Long-Term Asset Value (LTAV) method recently developed by the Vereinigung Hamburger Schiffsmakler und Schiffsagenten. This discounted cash flow method was developed in the aftermaths of the shipping crisis starting in the second half of 2008. It offers an alternative vessel valuation scheme for biased markets to determine an objective and sustainable long-term value. It is a suitable method that smoothes market volatility and counteracts market understatement as well as market exaggeration. The supposed future cash flow is (unless there is a long term charter contract in place) based on average historical charter rates, a fact which reveals the LTAV's weakness. By taking the average historical charter rate as a proxy for future income it smoothens the volatility, although it assumes implicitly that a similar kind of volatility will occur in future and therefore ignores potential changes of market fundamentals. Besides its orientation to the past, its results depend on the assumed discount interest rate. Even though the LTAV method has its justification, it can be criticized for not being based on actual market transactions, thus delivering a result that is of a somewhat hypothetical nature.

10.3 Algebraic Estimation on the Basis of "Last Done"

10.3.1 Three-Level Approach

In the following, we will derive the Algebraic Estimation based on Last Done (AELD). It is a tool setting an algebraic definition and giving a guideline on how to extract market values out of observed vessel transactions. The AELD method is based on a three level approach. In the first stage, utile comparison sales need to be identified and divided from those transactions that do not suit the criteria for serving as a benchmark for the vessel to be valued. The more analogous the sales of the vessels are the more appropriate they are for our purpose. This selection process is crucial for the validity of the result attained in the end.

After the benchmark transactions have been chosen carefully every real market sale needs to be adjusted to the vessel whose market value is supposed to be evaluated. In a second step, we will adjust the vessel to the trait that has a major influence on a vessel's value. A vessel's age is essential for its trading perspective and therefore for its earning potential and its value.

In a third step all other attributes that have an influence on the vessel's value need to be identified and the respective transaction prices need to be adjusted according to the ratio of the vessel of comparison and the vessel to be valued. There are various attributes such as size (measured in dwt, GT, NT or TEU), efficiency, and other special features like e.g. reefer plugs or auxiliary engines that can be part of the ratio equation. After all vessels of comparison have been assessed concerning their age and their other attributes, the mean of all the values can be calculated according to a special formula.

10.3.2 Identification of Sales of Comparison

In a first step, those vessels out of the recorded secondhand sales will be chosen that suit best to serve as a benchmark for the vessel that needs to be valued. For this purpose, we will define a procedure to adjust the transaction price according to the vessel's attributes, thereby increasing the valuation result's accuracy if attributes are as similar as possible. In the following, we will take it for granted that an accurate and complete set of data on second-hand transactions is available. However, it is essential to ensure the quality of this information.

The main selection criterion is a vessel's (nominal or homogeneous) capacity. As a rule, one can state that the more similar in kind the vessel of comparison is, the more precise the result will be. It would be unrewarding to define a maximum capacity difference (between comparison vessel and valuation vessel) that barely leads to a reliable result. It rather depends on the vessel type and on the specific vessel segment. For example, it makes sense to compare a container feeder vessel of a nominal capacity of 1,600 TEU and 1,700 TEU because both vessels are employable on the same routes. Hence, both types will face similar demand. However, it would not make sense to compare a handysize bulker with a capesize bulker because both ship types operate in totally different markets. Whether to accept a certain capacity difference or not depends on the specific market situation and on the available comparison sales.

Another criterion is time. The smaller the time lag between the observed comparison sale and the vessel's valuation is the more precise the result will be. Even though later on we will develop a method to incorporate the market change between the time of the comparison sale and the valuation date, a big time lag may interfere with the result's accuracy. Consequently, long time lags should only be taken into account if more recent comparison sales are not available.

A rather obvious criterion is the equipment with gear. Even though two vessels have an identical capacity but one is gearless and the other is geared, the two vessels are designed for different trades and might operate in totally different markets. In this case, they are not comparable.

Notwithstanding the age adjustment procedure that we will develop subsequently, the comparison vessel's age also needs to be regarded as a selection criterion. This is particularly the case if we have many comparison sales with a small time lag. In this case, it can be worth considering just those vessels that have a relatively small age difference to the assessed vessel because even here the rule of thumb pertains that a bigger age difference will decrease the probability of an accurate result.

Other criteria can be e.g. design, kind of propulsion or place of construction. Whether to consider those or other criteria always depends on the specific market and market situation. For example, in a market with high HFO bunker prices and relative low LNG prices, a vessel of the same size having a different kind of propulsion cannot simply be compared.

10.3.3 Age Adjustment

After having selected those vessels whose sale will serve as a benchmark for our valuation, we have to adjust the sales price according to the age difference between the vessel sold and the vessel that is supposed to be assessed. To adjust the age we need to define a rate of depreciation. In reality, the depreciation is gradual rather than steady, especially because of the cost expensive special survey.[1] Furthermore, if we defined a function of market value depreciation the rate of depreciation would change over time depending on the current market situation. In a boom market, even the oldest vessel bears a certain earning potential. Thus, market participants would be willing to pay more for an old vessel; even though it may be more cost-intensive and inefficient, it promises an undeniable short-run return. In such a case, the rate of

[1]The Special Survey has normally to be carried out every 5 years. In recent years there appeared to be special permits demanding a special survey every 7 years.

Table 10.1 Data of the ship under scrutiny

Name	TEU	Reefer	Gear	Built	Date	Price
Titanic Voyager	1,710	150	Geared	2001	April 13	?

vessel value depreciation would be low. In a depressed market rate of vessel value depreciation would be high. As a good profit on the purchase of an old vessel in the short-term is highly improbable, it is not worth much more than its scrap value. It is consensus among brokers that in a prosperous market a vessel's age-related attrition is around 5 % per annum. For practical reasons we will assume for the moment that we are facing such a prosperous market where a vessel devaluates by 5 %.

Hence, we can create the following formula to adapt the sales price of observed transactions to the age of the vessel we want to valuate:

$$\begin{aligned} &\text{If } \mathrm{AC}_i \geq \mathrm{AR} \text{ and } \mathrm{AAP}_i > \mathrm{SV}_i \rightarrow \text{ then } \mathrm{AAP}_i = \mathrm{PC}_i \times 1.05^{(\mathrm{AC}_i - \mathrm{AR})} \\ &\text{else if } \mathrm{AC}_i < \mathrm{AR} \text{ and } \mathrm{AAP}_i > \mathrm{SV}_i \rightarrow \text{ then } \mathrm{AAP}_i = \mathrm{PC}_i \times 0.95^{(\mathrm{AR} - \mathrm{AC}_i)} \\ &\text{else } \mathrm{AAP}_i = \mathrm{SV}_i = \mathrm{ldt}_i \times \mathrm{SP} \end{aligned} \tag{10.1}$$

where:

- AAP_i = age adjusted price of vessel i
- PC_i = price of comparison vessel i
- AC_i = age of comparison vessel i
- AR = age of rated vessel
- SV_i = scrap value of vessel i
- SP = scrap price per light displacement ton
- ldt_i = light displacement tons of vessel i

Intuitively, we appreciate the value of the transaction price of a comparison vessel by 5 % for every year that the comparison vessel is older than the vessel that needs to be evaluated. For every year, that the comparison vessel is younger than the evaluated vessel the transaction price needs to be depreciated by 5 % unless the vessel's scrap value is reached.

- **Numerical Example**

To give a numerical example, we assume that we want to estimate the market value of the fictitious vessel Titanic Voyager. As per Table 10.1, it is a geared feeder vessel built in 2001 with 1,710 TEU and 150 reefer plugs. The task is to estimate the value in April 2013. Since the beginning of the year 2013 there have been eight suitable comparison transactions, which are listed in the overview Table 10.2.

Table 10.2 Data of suitable comparison transactions

Name	TEU	Reefer	Gear	Built	Date	Price
Vessel A	1,740	300	Geared	2006	January 13	$13,500,000
Vessel B	1,645	120	Geared	1997	January 13	$4,000,000
Vessel C	1,730	200	Geared	1997	February 13	$4,000,000
Vessel D	1,730	200	Geared	1998	February 13	$4,500,000
Vessel E	1,730	250	Geared	2002	March 13	$7,140,000
Vessel F	1,620	145	Geared	2003	March 13	$7,500,000
Vessel G	1,620	145	Geared	2003	March 13	$7,500,000
Vessel H	1,620	145	Geared	2003	March 13	$7,500,000

- **Age Adjustment**
  Thus, to calculate the age-adjusted price for each vessel we need to apply the above formula. For PC_i we plug in the respective sales price [see Eq. (10.2)]. In the exponent, we put the respective age difference between the comparison vessel and the Titanic Voyager.

$$
\begin{aligned}
AAP_{\text{Vessel A}} &= \$13{,}500{,}000 \times 0.95^{(2006-2001)} \approx \$10{,}446{,}000 \\
AAP_{\text{Vessel B}} &= \$4{,}000{,}000 \times 1.05^{(2001-1997)} \approx \$4{,}862{,}000 \\
AAP_{\text{Vessel C}} &= \$4{,}000{,}000 \times 1.05^{(2001-1997)} \approx \$4{,}862{,}000 \\
AAP_{\text{Vessel D}} &= \$4{,}500{,}000 \times 1.05^{(2001-1998)} \approx \$5{,}209{,}000 \\
AAP_{\text{Vessel E}} &= \$7{,}140{,}000 \times 0.95^{(2002-2001)} \approx \$6{,}783{,}000 \\
AAP_{\text{Vessel F}} &= \$7{,}500{,}000 \times 0.95^{(2003-2001)} \approx \$6{,}769{,}000 \\
AAP_{\text{Vessel G}} &= \$7{,}500{,}000 \times 0.95^{(2003-2001)} \approx \$6{,}769{,}000 \\
AAP_{\text{Vessel H}} &= \$7{,}500{,}000 \times 0.95^{(2003-2001)} \approx \$6{,}769{,}000
\end{aligned} \tag{10.2}
$$

- **Attribute Adjustment**
  Having adjusted the comparison vessels' transaction prices for their major attribute, we still need to adjust the vessels for some minor attributes. Those attributes can be manifold and it always lies in the eye of the beholder which attributes to include or not to include in this adjustment process. Usually those attributes can be e.g. (nominal or homogeneous) capacity, building land (as far as that refers to the vessel's quality), consumption (especially in times of expensive fuel), auxiliaries, reefer plugs, etc. Whether to include an attribute in the valuation and how to weigh this attribute is a crucial issue that will influence our result. Hence, quite some time should be invested in this decision. The attribute selection could be based on experience or on quantitative methods.[2]

[2]For example application of econometric methods such as Ordinary Least Square, Instrument Variable Approach, or Natural Experiment to estimate the influence certain attributes have on the transaction price of vessels.

To simplify we will take for granted that in our market only two attributes have a significant influence on the price of the vessel: nominal capacity (in some cases it could make sense to judge by the homogeneous capacity) and reefer plugs. Additionally, we assume a weight of 30 for the nominal capacity and a weight of one for the reefer plugs. In the following, we will deploy a trivial formula that adjusts the age adjusted prices by the missing significant attributes.

$$\mathrm{AP}_i = \frac{\frac{\mathrm{TEU}_r \times 30}{\mathrm{TEU}_{c_i}} + \frac{\mathrm{REEFER}_r}{\mathrm{REEFER}_{c_i}}}{31} \times \mathrm{AAP}_i$$

$$\mathrm{PR} = \frac{\sum_{i=1}^{N} \mathrm{AP}_i}{N} \tag{10.3}$$

where:

- AAP_i = age adjusted price of vessel i
- PR = price rated vessel
- TEU_r = TEU of rated vessel
- TEU_{c_i} = TEU of comparison vessel i
- REEFER_r = Reefer plugs of rated vessel
- REEFER_{c_i} = Reefer plugs of comparison vessel i
- AP_i = adjusted price of vessel i
- N = number of comparison vessels

In a first step, we multiply the age-adjusted price of each comparison vessel with the weighed ratio of the other attributes. This grants the "adjusted price" for each vessel. In a final step, we take the mean of the adjusted prices for each vessel, which equals the price of the rated vessel or more precisely the estimated market value of the evaluated vessel. Plugging in the numbers of our previous example we derive the following numeric equations [see Eq. (10.4)]:

$$\mathrm{AP}_{\text{Vessel A}} = \frac{\frac{1{,}710 \times 30}{1{,}740} + \frac{150}{300}}{31} \times \$10{,}446{,}000 \approx \$10{,}103{,}000$$

$$\mathrm{AP}_{\text{Vessel B}} = \frac{\frac{1{,}710 \times 30}{1{,}645} + \frac{150}{120}}{31} \times \$4{,}862{,}000 \approx \$5{,}087{,}000$$

$$\mathrm{AP}_{\text{Vessel C}} = \frac{\frac{1{,}710 \times 30}{1{,}730} + \frac{150}{200}}{31} \times \$4{,}862{,}000 \approx \$4{,}768{,}000$$

$$\mathrm{AP}_{\text{Vessel D}} = \frac{\frac{1{,}710 \times 30}{1{,}730} + \frac{150}{200}}{31} \times \$5{,}209{,}000 \approx \$5{,}109{,}000$$

$$\mathrm{AP}_{\text{Vessel E}} = \frac{\frac{1{,}710 \times 30}{1{,}730} + \frac{150}{250}}{31} \times \$6{,}783{,}000 \approx \$6{,}620{,}000$$

$$AP_{\text{Vessel F}} = \frac{\frac{1,710\times 30}{1,620} + \frac{150}{145}}{31} \times \$6,769,000 \approx \$7,140,000$$

$$AP_{\text{Vessel G}} = \frac{\frac{1,710\times 30}{1,620} + \frac{150}{145}}{31} \times \$6,769,000 \approx \$7,140,000$$

$$AP_{\text{Vessel H}} = \frac{\frac{1,710\times 30}{1,620} + \frac{150}{145}}{31} \times \$6,769,000 \approx \$7,140,000$$

$$PR = \frac{\sum_{i=1}^{N} AP_i}{8} =$$

$$= \frac{1,000 \times (10,103 + 5,087 + 4,768 + 5,109 + 6,620 + 7,140 + 7,140 + 7,140)}{8}$$

$$\Rightarrow PR \approx \$6,639,000 \tag{10.4}$$

By adjusting the values of the suitable second-hand transactions observed we have derived the current market value of the Titanic Voyager. Based on the observed transactions its market value is approximately $6,639,000.

10.3.4 Criticism

So far we have derived a simple method that instructs us in how to approximate the market value of a given vessels by adjusting transaction prices of suitable comparison vessels. Compared to the rather intuitive approach of common broker evaluation this approach has the advantage that the evaluation follows a mathematically and precisely defined algorithm, and if applied properly it delivers robust results. Compared to the LTAV method, it is of non-hypothetical nature, as the values are orientated on real-market transactions.

However, this evaluation method has its weaknesses. For a start, it is a past-orientated method. As it utilizes comparison sales that occurred in "past months", the result is the value the respective vessel had at the time the comparison vessels were sold. However, unless we are conducting an ex-post valuation we are interested in the value it has at present. It is quite likely that the market level has changed since the comparison sales were transacted. So far, the AELD does not consider this.

Another weakness of the approach is that the age adjustment is static. Age-related attrition of a vessel depends on several factors.[3] However, as described above, the major factor of change in the pace of attrition is the market situation. In a "good

[3]Even though age related attrition does mainly depend on the market situation, it also depends among others on factors like cruise area, maintenance performance and steel quality.

market", vessels will devaluate more slowly than in a "bad market". Nevertheless, as it stands the AELD assumes 5 % of devaluation per annum.

Moreover, it has to be noted that the influence of the attributes on the transaction price may differ in reality and thus could bias the assessment result. Furthermore, the validity of the result depends on the choice of the comparison vessels.

10.4 Qualitative Adjusted and Audited Algebraic Estimation on the Bas is of "Last Done"

Even though we have developed a method that delivers robust results, the AELD still faces a couple of weaknesses as shown in the criticism above. In the following, we will elaborate our method further. We will demonstrate how to test the validity of an age adjustment factor and how to factor in a change of age related attrition. We will show how to incorporate possible market change since the observation of comparison transactions, enabling the estimation of current market values. Furthermore, we will briefly introduce a statistical method of testing attributes significance. Finally, we will discuss methods of ex-post auditing to ensure the result's validity.

10.4.1 Incorporating Market Changes

Unfortunately, we do not always have comparison sales available to judge a vessel's value today. It is quite possible that the last observed transactions date back a couple of months or even years. Normally some time has passed since the last realized transactions that suit as benchmark sales. However, it is likely that the market level has moved since then. To allow for the market movement between the time of the comparison vessel's transaction and the present, we have to incorporate market change. Hence, we will construct a factor that compensates the market movement between the time of observed comparison transaction and time of market value assessment. To value the change in market level we make use of the significant correlation between the charter and the second-hand market. While the second-hand market reveals just a few transactions, the charter market is (for most vessel sizes) more vibrant and delivers a continuous flow of fixtures and thus information on the market level. Hence, the charter market movement is the best available proxy for the change of second-hand market level.[4]

---

[4]It could be argued that the development of second-hand prices of vessels depends on charter market expectations rather than on the current charter market level. However, expectations are difficult to measure. Therefore, charter rates represent the best available proxy for second-hand price development.

Before constructing the market change factor, we have to reconsider the issue of age adjustment. As it is not likely that all comparison vessels were sold at the same point of time and therefore not at exactly the same market level, we would – to be exact have to adjust every comparison sale with its individual factor of market change. Unfortunately, this would bias the determination of the age adjustment factor. To avoid this bias we have two options: The first option is to estimate the age adjustment factor based on the last two sales of the sample of comparison transactions before adjusting them by market change. On the one hand, this would give us the most up-to-date idea of the age adjustment factor. On the other hand, the construction of the age adjustment factor would just be based on two sales that would endanger the quality of the result. The second option is to apply the same factor of market change to all comparison sales. This could lead to a more imprecise adaption of the market level, but would base the estimation of the age adjustment factor on a broader sample. Pondering both options, the latter seems more favorable.

The market change factor MCF is the quotient of the present charter market level ML_p and the average market level during the time of the comparison sales $\mathrm{ML}_{(p-1)}$, as per Eq. (10.5).

$$\mathrm{MCF} = \frac{\mathrm{ML}_p}{\mathrm{ML}_{(p-1)}} \tag{10.5}$$

The present market level ML_p is the mean of all charter rates (CR) fixed in the respective segment, where M represents the total amount of fixtures in the respective segment in period p, as per Eq. (10.6).

$$\mathrm{ML}_p = \frac{\sum_{i=1}^{M} \mathrm{CR}_{ip}}{M} \tag{10.6}$$

The average market level during the time of the comparison sales $\mathrm{ML}_{(p-1)}$ equals the mean of all charter rates (CR) fixed in the period when all comparison sales have been sold $p-1$, while O denotes the total amount of fixtures in period $p-1$, as per Eq. (10.7).

$$\mathrm{MP}_{(p-1)} = \frac{\sum_{i=1}^{O} \mathrm{CR}_{ip-1}}{O} \tag{10.7}$$

Setting in both formulas, we derive the following equation of market change. Intuitively it is the average charter rate of the respective segment in period p divided by the average charter rate of the respective segment in period $p-1$, as per Eq. (10.8).

$$\mathrm{MCF} = \frac{\mathrm{ML}_p}{\mathrm{ML}_{(p-1)}} = \frac{\frac{\sum_{i=1}^{M} \mathrm{CR}_{ip}}{M}}{\frac{\sum_{i=1}^{0} \mathrm{CR}_{ip-1}}{O}} \tag{10.8}$$

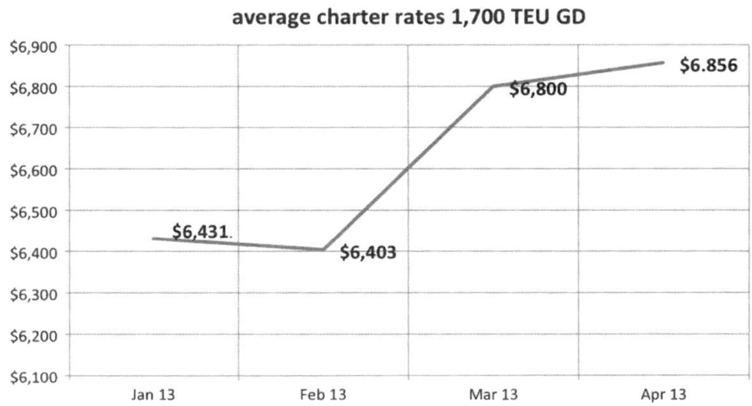

Fig. 10.1 Development of average charter rate January until April 2013

Now we can simply multiply each price of the comparison sale with the market change factor MCF before conducting the AELD. This procedure will make our result more present-orientated.

Recalling the numerical example of Sect. 10.3.3, it requested to estimate the value of the Titanic Voyager in April 2013. However, the comparison sales took place between January and March 2013. As the graph (Fig. 10.1) shows the charter market has improved during this time.

The average current charter rate for April equals \$6,856, as per Eq. (10.9), while the average charter rate for the first quarter of 2013 (January till March) equals \$6,503, as per Eq. (10.10). The market change factor equals the current average charter market level divided by the charter market level during the time of the comparison sales (in this case the first quarter of 2013), as per Eq. (10.11).

$$\mathrm{ML}_p = \frac{\sum_{i=1}^{M} \mathrm{CR}_{ip}}{M} \approx \$6{,}856 \tag{10.9}$$

$$\mathrm{ML}_{(p-1)} = \frac{\sum_{i=1}^{O} \mathrm{CR}_{ip-1}}{O} \approx \$6{,}503 \tag{10.10}$$

$$\mathrm{MCF} = \frac{\mathrm{ML}_p}{\mathrm{ML}_{(p-1)}} = \frac{\frac{\sum_{i=1}^{M} \mathrm{CR}_{ip}}{M}}{\frac{\sum_{i=1}^{0} \mathrm{CR}_{ip-1}}{O}} = \frac{\$6{,}856}{\$6{,}503} \approx 1.054 \tag{10.11}$$

By multiplying the observed comparison price with the market change factor MCF, the market-adjusted comparison price (MACP) is obtained (Table 10.3).

Table 10.3 Market-adjusted comparison price (MACP) of suitable comparison transactions

Name	TEU	Reefer	Gear	Built	Date	MACP
Vessel A	1,740	300	Geared	2006	January 13	$14,229,000
Vessel B	1,645	120	Geared	1997	January 13	$4,216,000
Vessel C	1,730	200	Geared	1997	February 13	$4,216,000
Vessel D	1,730	200	Geared	1998	February 13	$4,743,000
Vessel E	1,730	250	Geared	2002	March 13	$7,526,000
Vessel F	1,620	145	Geared	2003	March 13	$7,905,000
Vessel G	1,620	145	Geared	2003	March 13	$7,905,000
Vessel H	1,620	145	Geared	2003	March 13	$7,905,000

10.4.2 Adjusting the Age Adjustment Factor

Previously we assumed that a vessel would depreciate at a rate of 5 % per annum. However, this assumption is unrealistic because the pace of age-related attrition changes over time depending on the market situation. If we could define a function of age-related attrition depending on the market situation, the slope of the function would equal the rate of depreciation. If we assume exponential depreciation, it is relatively easy to estimate the function of vessel value development if you have at least two comparison sales (or the new building price). It is the negatively sloped function that minimizes the squares of the distance between the sales and mean. When the vessel's value reaches its scrap value, the value will remain equal to the scrap value. Hence, we will change our age adjustment function slightly by introducing the variable that denotes the annual change in percent.

$$\begin{aligned} &\text{If } \mathrm{AC}_i \geq \mathrm{AR} \text{ and } \mathrm{AAP}_i > \mathrm{SV}_i \rightarrow \text{ then } \mathrm{AAP}_i = \mathrm{PC}_i \times (1+\alpha)^{(\mathrm{AC}_i - \mathrm{AR})} \\ &\text{else if } \mathrm{AC}_i < \mathrm{AR} \text{ and } \mathrm{AAP}_i > \mathrm{SV}_i \rightarrow \text{ then } \mathrm{AAP}_i = \mathrm{PC}_i \times (1-\alpha)^{(\mathrm{AR} - \mathrm{AC}_i)} \\ &\text{else } \mathrm{AAP}_i = \mathrm{SV}_i = \mathrm{ldt}_i \times \mathrm{SP} \end{aligned} \tag{10.12}$$

The function $f(t)$ is the function of age-related attrition. While y_0 stands for the vessel's value at $t = 0$, t denotes the respective age and α is the rate of depreciation.

$$f(t) = y_0 \cdot (1-\alpha)^t \tag{10.13}$$

So if we recall our example of Sect. 10.3.3, we will have to test the age adjustment process. We have to find out whether the assumed 5 % were appropriate.

Before we can check the pace of depreciation, we have to adjust the price according to the ratio of the other attributes. Recalling the formula 10.3 of attribute adjustment, we need to replace the age adjusted price (AAP) by the price of the comparison vessel (PC) and we get the attribute adjusted price (ATAP). That is the sales price of each comparison vessel adjusted by other attributes (capacity and reefer plugs), but without age adjustment.

Table 10.4 Age, price, and attribute-adjusted price (ATAP) of comparison vessels

Name	Age	Price	ATAP
Vessel A	7	\$13,500,000	\$13,057,000
Vessel B	16	\$4,000,000	\$4,185,000
Vessel C	16	\$4,000,000	\$3,923,000
Vessel D	15	\$4,500,000	\$4,413,000
Vessel E	11	\$7,140,000	\$6,968,000
Vessel F	10	\$7,500,000	\$7,912,000
Vessel G	10	\$7,500,000	\$7,912,000
Vessel H	10	\$7,500,000	\$7,912,000

$$\mathrm{ATAP}_i = \frac{\frac{\mathrm{TEU}_r \times 30}{\mathrm{TEU}_{c_i}} + \frac{\mathrm{REEFER}_r}{\mathrm{REEFER}_{c_i}}}{31} \times \mathrm{PC}_i \tag{10.14}$$

If we do this adjustment for every vessel, we will obtain the following table of age and attribute adjusted prices (ATAP), as per Table 10.4.

An appropriate method to estimate the age-related attrition of a vessel's value is the ordinary least square method.[5] Recalling the formula of age-related attrition [Eq. (10.13)], we notice that it is a non-linear function. Thus, we have to transform it into logarithmic form to apply the ordinary least square method [Eq. 10.15].

$$f(t) = y = y_0 \cdot (1-\alpha)^t \Rightarrow \log y = \log y_0 + t \cdot \log(1-\alpha) \tag{10.15}$$

$$Y = \beta + t \cdot \lambda \tag{10.16}$$

In a first step we calculate the residual sum of squares for the logarithm of the attribute adjusted price (Y) and the age (t). In detail we calculate the mean for Y and t, calculate for every Y and every t the squared distance to the respective mean and cumulate the results. Afterwards we have to calculate the covariation of t and Y. This is the sum of the multiplier of the distance between a vessel's t and its mean and the distance of a vessel's Y and its mean.

$$\begin{aligned} S_{YY} &= \sum (Y_i - \hat{Y})^2 \\ S_{tt} &= \sum (t_i - \hat{t})^2 \\ S_{tY} &= \sum (t_i - \hat{t}) \cdot (Y_i - \hat{Y}) \end{aligned} \tag{10.17}$$

Finally, we have to estimate the estimators λ and β according to the following formula. The λ equals the covariation of t and Y divided by the sum of squares of t. The β equals the mean of Y minus λ times the mean of t.

[5]The ordinary least square method is presented and analyzed in standard textbooks of statistics and econometrics.

Table 10.5 Age (t) and logarithm of attribute-adjusted price (Y) of comparison vessels

Name	t	Y
Vessel A	7	7.115
Vessel B	16	6.621
Vessel C	16	6.593
Vessel D	15	6.644
Vessel E	11	6.843
Vessel F	10	6.898
Vessel G	10	6.898
Vessel H	10	6.898

$$\lambda = \frac{S_{tY}}{S_{tt}}$$
$$\beta = \hat{Y} - \lambda \cdot \hat{t} \qquad (10.18)$$

Assuming no disturbance variable, we can now calculate the market value of each vessel depending on its age. To calculate residuals (estimate error terms denoted $\overline{u}$), we have to subtract the estimated prices $\overline{Y}$ from the observed prices Y. Finally, we calculate the sum of squared residuals $S_{\overline{uu}}$, which serves as a measure for the goodness of the model.

$$\overline{u}_i = Y_i - \overline{Y}_i$$
$$S_{\overline{uu}} = \sum \overline{u}_i^2 \qquad (10.19)$$

One could criticize the assumption of a constant rate of age-related attrition as unrealistic, because it may differ over a vessel's life cycle. Even though this criticism may be justifiable in some cases, for our purpose it is sufficient to assume a constant rate of age-related attrition.

To perform the ordinary least square method with our example, we have to transform the value of the attribute adjusted prices into the logarithmic form. While t represents the vessel's age, Y is the logarithm of attribute adjusted price (ATAP).

Based on Table 10.5 the mean of t ($\hat{t} = 11.875$) and the mean of Y ($\hat{Y} = \$6.814$) are estimated; and apply the above formula to derive the residual sum of squares for the logarithms of attribute adjusted price (Y) and age (t).

$$S_{YY} = \sum (Y_i - \hat{Y})^2 \approx 0.227$$
$$S_{tt} = \sum (t_i - \hat{t})^2 \approx 78.875 \qquad (10.20)$$
$$S_{tY} = \sum (t_i - \hat{t}) \cdot (Y_i - \hat{Y}) \approx -4.202$$

Finally, we have to estimate the estimators λ and β by plugging in the calculated values.

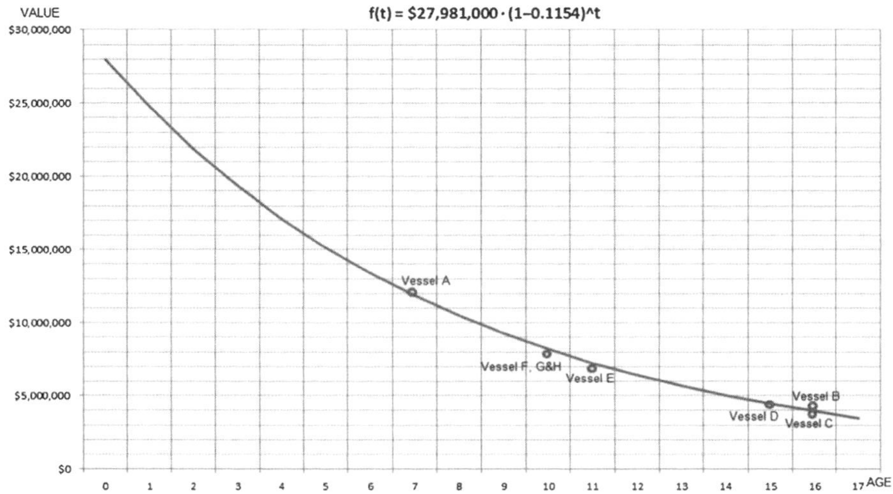

Fig. 10.2 Estimated function of the "Titanic Voyager's" value depending on age

$$\lambda = \log(1-\alpha) = \frac{S_{tY}}{S_{tt}} = \frac{-4.202}{78.875} \approx -0.0532$$

$$\beta = \log y_0 = \hat{Y} - \log(1-\alpha)\cdot\hat{t} = 6.814 + 0.0532 \times 11.875 \approx 7.45 \qquad (10.21)$$

For simplicity, we waive to calculate the residuals and simply retransfer the logarithms.

$$\begin{aligned} (1-\alpha) &= 10^{\log(1-\alpha)} = 10^{-0.0532} \approx 0.8846 \\ \alpha &= 1 - 0.8846 = 0.1154 \\ y_0 &= 10^{\log(y_0)} = 10^{\$7.45} \approx \$27,981,000 \end{aligned} \qquad (10.22)$$

The y_0 denotes the fixed parameter of our equation, α represents the slope. According to our model, the age related attrition is at 11.54 % p.a. In the depressed market situation, which was prevalent in the first half of 2013 the age related attrition was much faster than originally anticipated. This is congruent with our expectations. According to our model the new building price is slightly below $28 million (see Fig. 10.2). Even though this is almost three million US dollars higher than the actual new building price, it is still a good estimation considering it is just based on second-hand sales. It could be considered to include the new building price in our sample, but for estimating the rate of age related attrition of a second-hand vessel, this seems rather unfavorable because it would rather bias the estimation.

Now, we can carry out our adjustment under the assumption of a depreciation of approximately 11.54 %. In a first step we form the age-adjusted price of the market-adjusted comparison price (MACP) for each vessel, which we calculated above.

$$
\begin{aligned}
AAP_{\text{Vessel A}} &= MACP_{\text{Vessel A}} \times (1-0.1154)^{(2006-2001)} = \$14{,}229{,}000 \times 0.8846^5 \approx \\
&\approx \$7{,}707{,}000 \\
AAP_{\text{Vessel B}} &= MACP_{\text{Vessel B}} \times (1+0.1154)^{(2001-1997)} = \$4{,}216{,}000 \times 1.1154^4 \approx \\
&\approx \$6{,}526{,}000 \\
AAP_{\text{Vessel C}} &= MACP_{\text{Vessel C}} \times (1+0.1154)^{(2001-1997)} = \$4{,}216{,}000 \times 1.1154^4 \approx \\
&\approx \$6{,}526{,}000 \\
AAP_{\text{Vessel D}} &= MACP_{\text{Vessel D}} \times (1+0.1154)^{(2001-1998)} = \$4{,}723{,}000 \times 1.1154^3 \approx \\
&\approx \$6{,}582{,}000 \\
AAP_{\text{Vessel E}} &= MACP_{\text{Vessel E}} \times (1-0.1154)^{(2002-2001)} = \$7{,}525{,}560 \times 0.8846^1 \approx \\
&\approx \$6{,}657{,}000 \\
AAP_{\text{Vessel F}} &= MACP_{\text{Vessel F}} \times (1-0.1154)^{(2003-2001)} = \$7{,}905{,}000 \times 0.8846^2 \approx \\
&\approx \$6{,}186{,}000 \\
AAP_{\text{Vessel G}} &= MACP_{\text{Vessel G}} \times (1-0.1154)^{(2003-2001)} = \$7{,}905{,}000 \times 0.8846^2 \approx \\
&\approx \$6{,}186{,}000 \\
AAP_{\text{Vessel H}} &= MACP_{\text{Vessel H}} \times (1-0.1154)^{(2003-2001)} = \$7{,}905{,}000 \times 0.8846^2 \approx \\
&\approx \$6{,}186{,}000
\end{aligned}
\tag{10.23}
$$

Now we have to adapt the age-adjusted price (AAP) of each vessel according the ratio of the Titanic Voyager and the respective comparison vessel to calculate the adjusted price (AP) for each vessel.

$$
\begin{aligned}
AP_{\text{Vessel A}} &= \frac{\frac{1{,}710 \times 30}{1{,}740} + \frac{150}{300}}{31} \times \$7{,}707{,}000 \approx \$7{,}455{,}000 \\
AP_{\text{Vessel B}} &= \frac{\frac{1{,}710 \times 30}{1{,}645} + \frac{150}{120}}{31} \times \$6{,}526{,}000 \approx \$6{,}828{,}000 \\
AP_{\text{Vessel C}} &= \frac{\frac{1{,}710 \times 30}{1{,}730} + \frac{150}{200}}{31} \times \$6{,}526{,}000 \approx \$6{,}400{,}000 \\
AP_{\text{Vessel D}} &= \frac{\frac{1{,}710 \times 30}{1{,}730} + \frac{150}{200}}{31} \times \$6{,}582{,}000 \approx \$6{,}455{,}000 \\
AP_{\text{Vessel E}} &= \frac{\frac{1{,}710 \times 30}{1{,}730} + \frac{150}{250}}{31} \times \$6{,}657{,}000 \approx \$6{,}497{,}000
\end{aligned}
$$

$$\text{AP}_{\text{Vessel F}} = \frac{\frac{1{,}710\times30}{1{,}620} + \frac{150}{145}}{31} \times \$6{,}186{,}000 \approx \$6{,}525{,}000$$

$$\text{AP}_{\text{Vessel G}} = \frac{\frac{1{,}710\times30}{1{,}620} + \frac{150}{145}}{31} \times \$6{,}186{,}000 \approx \$6{,}525{,}000$$

$$\text{AP}_{\text{Vessel H}} = \frac{\frac{1{,}710\times30}{1{,}620} + \frac{150}{145}}{31} \times \$6{,}186{,}000 \approx \$6{,}525{,}000$$

$$\text{PR} = \frac{\sum_{i=1}^{N} \text{AP}_i}{8} =$$

$$= \frac{1000 \times (7{,}455 + 6{,}828 + 6{,}400 + 6{,}455 + 6{,}497 + 6{,}525 + 6{,}525 + 6{,}525)}{8}$$

$$\Rightarrow \text{PR} \approx \$6{,}651{,}000 \tag{10.24}$$

Hence, the estimated market value of the Titanic Voyager is approximately \$6,651,000.[6]

10.4.3 *Incorporation of Other Attributes and Adaption of the Attribute Adjustment*

If we recall the attribute adjustment conducted before, we only considered capacity, and to a minor degree the special feature of reefer plugs to have an influence on the price besides the major factor of age. Although this composition of the attribute adjustment factor can be justified in this case, the influence of the attributes can change over time. Thus, we need to evaluate the influence of attributes on the sales price at times. By constructing a simple multiple linear model of the influence of attributes on price, we can apply the ordinary least square method to estimate the respective influence of attributes on sales prices. While P constitutes the endogenous variable price, x denotes the respective attribute and β the attribute's influence on price. The letter σ is the error term which represents the price's non-explicable part.

$$P = \alpha + \beta_1 x_1 + \beta_2 x_2 + \cdots + \beta_n x_n + \sigma \tag{10.25}$$

By applying hypothesis testing, we can see whether the respective attribute has a significant influence on the price or not. In the latter case, we can ignore the attribute for our attribute adjustment. The estimated individual β gives us

[6]The results of AELD and QAAELD calculated in our example are almost identical because the increased age-related attrition is compensated by the risen market level.

an estimation of the weight the respective attribute should have in the attribute adjustment factor. Multiple linear regressions via ordinary least square method and testing of hypothesis can relatively easily be conducted with the help of econometric software packages. However, it requires some experience as well as econometric expertise to perform the process of estimation, testing and readapting of the linear model. A more detailed explanation of this procedure would go beyond the scope of discussion.

10.4.4 Ex-Post Auditing of the Result

After having conducted this procedure, it is important not to take the obtained result for granted, but to test its validity also on a qualitative basis. We have to question the result and ask whether it is realistic. Does it make sense compared to other available data as new building prices, charter markets, different segments etc.? Here should be utilized what could be called "broker's intuition". The result should be challenged concerning relevant market information. Such information can be among others different opinions, ongoing negotiations or market sentiment.

Reviewing our example, we can resume that our result is realistic. The underlying model of age related attrition does illustrate adequately the lifecycle development of a 1,700 TEU container vessel in the depressed market of 2013. Considering the observed market transactions and the attribute differences the market value of $6,651,000 is a reasonable estimate of a vessel that has the characteristics of the Titanic Voyager.

10.5 Conclusion

In this chapter, we derived a method of assessing the value of an ocean-going vessel. It is mathematically defined and delivers robust results based on actual market transactions. Through the adaption of the age-adjustment factor and the incorporation of market change, the model allows for market dynamics. Thus, the result is present-orientated and factors in age-related attrition and other influences of attributes on the market price accurately. However, the goodness of the result depends to a certain degree on the available comparison sales.

The Qualitative Adjusted Algebraic Estimation on basis of the Last Done (QAAELD) approach offers a reasonable alternative to ordinary desktop valuation and the LTAV method. Concerning the first, QAAELD is precisely defined, delivers results that are more robust, and is less likely to be arbitrary. Compared to the LTAV method, QAAELD has the advantage that it is present-orientated and based on real market transactions, while the LTAV is past-orientated and its results are in danger of being hypothetical. However, these different approaches should not necessarily be considered as competing with each other but should rather be viewed as complementary alternatives of vessel valuation.

Part IV
Institutional Framework

Chapter 11
Shipping Finance in Greece

Vera P. Alexandropoulou

Abstract Shipping has always played a vital role in the Greek economy. Through the years, it has been—and still remains—one of the few industries (if not the only one) where Greece has the lead in the world. According to the 2012 UN Review of Maritime Transport (UN Conference on Trade and Development – UNCTAD (2012) Review of Marine Transport 2012. ISBN 978-92-1-112860-4), Greece continues to have the largest merchant fleet in the world as a percentage of the world's total deadweight tonnage (dwt). The following analysis takes a look at the different financing options available to shipping companies in Greece, including the necessary conditions and procedures for obtaining approval of a shipping loan. It focuses, in particular, on the modern financial instruments and methods that shipping companies employ to fund their investment projects.

11.1 History of Shipping and Ship Finance in Greece

Like most industries, Greek shipping has relied on both traditional and less traditional methods of financing. Historically, ship financing came from the private funds of emerging strong maritime families, mainly from the islands of the Aegean. The use of these "savings," coupled with the ability of the Greeks to share their expertise with respect to international markets for trade, insurance and financing, as well as by pooling resources whenever needed, led to the impressive expansion of the Greek merchant fleet.

Following the Greek revolution, when Greek independence was achieved in 1832, the Greek merchant navy had around 700 ships. This number doubled to 1,450 within 20 years due to the increased shipbuilding activity at major yards within Greece. Around 1870, the Greeks became aware of the fact that they, too, had to

V.P. Alexandropoulou (✉)
Law Firm, Lawyer and Solicitor, Theatrou 53, Pireaeus, Greece
e-mail: vera_alex@post.harvard.edu

O. Schinas et al. (eds.), *HSBA Handbook on Ship Finance*,
DOI 10.1007/978-3-662-43410-9_11,

purchase steam-driven vessels to maintain their standing as a maritime nation even though steamships had been introduced more than 50 years earlier. However, these new vessels did not come cheap. Although the government ordered several vessels, private shipping companies used traditional financing methods, like grouping the resources of owners, captains, seamen and their relatives, so that they would be able to expand.

More often than not, they also had to look for older vessels, because funding was scarce, and older vessels were less expensive. Greek seamanship was of a very high quality and the Greeks were able to run their ships more efficiently and with smaller crew, with the owners themselves often sailing with the vessels. The result was that by 1901, Greece had over 1,150 sailing ships and 150 steamships.

Following World War I, when nearly 60 % of the Greek merchant fleet was destroyed, and then the Great Depression of 1929, Greek shipping again faced very challenging times. At the end of World War II, the Greek government provided funding for Greek ship-owners in the form of guarantees, and over 100 Liberties and seven T2 tankers were bought by various owners. Liberty-type ships had been built during WWII in the US and were lying idle as surplus war equipment. This, in essence, was the beginning of modern Greek shipping, and over the next 40 years, Greece came to control the largest merchant fleet in the world.

Additionally, the adaptability of the Greeks to changing markets and political and legislative requirements, and even their readiness to relocate, depending on where the business for shipping was primarily located, have proved to be exceptionally effective over time (Polemis 1995).

Today, the Greek shipping industry is the global leader in terms of both tonnage controlled and the nation's contribution to global transportation, logistics, and world trade. In 2011, there were a total of 762 shipping companies based in Greece. The number of Greek vessels was 4,714 and the 30 largest owners held 52 % of the Greek fleet (Bockmann 2012). The cyclical nature of shipping, both in terms of freight rates, vessel values, shareholder returns and financing, constantly presents new challenges in an increasingly complex and competitive setting.

11.2 Types of Ship-Owning Companies

Shipping is a genuinely global trade market. The tax regime prevailing for international shipping in Greece is particularly favorable to shipping companies. The types of companies through which this activity may be pursued are:

1. General commercial companies:

   (a) Companies limited by shares (S.A.) (which operate in accordance with the provisions of Law 2190/1920, as amended).
   (b) Limited partnerships (Ltd) (which operate in accordance with the provisions of Law 3190/1955).
   (c) General partnerships and limited partnerships (which operate in accordance with the provisions of the Civil Code and the Commercial Law).

2. Commercial companies that are designed for maritime activities
   (a) Greek Maritime Company (NE) (Law 959/1979), for all types of ships;
   (b) Special Maritime Enterprise (ENE) (Art. 16 and Art. 13 L.D. 2687/1953 and Law 959/1979, as amended by Law 2987/2002) for oceangoing vessels;
   (c) Shipping Company for Pleasure Yachts (NEPA) (Law 3182/2003) used for professional pleasure yachts;
   (d) Investment Company in Oceangoing Vessels (EEPN) (Law 2823/2000), a type of holding company mainly for listing its shares on the Athens Stock Exchange;
   (e) Partnership for co-ownership of vessels (Art. 10 of the Code of Private Maritime Law), occasionally used for small local vessels; and
3. Offshore companies:
   This is perhaps the most widely used company type for oceangoing vessels under the Greek flag or foreign flags, based mainly in Liberia, the Marshall Islands, Panama, Malta, Cyprus, and the British Virgin Islands.

11.3 Legal Framework

11.3.1 The Three Main Pillars

The first piece of legislation that contributed to the development of shipping was legislative decree L.D. 2687/1953 (Investment and protection of foreign capital). Article 13 of L.D. 2687/1953 considered ships over 1,500 GRT as foreign capital. It allowed their registration under Greek flag in the ownership of a non-Greek enterprise but controlled by Greek nationals to at least 51 % of their capital stock, and provided extended privileges and protection to mortgagees. The provisions of L.D. 2687/1953 allowed ship-owners to change the flag of the ships and to sell, mortgage or charter them freely to foreigners without requiring any additional license.

Moreover, L.D. 2687/1953 offered assistance, dispensations and guarantees to ship-owners and mortgagees as to the free disposal of foreign exchange, derived from the management or sale of the ships, the composition of the crew, the taxation, the fitting, the administration and management of the shipping business and the settlement of cases arising from the application of these provisions by arbitration. In addition, the formalities related to the registration of the ships or to the registration or discharge of mortgages were simplified.

Historically, L.D. 2687/1953 (which falls within the protection afforded by Article 107 of the Greek Constitution) was intended to protect foreign investments in Greece and had constitutional status. It overrides common law, cannot be replaced or amended by a legislative Act, and, therefore, offers a secure legal framework through the registration and operation of vessels under the Greek flag.

The second piece of legislation consists of two major statutes that were introduced into the Greek maritime reality in 1967 and 1968 (Law 89/1967—the companies formed under these laws are widely known as Law 89 companies - and Law 378/1968). These allowed foreign shipping companies that operate in Greece through a management company to establish a branch office in Greece under favorable tax treatment and other benefits. This legislation, which now applies only to shipping and related enterprises, has withstood the test of time and practically all shipping companies are established and are operating under this regime. Provided that a shipping company is created under the legal structures of Law 89, it is exempt from any corporate income tax related to the shipping activity.

Law 89/1967 has been replaced by Article 25 of Law 27/1975, the third piece of legislation favorable to shipping. A typical ship management company in Greece is a foreign company (usually based in Liberia or the Marshall Islands) which has an office in Greece, according to Article 25 of Law 27/1975, as amended (former Law 89/1967). A Law 89 company is probably one of the most attractive forms for shipping enterprises, mainly because of the straightforward method where they can be established, and the tax benefits it provides to them and the stable legal environment where it operates. The main features of this law are as follows:

1. The established branch or office shall engage only in:
   (a) The administration, management, chartering, brokerage of vessels under Greek or foreign flag of registered tonnage over 500 tons (Excluding passenger and commercial vessels operating on domestic routes);
   (b) The representation of ship-owning companies or other foreign enterprises engaged in the same business as the above; and
   (c) The ownership or management of salvage tugs or tugboats under foreign flag of any tonnage.
2. The establishment permit is granted by a Ministerial Decision and is valid for 5 years (and is automatically renewed).
3. The application for the permit is submitted along with the supporting documents.
4. Within two (2) months from the publication of the ministerial decision approving the establishment, the company must deposit a bank guarantee of US$10,000 as security for the company's compliance with the provisions of Law 27/1975.
5. The Company should import a minimum of US$50,000 foreign exchange annually to cover all expenses of its office in Greece, and the income derived from its business activities is not subject to any taxation.

11.3.2 Registration Issues

Vessels may be registered under the Greek flag through the Greek register as well as under foreign flags through local shipping registries. Registration under the Greek flag may take place in two ways:

1. Registration pursuant to the Code of Public Maritime Law: all coastal shipping vessels (unlike oceangoing vessels) are registered through this method; and
2. Registration of a vessel as a foreign investment, pursuant to Art. 13 of L.D. 2687/1953, a method most commonly used for oceangoing vessels. Vessels may be registered under foreign flags in Greece through local or correspondent offices (consulates and maritime administration authorities) subject to the respective requirements of each jurisdiction. Typically, the flags of Malta, Liberia, the Marshall Islands, Panama, Bahamas, and Cyprus are preferred.

11.4 Taxation

Although both LD 2687/1953 and Law 89/1967 provide tax incentives for shipping, Law 27/1975 is the main legislative instrument dealing with the taxation of shipping.

One of the differences of the shipping industry in Greece, if not the main one, with all other industries, is how shipping is taxed. Unlike other sectors, where taxation is imposed on profits made, shipping follows a tonnage tax system. Under Greek law, income from shipping activities is taxed based on the gross registered tonnage of the ship. In simple terms, the tax in shipping is calculated not according to the profit earned, but according to the tonnage of each ship. Whatever tax is due, based on the tonnage of the ship, is the only tax the ship-owner has to pay, and no other. Payment of this tax results in exemption from any other obligation of corporate/income tax, and this exemption also applies to shareholders. The exemption also extends to cover income earned from the sale of the vessels as well as any insurance indemnity claimed.

This tonnage tax system has many advantages for businesses. First, it is very simple and easy to understand. There are no complications, it is a streamlined process, which reduces the possibility of error and more importantly, the running costs of the business. Second, it offers certainty as it involves a one-off calculation without the need to re-examine it at the end of each tax year. Unlike other tax rules that change frequently, the tonnage tax systems remains consistent. Third, tax rates payable under the tonnage tax systems are very competitive in comparison to the conventional tax rates. Like the tonnage tax system itself, the reason behind its existence is also simple: to bring and keep shipping business in Greece.

Greek flag vessels pay only a fixed tonnage tax (depending on the tonnage of the ship) without the need to file another tax return with local tax authorities regarding their annual income (Law 27/1975). Once this tax is paid, no (income) tax is due in relation to the profits arising out of the operation of a vessel or capital gains in case of sale of the ship, either by the ship-owning company or its shareholders up to the level of individual (natural person) shareholders.

Until recently, foreign flagships' shareholders were also exempt from any income tax in Greece, provided these ships are managed in Greece by a foreign company commonly established in Greece pursuant to Law 27/1975. This regime was constitutionally protected (Art. 107 of the Constitution) i.e. it cannot be altered even by an Act of Parliament. Transactions relating to a vessel registered under Art. 13, such as registration, sale and purchase, mortgage, deletion, etc. were free of any tax, charge, or dues. A similar (but not constitutionally protected) regime applies to vessels under foreign flag managed by a Law 89 Company.

However, such tax exemption, enjoyed by foreign flagships until now, has recently come to an end. Law 4110/23.1.2013, which was ratified by the Greek Parliament, has brought changes to the tax regime applicable to shipping activities. The changes concerned foreign-owning companies with vessels flying a foreign flag that are managed by companies based in Greece (Article 26 of Law 27/19.7.95). Under the new legislation, tax based on the tonnage tax system is now applicable to foreign flagships in the same way that it is applicable to Greek flagships. The assessment of tonnage tax is subject to a 5-year prescription period. This development has taken place following the agreement of the Union of Greek Shipowners, which voluntarily agreed to the imposition of the new tax.

Furthermore, Greek flag vessels owned by Greek legal entities that make calls on US ports are also exempt from US income tax pursuant to a bilateral treaty between Greece and the US.

Following the recent economic crisis, which has hit Greece particularly hard, there have been many voices in Greece calling for a change in the shipping tax status quo. The main argument put forward is that with new taxes being imposed daily on all other forms of economic activity, it seems strange, to say the least, that shipping remains unscathed. Some even go as far as to argue that imposing a tax on shipping income earned abroad would be the obvious solution to Greece's debt problems. The country's ship-owners transferred €140 billion ($173 billion) in untaxed receipts to the country in the 10 years to 2010, the Union of Greek Shipowners said in its annual report, citing central bank data. The figure compares to Greece's €280 billion government total debt at the end of March 2012 (Geiger 2012).

Thus, if there were ever any intention to change the shipping tax regime in Greece, there would be no better opportunity than the one presented by the economic crisis. Despite these calls, though, Greek governments have refused to bring about any changes in this area and the reason for this is twofold. First, the tax imposed on shipping in Greece is no different from the shipping tax regimes across Europe or other countries like, for example, Dubai. Second, shipping is a very mobile industry, with many shipping companies having international offices. Governments are concerned that the imposition of taxes on shipping income would cause the shipping companies to relocate to more favorable tax regimes. As a fallout, thousands of employees could be made redundant, not only from the shipping companies, but also from all the supply and service companies surrounding shipping. The most important reason is that shipping accounts for more than 50 % of foreign exchange receipts in Greece, without which the country would collapse. Therefore, it seems that a change in the shipping tax regime is unlikely.

11.5 Financing

Shipping is capital-intensive. Intensified competition in the shipping markets has led shipping companies to constantly pursue operational flexibility, managerial efficiency, and robust financial liquidity. A shipping company can attain business growth following either an internal or external growth path. Subject to freight market conditions, shipping companies can expand their fleet by building new vessels or purchasing second-hand vessels. On the other hand, mergers, acquisitions, and strategic alliances (pools) can be an alternative path to internal growth. Nevertheless, these growth strategies, in addition to the need for replacement of older vessels, require substantial capital support and careful financial planning.

Two broad approaches can be distinguished in shipping capital financing: self-sustained (internal) financing and external financing. Although traditionally, Greek shipping companies have relied on internal financing, using their cash reserves for funding, as they looked to expand, more modern and complex methods of financing became necessary. In the second financing approach, the company turns to the international capital markets to raise the required investment funds. Fund raising then can be realized through a combination of traditional bank lending, private placements, public issues of equity and bonds, commercial paper and, more recently, securitization.

Greek shipping companies employ a combination of traditional and modern financing instruments and even proceed to innovative hybrid financing combinations. Major financing tools for Greek shipping companies include new forms of bank lending, leasing, and syndication, initial public offerings (IPOs) in international equity markets, private equity funding, and high-yield bond issuances.

11.5.1 Loans

The most widely accepted form of company financing is through loans, particularly the ones that use a combination of funding projects and assets. The basic elements of a standard ship loan arrangement are relatively simple and straightforward. There are three basic types of borrowing:

1. The standard ship mortgage loan, with or without assignment of charter income.
2. Financing up to 100 % through a lease or bareboat/hire-purchase arrangement.
3. The commercial banks' loan policies as a whole follow the same pattern; however, different factors affect the behavior of each bank. All financial institutions tend to specialize in specific types of loans, and markets operating a structured loan portfolio develop their experience and confidence in their ability to manage credit risk.

A number of core issues are important for shipping loans. External finance (debt) should come up to a level and term-horizon (length of repayment period) such that prospective investment cash flows can sufficiently meet financing expenses. This point is interrelated to newbuilding price trends, second-hand vessel price prospects, and freight rate trends. The cost of funding, as reflected in ship lending interest rates, is a key issue of major concern. Despite the low interest rates in recent years, shipping is a highly volatile and cyclical industry and risk premiums on shipping loans have remained relatively tight. Currency risk is another important issue, associated particularly with potential credit facilities originating from shipyards. To this end, modern hedging instruments, including currency derivatives and currency swaps of varying durations, can contribute to foreign exchange risk control (Syriopoulos 2007). Ship-owners mainly prefer bank loans. At the moment, banks have limited capacity to provide loans for the well-known reasons pertaining to the credit markets' systemic problems. Shipping companies have difficulties meeting their obligations and most of them are already negotiating with the banks to reschedule their loans.

The most common form of ship finance is a secured bilateral or syndicated loan (in the form of a short or medium term loan, revolving credit facility or, less often, an overdraft) provided by Greek and/or international financial institutions for the financing or refinancing of:

1. The construction of one or more new vessels; or
2. The acquisition of one or more second-hand vessels. In case of refinancing, it is now common to encounter mezzanine finance provided typically by international private equity firms or hedge funds.

The upward trends in ship values and the volatile behavior of the shipping markets have led individual banks to pursue the sharing of lending obligations in shipping loans with other peers, thereby forming syndicated shipping loan schemes. This may derive from (internal/external) regulatory requirements, limited bank capital adequacy, lending constraints in certain markets and industries or, fundamentally, from a risk diversification approach.

Overall, banks prefer sharing shipping loan risks instead of bearing them alone, because funding required in shipping is rising exponentially.

11.5.2 Regular Type Structure of Term-Loan Ship Finance

This form includes the loan agreement and the security documents: a mortgage on the vessel(s), general and specific assignment of earnings, assignment of insurance, bank account pledges, (occasionally) share pledges, guarantees by the holding and/or managing companies and/or all or certain individual shareholders, who are the ultimate beneficial owners. Personal guarantees are also included. Currency and/or interest hedging arrangements have become usual practice in ship financing.

Against the advance of the loan amount, the bank requires as primary security a mortgage on the ship. The bank may issue mortgages on ships other than the one for which the funding is indented. It will normally take an assignment of any time charter and of the earnings of the ship so that it may benefit as assignee. The bank will also take an assignment of insurance policies so that in the event of a total or partial loss of the ship, the debt is suitably secured, and the bank is protected. This practice aims to ensure that the bank is almost completely secured, in that it will have priority over all other claims of other creditors.

11.5.3 Mortgage

In Greece, to make a mortgage more attractive to financiers, L.D. 2687/1953 provided for enhanced rights for the mortgagee. It allowed the mortgagee to take over the management of the ship in case of default. L.D. 3899/1958 introduced the concept of preferred mortgage, which further enhanced the rights of mortgagees.

There are two types of ship mortgage: (a) the mortgage pursuant to Articles 195–204 of the Code of Private Maritime Law (Law 3816/1958), and (b) the preferred mortgage, which is granted pursuant to Law 3899/1958 on vessels over 500 tons. In both cases, the mortgage is granted for a specific amount by notarial deed and is registered with the ships register; it constitutes a title giving the mortgagee a right in rem running in priority over any unsecured claims and constitutes an enforceable title.

A mortgagee may liquidate the mortgaged asset (i.e. the vessel) in a private sale or public auction and, in case of a preferred mortgage, the mortgagee has the right to assume management of the vessel. The standard Greek mortgage resembles mortgage on immovable property. However, such mortgages are not flexible.

11.5.4 Alternative Forms of Financing

As elsewhere in the world, in Greece, too, the most known alternative forms of financing have found favor with the shipping businesses. These include Leasing, Listing, Private Equity, and Bonds. As the business environment changes dynamically in the shipping industry, shipping companies are turning to new financial instruments and markets to finance their investment plans. Leasing is an alternative method in shipping finance that bears some similarities to bank lending. As mentioned, Greek shipping has stood out for its ability to adapt, rapidly and effectively, to market changes over time. In recent years, several shipping companies have seized the opportunity to grow their business or obtain additional financing by listing on international stock exchanges, primarily in the US, but also in the UK. The main source has been Initial Public Offerings (IPOs) and Follow-on Offerings. For example, Costamare's initial public offering at $12/sh took place in November 2010. At the time, CMRE boasted a current fleet of 41 vessels, with contracts for 4 additional vessels, and 3 newbuildings.[1] In March 2012, Costamare conducted a secondary public offering at $14 m.

This has also changed the shipping business, which has traditionally been cash-rich and family-run, and created corporate-profile businesses, which have succeeded in both attracting investors and securing finance. Similar transactions include Special Purpose Acquisition Companies (SPAC), which have also proved successful in raising equity and completing business transactions. A case in point is Nautilus Marine Acquisition Corporation.

Nautilus Marine Acquisition Corporation has listed shares on Nasdaq under the ticker NMAR after offloading 4.8 million units at US$10.00 a piece.[2] In July 2011, Nautilus Marine Acquisition Corporation, the newly-organized blank check company formed for the purpose of acquiring or merging with an operating business, announced the pricing of its initial public offering of 4,800,000 units at a price of US$10.00 per unit for gross proceeds of US$48,000,000. Each unit issued in the initial public offering consists of one share of common stock and one warrant to purchase one share of common stock at an exercise price of US$11.50 per share. In August 2011, the company announced that pursuant to its initial public offering, which was consummated on July 20, 2011, the units issued in the initial public offering automatically separated into the common stock and warrants underlying the units. Other examples of companies using SPACs include Navios/International Enterprises, Trinity Partners Acquisition Company/Frees eas, Ink and Star Maritime Acquisition Corp.[3]

In early November 2012, Aquasition Corp. announced the closing of its initial public offering. The initial public offering was for an aggregate of 5,000,000 units at US$10.00 per unit. Each unit consists of one share of common stock and one warrant. In addition, the underwriters had a 45-day option to purchase up to an additional 750,000 units from the Company at the initial public offering price to cover over-allotments, if any. The Company also announced the completion of a private placement of 337,750 units at US$10.00 per unit to founding shareholders and certain of their designees.[4] However, equity markets are cyclical and dependent

[1] See also COSTAMARE, News Releases 2010. Available via http://ir.costamare.com/news/2010

[2] See also Nautilus Marine Acquisition Corp, Akis Tsirigakis. Available via http://www.nautilusacquisition.com

[3] See also Special Purpose Acquisition Corporation (SPAC) Overview. Available via http://amershipfinancepartners.com/spac.htm.

[4] See also US Securities and Exchange Commission, File No.: 001-35715, Film No.: 121187753. Available via http://www.sec.gov/Archives/edgar/data/1546383/000114420412060152/0001144204-12-060152-index.htm.

on both the local and global economies. Shipping is an international business, and more recently, capital raising has proven to be difficult and sometimes impossible. However, listed Greek shipping companies are now firmly on the radar screen of the main markets, and followed closely by analysts across the globe.

Other forms of financing, which have also been used to finance the gap left by the traditional bank financing, have been the sale-and-leaseback deals and mezzanine finance. These forms of finance, nevertheless, still require significant equity participation by the owner and tend to be expensive. Sale-and-leaseback is also an effective way of freeing up capital in vessels, by selling them and then taking them back on time charter or bareboat charter (more often) over a long period. This enables the owner to close a back-to-back deal, show liquidity, and strengthen his/her balance sheet.

China has recently taken a much more active role in providing ship financing for Greek shipping companies. Following the spate of newbuilding orders of the last few years and in an effort to support their shipyards and related businesses, Chinese banks are offering attractive terms to owners willing to place orders at Chinese shipyards. Similarly, some shipyards have agreed to extend payment terms or even take equity positions in ships to secure orders, something that is attractive to Greek owners, and this form of seller's credit is becoming more popular.

At the beginning of 2012, a lot of hype was created about the signing of the Export Buyer Credit Syndicated facility between China Development Bank and Dryships, which took place on February 13, 2012. The facility was part of the US$5 billion Sino-Greek Shipping Finance Special Scheme that was announced by the Chinese Prime Minister, Mr. Wen Jiabao, during his visit to Greece in October 2010. The US$5 bn funding initiative aimed to strengthen the economic vitality of Chinese shipyards that were going through a rough time as a result of the global economic crisis, by increasing the sale of ships built in China. By the middle of the summer of 2012, though, the hype had subsided as the expected surge of new orders never came. Owners refrained from new orders after rates plunged and the combined capacity of oil tankers, container ships, and commodity carriers reached a record. Earnings from the industry averaged the lowest since 1999, according to the ClarkSea Index, a measure of freight rates for different vessel types published by Clarkson (Petrofin Research 2011). Some say that it is still early to draw conclusions, but everyone is certain that China is expected to take a more active role in ship financing in the coming years.

Furthermore, we have also seen the emergence of shipping funds, created in various jurisdictions, which also play an important role in attracting investments in Greek shipping. Funds act as a vehicle that provide a transparent structure and attract investors who would otherwise not contemplate investing in shipping. Although only a handful of these structures, which are directly related to Greek shipping, exists at present, their numbers will increase as investor appetite returns to the markets.

11.5.5 The Global Economic Crisis and the Effect on Ship Financing

Lately, as a result of the global financial crisis, ship financing has been going through one of the most turbulent periods in recent history. Difficulties such as the poor shipping market, reduced earnings and the falling values of vessels, over-supply of vessels, and slow demand for raw goods and finished products across all sectors have made the shipping business even more challenging than usual.

The above has been accentuated by further problems encountered within the Eurozone area, which have severely affected the ability of banks to lend as well as the cost of lending. However, it is not all doom and gloom. Financing of Greek shipping companies has increased overall from 2010 to 2011, due mainly to the increased appetite of non-Greek banks, which traditionally had either no exposure or very little exposure to shipping. This has been capitalized upon by the larger Greek shipping companies, which have been successful in obtaining uninterrupted financing, although under terms which are far less favorable than before the crisis (50 % loan-to-value (LTV) and 300–400 bps spread), but still enough to be able to sustain profitability. The case is not the same, though, for small and medium-sized operators, to whom the lending market is essentially closed. For these, self-funding is the only available way forward.

The recent decision of Commerzbank-Deutsche Schiffsbank to stop funding shipping businesses added to the difficult times shipping worldwide is facing. According to a recent article in the German financial newspaper Das Handelsblatt, the weaknesses of the German shipping businesses in covering additional funding, will benefit Greek and Chinese ship-owners (Kontogiannis 2012), as they might go into the German market to purchase ships on favorable terms.

Despite these positive glimpses, however, the agreement of the recent Private Sector Involvement (PSI program) has had serious effects on the ability of Greek banks to provide financing for shipping companies. The Greek government imposed a heavy haircut on Greek sovereign debt holders, which as a consequence, left Greek banks scrambling for liquidity. This, combined with the recession and the high cost of liquidity, has meant that Greek banks have been left almost dry of fresh funds for financing.

In the period between 2010 and 2011, funds made available for shipping by the four top Greek shipping banks fell by over 60 %. In addition, as a result of the high interest rates charged by the banks, the cost of borrowing has increased substantially. The future is also uncertain, with the capitalization of the banks due this autumn (2012) with over EUR 55 bn of fresh equity. The banks will be looking to lend profitably as well as maintain adequate reserves for their own future.

Greek banks account for about 25 % of the lending for Greek shipping portfolios, with the remaining 75 % coming mostly from other European banks. With the Eurozone crisis also well under way, this has meant that drawn funds have also been limited and expensive.

11.5.6 Examples of Ship Finance Transactions Involving Greek Companies

The examples provided below are selected from related business sources (Marine Money International 2010, 2011, 2012).

- **Selected Equity Deals 2010**
  - Example 1
    Issuer: Costamare Inc.—US$160 m Issued 13.3 m shares priced at US$12, below the expect range of US$15–17/share. The offering represents 22.1 % of the o/s shares. Proceeds will be used for general purposes and future vessel acquisitions. Quarterly dividend at US$0.25/share equating to 6.3 % yield. Greenshoe of 1.995 m shares.
  - Example 2
    Issuer: Tsakos Energy Navigation Limited—US$86 m. In a bought deal, CS purchased 6.7 m of the 7.6 m shares offered, with the Tsakos family buying the balance. The shares were paid at US$11.30, a discount of 8.3 % from the prior close. Proceeds will be used for fleet expansion and general corporate purposes.
  - Example 3
    Issuer: Navios Maritime Partners L.P.—US$112 m. Follow-on offering of 5.5 m shares at US$17.65, a discount of 5.1 % from prior close. Proceeds to fund fleet expansion and/or general partnership purposes. Greenshoe of 0.8 m shares exercised.
  - Example 4
    Issuer: Navios Maritime Acquisition Corporation—US$500 m. Filed self-registration to sell US$500 m of common stock, preferred stock, warrants and/or debt securities. Effective self-registration enabling company to sell up to US$500 m of common stock, preferred stock, warrants, and/or debt securities.

- **Selected Mergers and Acquisitions in 2010**
  Acquirer: Navios Maritime Acquisition Corp. US$587, Vessel Acquisition. Acquisition of seven Very Large Crude Carriers (VLCCs) from Shinyo. Financed by assumption of US$453 m of bank debt, the issuance of US$11 m of shares to the seller with the balance cash. Average age of fleet is 8.6 years with charter coverage of 8.8 years at US$40.4 K/day, plus profit sharing on five of the vessels.
- **Selected Loan Agreements**
  In Tables 11.1, 11.2 and 11.3 selected bilateral loans are presented.

Table 11.1 Bilateral loans 2010

Bank	Borrower (SPC)	Owner	Amount in m US$
Nouvelle Gedispa	Prime International Investor Group	Teamworks International S.A Greece	$1.0
Aegean Baltic Bank		Dynacom Tanker Management Ltd	$20.0
Aegean Baltic Bank		AVIN International SA	$10.0
Aegean Baltic Bank		Ciel Shippmanagement SA	$3.6
Emporiki Bank of Greece SA	Virgilia Ship Management Ltd		$40.4
Emporiki Bank of Greece SA	Virgilia Ship Management Ltd		$46.4
Emporiki Bank of Greece SA	SYRA Navigation Ltd		$10.7
Piraeus Bank AE	Ellie Shipholding Limited	Endeavour Shipping Co. SA Greece	$2.0
Martin Egnatia Bank SA	Brave Maritime		$22.4
Pancretan Cooperative Bank	Kalan Shipping Limited		$5.0
Bremer Landesbank Kreditanstalt	Babylon Shipping Company	Union Commercial, Greece	$11.0
Martin Egnatia Bank SA	Rema Maritime Ltd	Roussos Shipping SA	$15.0
FBB First Business Bank SA	Malena Shipping Com	Blue Ocean Maritime	$15.9
Emporiki Bank of Greece	Rumor Holding Ltd	Navios Maritime Holdings	$130.0

Source: Marine Money International (2010)

11.6 Concluding Remarks

Very few will doubt that Greek shipping, like most other economic activities, is going through some turbulent times. No one can be certain whether Greeks will maintain their leading position in world shipping and what damage they will sustain as a result of the economic crisis. It can certainly be expected that not everyone will come out of it unscathed. However, history has shown that Greek ship-owners have profound, first-hand experience, deep-rooted knowledge, the determination to meet any challenge, and to make the best of a difficult situation. How much difficult the situation is will be seen in the years to come.

Table 11.2 Bilateral loans 2011

Bank	Borrower (SPC)	Owner	Amount in m US$
Generosity Investments Inc	Perfetto Investments Inc	TMS Dry Ltd	$10.0
Cyprus Popular Bank Public Co. Ltd	Bugle Shipping Company Ltd	Niki Shipping Co. Inc.	$379.1
Credit Suisse AG	Phoenix Accord	Phoenix Energy Navigation	$64.6
Deutsche Bank	Phoenix Concord Inc	Phoenix Energy Navigation	$46.9
EFG Eurobank Ergasias SA	Shark Maritime SA	Sifnos Navigation SA	$18.5
EFG Eurobank Ergasias SA	Shark Maritime SA	Sifnos Navigation SA	$1.0
EFG Eurobank Ergasias SA	Blaze Shipping Ltd		$2.0

Source: Marine Money International (2011)

Table 11.3 Bilateral loans 2012

Bank	Borrower (SPC)	Owner	Amount in m US$
Wells Fargo Bank	Shikhar Ventures SA	Navios Maritime Holdings	$488.0
Cyprus Popular Bank Public Co	Monsoon NavigationCorporation	Elmira Tankers Mgmt SA	$13.1
Generosity Investment Inc	Perfetto Investments	TMS Dry Ltd	$10.0

Source: Marine Money International (2012)

References

Bockmann M (2012) China's shipyards fail to win orders as Greek owners Shun loans. Available via http://www.bloomberg.com/news/2012-06-07/china-s-ship-yards-fail-to-win-orders-as-greek-owners-shun-loans.html

Geiger F (2012) Greek shipping gets a free ride. World Street Journal Blogs. Available via http://blogs.wsj.com/eurocrisis/2012/08/15/greek-shipping-gets-a-free-ride

Kontogiannis P (2012) Greek ship owners cashing in on economic crisis. Europe Greek Reporter. Available via http://eu.greekreporter.com/2012/08/07/greek-ship-owners-cashing-in-on-economic-crisis/

Marine Money International (2010) Volume 26, Number 8, November/December 2010

Marine Money International (2011) Volume 27, Number 3, April/May 2011

Marine Money International (2012) Volume 28, Number 4, June/July 2012

Petrofin Research (2011) Greek shipping companies. Available via http://www.petrofm.gr/en-gb/mNews.aspx?ElementId=9a27528b-4100-427a-b0f3-185fcac00bd6

Polemis S (1995) The history of Greek shipping. The Poseidon Voyage. Available via Hellenic Electronic Center

Syriopoulos T (2007) Financing Greek shipping: modern instruments, methods and markets. In: Pallis A (ed) Maritime transport: the Greek paradigm. Research in transportation economics series. Elsevier, London

UN Conference on Trade and Development – UNCTAD (2012) Review of Marine Transport 2012. ISBN 978-92-1-112860-4

Chapter 12
New Turkish Law on Ship Finance

Kerim Atamer

Abstract On 1 July 2012, the new Turkish Commercial Code, as well as the Turkish Code of Obligations, has come into force. Later the same year, the Code on Financial Leasing, Factoring and Financial Institutions has been adopted. These legislative moves have brought about significant changes to the Turkish law regarding the finance of ships and new building. The purpose of this paper is to introduce the new legal framework with a view to establish interest and confidence in the Turkish market.

12.1 Introduction

The Turkish ship financing industry has witnessed significant legislative changes and various fundamental changes over the past three decades. In particular, with the new "Turkish Commercial Code[1]" ("N-TCC") coming into force on 1 July 2012, the law on ship finance has been substantially modernized.[2] The purpose of this paper is to shed some light on these issues. However, since the new Turkish legislation and the enforcement of ship mortgages have been outlined elsewhere recently (Atamer 2012, p. 75), the following overview will be limited to those substantive aspects of ship finance which have not been covered earlier.

[1]Türk Ticaret Kanunu, Tarih ["T"]: 13.1.2011, Sayı ["S"]: 6102, Resmi Gazete ["RG"] T: 14.2.2011, S: 27846.

[2]As for details on the new Turkish Maritime law see in English: several contributions in Turkish Maritime Law Association (2012), Günay (2007); in German: Atamer (2011), Atamer (2010), Atamer (2009, p. 91); in French: Ünan and İzzet et al. (2011); in Spanish: Atamer (2007, p. 479)

K. Atamer (✉)
Department of Maritime and Insurance Law, Istanbul University, Law School, 34116 Beyazit, Istanbul, Turkey
e-mail: kerimatamer@yahoo.com

O. Schinas et al. (eds.), *HSBA Handbook on Ship Finance*,
DOI 10.1007/978-3-662-43410-9_12,

References have been made in the course of this paper to several International Conventions and a number of legal sources from Germany, Switzerland, and Turkey. To highlight the point that two or more provisions of these different legal sources are identical or, at least, similar, the "equal to" sign (=) is used. Given that most of the terminology of Turkish Private and Procedural law has been adopted from German and Swiss sources, some of the original German terms and phrases have been included in the footnotes. This should make the information more accessible to readers from a German-speaking jurisdiction.

The law is stated as being applicable from 1 July 2012, which is the date when the new legislation has come into force.

12.2 Sources of Law

12.2.1 International Conventions

The new Turkish Maritime law has been primarily prepared on the basis of the latest International Conventions.[3] With regard to ship finance, two significant Conventions have been adopted[4]: the "International Convention on Maritime Liens and Mortgages[5]" ("ICLM"), made at Geneva on 6 May 1993, and its sibling, the "International Convention on Arrest of Ships[6]" ("ICAS"), made at Geneva on 12 March 1999. The provisions of these two Conventions have been incorporated into the N-TCC. Currently, the legislative preparations for Turkey's accession to these Conventions are underway. Both Conventions apply as a matter of *lex fori*.[7]

12.2.2 Conflict of Laws

12.2.2.1 The Code

The Turkish rules on Conflict of Laws are set out in the "Code of International Private and Procedural Law[8]" ("CIPL"). All legal affairs that contain a foreign element are governed by the CIPL.

[3] A full list of such Conventions with a comparison to the Conventions applicable in EU Countries is available at Atamer (2009, p. 114).

[4] Details in this respect have been set out at Atamer (2012, p. 76).

[5] As for detailed information on this Convention see Berlingieri (1996, 1995), Czerwenka (1994), Wersel (1996).

[6] As for detailed information on this Convention see Berlingieri (2011).

[7] Art. 13(1) ICLM, Art. 8(1) ICAS.

[8] Milletlerarası Özel Hukuk ve Usul Hukuku Hakkında Kanun (T: 27.11.2007, S: 5718), RG T: 12.12.2007, S: 26728. As for detailed information in English about this new Code see Tekinalp (2007, p. 313), Atamer (2010).

12.2.2.2 Rights *In Rem*

The "rights *in rem*[9]" on ships are governed by the law of the place of registration. This rule covers ownership, mortgages, usufruct, rights of retention, and other rights *in rem*. Taking into consideration the shipping practice of flagging-in and flagging-out, the "place of registration[10]" is further specified as the "register where the rights *in rem* are registered". Accordingly, where a ship under a foreign flag is allowed temporarily to fly the Turkish flag, the rights *in rem* on such a ship are still governed by the principal register. The same applies also in respect of ships registered in Turkey which are temporarily allowed to fly a foreign flag.

12.2.2.3 Maritime Liens

A new provision has been introduced in the N-TCC in respect of the law governing maritime liens. According to this rule,[11] which has been lifted from the ICAS,[12] maritime liens are subject to Turkish law if proceedings were brought in Turkey.[13] This solution corresponds to the consistent practice of the Turkish Supreme Court.

12.2.2.4 Contracts

The parties are left free to agree on the applicable law at the time of conclusion of the contract, or at any time thereafter.[14] In the absence of such a choice, the "closest connection" criterion applies. It is presumed that the contract is most closely connected with the law of the place where the party, which is to perform the characteristic obligation, has its principal place of business at the time of conclusion of the contract.[15]

---

[9]"Dingliche Rechte".

[10]Art. 22 CIPL. This provision has been adopted from Art. 45 of the German "Einführungsgesetz zum Bürgerlichen Gesetzbuch", as included by Art. 1 of the "Gesetz zum Internationalen Privatrecht für außervertragliche Schuldverhältnisse und für Sachen", Bundesgesetzblatt ["BGBl".] 1999 I 1026; as to which see Bundestags-Drucksache 14/343, p. 6. See Tekinalp (2007, p. 328).

[11]Art. 1320(3) N-TCC; see Atamer, (2011, p. 104 (II 1)).

[12]Art. 3(1)(e) ICAS

[13]As for the impact of this rule, see Atamer (2012, p. 78)

[14]Art. 24(1) and (3) CIPL

[15]Art. 24(4) CIPL; see Tekinalp (2007, p. 320)

12.2.3 *National Law*

12.2.3.1 Civil Law

Turkish Civil law is primarily based on Swiss law.[16] In particular, the "Turkish Civil Code[17]" ("TCivC") has been largely translated and adopted from the "Swiss Civil Code[18]" ("ZGB"). Again, the "Turkish Code of Obligations[19]" ("TCO") is essentially an abridged translation of the "Swiss Code of Obligations[20]". As such, the Turkish law of Rights *in rem* and Obligations is generally in line with the Swiss law on these subjects. In addition, supplementary legislation on, say, financial leasing, banking transactions, pledge on motor craft and the like, has also been developed on the basis of the Swiss–Turkish general provisions of Civil law.

12.2.3.2 Maritime Law

Until midnight of 30 June 2012, the primary source of Maritime law has been the "Turkish Commercial Code[21]" ("TCC") of 1956. The TCC had been drafted by the late Prof. Dr. Ernst Hirsch, who had been among the German academics those immigrated to Turkey before the Second World War. He has reported extensively about his work on Turkish law and legislation.[22] In respect of the rights *in rem* on ships, Hirsch chose as his source the respective pieces of German legislation of 1940, including the "Act Concerning Rights on Ships and Ships under Construction[23]" ("SchRG"), the "Ship Register Directive[24]" ("SchRegO") and other incidental legislation.[25] Hirsch has translated the essential rules from these German

---

[16]As for detailed information see Atamer (2008, p. 723), Damar and Rösler (2011, p. 617), Atamer (2009, p. 1505), Bandak (2008), Baysal (2008, p. 159), Buz (2007, p. 31).

[17]Türk Medeni Kanunu T: 22.11.2001, S: 4721, RG T: 8.12.2001, S: 24607; replacing: Türk Kanunu Medenisi T: 17.2.1926, S: 743.

[18]Schweizerisches Zivilgesetzbuch (10.12.1907), SR 210.

[19]Türk Borçlar Kanunu, T: 11.1.2011, S: 6098, RG T: 4/2/2011, Sayı: 27836; replacing: Borçlar Kanunu, T: 22.4.1926, S: 818, RG T: 8.5.1926, S: 366.

[20]Bundesgesetz (30.3.1911) betreffend die Ergänzung des Schweizerischen Zivilgesetzbuches (Fünfter Teil: Obligationenrecht), SR 220.

[21]Türk Ticaret Kanunu T: 29.6.1956, S: 6762, RG T: 9.7.1956, S: 9353.

[22]See Hirsch (1938, p. 369), Hirsch (1954, p. 201), Hirsch (1956, p. 157), Hirsch (1982) and finally Hirsch (2008).

[23]Gesetz über Rechte an eingetragenen Schiffen und Schiffsbauwerken (15.11.1940), Reichsgesetzblatt ["RGBl".] 1940 I 1499.

[24]Schiffsregisterordnung (19.12.1940), RGBl. 1940 I 1591.

[25]Namely: Verordnung zur Durchführung des Gesetzes über Rechte an eingetragenen Schiffen und Schiffsbauwerken (21.12.1940), RGBl. 1940 I 1609; Einrichtung und Führung des Schiffsregisters und des Schiffsbauregisters (23.12.1940), Deutsche Justiz ["DJ"] 1941, 42; Durchführung der Schiffsregisterverfügung (27.12.1940), DJ 1941, 62.

sources and used them, mostly verbatim, for the Turkish provisions. The N-TCC, which has come into force on 1 July 2012, has generally retained the same rules and provisions. Some changes and new rules have been introduced in connection with the incorporation of the ICML and ICAS into the N-TCC. Other changes reflect the explicit intention to create more harmony with the original German provisions. The provisions of the N-TCC are supplemented by the "Ship Register Directive[26]" ("SRD") of 1957, which is basically a translation of the SchRegO.[27]

Together with the N-TCC, the new "Code of Implementation and Enforcement of the N-TCC[28]" ("N-CIE") has also been adopted.[29] This Code sets out the transitional provisions.[30] As of 1 July 2012, all references to the TCC are deemed to have been made to the corresponding provisions of the N-TCC.[31] Other rules on Maritime law are to be found in particular Acts regarding, say, the International Register, financial leasing, and other incidental issues. These Acts will be considered later in their respective contexts.

12.3 Rights *In Rem*

12.3.1 Definition and Legal Qualification of "Ship"

Previous and new Turkish law does not settle on a singular definition of the term "ship". Rather, most pieces of legislation say in their respective provisions on "definitions" as to what qualifies as a ship within the meaning of that legislation. However, the new law finally clarifies a legal discussion that had been going on for a long time. Under previous laws and practices, it was believed, particularly by the Supreme Court, that ships registered in Turkey are to be treated as "immovable property" ("real estate"). This erroneous assumption has been set aside by explicit provisions of the new law, which state clearly that as a general rule, all Turkish and foreign "ships are movable property[32]". As such, all doubts as to whether ships might legally qualify as real estate have finally been abandoned. There are only few exceptions to this general principle, whereby Turkish and foreign ships are

---

[26]Gemi Sicili Nizamnamesi, RG T: 4.2.1957, S: 9526.

[27]It is expected that the SRD will be revised in due course so as to achieve full harmony with the N-TCC.

[28]Türk Ticaret Kanununun Yürürlüğü ve Uygulama Şekli Hakkında Kanun, T: 14.1.2011, S: 6103, RG T: 14.2.2011, S: 27846.

[29]The N-CIE is complementary to the N-TCC, and corresponds to what is known in German law as an "Einführungsgesetz".

[30]As for details see Atamer (2012, p. 86).

[31]Art. 7(1) N-CIE.

[32]Art. 936(1), Art. 1351(1) N-TCC, Art. 23(2) N-CEB introduced according to Art. 41(2)(a) N-CIE.

held subject to specifically identified provisions governing immovable property,[33] to take due account of registration issues. However, in each of those cases, it has been carefully reviewed whether any conflict is created thereby with the specific rules on ships, and if so, additional provisions have been introduced to remedy any such conflict.

12.3.2 Registration

Five different means of registration for ships are recognized under previous and new Turkish laws. These are introduced as follows.

12.3.2.1 National Ship Register

Introduction

The oldest is the "National Ship Register" ("NSR"), which is subject to the provisions of the N-TCC and SRD. NSRs are maintained at ten Turkish ports, including Istanbul and Izmir.[34] The legal provisions regarding the NSR have been compiled from the German sources listed earlier.[35] Ships admitted for registration at the NSR are defined on the basis of a decision of the German Federal Supreme Court[36] from 1951.

Rights to be Registered

In accordance with the German sources, Turkish law explicitly admits the registration of only four rights *in rem* in the NSR[37]:

1. The property (ownership) in the ship;
2. A ship mortgage;
3. A right on the ship mortgage, such as a pledge;
4. A usufruct.

---

[33]Art. 937(1), Art. 1351(1) N-TCC.

[34]Art. 1 SRD.

[35]See Sect. 12.2.3.2.

[36]Bundesgerichtshof (14.12.1951), LM §4 BinnSchG Nr. 3 ("Unter einem Schiff im Rechtssinne ist jedes schwimmfähige, mit einem Hohlraum versehene Fahrzeug von nicht ganz unbedeutender Größe zu verstehen, dessen Zweckbestimmung es mit sich bringt, daß es auf dem Wasser bewegt wird".).

[37]§15 SchRG = Art. 884 TCC = Art. 974 N-TCC.

In addition, a priority notice[38] may be recorded to protect any of the four rights *in rem*.[39] On the contractual side, financial leasing agreements in respect of ships must be registered.[40] Finally, the registration in the NSR of bareboat charters has been explicitly admitted under the new law.[41]

Turning to proceedings of maritime enforcement, the following steps will be notified to and entered with the NSR: the arrest of a ship,[42] a judgement upholding or setting aside a right *in rem*,[43] the passing of title to the purchaser upon the judicial sale of a ship,[44] and the deletion of registered rights *in rem* upon the judicial sale of a ship.[45]

Effect of Registration

The legal effect of entries made at the NSR is governed by provisions which have been translated from German rules.[46] The general principle is set out to the effect that where a party is registered as the owner, mortgagee, holder of a right on the mortgage, or the usufruct holder of the ship, it will be presumed that such entry is correct.[47] Therefore, third parties are allowed to rely upon the correctness of the NSR.[48] It follows that the NSR protects the positive reliance on the existence of registered rights and therefore admits the acquisition in good faith of the ship mortgage from a person having no or defective legal title to such ship.

However, it ought to be emphasized that the Turkish ship mortgage is identical with the German ship mortgage in that the registration does not provide any *prima facie* or conclusive evidence in respect of the claim that is secured by the mortgage.[49] As such, to give another example, if the claim ceased to exist, the transfer of the mortgage to a third party will not confer on that third party the right to enforce the mortgage for such claim that no longer exists. However, the parties are

---

[38]"Vormerkung".

[39]§10 SchRG = Art. 879 TCC = Art. 977 N-TCC.

[40]Art. 22(1) of the Financial Leasing Act (2012) (Finansal Kiralama, Faktoring ve Finansman Şirketleri Kanunu [T: 21/11/2012, s:6361])

[41]Art. 1121(1) N-TCC.

[42]Art. 1366(4) N-TCC.

[43]Art. 31/a(2) and (7) N-CEB introduced according to Art. 41(2)(e) N-CIE.

[44]Art. 135(1) N-CEB applicable according to Art. 136 N-CEB amended as per Art. 41(2)(ğ) N-CIE.

[45]Art. 144/a(2) N-CEB introduced according to Art. 41(2)(h) N-CIE.

[46]§§15–21 SchRG, which in turn have been adopted from §§891–902 BGB.

[47]§891 BGB = §15 SchRG = Art. 884(1)-(3) TCC = Art. 974(1)-(3) N-TCC.

[48]§892(1) BGB = §16(1) SchRG = Art. 885(1) TCC = Art. 983(1) N-TCC. The same rule applies in respect of mortgages on real estate (Art. 974(1) ZGB = Art. 1024(1) TCivC).

[49]Third sentence of §8(1) SchRG = implied in Art. 875 TCC = explicit in Art. 1014(2) N-TCC.

free, as in German law, to create the ship mortgage for an abstract acknowledgement of debt[50] to overcome any problems associated with this legal position.

On the other hand, the negative reliance is also protected in that a right, which is not registered, is presumed not to exist.

12.3.2.2 Register for New Buildings

The "Register for New Buildings[51]" ("NBR") has been established as of 1 January 1957 under the provisions of the TCC, which is now kept pursuant to the N-TCC. Additional provisions are to be found in the SRD. The Turkish provisions[52] have been generally adopted from the corresponding German provisions regarding the NBR.[53]

Under current German and previous Turkish law, the registration of a "ship under construction" (= "new building") is admitted only if and whenever a mortgage or arrest is to be simultaneously registered.[54] This limitation is abandoned under the new Turkish law, which finally gives leave to the registration of new buildings for the sole purpose of making the ownership public.[55] This had been recognized as a pressing need in Turkish practice, because it was noted on several occasions that the ownership in the new building requires public information in cases where a person other than the shipyard is the owner. Particularly, if the shipyard went bankrupt, the prior registration of the ownership would ensure that the owner of the new building is protected against the creditors of the shipyard.

The information to be registered is identical with German law.[56] A ship under construction might even be registered if the owner was a foreign person or entity.[57] Other than the ownership, the only right *in rem* that might be entered with the NBR is the mortgage on a new building.[58] The registered mortgage on a new building carries the same legal effect as the ship mortgage.[59] Finally, priority notices are also admitted in respect of the NBR. The notices to be made to the NSR in enforcement proceedings apply to the NBR as well.

---

[50]"Abstraktes Schuldversprechen".

[51]İnşa Hâlindeki Gemilere Mahsus Sicil.

[52]Art. 858–863 and Art. 941–944 TCC; Art. 986–992, Art. 1010–1011 and Art. 1054–1058 N-TCC; Art. 76–84 SRD.

[53]§§76–81 SchRG and §§65–74 SchRegO.

[54]§66 SchRegO = Art. 858(1) TCC.

[55]Art. 986(1) N-TCC.

[56]§69(1) SchRegO = Art. 860(1) TCC = Art. 988(1) N-TCC.

[57]Art. 822(2)(3) TCC = Art. 935(2)(b) N-TCC.

[58]§66 SchRegO = Art. 858(1) TCC = Art. 986(1) N-TCC.

[59]Art. 991(2) N-TCC.

12.3.2.3 Special (Flag-in) Register (Roll)

On the basis of German law,[60] Turkish law also recognizes the options of flagging-in and flagging-out of ships.[61] Foreign ships that are temporarily allowed to fly the Turkish flag are recorded in a "Special (Flag-in) Register[62]". Technically, however, this list of ships is not a register, but simply a "roll[63]" of the ships using this option. Therefore, rights *in rem*, such as mortgages, cannot be created or transferred by way of entry into this roll.[64]

In Turkish practice, this roll is usually referred to as a "bareboat register," because the bareboat charter is generally considered the primary agreement under which the ship may be let out to a Turkish interest. However, as a matter of law, the agreement may also be a financial leasing agreement[65] or a usufruct. In all these cases, the ownership in the vessel will still be maintained in the foreign principal register, whereas the possession will pass to a Turkish interest, enabling it to obtain permission to fly the Turkish flag. Therefore, this roll is better described with reference to the flag-in procedure rather than the underlying type of agreement.

In this connection, Art. 16 of ICLM ought to be given due consideration whenever the Convention comes into force for Turkey.

12.3.2.4 Turkish International Ship Register

Introduction

In 1999, the "Turkish International Ship Register[66]" ("TISR") was introduced under the provisions of the "Act on the Turkish International Ship Register" ("TISR-A"). This Act is supplemented by the provisions of the "Regulation on the Turkish International Ship Register[67]" ("TISR-R"). The TISR has been established in Istanbul with a branch office in Izmir.[68]

[60] §7, §§11–12 Gesetz über das Flaggenrecht der Seeschiffe und die Flaggenführung der Binnenschiffe (Flaggenrechtsgesetz) (8.2.1951), BGBl. 1951 I, S. 79 = BGBl. 1951 II, S. 6.

[61] Art. 824 TCC = Art. 941 N-TCC.

[62] "Verzeichnis der gecharterten Schiffe"; §12(2) Flaggenrechtsgesetz = Art. 824(3) TCC = Art. 941(3) N-TCC.

[63] "Verzeichnis".

[64] See also the corresponding rule on the applicable law, as described earlier in Sect. 12.2.2.2.

[65] Art. 5(2) TISR-A and Art. 11 TISR-R.

[66] Türk Uluslararası Gemi Sicili Kanunu ile 491 Sayılı Kanun Hükmünde Kararnamede Değişiklik Yapılmasına Dair Kanun, T: 16.12.1999, S: 4490, RG T: 21.12.1999, S: 23913, as amended by the Act of 2.12.2004, S: 5266, RG T: 9.12.2004, S: 25665.

[67] Türk Uluslararası Gemi Sicili Yönetmeliği, RG T: 23.6.2000, S: 24088; as amended in: RG T: 22.8.2002, S: 24854; T: 19.1.2005, S: 25705; T: 17.9.2006, S: 26292.

[68] Art. 3(1) TISR-A, Art. 5(2) TISR-R.

Incentives

From a financial point of view, registration with the TISR is extremely advantageous.[69] All transactions related to ships registered, or to be registered, with the TISR, such as sale and purchase agreements or mortgages, are exempted from all types of taxes, levies, and dues. More importantly, the owners of such ships are free from paying corporate income taxes. Several incentives have also been allowed in respect of crew wages and social security arrangements.

Ships Admitted for Registration

Rather than provide a definition of ships that may be registered, a more pragmatic solution has been chosen for the TISR.[70] Accordingly, the TISR is open only for ships that are used for commercial purposes, such as the carriage of goods or passengers, or for fishing. A tonnage limitation applies to ships imported from abroad to protect the national shipbuilding industry and coastal carriage. Special purpose ships and other craft are admitted on the basis of a list, which is prepared and updated by the Ministry. As for the details of the registration, reference is made[71] to the rule governing the NSR.[72]

Applicable Provisions

The rules regarding the rights *in rem* on ships, including registration, are to be defined by the TISR-R.[73] However, this Regulation provides only for a minimal number of rules, and refers to the SRD for all other issues that are left open.[74] It follows that the rules and provisions of the N-TCC and the SRD also govern the TISR, to the extent that the TISR-A and the TISR-R do not set out specific provisions. Indeed, the provisions on the TISR have been clearly reserved in the N-TCC as well.[75] This means that the particular provisions of the TISR-A and TISR-R will apply with priority. However, as for matters left open in those two sources, the provisions of the N-TCC and the SRD will be applicable.

[69] Art. 12 TISR-A.

[70] Art. 2 and 4 TISR-A, Art. 2 TISR-R.

[71] Art. 6(1) TISR-A.

[72] §11(1) SchRegO = Art. 845 TCC = Art. 960 N-TCC.

[73] Art. 6(2) TISR-A.

[74] Art. 14 TISR-R.

[75] Art. 995 N-TCC.

Rights to be Registered

The following rights *in rem* have been admitted for entry with the TISR:

1. The property (ownership) of the ship;
2. A ship mortgage[76];
3. A right on the ship mortgage, such as a pledge.

However, the usufruct has not been mentioned for ships registered in the TISR. Priority notices, as well as the notices in enforcement proceedings, as considered earlier, are applicable to the TISR as well.

Turning to contracts, financial leasing agreements in respect of ships are admitted for registration,[77] whereas bareboat charters are not.[78] Financial leasing agreements concluded with a foreign lessor may also be registered with the TISR.[79] As such, there is no need in such cases to apply the flag-in procedure described earlier, as the ship will be entitled to fly the Turkish flag upon registration with the TISR.[80]

12.3.2.5 Home Port Log

Finally, a package of legislative measures adopted in 2009 has established yet another register that may be translated as the "Home Port Log[81]" ("HPL"). The HPL is primarily intended for the registration of pleasure boats, yachts, other water craft, as well as all ships and vessels of inland navigation. As the result of a severe error made by the legislative bodies, mortgages cannot currently be entered with the HPL. Also, the legal qualities attached to the NSR, NBR and TISR have not been explicitly repeated in respect of the HPL. As such, the HPL will not be of any interest to international financial markets, and will therefore not be further considered in this paper.

12.3.2.6 Statistics

According to the latest official statistics,[82] the number of vessels registered with the NSR totals 11,328 with a total deadweight tonnage (DWT) of 864,315. On the other hand, whereas the total number of ships entered with the TISR is only 1,362,

---

[76] Art. 6(3) TISR-A, Art. 14 TISR-R.

[77] Art. 22(1) of the Financial Leasing Act (2012); Art. 5(2) TISR-A, Art. 11 TISR-R.

[78] Art. 12 TISR-R.

[79] Art. 5(2) TISR-A.

[80] Art. 7(1) TISR-A.

[81] As for detailed information in respect of this new register and the underlying legislation see (in Turkish) Atamer (2009, p. 301).

[82] Published at http://www.denizcilik.gov.tr/tr_/istatistik/Guncel_Filo.asp?rf=ybs (last access: 25.1.2012).

their collective DWT of 9,089,000 is roughly 11 times higher compared to the ships registered with the NSR.

12.3.2.7 Authority

Following a recent restructuring in the Government, the "Undersecretariat of Shipping" has been merged, as of 1 November 2011, into the Ministry of Transportation, which has formally assumed the name of the "Ministry of Transportation, Shipping Affairs and Communication[83]". One of the administrative units established within this Ministry is the "General Directorate of Maritime Affairs[84]". The list of duties assigned to this Directorate includes all issues relating to the registration of ships and all other water craft.[85] It follows that, as of 1 November 2011, the five registers described above are all kept under the authority of the Ministry of Transportation, Shipping Affairs and Communication.

12.3.2.8 Public Registers

In a direct adaptation of the German rule, the NSR, NBR, and TISR are all described explicitly as public[86] registers.[87] Accordingly, any person can review the entries in the NSR. However, as for the NBR and TISR, it is additionally required that a legitimate interest[88] is demonstrated.[89] To obtain certified copies from the NSR and NBR, it is required in accordance with the German original that a legitimate interest can be shown.[90]

12.3.2.9 State Liability

Concerning the State's liability for properly keeping and maintaining the registers, the NSR, NBR, and the TISR are all governed[91] by the general provisions of Civil

[83]The relevant Decree is published as: Ulaştırma, Denizcilik ve Haberleşme Bakanlığının Teşkilat ve Görevleri Hakkında Kanun Hükmünde Kararname, T: 26.9.2011, S: KHK/655, RG T: 1.11.2011, S: 28102 (1. Mükerrer).

[84]Art. 6(d) of the Decree referred to in the preceding footnote.

[85]Art. 11(ğ) of the Decree referred to in the preceding footnote.

[86]"Öffentlich".

[87]§8(1) SchRegO = Art. 842(1) TCC = Art. 973(1) N-TCC; Art. 6(c) TISR-R.

[88]"Berechtigtes Interesse".

[89]§65(2) SchRegO = Art. 858(3) TCC = Art. 991(1) N-TCC; Art. 6(c) TISR-R.

[90]NSR: §8(2) SchRegO = Art. 842(2) TCC = Art. 973(2) N-TCC; NBR: §65(2) SchRegO = Art. 858(3) TCC = Art. 991(1) N-TCC.

[91]Pursuant to the explicit references set out in Art. 839(3) TCC = Art. 954(3) N-TCC.

law.[92] As such, the State is liable for all damages arising from maintenance of the registers. It is settled under Swiss and Turkish law that this provision calls for the strict liability of the State. As such, any negligence of the registrar is not required to be proved for such liability to arise. However, it must be shown that the registrar must have acted in breach of the law.[93] These principles apply in exactly the same terms to the NSR, NBR, and TISR. Where liability is established in accordance with these provisions, it is ultimately the Turkish Treasury that will pay out any indemnity adjudged by the Court.

12.3.3 Ownership

The scope and protection of ownership in a ship or new building is subject to the general provisions.[94] However, particular provisions are available for the passing and abandoning of ownership in ships and new buildings. Under the new law, the transfer of ownership in ships[95] and new buildings,[96] which are registered in Turkey, has been brought in line with international practices. Accordingly, the validity of the transfer now requires two steps. On the one hand, the transfer must be recorded in a formal document to be signed by the parties, and the signatures must be authenticated by a notary public. Such a document may also be drawn up at the NSR, NBR, or TISR.

In practice, this document will invariably correspond to the Bill of Sale used in international practice, with the additional requirement that the signature of the buyer must also be inserted. On the other hand, delivery of the possession of the ship has been introduced as an additional requirement. As a matter of practice, this will be achieved invariably by substitution of the captain and crew with the simultaneous production of the Protocol of Delivery and Acceptance. Included in such a transfer are also the ship's appurtenances, unless the parties have agreed otherwise, or these belong to third parties.[97]

---

[92] Art. 955 ZGB = Art. 1007(1) and (2) TCivC. The Turkish provision incorporates a third paragraph to the effect that the Court at the place of the respective register has jurisdiction to hear any indemnity action.

[93] "Rechtswidriges Verhalten".

[94] ZGB Art. 641–654 = TCivC Art. 683–703.

[95] Art. 1001(1) and (2) N-TCC.

[96] Art. 1011(1) N-TCC.

[97] Art. 1002 N-TCC.

12.3.4 Usufruct

Under current German and previous Turkish law, the application of the usufruct on ships is strictly limited to two specific cases.[98] However, under new Turkish law, these restrictions have been abandoned, and the usufruct is made generally available.[99] It remains to be seen whether this option will be of interest in practice. As for the details of the usufruct on ships, only a few specific provisions have been set out, with a reference being included[100] to the general provisions.[101]

12.3.5 Mortgage on Ships and New Buildings

12.3.5.1 Sources

As was mentioned already, previous and new Turkish law of ship mortgages[102] is largely based on the German reform legislation of 1940. Considering further the fact that the German provisions on the ship mortgage have been copied directly from the "security mortgage on real estate[103]" of the "German Civil Code[104]" ("BGB"), it follows that the current Turkish ship mortgage is essentially identical with the German security mortgage on ships and real estate. Only a few exceptions have been admitted. Indeed, to achieve some degree of harmony with the general rules of Turkish law on real estate mortgages as set out in the TCivC, a few references were made to those rules. Notable examples are the provisions on the ranking and scope of Turkish ship mortgages. However, as those provisions have their origins in the ZGB, the Turkish ship mortgage can be qualified as a German "security mortgage on ships and real estate[105]" with a flavor of the Swiss "mortgage on real estate[106]". Nevertheless, the principal nature and character of the Turkish ship mortgage as an offspring of the German original is no way prejudiced. This legal state of affairs has been generally retained in the N-TCC. However, several amendments have

[98]§9(1) SchRG = Art. 878(1) TCC.

[99]Art. 1059(1) N-TCC.

[100]Art. 1060(1) N-TCC.

[101]ZGB Art. 745–769 = Art. 794–817 TCivC.

[102]As for detailed information in English on the previous Turkish law of ship mortgages see Sözer (2007). In Turkish see in particular Akinci (1958), Kalpsüz (2004), Sözer (2011).

[103]"Sicherungshypothek an Grundstücken".

[104]Bürgerliches Gesetzbuch, in der Fassung der Bekanntmachung vom 2. Januar 2002 (BGBl. I 42, 2909; 2003 I 738), zuletzt geändert durch Artikel 1 des Gesetzes vom 27. Juli 2011 (BGBl. I 1600).

[105]"Sicherungshypothek an Grundstücken und Schiffen".

[106]"Grundpfandverschreibung".

been made to bring the Turkish provisions even closer in line with the German originals.

12.3.5.2 Legal Character

The original Turkish name for a ship mortgage is "gemi ipoteği". As the word "ipotek" implies, it is a translation of the German word "Hypothek". As a matter of law, "Hypothek" denotes the Roman law terminology that a pledge is created without transfer of possession.[107] As such, the widespread practice to translate the term "Hypothek" as "mortgage" into English is not necessarily accurate. A better translation would be "hypothèque" as is used in Art. 1 ICLM. Nevertheless, to follow established practice, the Turkish "ipotek" will be described as a "mortgage" in this paper, as well.

The ship mortgage is defined on the basis of the German original[108] as a right created to secure a claim, which right entitles the mortgagee to seek recovery from the proceeds of the ship.[109] It follows that the mortgage grants the mortgagee a right *in rem* in the ship as opposed to a mere contractual claim against the ship-owner. Indeed, a ship-owner may agree to a mortgage on his/her ship for a debt, for which he/she is not personally liable, in which case the owner will be held liable exclusively to tolerate enforcement[110] into the ship. The extensive scholarly discussions on this important point in German law[111] are obsolete in Turkish law because if the proceeds of the judicial sale do not fully cover the claim, a "certificate of insolvency[112]" will be issued only as against the personal debtor, not the owner of the real estate or ship on which the mortgage was created. Accordingly, the owner of a ship who agrees to provide a mortgage for a third party's debt does not become thereby personally liable for that debt.

The mortgage and the claim secured thereby are strictly intertwined. Accordingly, one cannot be transferred without the other.[113]

[107] D. 13, 7, 1 *pr.*; D. 13, 7, 9, 2; Inst. 4, 6, 7.

[108] §§1113(1) and 1184(1) BGB; §8(1) and (3) SchRG.

[109] First two sentences of both Art. 875 TCC and Art. 1014(1) N-TCC.

[110] "Duldung der Zwangsvollstreckung".

[111] As to which see Staudinger/Wolfsteiner (2009).

[112] "Pfandausfallschein"; see Art. 152(2) CEB. Under general law, this certificate will entitle the mortgagee to commence bankruptcy or ordinary arrest proceedings against the debtor. If such proceedings were commenced within 1 year, no further service of proceedings will be required. In respect of ships, the foreclosure of the mortgage will already include the arrest of the ship. As such, the certificate will be of use only to commence bankruptcy proceedings or ordinary arrest proceedings against any other property that the shipowner may have.

[113] §1153(2) BGB = §51(2) SchRG = Art. 921(2) TCC = Art. 1038(2) N-TCC.

12.3.5.3 Creation of Ship Mortgage

Agreement

A ship mortgage is created by the agreement of the parties and registration. Turkish law does not impose any standard type of agreement. In practice, there are probably as many forms in circulation as there are foreign and local law firms involved. Most of these forms are based on English standard texts, whereby attention ought to be paid to achieving full harmony with the applicable Turkish law(s).

Ship mortgage agreements must be concluded in writing and the signatures of the parties must be certified by a notary public.[114] Under the new law, the mortgage agreement may also be concluded at the NSR, NBR or TISR.[115] This will confer on the mortgagee an important advantage in enforcement proceedings.[116] The notarial certification may as well be obtained abroad, in which case Apostilles from the respective Authorities would be required. The agreement may be concluded abroad in a foreign language. If so, however, a certified Turkish translation would have to be submitted to the registrar.

Registration

Following conclusion of the agreement, it is effective as between the parties thereto. However, to achieve validity as against third parties, the mortgage must be registered.[117] The place of registration will be the NSR, NBR or TISR. In addition, Turkish law provides for an option that has been inspired by the famous work of the German maritime law legend, the late Prof. Dr. Hans Jürgen Abraham (Abraham 1950, p. 210). Indeed, a ship mortgage may also be created by entry into the flag certificate in cases where the ship was purchased from abroad and not yet registered in Turkey.[118] Upon registration of the ship in Turkey, the ship mortgage will be transferred to the NSR or TISR, as the case may be. The contents of the registration are set out in accordance with German law.[119]

[114] Art. 876(2) TCC = Art. 1015(2) N-TCC. It will be noted that the Turkish requirement is slightly different from the provisions of §3(1) and (2) SchRG.

[115] Art. 1015(2) and 10551(1) N-TCC.

[116] Art. 1377(2) N-TCC

[117] Art. 876(2) TCC = Art. 1015(2) N-TCC; here the principle of German law (§8(2) referring to §3(1) SchRG) is maintained.

[118] Art. 876(1) TCC = Art 1015(5) N-TCC.

[119] See §24(1) SchRG = Art. 893(1) TCC = Art. 1016(1) N-TCC.

12.3.5.4 Claims Secured

The Applicable Rule

As for the claims that are secured by the ship mortgage, the general provisions of civil law[120] are applicable.[121] Accordingly, the following amounts are secured, as a matter of law, by the ship mortgage.

Principal Claim

The mortgage secures, first of all, the outstanding debt. The debt might be specified. However, the amount so secured may also be agreed as a maximum upper limit,[122] with the actual amount of debt to be determined at the time of maturity.[123] The debt may as well be expressed in foreign currency or gold.[124] The new rules on this point have been copied from the general provisions in respect of real estate mortgages.[125] The foreign currencies which can be admitted are to be determined by the Undersecretariat of the Treasury. The conversion rate will be the buying exchange rate of the Turkish Central Bank as on the date of calculation. Several mortgages within the same rank cannot be established in different currencies. Whereas real estate mortgages in foreign currencies are available only to financial institutions,[126] such a restriction has not been adopted for ship mortgages.[127] The claim secured by the ship mortgage might arise in the future, or might be conditional.[128] Moreover, Turkish law adopts the principle of Swiss law to the effect that a ship mortgage may even be created to secure non-pecuniary claims, provided that the maximum amount covered by the mortgage is registered.

Interest, Accessory Claims and Enforcement Costs

The ship mortgage also provides security for the costs relating to enforcement proceedings and default interest, as well as for 3-year interest which is due and payable as at the date on which bankruptcy proceedings have been initiated or foreclosure of the mortgage has been requested, and for interest running as of the

---

[120] Art. 875(1) and Art. 876 TCivC, as translated from Art. 818(1) and Art. 819 ZGB.

[121] By virtue of the explicit references in Art. 899(1) TCC = Art 1018(1) N-TCC.

[122] "Höchstbetragsschiffshypothek".

[123] §75(1)(2) SchRG = Art. 893(2) TCC = Art. Art. 1016(3) N-TCC.

[124] Art. 939–940 TCC = Art. 1016(2)(4)(5) N-TCC

[125] Art. 851(2)-(4) TCivC.

[126] Art. 851(2) TCivC.

[127] Cf. Art. 939 TCC and Art. 1016(4) N-TCC.

[128] "Zukünftige oder bedingte Forderung"; §8(1) SchRG = Art. 875 TCC = Art. 1014(1) N-TCC.

same date. The costs of enforcement proceedings enjoy the first rank in the list of priorities.[129] On the other hand, where the mortgage was created for a maximum amount secured, any interest payable on the claim is included in the upper limit registered.[130]

12.3.5.5 Property Subject to the Mortgage

The Ship with All Appurtenances

As a matter of law,[131] the mortgage attaches to the ship together with all appurtenances (*i.e.* things belonging to the ship) such as the engine, hatch covers, navigational instruments, lifeboats, furniture and anchor chains. However, other property on board that is not owned by the ship-owner, such as cargo, leased containers or time charterers' fuel, will not be subject to the mortgage.

Hire

The mortgage attaches, as a matter of law,[132] to hire payable under a bareboat charter to the ship-owner as well. However, an assignment of earnings must be obtained in respect of any time charter hire or freight payable under voyage charters or bills of lading to the ship-owner.

Indemnities

Under the new law, the mortgage attaches to indemnities payable to the owner for loss of or damage to the ship and to payments made to the owner if the ship was seized by the government for public purposes.[133]

Insurance Indemnity

The detailed German provisions in respect of the mortgagee's rights on the insurance indemnity have been translated and adopted in Turkish law.[134] According to the

[129] Art. 1390(1) N-TCC; see Atamer (2012, p. 84).

[130] §75(2) SchRG = Art. 893(2) TCC = Art. 1016(3) N-TCC.

[131] Art. 900(1) TCC and Art. 1020(1) N-TCC referring to Art. 862, which provision has been translated from Art. 805 ZGB. This rule is in line with §31(1) SchRG.

[132] Art. 900(1) TCC and Art 1020(1) N-TCC referring to Art. 863 TCivC, which provision has been translated from Art. 806 ZGB.

[133] Art. 1020(4) N-TCC.

[134] §§32–38 SchRG = Art. 901–908 TCC = Art. 1022–1029 N-TCC.

general principle, where the interest of the ship-owner in any item that is subject to the mortgage has been insured, any insurance indemnity payable in respect of such items is also subject to the mortgage. As such, the indemnity cannot be paid to anyone without the mutual consent of the ship-owner and the mortgagee. The mortgage will attach exclusively to indemnities payable to restore the ship-owners interest in the ship. As such, indemnities payable under liability insurances of the ship-owner are not available to the mortgagee.

Moreover, the mortgagee is protected under the insurance even if the insurer ought to be free from its obligations as against the ship-owner. Accordingly, the position under Turkish law is in line with the solutions adopted under German law.[135] Therefore, the insurer will remain liable to pay the indemnity to the mortgagee, even in the event of, to name but one example, scuttling.[136]

A most important new provision finally clarifies that the holders of maritime liens are not entitled to follow any insurance proceeds payable to the ship-owner.[137] As such, the protection of the mortgagee has been significantly advanced.

12.3.5.6 Rank

The only material difference between the German and Turkish provisions is to be found in respect of the ranking system.[138] Whereas German law of real estate and ship mortgages follows the principle of the sliding ranks,[139] Swiss–Turkish law of real estate and ship mortgages adopt the principle of constant ranks.[140] Indeed, as for the ranking of ship mortgages, the general provisions on real estate mortgages are applicable.[141] According to these principles, each mortgage is registered at the rank that the parties have chosen and that is free at the time of registration. The ship-owner is entitled to reserve free ranks for subsequent registrations. In such a case, the maximal amount secured under such free rank must be registered.

Where several mortgages are registered, their priorities will be determined by the ranks assigned to them on registration. If a mortgage is deleted, subsequent mortgages will not automatically move up. However, the ship-owner and any given mortgagee may provide in the mortgage agreement that the mortgage shall automatically move up if and whenever the preceding mortgage is deleted. It ought

---

[135]Details available at Hungar (1998, p. 172) with further references.

[136]§36(1) SchRG = Art. 906(1) TCC = Art. 1027(1) N-TCC. As for German law, see Hungar (1998) citing in footnote 608 a decision of the BGH (NJW 1970, 753) to the effect that scuttling would be covered by §36(1) SchRG.

[137]Art. 1321(2) N-TCC.

[138]As for the ranking of ship mortgages in the list of priorities, see Atamer (2012, p. 85).

[139]"Gleitende Rangstellen".

[140]"Feste Rangstellen".

[141]Art. 894 TCC = Art 1017(1) N-TCC referring to the general provisions of Art. 870–872 TCivC, which have been translated from Art. 813–815 ZGB.

to be emphasized that the *in rem* effect[142] of such an agreement as against third parties depends on its registration together with the mortgage in favor of which it is agreed.[143] Therefore, for such an agreement to be enforceable as against third parties, it must be registered.

Attention ought to be paid to the principle that several mortgages within the same rank will share *pro rata*, and not in accordance with any priorities.[144] It follows that several creditors might be entered within a single rank. However, such mortgages within the same rank will share *pro rata*, irrespective of any priority that is assigned to them in their respective mortgage agreement. Therefore, the registration of mortgages marked "first rank, first priority" are dangerous for the mortgagee, and should be avoided unless the mortgagee is prepared to share *pro rata* with a "first rank, second priority" mortgage rather than taking ahead of a "second rank" mortgage. To create priorities within a rank, the registered consent is required of all creditors who are entered within the same rank.

12.3.5.7 Protection Against Deletion

The mortgagee is protected against deletion of the mortgage from the register without its prior written approval.[145] Accordingly, the registrar is not entitled to delete the mortgage without the consent of the mortgagee. Should the mortgage be deleted without such prior approval, the liability of the State will arise. The same rules also apply in respect of the deletion of the ship from the ship register.[146]

12.3.5.8 Ships Under Construction

A ship mortgage may also be created in respect of a ship under construction. However, such mortgage may only be registered whenever the keel is laid and the new building has been marked clearly by name or[147] number.[148] A mortgage on a new building is not admitted if the ship will be less than 18 gross register tonnage (GRT[149]) upon completion.[150] The mortgage on a new building is subject to the

---

[142]"Dingliche Wirkung".

[143]Art. 814(3) ZGB = Art. 871(3) TCviC.

[144]Art. 817 ZGB = Art. 874 TCivC.

[145]§29 SchRegO = Art. 21 SRD.

[146]§§20–21 SchRegO = Art. 851–852 TCC = Art. 965–966 N-TCC; §29 SchRegO = Art. 21 SRD; Art. 6(3) TISR-A.

[147]Art. 1054(2) N-TCC requires that name and number are marked; however, this is a printing mistake, and the provision ought to be understood as providing for alternatives.

[148]§76 SchRG = Art. 941(2)(3) TCC = Art. 1054(2)(3) N-TCC.

[149]That is the equivalent of the German requirement of 50 cubic meters.

[150]§76(2) SchRG = Art. 941(3) TCC = Art. 1054(3) N-TCC.

rules of the ship mortgage, except where provided otherwise. Accordingly, the above information applies to the mortgage of a new building.

12.3.5.9 Mortgage Bonds

Where the mortgagee has issued mortgage bonds, a pledge on the ship mortgage may also be registered. Such a pledge will confer priority on the holders of the bonds on any sums payable to the mortgagee upon judicial sale of the ship, or otherwise. This issue has already been covered elsewhere in detail (Atamer 2012, p. 90).

12.3.5.10 Enforcement

This topic has also been discussed already (Atamer 2012, p. 80). Suffice it to say here that claims secured by a ship mortgage are included in the list of "maritime claims[151]". Accordingly, any mortgagee is entitled to arrest the ship to obtain security or to initiate foreclosure.[152] The mortgagee is entitled to commence proceedings to enforce the mortgage following arrest of the ship, or directly. Under the new law, a distinction will be made thereby as between ship mortgages where the agreement was concluded at the NSR, TISR or NBR, and those that were not. If the agreement was concluded at either register, the mortgagee will be entitled to serve directly an "enforcement order[153]". Upon this order being served, the debt must be paid within 30 days or a stay of action be obtained from the Court. Otherwise, the judicial sale of the ship can be initiated promptly at the expiry of the period.

Another alternative for proceeding directly on the basis of an enforcement order is provided for in Art. 1377(2) N-TCC. According to this provision, in conjunction with Art. 38 CEB, an enforcement order may also be served if the mortgage and the acknowledgement of debt have been recorded in a document, which has been formally drawn up by a notary public. Such a document is to be contrasted to a document drawn up by the parties, where the notary public simply certifies the authenticity of the signatures and authorizations of the signatories. In the latter case, service of an enforcement order will not be admitted.

What is probably among the most striking features of the new law is that the special enforcement procedure granted to creditors of loan agreements[154] has now been made explicitly available for ship mortgages as well.[155] According to this remedy, an enforcement order will also be served in all cases where the debt arose under a loan agreement and the creditor served through the notary public a notice

---

[151] Art. 1(1)(u) ICAS = Art. 1352(1)(v) N-TCC.

[152] Art. 1353(1) and (2), Art. 1381(1) N-TCC.

[153] Art. 149 CEB; "Vollstreckungsbefehl" in Swiss law, "Vollstreckungsbescheid" in German law.

[154] Art. 150/ı CEB.

[155] Art. 153/a(3) N-CEB introduced in accordance with Art. 41(2)(ı) N-CIE.

according to which payments fell due. This expedited and simplified procedure had been introduced in 1988 specifically for banks and other financial institutions. However, extension of its application to ship mortgages had been forgotten. This has now been rectified.

If the ship mortgage agreement was not concluded at either register, or the mortgagee did not wish to apply the procedure under Art. 150/ı CEB, then the mortgagee will be entitled to serve a "payment order[156]". Upon service of this order, the debt must be paid within 30 days or objections against the debt must be filed within 7 days as of the date of service. However, no objections will be admitted against the ship mortgage.[157] If neither payment was effected, nor objections were filed, the judicial sale of the ship can be initiated promptly at the expiry of the period of 30 days. If objections were filed against the debt within 7 days, the mortgagee would have to apply to the Court to have the objection set aside.

12.3.6 *Maritime Liens*

Previous Turkish law contained an extensive catalogue of maritime liens.[158] However, under the new law, the rules of the ICLM have been adopted.[159] As such, the list of maritime liens, which have priority over the ship mortgage, has been reduced to five classes. These are the following:

1. Claims for wages and other sums due to the master, officers and other members of the ship's complement in respect of their employment on the ship, including costs of repatriation and social insurance contributions payable on their behalf;
2. Claims in respect of loss of life or personal injury occurring, whether on land or on water, in direct connection with the operation of the ship;
3. Claims for reward for the salvage of the ship, excluding claims for special compensation;
4. Claims for port, canal, and other waterway dues and pilotage dues;
5. Claims based on tort arising out of physical loss or damage caused by the operation of the ship other than loss of or damage to cargo, containers and passengers' effects carried on the ship.

As a result of this significant change of law, the number of maritime liens has been significantly reduced. Therefore, far less a number of creditors will take ahead of the ship mortgage. Moreover, it ought to be noted that the claims in categories (2) and (5) are secured under new Turkish law by way of compulsory liability insurance.

---

[156] Art. 149/b CEB; "Zahlungsbefehl" in Swiss law, "Mahnbescheid" in German law.

[157] Art. 150 CEB.

[158] As for detailed information in English on the previous Turkish law of maritime liens see Atamer (1998, p. 1392).

[159] Art. 4(1) ICML = Art. 1320(1) N-TCC.

As such, those claims are likely to be satisfied by the respective liability insurer, thereby leaving the mortgage on the "carrying ship" unaffected.

One additional lien has been admitted in accordance with the right granted under Art. 6 ICLM. Indeed, claims for general average contribution have also been given the status of maritime liens[160]; however, this maritime lien ranks after all registered mortgages.[161] As such, these claims will only be paid out if and whenever anything is left after the mortgagees have been satisfied. Therefore, such a lien will be admitted only after the ship mortgage.[162]

12.4 Contractual Agreements

12.4.1 Shipbuilding

The Turkish shipbuilding industry has seen an enormous development over the past 20 years or so. New areas designated for shipbuilding, innovative technologies and a wealth of experience have put Turkish shipyards firmly on the map. The contract for the construction or repair of a ship is generally qualified as a *locatio conductio operis*. However, the distinction between sales contracts and the *locatio conductio operis* may occasionally cause problems. As a matter of practice, most shipyards use standard contracts, which have been adopted directly from, or developed on, the basis of the standard SAJ and AWES forms. A written form is not mandatory for the validity of the contract; however, it is invariably applied in practice. In the absence of particular provisions for shipbuilding contracts, the general provisions[163] govern these contracts as well, provided of course that the parties have not chosen another law as applicable.

12.4.2 Ship Sale and Purchase

No particular provision has been adopted for the sale and purchase of ships registered with the NSR, NBR and TISR. Notwithstanding that Turkey is a party to the CISG, this Convention does not apply to the sale of ships and new buildings.[164]

---

[160] Art. 1320(1)(f) N-TCC.

[161] Art. 1323(2) N-TCC.

[162] Art. 1395(1) N-TCC.

[163] Art. 470–486 TCO, which provisions have been generally adopted from the corresponding provisions of the OR.

[164] Art. 2(e) CISG.

Ships being qualified explicitly as movable property,[165] the general provisions on the sale and purchase of movables[166] are applicable. Some of those provisions are mandatory. Accordingly, when Turkish law governs the contract, clauses in standard forms of documents must be considered in respect of their applicability. In practice, the Norwegian Memorandum of Understanding, codenamed Saleform, is the most widely used document for the conclusion of such agreements.

12.4.3 Financial Leasing

Following the introduction of the "Financial Leasing Act[167]" in 1985, which has recently been renewed,[168] such agreements have become widely used in the Turkish market. In respect of ships, the lessee will choose a ship, which will be purchased by the lessor.[169] Alternatively, the new Act gives leave to "sale and lease back" agreements,[170] which were alien to the previous Act. The lessor will register the ship with the NSR or TISR in its own name.[171] Whereas the "legal ownership" remains with the lessor,[172] the lessee is qualified as the "economic owner" of the ship and obtains possession.[173] At the expiry of the leasing period, the lessee is entitled to request transfer of ownership. The lessee is prohibited from creating any rights *in rem* on the ship. However, maritime liens will attach to ships even under a financial leasing agreement.

These rules govern leasing agreements that have been concluded with a lessor that is admitted to practice in Turkey. However, if the lessor was a non-resident foreign company, then Turkish law would apply only if so chosen by the parties. It has already been considered that ships leased by a foreign lessor might be registered with the TISR. If this alternative was not applicable, then the flag-in procedure must be applied.

---

[165] See earlier Sect. 12.3.1

[166] Art. 207–208 and 209–236 TCO, which provisions have been generally adopted from the corresponding provisions of the OR.

[167] Finansal Kiralama Kanunu, T: 19.6.1985, S: 3226.

[168] Finansal Kiralama, Faktoring ve Finansman Şirketleri Kanunu, T: 21.11.2012, S: 6361.

[169] Art. 4 of the Financial Leasing Act (1985) = Art. 18 of the Financial Leasing Act (2012).

[170] Art. 18(1) of the Financial Leasing Act (2012).

[171] Art. 8(1) of the Financial Leasing Act = Art. 22(1) of the Financial Leasing Act (2012); Art. 4(k) TISR-R.

[172] Art. 17(1) of the Financial Leasing Act = Art. 23(1) of the Financial Leasing Act (2012).

[173] Art. 4 and 13(1) of the Financial Leasing Act = Art. 24(1) of the Financial Leasing Act (2012).

12.4.4 Bareboat Charter and Temporary Change of Flag

The basic rules have been introduced in the N-TCC in respect of bareboat charters.[174] These provisions have been drafted comparing French, Norwegian, and Dutch legislation, as well as the BARECON 2001 standard form of agreement. Under a bareboat charter, the ship-owner undertakes to let the ship against payment of hire to the charterer.[175] The ship must be delivered in a seaworthy condition.[176] However, the charterer must then maintain the seaworthiness of the ship. The charter may be registered with the NSR, but not the TISR. Should the parties wish to temporarily flag-out a Turkish ship or flag-in a ship registered abroad, they may do so by concluding a bareboat charter and by obtaining formal permission. As discussed earlier, ships so flagged-in will be listed in a roll kept by the government.

12.5 Outlook

In the course of the preparations for the new Turkish law, the legislative bodies have been conscious of the need to improve conditions for ship financing to ensure the development of the national merchant fleet. Against this background, the provisions of the ICLM and ICAS have been incorporated into the N-TCC. As for matters left open in these Conventions, the legislation of Germany as one of the leading ship financing nations has been adopted as a model in respect of rights *in rem* on ships and new buildings. Also, significant changes and original remedies have been introduced to ensure a quick and rewarding enforcement of ship mortgages. As such, the new law is supposed to provide a solid basis for the development of the ship finance market in Turkey. It remains to be seen the extent to which this aim is achieved in practice.

References

Abraham HJ (1950) Die Schiffshypothek im deutschen und ausländischen Recht. Übersee-Studien zum Handels-, Schiffahrts- und Versicherungsrecht Heft 20. W. Kohlhammer, Stuttgart
Akinci S (1958) Türk Hukukunda Gemi İpoteği, Ankara
Atamer K (1998) Maritime liens: Turkey. In: Tetley W, Wilkins RC (eds) Maritime liens and claims, 2nd edn. International Shipping Publications, Montreal
Atamer K (2007) Legislación, Jurisprudencia y Bibliografía en Derecho Marítimo Turco 2004–2006. In: Arroyo I (ed) Anuario de Derecho Maritimo 2007, vol XXIV

[174] Art. 1119–1130 N-TCC.
[175] Art. 1119(1), Art. 1128(1) N-TCC.
[176] Art. 1123(1) N-TCC.

Atamer K (2009) Reform des Seehandelsrechts im Entwurf des Türkischen Handelsgesetzbuchs. In: Atamer YM, Hopt KJ (eds) Kompatibilität des türkischen und europäischen Wirtschaftsrechts – Der neue türkische HGB-Entwurf und benachbarte Rechtsgebiete. Tübingen Mohr Siebeck, Tübingen

Atamer K (2009) Bağlama Kütüğü: Yasama Amacı, Uygulama Alanı ve Özel Hukuk Kurallarına Etkisi (The home port log: legislative purpose, scope of application and impact on private law provisions). Banka ve Ticaret Hukuku Dergisi (Banking and Commercial Law Journal, Ankara, cited in the Index to Foreign Legal Periodicals) 2009, vol XXV, issue 4 (Dedicated to the Memory of Prof. Dr. Reha Poroy)

Atamer K (2010) Reform des türkischen Transport-und Seefrachtrechts. Transportrecht ("TranspR")

Atamer K (2011) Das neue türkische Handelsgesetzbuch. Transportrecht ("TranspR")

Atamer K (2012) New Turkish law of ship mortgages and enforcement. In: Turkish Maritime Law Association, Deutscher Verein für Internationales Seerecht (eds) Recent developments in maritime law. Istanbul

Atamer Y (2008) Rezeption und Weiterentwicklung des Schweizerischen Zivilgesetzbuches in der Türkei. Rabels Zeitschrift für ausländisches und internationales Privatrecht, vol 72, number 4

Atamer Y (2009) Türkisches Zivilgesetzbuch und Obligationenrecht. In: Basedow J, Hopt K, Zimmermann R (eds) Handwörterbuch des Europäischen Privatrechts, Band II

Bandak H (2008) Die Rezeption des schweizerischen Zivilgesetzbuches in der Türkei. Ernst und Werner Gieseking, Würzburg

Baysal B (2008) Die Rezeption des westlichen Rechts im Allgemeinen und des ZGB im Besonderen im Modernisierungsprozess der Türkei nach 1926. In: Kieser H-L, Meier A, Stoffel W (eds) Revolution islamischen Rechts - Das Schweizerische ZGB in der Türkei

Berlingieri F (1995) The 1993 convention on maritime liens and mortgages. Lloyd's Maritime Commercial Law Quarterly 1995 ("LMCLQ")

Berlingieri F (1996) The convention on maritime liens and mortgages, 1993. Comité Maritime International (CMI) Yearbook 1996

Berlingieri F (2011) Berlingieri on arrest of ships, 5th edn. Informa Law, London

Buz V (2007) Die Rezeption des Schweizerischen OR in der Türkei. In: Sirmen L, Kırca Ç, Buz V (eds) Symposium anlässlich des 80. Jahrestages des Inkrafttretens des Türkischen Zivilgesetzbuches

Czerwenka B (1994) Internationales übereinkommen von 1993 über Schiffsgläubigerrechte und Schiffshypotheken. Transportrecht ("TranspR")

Damar D, Rösler H (2011) Türkisches Zivil-, Handels- und Kollisionsrecht im Zeichen der Modernisierung - Reform- und Systemfragen. Zeitschrift für Europäisches Privatrecht 19

Günay B (2007) Turkish law of ship arrest and the Draft Turkish Commercial Code. J Maritime Law Commerce 38(83)

Hirsch E (1938) Der Zentralbegriff des Handelsrechts - Eine Vorstudie zur Reform des Türkischen Handelsgesetzbuchs. Annuario di Diritto Comparato e di Studi Legislativi, Seconda Serie, vol XIII, Parte I, Dottrina

Hirsch E (1954) Die Einflüsse und Wirkungen ausländischen Rechts auf das heutige türkische Recht. Zeitschrift für das Gesamte Handelsrecht ("ZHR") 116

Hirsch E (1956) Das neue türkische Handelsgesetzbuch. Zeitschrift für das Gesamte Handelsrecht ("ZHR") 119

Hirsch E (1982) Rezeption als sozialer Prozess - Erläutert am Beispiel der Türkei. Duncker & Humblot, Berlin

Hirsch E (2008) Als Rechtsgelehrter im Lande Atatürks. BWV Verlag, Berlin

Hungar J-U (1998) Die Rechtsstellung des Schiffshypothekengläubigers im Versicherungsfall. Diss. Hamburg 1998, Versicherungsrechtliche Studien Bd. 58, Frankfurt am Main

Kalpsüz T (2004) Gemi Rehni. Genişletilmiş 5. Baskı, Ankara

Sözer B (2007) Turkey - Part II. In: Breitzke C, Lux J, Verlaan P (eds) Maritime law handbook, suppl 29. International Bar Association

Sözer B (2011) Deniz Ticareti Hukuku: Gemi - Donatan - Taşıyan ve Deniz Ticareti Hukuku'nda Sorumluluk Rejimi, İstanbul

Staudinger/Wolfsteiner (2009) Einl 1 zu §§1113 ff

Tekinalp G (2007) The 2007 Turkish code concerning Private International Law and International Civil Procedure. Yearbook of private international law 2007, vol IX

Turkish Maritime Law Association, Deutscher Verein für Internationales Seerecht (2012) Recent developments in maritime law. Istanbul

Ünan S, İzzet H (2011) La nouvelle réglementation du droit maritime en Turquie. Droit Maritime Français

Wersel C (1996) Das übereinkommen über Schiffsgläubigerrechte und Schiffshypotheken vom 6. Mai 1993. Schriften zum Seehandelsrecht, Hamburg

Chapter 13
Double Tax Treaties: Practical Problems in Article 8 of the OECD Model Convention

Florian Haase

Abstract Article 8 of the OECD Model Convention is a special provision in the Model Convention. It prevails over the permanent establishment principle of Article 7 and deals with the taxation of profits from the operation of ships in international traffic. The scope of this provision is confined to business operations in the maritime sector, but is of particular importance. The tax structures of many large shipping companies rely on Article 8 of the OECD Model Convention. Surprisingly, however, several questions remain unsolved. Court rulings hardly exist. Moreover, the OECD Commentary to Article 8 of the Model Convention is rather outdated; it has been amended only on rare occasions in the past. The main problems of Article 8 of the OECD Model Convention relate to the treatment of preparatory and ancillary activities, the use of containers, bareboat chartering and the definition of "international traffic".

13.1 Introduction

Article 8 of the OECD Model Convention deals with the taxation rights of states that have concluded double tax treaties with other contracting states regarding profits from the operation of ships in international traffic. Whether a state has permission to tax the respective profits inevitably influences the way how investors finance their investment. This is important for the state where the investment is financed as well as the vehicle through which it is financed; it is sensible to have the possibility of interest deduction in the same state where the profits are generated and taxed. This is true in principle, even if a tonnage tax regime is applicable.

F. Haase (✉)
Rödl & Partner, Kehrwieder 9, 20457 Hamburg, Germany
e-mail: florian.haase@roedl.com

O. Schinas et al. (eds.), *HSBA Handbook on Ship Finance*,
DOI 10.1007/978-3-662-43410-9_13,

13.1.1 Purpose of Double Tax Treaties

In today's ever-developing economy, taxpayers are increasingly affected by the tax laws of more than one country. Most international businesses—from the individual entrepreneur to a large multinational corporate group—need occasional foreign tax advice or may even have to pay taxes abroad and not just in their home country. This is true for any business in the shipping industry, as this remains a truly international environment. Vessels, sailing boats and cruise ships of all kinds and sizes travel constantly across the oceans. A significant part of global trade is still carried out through boats.

The inherent trouble with multinational tax effects is that the tax laws of different autonomous countries are almost never coordinated; they are simply not "in tune". This can result in double taxation for a specific taxpayer if two or more countries want to tax the same fact pattern at the same time. Naturally, double taxation has a harmful effect on the exchange of goods and services as well as on the movement of capital, technology and people. Even a double non-taxation may have a harmful effect, but such cases are hardly ever discussed in public. Removing the obstacles brought about by double taxation is unquestionably the only way of building economic relations between two or more countries.

This is where double tax treaties come into play. They aim at eliminating double taxation by dividing and distributing taxation rights among the contracting states. The state of residence usually has the sole taxation right. This state must also apply one of the two internationally recognized methods of avoiding double taxation—i.e. the exemption method and the tax credit method. The state of source, on the other hand, is usually entitled to either a restricted taxation right or no taxation right at all.

Within this setting, the "shipping article"—i.e. Article 8 of the OECD Model Convention—provides special rules regarding the elimination of double taxation on profits from the operation of ships in international traffic. The OECD Model Convention, which was first published in 1955, is recommended by the Council of the OECD and serves as a uniform basis for the most common problems arising from international double taxation. The Model Convention and the accompanying Commentary standardize, clarify and confirm the fiscal situation of taxpayers who are engaged in commercial, industrial, financial or other activities in other countries through the application by all countries of common solutions to identical cases of double taxation. Germany, for instance, has concluded more than 90 double tax treaties, most of which follow the suggestions of the OECD Model Convention. The same is true for most EU/EEA member states, but worldwide, states frequently use other models like the UN model or the US model. It is not mandatory for states to use any one of the models and a country faces no sanctions in case it negotiates its treaties in a way that differs from the model.

From the German point of view, the Commentary is crucial for taxpayers, particularly with respect to Article 8 of the OECD Model Convention, because there is hardly any German case law on it. Therefore, the Commentary provides guidance and help with respect to the interpretation of Article 8.

13.1.2 Brief History of Article 8 of the OECD Model Convention

Article 8 of the OECD Model Convention has a long history. As early as 1920, when the League of Nations first started working on international double taxation, the shipping industry had already experienced a major tax dispute between states. The United States and the UK had introduced special tax rules for the shipping industry, and Japan, Norway, Italy and France followed suit. Immediately after World War I, some states concluded bilateral treaties regarding the free transit of vessels navigating through international waters. These treaties included tax provisions for foreign shipping companies. In 1923, the Financial Committee of the League of Nations submitted a Report on Double Taxation with particular focus on maritime and air transport activities. The report was revised in 1925 by the resolution of a group of technical experts. These technical experts also published the first draft of a bilateral convention for the prevention of double taxation in 1927.

In 1931, the first draft of a multinational tax treaty was published. This convention reaffirmed the "centre of real management" as the decisive criterion for taxation rights in the shipping industry. In the following years, the Financial Committee of the League of Nations continued working on revisions of the existing draft conventions, but only in 1943 and 1946 were these discussions implemented into the Mexico and London Model Conventions. In these conventions, the "centre of real management" was still the crucial factor used to determine taxation rights. However, the Mexico Model Convention used the term "fiscal domicile" for the first time in history to represent the state where the shipping enterprise was incorporated. Naturally, placing emphasis on the place of incorporation rather than the place of effective management produces significantly different results.

In 1956, the Fiscal Committee of the OECD commenced work on double taxation, which led to the famous 1959 draft report. This report introduced the term, "place of effective management", which was incorporated into Article 8 of the OECD Model Tax Convention in the year 1963. Ever since, Article 8 has remained largely unchanged, even though the Commentary has been amended several times. The changes and amendments were made with respect to preparatory and ancillary activities and the special rules presented in paragraphs 3 and 4 of Article 8 of the OECD Model Convention, but the principle of paragraph 1 remains the same.

13.1.3 Reflection of Article 8 in German Tax Treaties

13.1.3.1 Paragraph 1 of Article 8

Regarding the general rule set forth in Article 8 paragraph 1 of the OECD Model Convention, it must be noted that Germany has concluded a significant number of tax treaties that deviate from this rule. According to these treaties, the decisive factor is not the place of management of the enterprise that operates a ship, but the residence of the enterprise or the entrepreneur (e.g. tax treaties with Azerbaijan, Australia, Iceland, Indonesia, Japan, Canada, Kenya, Lithuania, Sweden, Turkey, the United States, Russia, Malaysia, Liberia, Latvia and the Philippines).

Deviation from the OECD Model Convention can lead to difficulties in determining tax residency in case partnerships are used for the operation of ships (this is not unusual, particularly under the German tonnage tax system). From the German perspective, if a partnership operates a ship in international waters, only the partners can be tax residents within the meaning of Article 3 paragraph 1 lit. d and Article 4 of the OECD Model Convention. As the partnership is tax-transparent under German tax law, it cannot be a resident of a contracting state. Qualification conflicts may arise if foreign countries qualify a partnership differently, and these conflicts may eventually result in a double taxation that cannot be eliminated.

Tax treaties with Singapore and Korea state that tax exemptions on shipping income shall be granted only if domestic tax residents do not control a foreign enterprise. For instance, consider a Korean corporation that has German tax residents as shareholders with a qualifying shareholding of more than 25 % (Singapore: 50 %). This corporation may rely on the tax exemption in Germany only if it can prove that the tax levied equals the tax that is usually levied without any allowances or tax benefits. The old treaty with Cyprus provided for a similar rule, but the new treaty as of 7 November 2011 lacks such a provision, and with good cause: the German Foreign Tax Act with its add-back rules is applicable as a tax treaty anyway.

Many German treaties, particularly the older ones, have special clauses for the taxation of income resulting from the leasing of containers (e.g. Denmark, Poland, India, Japan, Canada, Korea, Croatia, Norway, Malta, Russia, Sweden, Ukraine, Italy, Romania, Singapore, the United States and the United Arab Emirates).

13.1.3.2 Paragraph 2 of Article 8

Many of the German tax treaties have no special provision for the operation of boats in inland waterways. It is small wonder that the list of countries primarily comprises states with which Germany shares no inland waterways (e.g. Australia, China, the UK, India, Italy, Japan, Canada, Malta, the United States and Cyprus).

13.1.3.3 Paragraph 3 of Article 8

Many German tax treaties have no special provision regarding the taxation of income if the place of effective management of a shipping enterprise or of an island waterways transport enterprise is aboard a ship or a boat (tax treaties with, e.g. Australia, Greece, the UK, Ireland, Japan, Norway, Russia, Sweden and the United States).

13.1.3.4 Paragraph 4 of Article 8

Most German tax treaties have a similar provision as seen in Article 8 paragraph 4 of the OECD Model Convention regarding participation in a pool, a joint business or an international operating agency. Only the tax treaties with France and Turkey lack such a special provision. However, the tax consequences are the same even in these rare cases because the income in question, in most cases, is closely connected to the income from the transport activities mentioned in the first three paragraphs of the OECD Model Convention and will follow the same rules. Therefore, Article 8 paragraph 4 of the OECD Model Convention has only a declaratory meaning in this respect.

13.2 Article 8 of the OECD Model Convention

13.2.1 General

13.2.1.1 Special Purpose Provision

Article 8 of the OECD Model Convention describes a special case of business profits (profits of an enterprise as defined in Article 3 paragraph 1 lit. c of the OECD Model Convention) as set forth in Article 7. The permanent establishment principle usually applies for the taxation of these business profits. This principle means that the only states entitled to tax the profits are those where an enterprise maintains a permanent establishment in the sense of Article 5 of the OECD Model Convention.

In the international shipping business, the permanent establishment principle would lead to a fragmentation of taxation rights. For instance, when a vessel cruises through the domestic waters of 42 countries on its way around the world, all these countries would be entitled to tax the arising profit. This is impossible from an administrative point of view, and many other practical problems would arise as well. Therefore, Article 8 paragraph 1 of the OECD Model Convention concentrates the sole taxation right for the entire profit in the state wherein the place of management of the enterprise is located. This clearly contravenes the general rule stated in Article 7 paragraph 1 sentence 2 of the OECD Model Convention.

In the shipping industry, Article 8 of the OECD Model Convention plays a crucial role. This is particularly true for the practice of ship financing through German closed-end funds. These funds, which are usually established in the legal form of a GmbH & Co. KG (limited liability partnership with a limited liability company as a general partner and investors as limited partners), have been blockbusters not only on the German market, but also abroad. Many foreign investors are nowadays limited partners in a German GmbH & Co. KG, and it is only thanks to Article 8 of the OECD Model Convention that such a KG actually benefits from the German tonnage tax system. The same is possible with other jurisdictions that provide beneficial tonnage tax regimes. Article 8 of the OECD Model Convention alone makes it possible to utilize such systems provided the place of management of an investment vehicle that operates or charters the ship is located in the respective country.

13.2.1.2 Ranking Compared to Other Treaty Provisions

Within its scope, Article 8 of the OECD Model Convention prevails over other provisions of the applicable double tax treaty, which is why particularly Article 7 of the OECD Model Convention cannot be applied. Income within the meaning of Articles 10 (dividends), 11 (interest payments) or 12 (royalties) of the OECD Model Convention may be taxed in accordance with the mentioned provisions provided they are not effectively connected to the shipping enterprise. If the underlying source of income can be allocated to a permanent establishment of the shipping enterprise in the other contracting state, the permanent establishment principle may apply again (Article 10 paragraph 4, Article 11 paragraph 4 and Article 12 paragraph 3 of the OECD Model Convention).

Article 8 of the OECD Model Convention does not cover profits arising from the sale of ships or boats that operate in international traffic. In this respect, Article 13 paragraph 3 of the OECD Model Convention would apply, but the consequences are more or less the same as if Article 8 of the OECD Model Convention had been applied. Lastly, Article 15 paragraph 3 of the OECD Model Convention refers to income from employment for duties carried out aboard a ship or boat.

13.2.2 Requirements (Paragraph 1)

According to Article 8 paragraph 1 of the OECD Model Convention, profits from the operation of ships in international traffic shall be taxable only in the contracting state wherein the place of effective management of the enterprise is situated. As mentioned above, the object of paragraph 1 concerning profits from the operation of ships is to secure that such profits will be taxed in one state alone to avoid a fragmentation of taxation rights.

13.2.2.1 Operation of Ships

Article 8 paragraph 1 of the OECD Model Convention deals with profits arising from the operation of ships. This covers situations where the respective "enterprise of a Contracting State" (as defined in Article 3 paragraph 1 lit. d of the OECD Model Convention) actually operates the ship itself, as well as situations where profits are generated by leasing a ship on charter fully equipped ("time charter"), crewed and supplied.

The profits covered by paragraph 1 consist primarily of profits directly generated by the enterprise from the transportation of passengers or cargo by the ships that it operates in international traffic. However, as international transport has evolved, shipping transport enterprises inevitably perform a large variety of activities to permit, facilitate or support their international traffic operations. Paragraph 1, therefore, covers profits from activities that are directly connected with such operations as well as profits from activities that are not directly connected with the operation of the enterprise's ships in international traffic as long as they are ancillary to such operations.

The wording of Article 8 paragraph 1 of the OECD Model Convention indicates that enterprises that are not exclusively engaged in shipping or inland waterways transport come within the scope of this paragraph with respect to profits arising from the operation of their ships or boats. If such an enterprise maintains a permanent establishment in a foreign country exclusively to monitor its shipping operations, the OECD sees no reason to treat such establishments differently from the permanent establishments of enterprises engaged exclusively in the above-mentioned activities. On the contrary, if a foreign permanent establishment maintains installations for operating the ships or incurs other costs in connection with the carriage of the enterprise's goods, its expenditure in the operation of the ships should be allocated not to the permanent establishment but to the enterprise itself because none of the profits generated through the carrying benefits the former.

13.2.2.2 International Traffic

The term "international traffic" is defined in Article 3 paragraph 1 lit. e of the OECD Model Convention with binding effect on both contracting states. According to this provision, international traffic means any transport by a ship (or aircraft) operated by an enterprise that has its place of effective management in a contracting state, except when the ship (or aircraft) is operated solely between places in the other contracting state.

According to the Commentary to Article 3 paragraph 1 lit. e of the OECD Model Convention (see paragraph 6 and, for the above as well as for the following, refer to the other paragraphs of the Commentary), the definition of the term "international traffic" is much broader than usually understood. The broader definition is intended to preserve for the state of the place of effective management the right to tax purely domestic traffic as well as international traffic between third states, and to allow the other contracting state to tax traffic solely within its borders.

A ship is operated solely between places in the other contracting state in relation to a particular voyage if the place of departure and the place of arrival of the ship are both in that other contracting state. However, the definition applies when the journey of a ship between places in the other contracting state forms part of a longer voyage of that ship involving a place of departure or a place of arrival outside that other contracting state.

13.2.2.3 Determination of Profit

Each contracting state decides independently, according to its national tax law, how to determine and assess profits from the operation of ships in international traffic. The contracting state where the place of effective management of the enterprise that operates the ships is located is in a position to determine the profit because it may tax it under the applicable double tax treaty. The other state also determines the profit according to its own national law, but only to determine which profit is exempt.

13.2.3 Consequences (Paragraph 1): Tax Exemption

Article 8 paragraph 1 of the OECD Model Convention concentrates the sole taxation right for the whole profit in the state where the place of management of the enterprise is located, which effectively results in a tax exemption. The taxation right is exclusive as explicitly indicated in the provision ("shall be only taxable"). A potential double taxation is technically eliminated directly through Article 8 of the OECD Model Convention so that particularly Article 23 of the OECD Model Convention is not applicable.

It must be noted that the tax exemption is granted only with progression, but whether the progression is reflected depends on the applicable national law (for Germany, see section 32b paragraph 1 sentence 2 no. 4 German ITA).

In case ships are operated through a foreign permanent establishment of the enterprise that operates the ships and that is not the effective place of management (as usual in practice), the following special rule applies: where ships are operated in international traffic, the application of Article 8 of the OECD Model Convention to the profits arising from such operation will not be affected by the ships being operated by a foreign permanent establishment that is not the effective place of management of the whole enterprise (e.g. ships put into service by the permanent establishment or figuring on the balance sheet of the permanent establishment).

13.2.4 Inland Waterways (Paragraph 2)

According to Article 8 paragraph 2 of the OECD Model Convention, profits from the operation of boats engaged in inland waterways transport shall be taxable only in the contracting state where the place of effective management of the enterprise is situated. The aim of paragraph 2 is to apply the same tax treatment to transport on rivers, canals and lakes as to shipping in international traffic. This is why the rules and problems explained with respect to the operation of ships in international traffic in this chapter also apply to profits from the operation of boats engaged in inland waterways transport.

The practical problems attached to the operation of boats engaged in inland waterways transport are frequently addressed specially in bilateral agreements. In many of these agreements, it is agreed that profits from the operation of vessels engaged in fishing, dredging or hauling activities on the high seas shall also be treated as income as per Article 8 paragraph 2 of the OECD Model Convention.

13.2.5 Place of Management Aboard (Paragraph 3)

If the place of effective management of a shipping enterprise or of an inland waterways transport enterprise is aboard a ship or a boat, then it shall be deemed to be situated in the contracting state where the home harbor of the ship or boat is situated, or if there is no such harbor, in the contracting state of which the operator of the ship or boat is a resident.

13.2.6 Pool Agreements, etc. (Paragraph 4)

According to Article 8 paragraph 4 of the OECD Model Convention, the provisions of paragraph 1 will also apply to profits arising from participation in a pool, a joint business or an international operating agency. This is because various forms of international cooperation exist in the shipping industry. In practice, international cooperation is often secured through pooling agreements or other conventions of a similar kind, which set forth specific rules for apportioning profits from the joint business. Although the Model Convention is very clear about such cooperation, many states have clarified the taxation position of the participant to the extent that paragraph 1 applies “only to so much of the profits so derived as is attributable to the participant in proportion to its share in the joint operation”.

13.3 Major Practical Problems

13.3.1 Preparatory and Ancillary Activities

Article 8 paragraph 1 of the OECD Model Convention covers profits from activities that are directly connected with the operation of a ship in international traffic as well as profits from activities that are not directly connected with the operation of the enterprise‘s ships in international traffic as long as they are preparatory or ancillary to such an operation. In practice, states sometimes debate over which activities are preparatory or ancillary and which ones are not. In some cases, the profits from these activities are higher than the profits from the operation of the ship, so it is a hot topic indeed.

For profits derived by an enterprise from the transportation of passengers or cargo otherwise than by ships that operate in international traffic, most states agree to an interpretation in a way that such transportation is directly connected with the operation and would thus be regarded as an ancillary activity. For instance, if an enterprise engaged in international transport conveys some of its passengers or cargo internationally through ships operated by other enterprises—e.g. under slot-chartering arrangements—this would be regarded as an ancillary activity.

Another example is of an enterprise that transports passengers or cargo by ships operating in international traffic and that undertakes to have those passengers or cargo collected in the country where the transport begins or transported and delivered in the country of destination by any mode of inland transportation operated by other enterprises. In such a case, most countries will agree to the following: any profits derived by the first enterprise from arranging such transportation by other enterprises are covered by Article 8 paragraph 1 of the OECD Model Convention even though the profits derived by the other enterprises that provide such inland transportation are not covered by the same article.

Paragraph 8 of the Commentary to Article 8 of the OECD Model Convention states that if an enterprise frequently sells tickets on behalf of other transport enterprises at a location that it maintains primarily for the purpose of ticket selling, such sale of tickets on behalf of other enterprises will be either directly connected with voyages aboard ships that the enterprise operates or ancillary to its own sales. Advertising provided by the enterprise for other enterprises in magazines offered aboard ships that it operates or at its business locations is ancillary to its operation of these ships; profits generated by such advertising will come under the scope of Article 8 paragraph 1 of the OECD Model Convention.

An enterprise that maintains assets or personnel in a foreign country for the purposes of operating its ships in international traffic may also derive income from providing goods or services in that country to other transportation enterprises. This would usually include, for instance, the provision of goods and services by engineers, equipment maintenance staff, cargo handlers, catering staff and customer service personnel. Where the enterprise provides such goods to or performs services for other enterprises and where such activities are directly connected or ancillary to the enterprise‘s operation of ships in international traffic, Article 8 paragraph 1 of the OECD Model Convention can be applied in most countries.

13.3.2 Containers

As stated in the Commentary and as can be seen in practice, containers are used extensively in international transport in today’s ever-developing economy. Such containers are also frequently used in inland transport. Profits derived by an enterprise engaged in international transport from the lease of containers are usually either directly connected or at least ancillary to its operation of ships in international traffic. The same conclusion would apply with respect to profits derived by such an enterprise from the short-term storage of such containers and from detention charges (penalties) for the late return of containers.

Whether the income from the lease of containers falls within the scope of Article 8 of the OECD Model Convention is of particular interest for enterprises that lease containers but do not operate any ships. Some tax treaties allow for such a situation if one takes the wording literally, but this interpretation is not in line with the approach of the OECD. The German tax authorities also do not share this view, which is why some existing German container funds are in serious trouble. Germany has expressed a reservation to the respective paragraphs of the Commentary.

In practice, the German tax authorities have laid down their view of the tax treatment of the use of containers and connected services in relation to shipping income in a rather early, but still valid, decree as of 15 April 1969 (Hessisches Finanzministerium, Handbuch des Aussensteuerrechts, C5 paragraph 15). The decree lists activities that are directly connected with the operation of ships in international traffic. Moreover, the German tax authorities are of the view that all activities rendered without monetary consideration come under the scope of Article 8 of the OECD Model Convention, provided the other contracting state agrees to reciprocity in this respect.

13.3.3 Bareboat Charter

As stated above, Article 8 paragraph 1 of the OECD Model Convention also covers profits that are generated by leasing a ship on charter fully equipped ("time charter"), crewed and supplied. However, only Article 7 of the OECD Model Convention (and not Article 8) applies to the profits that arise from leasing a ship on a bareboat charter basis, except when it is the ancillary activity of an enterprise in the international operation of ships. However, things may change with the new tax treaty between Cyprus and Germany. In its revised shipping article, the state explicitly allows an occasional bareboat charter.

13.3.4 International Traffic

Despite the definition in Article 3 paragraph 1 lit. e of the OECD Model Convention, the involved states sometimes debate over whether a ship is actually operated in international traffic. One example involves an enterprise of a contracting state that sells, through an agent in the other contracting state, tickets for a passage that is confined wholly within the first-mentioned state or, alternatively, within a third state.

In this case, Article 8 paragraph 1 of the OECD Model Convention prohibits the other states from taxing the profits of either voyage. The other state is allowed to tax such an enterprise of the first-mentioned state only when the operations are confined solely to places in that other state.

Some states feel that the definition of international traffic should refer to a transport as the journey of a passenger or cargo where any voyage of a passenger or cargo solely between two places in the same contracting state should not be considered as covered by the definition even if that voyage is made on a ship used in international traffic. Thus, the definition should not apply to a transport by an enterprise that has its place of effective management in one contracting state when the ship is operated between two places in the other state, even if part of the transport takes place in that state. For instance, if a cruise begins and ends in that other state without a stop in a foreign port, it does not constitute a transport of passengers in international traffic.

13.3.4.1 Investment Income

When international shipping companies invest liquid monies, the question arises whether such investment income (in most cases, capital income like dividends or interest) comes under the scope of Article 8 paragraph 1 of the OECD Model Tax Convention. In general, the investment income of shipping enterprises must be subjected to the treatment ordinarily applied to the respective class of income under the treaty, except where the investment that generates the income is an integral part of carrying on the business of operating the ships in international traffic in a contracting state. In the latter case, the investment is considered to be directly connected with such operations.

For instance, as stated in the Commentary, Article 8 paragraph 1 of the OECD Model Convention would apply to the interest income generated by the cash required in a contracting state for carrying on that business or by bonds posted as security where this is required by law to carry on the business. In such cases, the investment is necessary to allow the operation of the ships at that particular location. On the other hand, Article 8 paragraph 1 of the OECD Model Convention will not apply if the interest income is derived in the course of handling the cash flow or other treasury activities for permanent establishments of the enterprise to which the income is not attributable, nor for associated enterprises regardless of whether these are located within or outside the contracting state, or for the head office (centralization or treasury and investment activities). It will also not apply to interest income generated by the short-term investment of profits arising from the local operation of the business where the funds invested are not required for that particular operation.

13.4 Future Developments

While Article 8 of the OECD Model Convention remains unchanged, in the most recent Update 2010 to the Commentary, paragraphs 20, 21 and 38 were rephrased and paragraph 43 (new reservations) was added. The next Model Tax Convention Update is expected in 2015, but the OECD is yet to publish whether Article 8 of the Model Convention will also be in focus. Nevertheless, a change is doubtful because unlike other articles, Article 8 was not part of the discussion paper on the OECD Tax Agenda 2011, where the OECD outlined their view on articles that need revision soon.

Part V
Challenges and Advances

Chapter 14
Ship Leasing

Philip Clausius

Abstract In its most general definition "leasing" is a process by which one party obtains the use of a fixed asset for which it must pay a series of contractual periodic rentals to the owner of the fixed asset. The party obtaining the use of the asset is called the lessee, whereas the party providing the use of the asset is called the lessor. In this chapter, the focus is on the longer term ship leasing market, which is in fact an alternative finance market for the industry. The motivation for entering into a leasing transaction could be based on any single or combination of factors including cash management, funding diversification, cost, accounting and technological obsolescence risk mitigation. Compared to ship operators, the risk-return profile of the leasing business is more attractive and lessors can usually achieve higher financial leverage in debt markets that can drive returns on equity (ROEs) to attractive levels. Ship leasing transactions can be structured in several forms and each has its advantages and disadvantages. This is also discussed in the text in greater details. In pricing lease transactions, lessors typically focus on target project returns, equity returns and cash yield. The assumed residual value of the asset at lease maturity will have a significant impact on pricing. Lessors face three broad risks credit, asset and financial which need to be addressed appropriately through a disciplined risk management approach. The recent financial and shipping crises have posed significant challenges for the industry. Bank lenders have become highly selective in grading fresh credit and high profile defaults of companies, such as Sanko, Korea Line, Berlian Laju Tanker, Armada and Brittania Bulk, as well as complex restructurings of Torm, CSAV and CMA CGM, have shed light into the risk of off-balance sheet obligations. Significant developments to ship leasing are the proposed changes to lease accounting rules. If implemented, "lease buying

P. Clausius (✉)
Transport Capital Pte. Ltd., 3 Temasek Avenue, #21-00 Cantennial Tower, 039190 Singapore, Singapore
e-mail: pc@transportcapital.com

O. Schinas et al. (eds.), *HSBA Handbook on Ship Finance*, 245
DOI 10.1007/978-3-662-43410-9_14,

behavior" is likely to change since obligations that were heretofore treated off-balance sheet will henceforth be capitalized onto the balance sheet.

14.1 Overview

14.1.1 General Leasing Definition

In its most general definition "leasing" is a process by which one party obtains the use of a fixed asset for which it must pay a series of contractual periodic rentals to the owner of the fixed asset. The party obtaining the use of the asset is called the lessee, whereas the party providing the use of the asset is called the lessor.

14.1.2 Ship Leasing Definition

If one applies the above definition to shipping then any type of vessel charter agreement, regardless of type and term, is in fact a ship leasing transaction. At its most extreme, even a ship-owner trading his vessels in the spot market is a lessor, although he would never use that terminology. The lines are further blurred because many shipping companies charter vessels in as well as out. Hence, these companies are both lessor and lessee at the same time, and sometimes even in relation to the same asset. The latter, known as a sub-lease, is a transaction where the asset is re-leased by the original lessee to a third party, and the lease agreement between the two original parties remains in effect (as defined in Financial Accounting Standards, FAS 13).

Just consider the dry bulk market boom prior to the financial crisis. During that period, vessels were chartered and sub-chartered many times as the market kept rising. Every sublet involved a party taking the role of lessee and lessor at the same time, obviously with the expectation of earning a spread between charter-in and -out cost.

However, for the purposes of this book, we shall focus on the longer term ship leasing market, which is in fact an alternative finance market for the industry. Hence, the question is what the approximate lease term is with which opportunistic market-related chartering activity ends and more strategic finance-related leasing activity starts. Clearly there is no generally accepted rule for such dividing line. Based on many discussions with industry participants over the years the author believes that any chartering activity for a term of at least 5 years is of a strategic finance-related nature and therefore can be considered a substitute for a vessel purchase or ownership. Hence, this book will equate long term chartering activity for terms of 5 years or longer to the ship leasing definition.

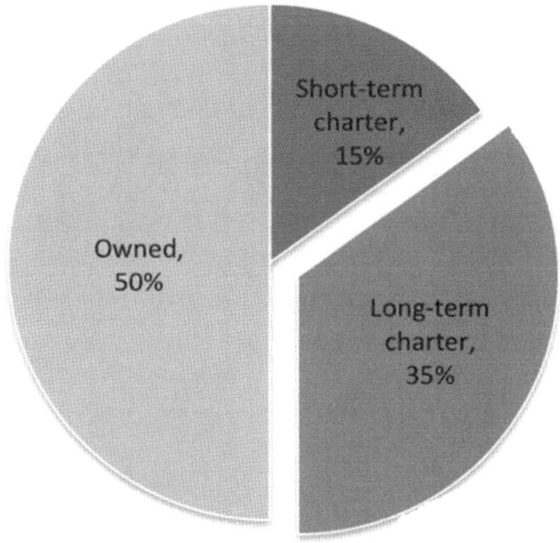

Fig. 14.1 Financing mix for container lines

14.1.3 Ship Leasing Market Size

There is no publicly available data that can reliably estimate the size of the ship leasing market because there is no consensus of what leasing constitutes in the shipping industry (see discussion above).

Of all shipping sectors, the most promising one for which to attempt estimating the ship leasing market size is the container vessel sector. We know from public disclosures of larger container lines that they charter about 40–60 % of their shipping capacity, with the balance being owned by them. Interestingly, this so called lease penetration ratio of 40–60 % is about the same for the commercial aviation industry. The chartered capacity by container lines includes vessels typically smaller ones—on shorter term charters (less than 5 years in duration). Whilst there are more ships on shorter term charters, the longer term charters of the larger ships are more important for the container liner industry in capacity terms. Hence, if we arbitrarily assume that 70 % of the chartered tonnage capacity is on long-term charters, then we would come to the following financing mix for container lines assuming an overall lease penetration rate of 50 %, see Fig. 14.1 (Garfield 2012, p. 3).

Whilst there is reasonably reliable data available for the container ship sector this is not the case for the two large commodity shipping sectors of dry bulk and tanker. However, it is safe to assume that the lease penetration rate for dry bulk and tanker is significantly lower than for the container sector. The main reason for this lower lease penetration rate is that dry bulk and tanker shipping companies have historically derived a significant portion of their investment return from the timely purchase and sale of the vessel itself, whereas container lines earn their return from operating a network, somewhat similar to the airline industry. One of the disadvantages of leasing in that context is that the leasing structure always entails a restriction in asset disposal flexibility, hence impeding the return potential for the operator through a timely asset sale.

14.2 Leasing Motivations

14.2.1 Lessee's Perspective

Why do companies generally and ship operators specifically enter into leasing transactions when presumably they could purchase or own the assets instead? The motivation for entering into a leasing transaction could be based on any single or combination of the below factors:

14.2.1.1 Cash Management

Especially for very capital intensive industries, such as shipping, cash management is the single most important motivator to enter into leasing transactions. Leasing effectively provides 100 % financing for an asset. On the other hand, the mainstay ship finance tool, the first priority ship mortgage, has typically provided financing for 60–80 % of a vessel's value. The balance would normally come from the operator's equity, which adds up to significant absolute investment amounts, especially in the context of multi-vessel newbuilding orders. Clearly the "incremental cash flow" value, which leasing provides, is greatest at times when conventional bank finance is constrained and limited to low leverage ratios on the asset's value.

14.2.1.2 Funding Diversification

The financially more sophisticated companies attribute value to funding diversification and consider leasing an integral part of that funding mix. In shipping this is most evident with the container liner companies. As we are witnessing right now during the financial crisis, bank funding sources can dry up very quickly and in such situations it is of great value to have access to different sources of capital, be it bank finance, capital markets or leasing.

14.2.1.3 Cost

Whether leasing is perceived to be cost competitive compared to ownership by a potential lessee, depends entirely on the comparison that is employed. In shipping there is still significant confusion over what the correct comparison is. If one compares the cost of a lease with the cost of debt finance, it is not a like for like exercise because it assumes that the cost of the operator's equity in the bank finance scenario is zero. The correct comparison is between the cost of the lease (IRR calculation taking into account the cost of the asset, rental stream and residual value) and the weighted-average cost of capital (WACC)[1] of the lessee company. It is interesting to note that in shipping, the great majority of companies, particularly but not only private ones have either never considered their cost of equity or have simply determined it at a level that is not commensurate with the risks and cyclicality of the industry. As such, ship lessors are still facing a great challenge in winning the cost argument when marketing transactions.

14.2.1.4 Accounting

Historically, accounting treatment of leases has been a significant motivation to consider leasing as opposed to ownership. Below, we describe the differences between a capital and operating lease and the lease accounting requirements by a lessee and lessor.

For financial accounting purposes, a lease must be classified, at its inception, as a capital lease or an operating lease. The classification criteria differ under various lease accounting standards. In general, a lease is considered a finance lease if it transfers substantially all the risks and rewards incidental to ownership. All other leases are classified as operating leases.

Table 14.1 describes the capital lease criteria established under currently applicable main accounting regimes, U.S. Generally Accepted Accounting Principles (U.S. GAAP) and International Financial Reporting Standards (IFRS).

If a lease, at its inception, meets any one of the four criteria listed under U.S. GAAP (FAS 13), it should be classified as a capital lease; otherwise the lease is considered an operating lease. Additionally for lessors, two other criteria must be met in order for a lease to be classified as a capital lease.

Under IFRS, a lease will be classified as a capital lease if it exhibits one or more of the situations listed under IAS 17 para 10 and IAS 17 para 11. Otherwise, the lease is considered an operating lease.

If a lease is classified as a capital lease, the lessee records the lease payments as liability and leased property as an asset on its balance sheet. The lessor, on the other hand, recognizes lease rentals and the unguaranteed residual value as a receivable in the balance sheet. Over the lease term, rentals are apportioned between a reduction in the receivable and finance income.

For an operating lease, the vessel cost is capitalized in the lessor's balance sheet and lease rentals are recorded as income during the period they are earned. For the lessee, rental payment is recognized as an expense in the income statement over the lease term.

Under U.S. GAAP and IFRS, even long-term leases for ships (up to 12 years for newbuildings) if structured correctly qualify as operating leases for accounting purposes. In other words, the transaction can stay "off-balance sheet". Only the

[1] WACC for a firm is calculated by weighting the cost of each source of funds by its proportion of the total market value of the firm.

Table 14.1 Capital lease criteria under U.S. GAAP and IFRS

U.S. GAAP (FAS 13)	IFRS (IAS 17)
1. The lease transfers ownership of the vessel to the lessee by the end of the lease term	
2. The lessee has the option to purchase the asset at a price which is sufficiently lower than the fair market value such that it is almost certain that the option will be exercised	
3. The lease term is ≥75 % of the estimated economic life of the asset	3. The lease term is for the major part of the economic life of the asset even if the title is not transferred
4. At inception of the lease, the present value of the minimum lease payments is ≥90 % of fair market value of the asset	4. At inception of the lease, the present value of the minimum lease payments amounts to at least substantially all of the fair value of the asset
Additional criteria for lessors:	
(a) Collectibility of the minimum lease payments is reasonably predictable	
(b) No important uncertainties surround the amount of unreimbursable costs yet to be incurred by the lessor under the lease	
	5. The assets are of a specialized nature such that only the lessee can use them without major modifications being made
	6. If the lessee is entitled to cancel the lease, the lessor's losses associated with the cancellation are borne by the lessee
	7. Gains or losses from fluctuations in the fair market value of the residual fall to the lessee
	8. The lessee has the ability to continue to lease for a secondary period at a rent that is substantially lower than market rent

annual rental payment is charged to the profit and loss account whereas the balance sheet will typically only contain a footnote disclosure setting out some detail of the future liabilities connected to the lease. To the superficial student of financial statements, the lessee company will appear less leveraged and likely more profitable than it actually is. More significantly, some loan agreements or bond indentures still exclude off-balance sheet obligations from their covenant test calculations. However, it is very important to note that experienced credit analysts will always capitalize off-balance sheet obligations back onto the balance sheet of the companies which they analyze, so as to get a true picture of risk and profitability. Financial covenants for new financings are today almost exclusively designed to take into account off-balance sheet obligations. But finally and most importantly U.S. GAAP and IFRS are working on the introduction of new lease accounting standards[2]), which will have a significant impact on "lease buying behaviour". Under the proposed changes to the lease accounting rules, all lease obligations will be capitalized on the balance sheets of the companies by calculating the net present

[2]Refer to the IFRS website for more information: http://www.ifrs.org/Current-Projects/IASB-Projects/Leases.

value of the remaining contracted lease obligations. (Refer to Section 7 for more on the change in "buying behaviour".)

14.2.1.5 Technological Obsolescence Risk Mitigation

In industries with a fast rate of technological change many companies prefer leasing to owning as they are concerned that the fixed assets might become outdated before the end of their anticipated useful economic lives. Leasing provides the option to allay the residual risk of these assets to a third party. In shipping, this is not a strong motivation to enter into a leasing transaction as technological change in the industry is only gradual and the premature obsolescence risk is therefore relatively small.

14.2.2 Lessor's Perspective

The following are the main factors that lessors consider as they conduct their business:

1. Attractive Risk/Return Profile:
   In many cyclical and capital-intensive businesses the risk-return profile of leasing companies is more attractive than that of the operators. The most prominent example in that respect is the relative financial success of aircraft leasing companies over several business cycles, which have far outperformed the airlines. The main advantage of the leasing business is that it typically has a diversified fixed revenue backlog and therefore is only via the credit risk of its customers—indirectly exposed to the cyclicality of the industry it serves. Even in the current shipping crisis we can observe that the few transparent ship leasing businesses are all financially outperforming the operators.
2. Capacity for Significant Financial Leverage:
   In view of the more secure revenue base, leasing companies are typically able to achieve higher financial leverage in the debt markets than most operators. That can drive returns on equity (ROEs) to attractive levels.
3. Residual Value Speculation:
   Some lessors hope or expect to derive significant "extra-return" through residual value realizations. The lessor's estimate of residual value naturally has a very significant impact on the lease pricing process (see discussion below).
4. Tax Benefits:
   Tax benefits have historically played a very significant role for the leasing business. For most lessors in most jurisdictions, debt finance costs and equipment depreciation are tax deductible items. In some jurisdictions, accelerated tax depreciations have been permitted or even encouraged (to boost investment) resulting in significant tax losses in the early years of a lease. These same tax losses could then be offset against accounting income from other operations,

hence lowering the near term tax burden of the lessor group. Over the years, these tax benefits have lured many institutions into the leasing business, although their core business had no connection whatsoever with the industry the leasing business was serving. In shipping, the most prominent tax leasing market was the UK in the years 2002–2004. Since then, the tax leasing business in shipping has almost vanished as tax authorities in the UK and elsewhere have clarified that to claim the significant tax benefits associated with the leasing activity, the lessor has to be "substantially at risk". In other words, the lessor has to assume significant residual risk in the transaction to claim the tax benefits. Bank lessors, especially those in the UK, have left the field as concerns over ownership connected liability, residual value and remarketing exposure, as well as the need to shrink balance sheets in light of the Basel III regulations, have taken center stage. On the other hand, the specialist ship lessors have all been established in low tax or no-tax jurisdictions and have no use for tax depreciation benefits. Shipping is unique in this aspect, as most lessors and operators are only marginally taxed on their profits.

14.3 Ship Lease Contract and Structure

14.3.1 Time Charter

Fundamentally, ship leasing activities can be either based on a bareboat charter or a time charter contract. Time charters, which might also be called full service leases or to use an aviation term wet leases,[3] are significantly more widespread than bareboat charters. Under a time charter the lessor provides the lessee the vessel "ready to trade" and all that is left for the lessee to decide is the direction of the vessel. Hence, the lessor provides for the operation of the vessel, including crewing, maintenance, insurance, docking etc. From the lessor's perspective the advantage of a time charter is the full operational control over the vessel which is particularly significant in a customer default scenario allowing the lessor to redeploy the vessel without having first to repossess it (as under the bareboat charter). This has to be weighed against the operational and technical performance risk that the lessor carries under such transactions. The lessor has priced into the lease structure the estimated vessel operating expenses. If the actual operating expenses overrun, there is no contractual basis for demanding a higher lease rate from the lessee. Hence, the return of the lessor might become negatively impacted. This is particularly significant in the case of very long term time charters (10 years or more) as it has been historically difficult to accurately determine operating cost inflation over such long time periods and

[3]A wet lease as defined in Title 14 (Aeronautics and Space) of the Code of Federal Regulations (14 CFR) is any leasing arrangement whereby a person agrees to provide an entire aircraft and at least one crewmember.

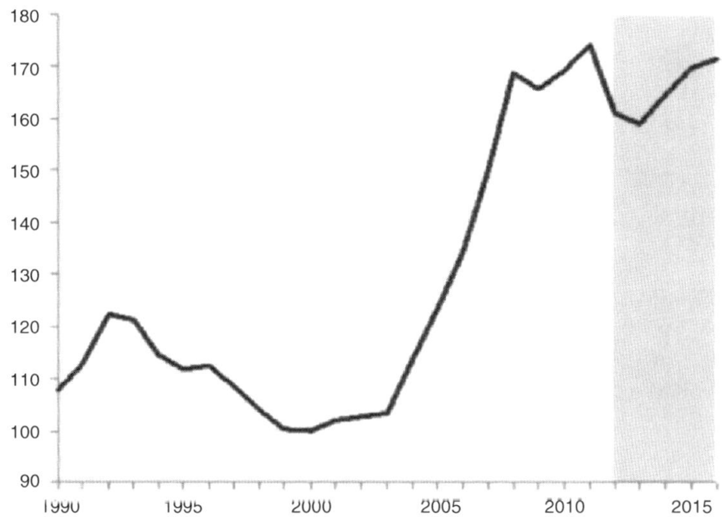

Fig. 14.2 Total operating costs

there are many cases of lessors having become "squeezed" especially in the years 2006–2008 when operating costs increased sharply as shown in Fig. 14.2 (Drewry Maritime Research 2012, p. 2).

Also, under the time charter the lessor provides for certain performance warranties in relation to the ship's abilities, such as cargo carrying capacity as well as speed and consumption. Should the vessel not be able to perform in line with these warranties for whatever reason, then the lessee might lodge performance claims against the lessor or declare the vessel off-hire ceasing the payment of charter hire. The long term time charter as contractual basis for a lease has proved to be particularly popular in the container liner industry as the liner companies have been very content to focus on their "network challenges" whilst the lessors were charged with running the ships and solving ship operational challenges, including sourcing for increasingly difficult to find ship officers. The time charter is typically documented on generally accepted industry form contracts such as New York Produce Exchange—for dry bulk vessels, Boxtime—for containerships or ShellTime—for tankers (Tiberias Management Consultants 2009).

14.3.2 Bareboat Charter

The alternative ship lease contract to the time charter is the bareboat charter. Under the bareboat charter the lessee is fully responsible for the operation of the vessel. The aviation equivalent is the dry lease which is by far the dominant leasing contract in aviation leasing. The advantages and disadvantages of this contract from the lessor's

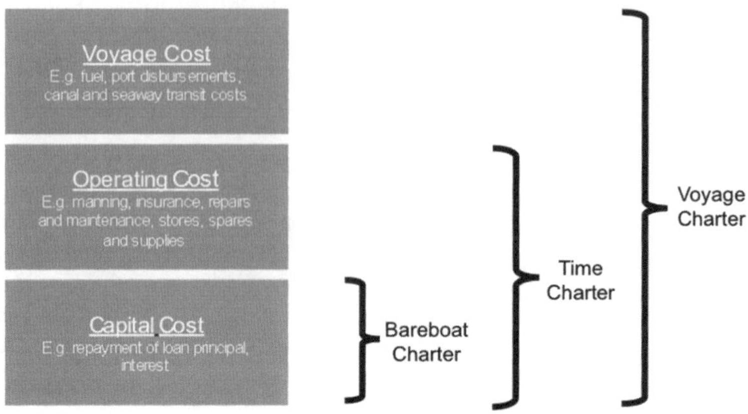

Fig. 14.3 Various costs associated to a ship-owner under different types of charters

perspective are the mirror image of those under the time charter. Under the bareboat charter the lessor does not carry the operational cost and vessel performance risk, resulting in a more predictable and stable cash flow. However, in the case of a customer default the lessor has to first secure repossession of the vessel. This could be time consuming depending on the maritime jurisdictions that are involved. Also, a customer default oftentimes goes hand in hand with a vessel that has not been maintained to an appropriate standard, such that the lessor upon repossession could face significant maintenance capital expenditures to get the vessel back into a "lease-ready" status. The bareboat charter has proven to be the lease contract of choice for the tanker industry as it is important for tanker operators to have control over the vessel because this is the service that they sell to their customers: the oil companies and traders. The background to this is that the tanker industry is facing the highest environmental and regulatory scrutiny within shipping, hence outsourcing ship operations to a lessor via a long term time charter is not an option for many operators. The industry accepted contract form for bareboat charters is the Barecon (see also Fig. 14.3).

14.3.3 "Hell and High Water" Bareboat Charter

The "hell and high water" contract is a sub-form of the Bareboat Charter and generally a higher contractual standard from the lessor's perspective than the standard bareboat charter. The concept literally applied says: *Come hell and/or high water the lessee has to pay.* This contract has emanated from the tax leasing industry where non-industry lessors wanted to make it contractually clear beyond any doubt that they do not carry any operational risks. The aim is twofold: To remove the lessor from any liability risk connected to the ownership of the vessel and to ensure the highest predictability of rental stream for the lessor. There is no standard industry form for "hell and high water" contracts. Lessors use either proprietary lease documentation, which is built around the "hell and high water" concept, or they insert an expansive "hell and high water" clause into the Barecon contract. A comparative analysis of some risks and parameters highlighting the differences between leasing and Barecon are available in Table 14.2.

14.3.4 Tax Leasing

Tax based leasing in shipping has so far been based on "hell and high water" bareboat charter contracts. The main contractual difference between a tax and non-tax lease is the inclusion or absence of a very onerous (on the lessee) tax indemnity provision. In a typical tax lease under the tax indemnity provision, the lessee indemnifies the lessor for any tax changes during the term of the lease which might negatively impact the after-tax return of the lessor. In other words, during the lease term the lessee guarantees the lessor an after-tax return. One reason why UK tax leases are no longer in such demand from lessees is that lessees have realized that over the years the lower lease rates (as a result of the high tax depreciation the lessor enjoys) at inception might come at a cost later when the tax law changes and the lessor makes use of the tax indemnity provision. It has been costly for lessees to unwind some aggressive tax lease structures upon the implementation of changes in tax law.

14.3.5 Sale and Leaseback Transaction

A sale and leaseback transaction can be conducted both on a time charter or a bareboat charter basis. It is a transaction where an operator sells its own vessel to the lessor and then charters its back. The rationale for the lessee is described in Sect. 2.1 with the most important considerations being cash flow and accounting treatment. For the lessor this transaction structure has the following benefits (Fig. 14.4):

1. It allows the lessor to immediately generate revenue upon acquisition of the vessel. In contrast, lessors that place newbuilding orders have cash outlays to the shipyards typically over a 2–3 years period before the ships are delivered and any income can be generated.
2. In a sale and leaseback transaction the lessor has typically to make no representation (in the case of bareboat charters) as to the vessel's specifications and performance, as the vessel was selected by the lessee in the first place and the lessee is more familiar with the ship than the lessor.

Table 14.2 Example of "hell and high water" lease vs. Barecon contract

	Example of "hell and high water" lease	Barecon contract
Risks and reward of ownership	– Mostly with the charterer	– Mostly with the owner
Lease duration	– Typically over a large portion of the useful life of the vessel	– Typically between 1–4 years, or more
Conditions precedent to performance by owner	– Extensive "loan agreement-style" list of conditions precedent	– Few, other than payment of any advance hire
Owner warranties	– No warranties. Vessel is delivered "as is where is" to charterer	Warranties of: – Sea worthiness – That vessel is in every respect ready in hull, machinery and equipment of service under charter – No latent defects at the time of delivery into charter
Charterer warranties	– Extensive warranties	– Limited warranties
Obligation to pay hire	– Obligation to pay hire is absolute and unconditional throughout the charter period – Obligation to pay charter is "hell and high water"	Payment of hire stops: – If vessel is lost or missing – If vessel is damaged – Any on-hire survey by Owner – Compulsory acquisition
Indemnities	– Extensive indemnities (e.g. tax indemnities, tax gross up, to Owner and related parties against all losses and liabilities arising or asserted in relation to the vessel before or after lease period)	– Limited indemnities indemnity to Owner for loss, damage, expense incurred by Owner arising out of or in relation to the operation of the vessel and against charterer liens
Insurances	– Charterer typically to maintain all insurances – Extensive insurance covenants	– Depends on duration of charter. Owner maintains insurances in short-term charters while charterer maintains insurance for longer-term charters – Insurances to be "satisfactory to the owner"
Corporate covenants	– Extensive "loan agreement-style" corporate covenants	– Limited or none

(continued)

Table 14.2 (continued)

	Example of "hell and high water" lease	Barecon contract
Requisition for hire	– Charterer's obligations will continue (including obligation to pay hire) until the end of a pre-agreed period (typically 90 days) whereupon an "Event of Loss" occurs	– Charterer's obligations (including obligation to pay hire) continues until the end of the charter term
Compulsory acquisition	– Charterer takes compulsory acquisition risk	– Owner takes compulsory acquisition risk
Charter termination events	– Extensive "loan agreement-style" termination events	– Limited termination events, relating to operational and payment issues
Effect of termination event	– Owner may withdraw vessel from charter and repossess the vessel	– Owner may withdraw vessel from charter and repossess the vessel

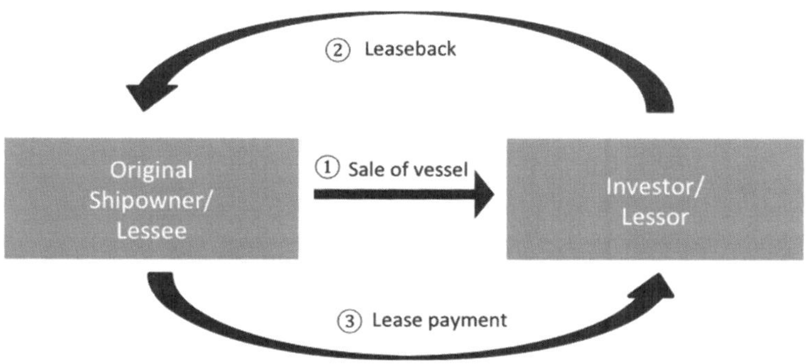

Fig. 14.4 Sale and leaseback transaction

The disadvantage for the lessor is that lease pricing becomes more transparent as the lessee knows the vessel acquisition cost of the lessor. Generally, sale and leaseback transactions have more of a "financing" rather than a "charter" character.

14.3.6 Optionality and Flexibility Features

As mentioned above, one of the greatest obstacles to a higher penetration rate for leasing in shipping is the limited asset disposal flexibility for the lessee as compared to outright ownership. Shipping is probably the only transportation industry where the timely acquisition and sale of a fixed asset makes up such a significant proportion of the total return the operator derives over an investment cycle. In other transportation sectors, the fixed assets are simply a basis to deliver a service. In shipping they are an important element of speculation themselves, and as important or more important than the shipping service that they are used for. As such, lessees have been pushing very hard over the years to include greater flexibility via such contract features as early buyout options during the lease term, purchase options at lease maturity and multiple lease extension options. During the liquidity boom when lessors were competing with each other, as well as other forms of financing, lessors were mostly willing to give away that flexibility "for free" just to secure the business. However, lessors have increasingly realized that this excessive optionality results in an asymmetric distribution of risk and reward between lessee and lessor. In other words, during a cyclical downturn for shipping it is likely that none of the options will be exercised and the lessor has to bear very high contract default risk in view of the industry's weak credit profile. During a cyclical upturn the most attractive option will be exercised by the lessee depriving the lessor of some or all of the return upside in the asset.

14.4 Lease Pricing

In pricing lease transactions, lessors will typically focus on target project returns, equity returns and cash yield. In the return calculations, the assumed residual value of the asset at lease maturity has a significant impact and as such is deserving of separate discussion.

14.4.1 Return on Asset/Return on Equity

Most lessors will start by targeting a minimum return on asset (ROA) or lease IRR. This measure is extremely useful as it will set a minimum return for the project, independent of the lessor's funding structure for the project. It can be misleading to talk about equity return targets without transparency on the underlying funding structure. In other words, a 20 % equity return for a project with 90 % leverage might be not sufficient compensation for the high financial risk, whereas that same return with 60 % leverage would be deemed extremely attractive. As a rule of thumb, most lessors will target ROAs ranging between 2–4 % premium over like term senior secured debt financings.

Table 14.3 can offers an example: the premium of 2–4 % over senior secured debt funding cost is the compensation for the 100 % financing offered in the lease project and the assumption of residual risk by the lessor.

Given that most lessors will operate with financial leverage of 60–80 % across their leasing portfolio, the above described ROA target will typically translate into ROE targets of 10–15 % per annum, depending on the prevailing cost of debt at the time.

Table 14.3 Targeted ROA/IRR for 8-year lease

Eight-year US$ swap rate	2.5 %
Senior secured debt credit margin	2.5 %
Like term senior secured debt funding cost	5 %
Targeted ROA/IRR for 8-year lease	7–9 %

In their return calculations, lessors will typically include all origination, closing and other transaction costs, but only very few lessors have a disciplined process to price in lessee specific credit costs.

14.4.2 *Cash Yield*

Another very important measure for lessors to analyze is the cash yield over the life of the lease. In simple terms, it is the annual bareboat charter (equivalent for time charters) income divided by the asset acquisition cost. Lessors that have a very low tolerance for residual risk will typically target very high cash yields (say as high as 15 % per annum) and might then provide the lessee with an attractive purchase option at lease maturity as compensation for the higher lease rentals during the lease term. Conversely, lessors that have significant faith in the residual upside of the asset might be satisfied with a more moderate cash yield (say as low as 10 % per annum) in the hope and expectation of an "extra-return" upon residual value realization.

14.4.3 *Residual Value Impact on Pricing*

Clearly the assumed residual value has a significant impact on return calculations in lease pricing. Most lessors will go to great length in estimating the future value of an asset, largely by studying historical value data from various industry sources, such as shipbrokers and risk management consultants. The greatest hedge against residual value volatility will always be a long lease term. The longer the lease term, the smaller the ex-post return impact of residual value variations. Here is an example to illustrate the point:

Consider a target IRR of 10 % for a $45 million vessel on two different lease terms 7 and 12 years. The graph below illustrates the sensitivity on IRR to changes in residual value. It is clear from the gradient of the graphs that a longer lease term structure would mitigate downside asset residual risk (see Fig. 14.5).

What the last shipping boom and bust clearly illustrated is that the accounting depreciation method of most shipping companies 25 years straight-line down to scrap value is not appropriate for lessors. This very simple method completely ignores the period in the cycle a vessel is bought, and hence how cheap or expensive the vessel is. Also, the method does not take into account the concave residual

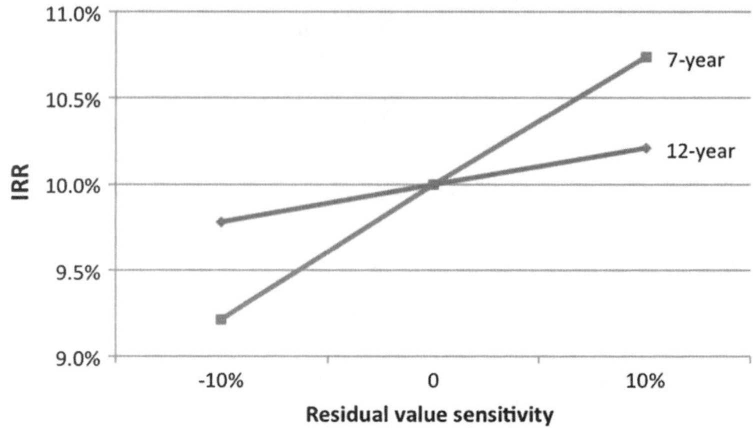

Fig. 14.5 Sensitivity on IRR to changes in residual value for 12- and 7-year lease term structures

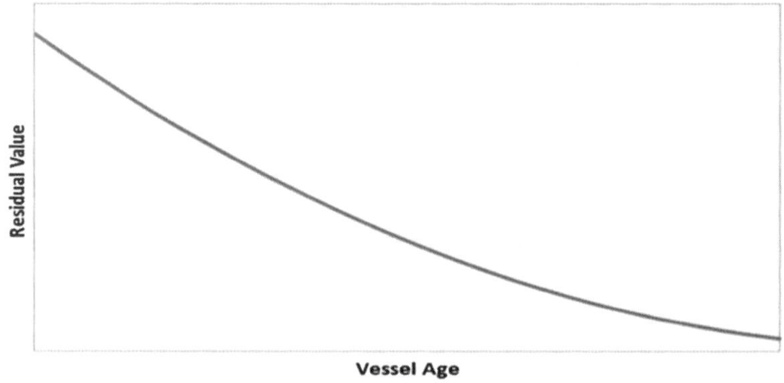

Fig. 14.6 Residual value against vessel age

value characteristics of most fixed assets including ships. In other words, everything else being equal, ships tend to use more of their value in the early years of their useful economic life before the value erosion moderates over the later years (see also Fig. 14.6).

14.5 Risk Management

Lessors face three broad risks credit, asset and financial which need to be addressed appropriately through a disciplined risk management approach.

14.5.1 Credit Risk

Credit risk, in this context, is the default risk by the customer during the lease term. Given that shipping is a highly cyclical and capital intensive industry with a largely sub-investment grade credit profile, professional credit analysis is of paramount importance. If validation for this thesis was needed then the recent high profile defaults by companies, such as Korea Line, Sanko Steamship, Brittania Bulk, Armada and Berlian Laju Tanker certainly provided it.

Proper credit risk management stretches from the pre-transaction analysis, over appropriate deal documentation to post-transaction credit monitoring throughout the life of the lease. The credit risk is a function not only of the lessee's own credit metrics, but also the specific market risks of the sector it operates in. The credit review of the lessee is or should be no different from the work that any bank lender would perform. Particularly important is for the lessor to gain a full understanding of all the lessee's on and off-balance sheet obligations, including other leases (which might be classified as off-balance sheet) and derivative contracts (freight and bunker rates and foreign exchange rates). In addition, it is critical to evaluate if the potential lessee has newbuilding commitments and whether funding has been obtained for the orderbook and on what terms. The lessor can also employ various credit risk mitigation strategies by enhancing the transaction structure with additional security, such as assignment of specific cargo/sub-charter contracts or cash security deposits. A lessor should have a system which allows for quantification of the credit risk so that this risk can be appropriately reflected in the lease pricing process.

14.5.2 Asset Risk

Generally, a proper asset risk management strategy has to consider two alternative scenarios:

1. Lease runs to maturity and the asset is returned to the lessor
   The lessor needs to conservatively estimate the residual value of the asset for lease pricing purposes. In doing so, it will take into account historical residual values for similar assets, expected technological changes (if any; currently fuel efficiency is very relevant), standardization level of the asset (the more specialized the asset the more cautious the lessor has to be in determining residual risk) and the asset age at lease maturity (the older the vessel at lease maturity the lower the residual value the lessor should assume).
2. Lease defaults
   Whilst credit risk management is primarily concerned with the probability of default, asset risk management will consider the exposure at default. The exposure will differ over the life of the lease as the asset is amortized but having a solid understanding of the exposure curve is very important for proper risk assessment.

In addition, asset risk management revolves around the technical and operational management of the vessel (for vessels on time charter) or the periodic monitoring of the lessee's maintenance and operational standards through inspections of vessels and reports (for vessels on bareboat charter). Another important aspect is ensuring proper insurance coverage for the asset throughout the lease term.

14.5.3 Financial Risk

A lessor potentially faces three key financial risks: funding, interest rates and foreign exchange.

1. Funding Risk
   Once a lessor has committed to an asset acquisition, it has to source for appropriate funding (in practice this process takes place concurrently with the asset acquisition). Most lessors will attempt to be as close as possible to being "match-funded". In other words, if a lessor leases a vessel for 10 years it would attempt to fund a portion of that acquisition cost with a 10-year term debt to be "match-funded". Given that banks increasingly have funding problems at the long end it has recently become very difficult to secure debt with terms longer than 7 years. Consequently, lessors might be facing a refinancing risk of the asset at the maturity of the debt term, since in this example the lease carries an "overhang term" of 3 years. Some lessors will try to roll over the risk to the lessee by including a lease re-pricing provision after 7 years, but that is typically difficult to achieve in a competitive market.
2. Interest Rate Risk
   Most ship leases tend to be fixed rate level payments. Bank debt is almost exclusively provided on a floating rate basis. Hence unless hedged, lessors are facing very significant interest rate risk. For lessors, an interest rate hedging program is a key consideration. The most conservative lessors will simply hedge the interest rate risk for the entire lease period (provided they can obtain a "match-funded" debt term), enabling them to earn a constant spread in the transaction. Other lessors will see the interest rate curve potentially as an additional profit source and will therefore deliberately take on interest rate risk.
3. Foreign Exchange Risk
   We have historically seen markets, particularly in Japan and Germany, where the currency in which some or all of the debt funding was denominated differed from the currency denomination of the lease. This introduces a significant foreign exchange risk into the leasing transaction. Again, most lessors will avoid such additional risk and try to be as best as possible "match-funded", but others have deliberately taken on the foreign exchange risk to become more competitive in the market. In many cases this aggressive stance has backfired.

14.6 Lessor Universe

We can segregate the shipleasing landscape along the following lines.

14.6.1 Specialists Versus Generalists

Specialist lessors are typically those which focus only on one sector of shipping. These lessors will in most cases conduct their business on a time charter basis as they feel that they have attained a certain operational expertise in managing vessels of a particular type. The lessors which conduct their business on a bareboat charter basis in most cases have no specific sector focus, as they are not required to operate the vessels. In a situation where the vessel is redelivered, these generalist lessors will typically outsource technical management to a professional third party.

14.6.2 Corporate Lessors Versus Project Leasing Structures

Corporate lessors are companies which fund individual transactions from one balance sheet and offer their debt funding providers recourse to a more diversified pool of assets and revenue streams. By contrast, the project leasing structures are dominated by lease arrangers that will fund transactions on an individual project basis, by raising equity and debt on a case by case basis. The dominant markets for these structures have historically been Germany, Norway and Korea.

14.6.3 Bank Lessors Versus Independent Lessors

During the height of the UK tax lease boom we saw many UK banks involved in the leasing market. However, as discussed above they have subsequently retreated from the market. That leaves today only two banks which are visibly active in shipleasing: Standard Chartered and DVB Bank. A list of lessors is provided in Table 14.4

14.7 Latest Developments and Outlook

14.7.1 Proposed Lease Accounting Changes

The proposed lease accounting rules for lessees will have a profound impact on "lease buying behavior". I believe that the appetite for leasing will continue to be

Table 14.4 List of ship lessors

	Company name	Specialist/generalist	Type of charters	Company type	No. of vessels
U.S. listed companies/master limited partnerships (MLP)					
1	Costamare	Specialist—containership	Time charter	Public	58
2	Danaos	Specialist—containership	Time charter	Public	64
3	Global Ship Lease	Specialist—containership	Time charter	Public	17
4	Seaspan	Specialist—containership	Time charter	Public	72
5	Ship Finance International	Generalist	Time and bareboat charter	Public	67
6	Teekay LNG Partners	Specialist—LNG carriers	Time and bareboat charter	Public	43
7	Teekay Offshore Partners	Specialist—offshore support vessels	Time and bareboat charter	Public	58
German listed companies					
8	HCI Hammonia Shipping AG	Specialist—containership	Time and pool charter	Public	13
9	Marenave Schiffahrts AG	Generalist	Time charter	Public	13
Singapore listed business trusts					
10	First Ship Lease Trust	Generalist	Time and bareboat charter	Public	25
11	Rickmers Maritime	Specialist—containership	Time charter	Public	16
Bank affiliated lessors					
12	Standard Chartered Bank	Generalist	Bareboat charter	Bank affiliated	22
13	Bank of Communications Leasing	Generalist	Bareboat charter	Bank affiliated	N.A.
14	China Development Bank Leasing	Generalist	Bareboat charter	Bank affiliated	N.A.
15	CMB Financial Leasing	Generalist	Bareboat charter	Bank affiliated	N.A.
16	ICBC Financial Leasing	Generalist	Bareboat charter	Bank affiliated	N.A.
17	Minsheng Financial Leasing	Generalist	Bareboat charter	Bank affiliated	>130
Norwegian KS houses					
18	Cleaves Marine Finance	Generalist	Time and bareboat charter	Private	16
19	Fearnleys	Generalist	Time and bareboat charter	Private	40
20	Ness Risan & Partners	Generalist	Time and bareboat charter	Private	34

21	Pareto	Generalist	Time and bareboat charter	Private	86
22	Platou	Generalist	Time and bareboat charter	Private	100
German KG houses					
23	Dr. Peters Group	Generalist	Time charter	Private	87
24	HCI Capital	Generalist	Time charter	Public	N.A.
25	König & Cie	Generalist	Time charter	Private	66
26	Lloyd Fonds AG	Generalist	Time charter	Public	N.A.
27	Nordcapital	Generalist	Time charter	Private	122
28	Salamon AG	Generalist	Time charter	Private	18
Investment funds					
29	Borealis Maritime	Generalist	Time and bareboat charter (mainly bareboat charter)	Private	9
30	Cypress Leasing	Generalist	Time and bareboat charter (mainly bareboat charter)	Private	N.A.
31	DVB Bank	Generalist	Time and bareboat charter (mainly bareboat charter)	Public	70
32	HI Investment & Securities	Generalist	Time and bareboat charter (mainly bareboat charter)	Private	N.A.
33	Icon Capital	Generalist	Time and bareboat charter (mainly bareboat charter)	Private	N.A.
34	Korean Maritime Fund	Generalist	Time and bareboat charter (mainly bareboat charter)	Government-linked	50
35	Northern Shipping Funds	Generalist	Time and bareboat charter (mainly bareboat charter)	Private	N.A.
36	Sole Shipping	Generalist	Time and bareboat charter (mainly bareboat charter)	Private	5
37	Tufton Oceanic	Generalist	Time and bareboat charter (mainly bareboat charter)	Private	N.A.

strong in light of the operator's increasing need for funding diversification, but the new lease accounting rules will sharpen the focus on lease term. Since obligations which were heretofore treated off-balance sheet will henceforth be capitalized onto the balance sheet, CFOs of the operators will push lessors to accept shorter lease terms. In the past, operators wanted the lowest possible lease rate in conjunction with off-balance sheet treatment. This has mostly resulted in lease terms of 10–12 years, the maximum term allowed in most accounting conventions for ship leases to still be considered off-balance sheet. Since off-balance sheet treatment will no longer be an option, there will in the future be an inherent conflict between the chartering/leasing department of the operator, which will continue to push for the lowest possible lease rate and the finance department, which will try to minimize liabilities on the balance sheet. A shortening of lease terms results in more residual/asset risk for lessors which will need to be managed appropriately.

14.7.2 Impact of Debt Funding Constraints

Obtaining debt finance for any type of shipping borrower has become very challenging since the onset of the financial crisis in 2008. It has become very clear that lenders have become highly selective when it comes to grading fresh credit. Some of the key factors that lenders look for in a borrower today are:

1. Solid balance sheet ratios with good equity base
2. Diversified "crisis-resistant" cash flows
3. Full transparency and proactive management
4. Promising cross-selling opportunities
5. Borrower with access to alternative sources of capital (capital markets)
6. Borrower with conservative business philosophy

Generally and in principle, this development favors ship lessors as they have a more conservative business model than the operators. However, that applies only to the larger corporate lessors. The arrangers of project leasing structures are finding it extremely difficult to source debt funding today as there are hardly any banks left who are willing to extend plain vanilla project finance. I believe that this trend will persist and not unlike the aircraft leasing sector the large corporate lessors in shipping will over time gain the status of "premium borrowers" in the market.

14.7.3 Impact of High Profile Industry Defaults

The recent high profile defaults of companies, such as Sanko, Korea Line, Berlian Laju Tanker, Armada and Brittania Bulk, as well as complex restructurings of Torm, CSAV and CMA CGM, have made it very clear that credit risk is as important a consideration for lessors as it is for bank lenders. In addition, these failures have shed light onto the risk of off-balance sheet obligations (particularly in the case of Sanko and Korea Line), an area that was previously neglected in the superficial credit analysis of most lessors. The new accounting rules will bring more clarity to this area. But generally, lessors that want to continue serving this market will have to improve their credit analysis skills not only to satisfy their shareholders but also their lenders. Since the number of lessors is likely to shrink given the debt funding constraints, it will mean that operators seeking lease finance will need to be as transparent with their lessors as they are with their bank lenders.

References

Drewry Maritime Research (2012) Shipping operating costs 2012–2013 annual review and forecast. Drewry Publishing, London (September 28)

Garfield G (2012) Orders plunge takes toll on profits. TradeWinds World Shipbuilding Report (August 29)

Tiberias Management Consultants (2009) Challenges in using Standard Form Charterparty Contracts. Available via http://www.tiberiasmc.com/index.php?option=com_content&view=article&id=111:charterparty&catid=49:latest-news&Itemid=13. Accessed 18 Sept 2012

Chapter 15
Pools in International Shipping

Basil Ph. Papachristidis and Phrixos B. Papachristidis

Abstract This paper examines the drivers and the rationale for pooling tonnage. Enhanced bargaining power and higher profitability are identified and further analyzed as the key reasons for independent owners to enter a pool. The benefits and the financial impact are also examined and critically assessed. A typical structure of a pool and the related flows of capital as well as relationships among the members are presented. The analysis concludes with the potential benefits of entering into pools to lenders and borrowers.

15.1 Background

Contract shipping, or the carriage of bulk commodities by sea, has undergone profound changes over the last 25 years. Historically, bulk shipping markets, wet and dry, were as close an approximation as one could find of perfectly competitive markets. They satisfied the four necessary and sufficient conditions of perfect competition:

1. Homogeneous product
2. Perfect information
3. Low entry barriers
4. Large number of buyers and sellers

B.P. Papachristidis (✉)
Hellespont Marine Services Ltd, 93 Poseidonos, 16674 Glyfada, Greece
e-mail: pbp1@hellespont.com

P.B. Papachristidis
Hellespont Ship Management GmbH & Co. KG, Beim Strohhause 27, 20097 Hamburg, Germany
e-mail: p.papachristidis@hellespont.com

O. Schinas et al. (eds.), *HSBA Handbook on Ship Finance*,
DOI 10.1007/978-3-662-43410-9_15,

Even in pre-1973 days of the "Seven Sisters" (Esso, Shell, BP, Mobil, Texaco, Gulf and National Iranian Oil Co), who controlled the vast majority of oil transported by sea, buyers of transportation services relied on an independently-derived transportation cost for pricing their traded cargoes and therefore saw no value in tampering with the spot market.

The loss by the oil companies of their own sources of production since that time—and the resulting reliance on traded oil to feed the oil industry's refineries—has changed charterer attitudes towards securing shipping services. Not knowing what their transportation requirements would be, and unwilling to repeat the costly mistake of controlling large owned and time-chartered fleets against a background of unstable demand, the oil majors began to rely on spot chartered tonnage for the majority of their transport needs. The pursuit of trading profits replaced long-term strategic considerations, and unleashed the overwhelming bargaining power of the oil-company in a market that had historically been characterized by a benign respect of the independent, competitive market place.

A similar imbalance between the bargaining power of buyers and sellers of transport services evolved in dry bulk markets. The growth, consolidation and global reach of major steel companies, iron-ore producers and grain houses, like in oil markets, left a fragmented shipping industry at a negotiating disadvantage *vis-à-vis* their customers.

Bulk shipping has historically been the domain of small, privately-owned enterprises in traditional maritime nations, often controlled by families with seafaring backgrounds. These small, fiercely independent entities, have been denied access to capital markets because of the cyclical nature of earnings and insufficiency of profits (i.e. absence of "pure rents") in the competitive environment where they pursued their trades.

However, the concentration on the buyers' side of both dry and wet markets, and the unbridled use of the lopsided bargaining power by charterers, has inspired a development that few would have thought possible of a fragmented industry a generation ago. Ship-owners, long-suffering victims of debilitating market cycles and exploitation by their charterers, began to see the merits of a more purposeful approach to deploying their fleets, marketing their services and raising capital. Conscious of the need for critical mass in pursuing these objectives, they began a long-overdue process of consolidation—financial, operational and commercial.

The last quarter century has witnessed a transformation of several small, privately-held companies into large IPO-driven consolidated fleets. Listed bulk shipping companies like Teekay, Frontline, Genmar, Nordic American, Diana, TEN and many others were nowhere to be seen 25 years ago but today own large fleets by comparison to shipping "tycoons" of years gone by.

The same period has seen an equally impressive consolidation process in the ship management side of the shipping business. Fleets of both private and listed owning entities have increasingly migrated to such management companies as V-Ships, Columbia, Hanseatic, Wallem, East Asiatic and other very large and focused professional ship management concerns, many of which manage hundreds of ships and offer significant economies of scale not available to small operators.

The commercial management of ships has matched the same consolidation process as has taken place in financial and ship management terms. Shipping pools, the principal vehicles for this consolidation process, have pervaded almost all sectors of bulk shipping, from the pedestrian crude oil and main dry bulk trades to high-end chemical, LPG and other specialized trades. They represent a departure from the traditional defeatist attitudes of despondent, price-taking ship-owners, who hitherto saw the purchase and sale of ships as their most realistic source of profit. The growth of shipping pools in the last 25 years is a testament to a new fighting spirit among ship-owners seeking to assert a legitimate claim to profitability through the discharge of the service they perform—that of carrying the world's commodities by sea.

This chapter discusses the philosophical underpinnings of shipping pools, their rules, workings and benefits.

15.2 Shipping Pools and Their *Raison d'Être*

Shipping pools have come to exist in every sector of bulk and even container shipping today. No less than about 5 % of the world's tanker fleet and about 10 % of the world's dry bulk fleet are commercially operated in pools.

Shipping pools can be briefly described as vehicles that enable the marketing of transportation services of different owners through a single chartering entity, with the sharing of pooled income on a pre-agreed basis.

Their primary *raison d'être* from a ship-owner's standpoint is the need to organize commercial operations purposefully, to enhance efficiency and to provide meaningful transportation services that can place an owner in a stronger bargaining position *vis-à-vis* charterers, thereby enhancing profitability.

While one might think pools are a potential threat to charterers' market influence, charterers have by and large reacted positively to their advent. The reason for this is the increasing tendency of industrial users to focus their resources and attention on their core activities and to out-source such services as transportation. To do so with confidence, they require a strong and financially stable shipping industry, the security of adequate availability of tonnage, and a level of transportation efficiency (with attendant stable and often lower cost) as can only be available from larger, professionally-managed fleets.

Seen from the perspective of lenders, shipping pools serve as a useful proxy for period employment and therefore significantly enhance the security of a shipping credit. Though pool distributions cannot replace the security of a fixed time charter arrangement, financial benefits to the owner mentioned hereunder operate to the benefit of the bank.

15.3 Benefits to Owners

As one would expect, the combination of fleets of smaller owners into a large fleet whose commercial operation is conducted under a single umbrella provides significant benefits.

1. The first of these is the higher visibility and market profile. This leads to a stronger customer and broker following, with resulting increase in "deal flow" and access to business that is not quoted.
2. Closely associated with higher market profile is the perception of reliability conveyed by a larger shipping operation. A larger fleet offers end users greater confidence as to the availability of tonnage to perform a contract. The perception of reliability also stretches to professionalism of service; the inevitably larger chartering, operations and accounting staff and supporting systems found in pool operations provide that confidence. Moreover, the perception of financial reliability (although not always justified) usually accrues to the larger, professionally-managed operations.
3. The third benefit is the ability to provide a larger range of shipping solutions, especially contracts of affreightment, to clients who are looking to outsource transportation services. There is considerable value in being able to provide transportation solutions of varying types, duration and volume on stable "industrial" terms, as opposed to simply being there to shift cargoes on an opportunistic ad hoc basis, which is all that many small owners can aspire to.
4. The fourth benefit is the commercial advantage that results from market visibility, reliability and flexibility of service. As a minimum, a larger pool operation has more bargaining clout than the small independent owner. However, the ability to add value and to serve transportation needs on a flexible, recurring basis endears a transportation provider to its customers and fosters closer relations between the two—relations that are often strong enough to eventually replace price as the main deciding factor.
5. Finally, but by no means least important, is the efficiency in fleet deployment that comes from being part of a larger fleet capable of providing both penetration and diversification (both geographic and functional) of markets. Ballast and waiting time is invariably reduced in a large operation with a multitude of customers, range of cargoes, contracts of affreightment and opportunity for positioning voyages. The gains in efficiency achieved by a large fleet can result in lower transportation cost to the customer while achieving higher time-charter-equivalent earnings for the owner.

15.4 Financial Impact of Pooling

As one would expect, the benefits achievable through the pooling of one's vessels translate into tangible results:

1. The first and most obvious result is the enhancement of earnings. The only exception to this is in a high market—or the early stages of a protracted high market—when lower-paying contracts need to be played out. However, over a complete market cycle, pools invariably produce higher earnings than the market for the reasons stated above.
2. The second result is the reduction in the volatility of earnings that accrues from a wider range of revenue sources and of type and maturity of employment engagements.
3. The third impact is the lower volatility of cash flows that results from participating in a larger, varied and therefore more stable aggregate stream of revenues.
4. The diversification of risk is another result that comes from having a wide variety of revenue sources.
5. Finally, the stable client relationships fostered by pools lead to better future earnings prospects.

The above contribute not only to direct financial results, but also to enhancing the "credit" of a participating owner.

15.5 Typical Pool Structure

Shipping pools are all, by and large, structured along very similar lines. Such a typical structure is briefly defined in this section.

Vessels are entered into a pool via a Commercial Management Agreement or Time Charter Party where the vessels are described and the responsibilities of the owner and operator are defined. In the case of Time Charters, the charter-hire is a variable amount pegged to aggregate Pool fleet earnings via weightings (*Pool Points*) ascribed to each Vessel (see below). These agreements are accompanied by a Pooling Agreement that sets forth the rules by which the Pool is run.

The Pool normally takes the form of a separate, single-purpose entity. It is the contracting party *vis-à-vis* the participating owners (*Members*), third-party owners of inward-chartered tonnage, and customers (*Charterers*). It typically does not have a staff of its own, but is managed by another (usually also single-purpose) entity, the Pool Manager.

The Pool Manager (*Manager*) provides services to the Pool under a Pool Management Agreement. The Manager is, more often than not, created by the founding member(s) of the Pool. The services provided by the Manager embrace chartering, operations, accounting, and reporting.

The staff of the Manager is either hired from third-party sources or seconded by participating owners. Even when run by staff of participating owners, the Manager is independent of any of the Members so as to ensure all members are treated in an even-handed manner in matters of pool point determination, off-hire and other operational matters.

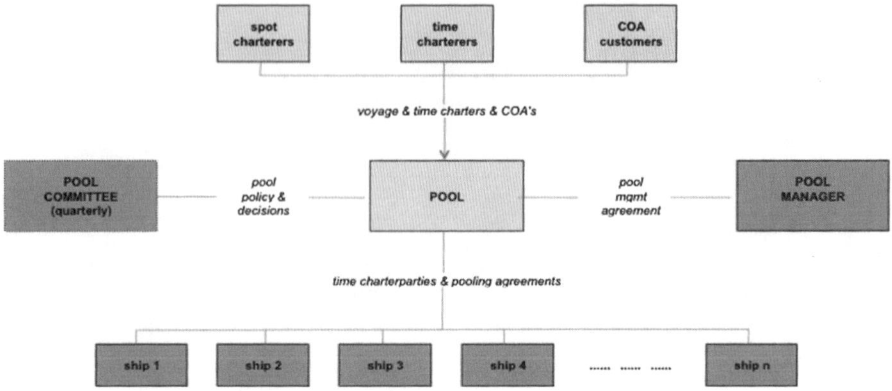

Fig. 15.1 Pool structure

Pool policy is established by the Pool Committee, and important commercial decisions are referred to it. The Pool Committee comprises representatives of all the Members. It typically convenes once a quarter. Voting power of each Member is typically pro rata according to the aggregate Pool Points of the vessels entered in the Pool by the Members.

All vessel earnings are paid into a single account (the *Pool Account*) in the name of the Pool and run by the Manager. As outlined below, all voyage costs and other Pool disbursements are made from this account before distributions are made to Members.

Vessels are awarded Pool Points according to objective criteria affecting earnings. These are described in the next section.

The structure of the Pool and the relationship between the above parties is depicted in Fig. 15.1.

15.6 Determinants of Pool Points

One would think the most contentious problem associated with pooling is the determination of Pool Points. The distribution of a finite quantum of fleet earnings is a zero-sum-game, with one vessel's gain resulting in another vessel's loss. The inevitably imprecise science by which Pool Points are determined could be forgiven for being a subject of recurring heated debated amongst Pool Members. Surprisingly, the experience of most pools is that Pool Point determination is relatively free of controversy. Imprecise as the science may be, it uses objective parameters the measurement of which is difficult to contest.

Pool Points are typically proposed by the Manager and ratified by the Pool Committee. The principal elements of the calculation are:

- Deadweight
- Draft
- Cubic capacity
- Dimensions (LOA, beam)
- Speed and consumption
- Coatings type and condition
- Number of cargo holds/tanks and/or segregations
- Pumps or cargo gear (number, type and capacity)
- Existence and level of ice class
- Existence and capacity of bow thruster
- Special design features (e.g. stern anchor or discharge line)
- Flag (and attendant trading flexibility)

All these elements are embraced in models based on vessel trades, range of cargoes carried, customer requirements etc. Vessel characteristics determine how a ship *freights out* (i.e. what its time-charter-equivalent *TCE* earnings are) on the typical voyages of the Pool fleet.

As optimal vessel speed is a function of market earnings and because ships have different *speed curves* (i.e. different consumptions at different speeds), the point of the market cycle is an important determinant of Pool Points. Hence, it is necessary to re-assess Pool Points periodically, especially in a volatile market.

15.7 Money Flows

All charter-hire, freight, demurrage and other fleet earnings are paid into the Pool Account. All voyage costs (fuel, port charges, canal tolls etc.), charter hire on inward charters, broker commissions and fees to the Manager are disbursed from the Pool Account before distributions are made to participating vessels (see Fig. 15.2).

Distributions are typically made on a semi-monthly or monthly basis in arrears, after a suitable retention of working capital to meet voyage-cost and other commitments.

15.8 Commercial Strategy

Market opportunities are invariably more important determinants of a contract carrier's business choices than purposeful business plans, even in the case of large pooled fleets. However, any commercial management activity has to begin with a plan or basic strategy, and the size of a pooled fleet significantly widens the strategy alternatives open to the Manager and Pool Committee.

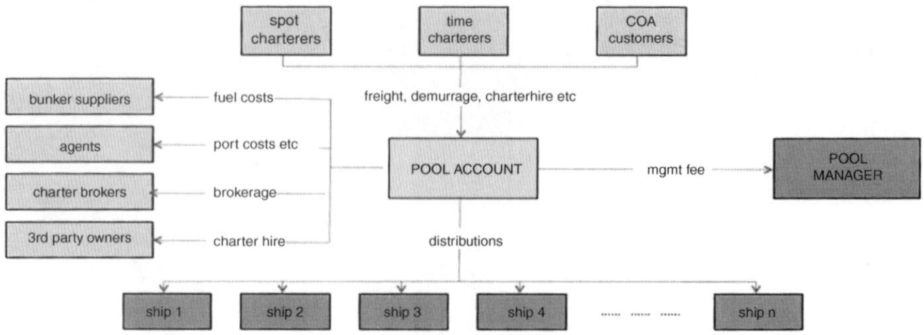

Fig. 15.2 Money flows

Commercial strategy decisions principally centre on the following choices:

1. Fleet Size: choice of optimal size of fleet as a function of:
   - Planned activity
   - Preferred commercial focus
   - Geographic spread
   - Expected customer needs etc.
2. Type of Employment Contracts: the extent to which the Pool wishes to:
   - Secure earnings by taking period cover via time charters
   - Ride shipping cycles by keeping its fleet in the spot market
   - Perform a transportation service (with an element of forward earnings cover) by taking of contracts of affreightment
3. Forward Revenue Cover: choice of period of forward revenue cover (closely related to the choice of employment engagements) whether via time charters, contracts of affreightment or consecutive voyage charters, according to
   - Perceived direction of markets
   - Risk posture of constituent owners
   - Customer preference, or
   - Element in fleet deployment strategy
4. Paper Hedging: the use of paper markets to hedge
   - Earnings exposure or
   - Bunker cost volatility
5. Inward Charter Strategy: the recourse to the inward charter of third-party vessels as a means of:
   - Increasing operational leverage
   - Asserting stronger presence in certain markets
   - Ensuring ability to perform contracts

6. Trading Areas: the choice of geographic theaters of operation (e.g. Atlantic, Pacific, Far East, Caribbean, North Sea etc.) where to locate one's fleet and focus activity, as a means of adopting a higher profile and mustering greater broker and charterer support
7. Cargoes: the choice of cargoes to carry (e.g. clean or dirty in case of coated tankers, or of chemicals or CPP in case of chemical carriers) to develop a specialization and market following
8. Customer Focus: the decision to concentrate marketing effort on specific customers to penetrate a certain trade.

Needless to say, the above commercial choices are interactive. For example, the decision to develop one's book of contracts of affreightment will have the following determining effects on the other commercial choices. To wit, it will

- Induce customer focus
- Involve forward cargo cover
- Determine fleet geographic location
- Force consideration of the size of the pooled fleet
- Possibly invoke need to charter in tonnage on either a period or ad hoc basis
- Force reliance on the spot market for positioning voyages, and
- Give rise to the need for bunker hedging.

Commercial strategies will also be highly sensitive to the point in the market cycle where they are perceived to be made and therefore need to be constantly reviewed. Needless to say, in a market felt to be falling, a pool manager will:

- Seek to secure forward cargo and earnings cover by whatever means available; time charter opportunities will become attractive to even the most die-in-the-wool COA operator determined to perform transportation services as opposed to being a provider of equipment
- Use paper markets to enhance forward revenue cover
- Eschew the temptation of chartering in tonnage to cover perceived needs, acting in the belief cheaper tonnage will be available to support contractual obligations as they arise
- Be prepared to relocate tonnage to higher paying theaters of operation
- Abandon rigid adherence to preferred cargo choices (e.g. be prepared to trade chemical carriers in clean petroleum product trades and switch product carriers to crude oil trades) in pursuit of higher paying cargoes.

Important commercial strategy decisions are typically referred to the Pool Committee for decision, or for ratification in the case of decisions having had to be taken urgently by the Manager.

However, the burden of responsibility for discerning shrewd (or necessary) commercial strategies and proposing them to the Pool Committee remains squarely with the Manager. As steward of the interests of participating owners, it is incumbent upon the Manager to be proactive in exploiting the critical mass entrusted in its hands and to pursue a more purposeful commercial operation than its constituent owners could if acting independently.

Apart from the obvious chartering and commercial operating responsibilities, a Pool Manager is expected to

- Engage in or interprete third party market research
- Gather and disseminate market intelligence to Pool Members
- Propose strategy alternatives to the Pool Committee, and
- Suggest and execute energetic marketing programs.

No concentration of tonnage in a Pool will derive the potential benefits to participating owners without the leadership of a proactive and competent Manager.

15.9 Pool Entry and Exit Rules

An important contributing factor to the success of pool is the set of conditions by which members are allowed to enter and exit pools.

The first of these has to do with entry criteria for an owner applying for pool membership. Components of the decision as to the suitability of an aspiring owner are the following:

- Approach to broad commercial goals and strategies, so as to avoid impasses in pursuing commercial plans
- Commitment to quality of, and ethical standards in, the technical management of vessels
- Respect of confidentiality of commercial information shared by pool members
- Exclusive commitment of all controlled tonnage (in the particular category) to the pool, and
- Attitude towards conflict of interest, in relation to exclusive commitment (above) and withdrawal of vessels (below).

The second entry requirement concerns the acceptability of an owner's ships. This decision will obviously depend on:

- The type, size and characteristics of the vessel, and its conformity with the requirements of the pool
- The age and condition of the vessel, as this may affect the reputation of the pool and acceptability of the fleet, and
- The vessel's technical manager.

The contribution of working capital is a further component of the entry requirements to be met by prospective pool members. Unlike the case of conventional time charters, where the charterer is a profit center acting at arm's length with controlled tonnage and, therefore, is self funded, a pool is a purely non-profit-making instrument of participating owners designed to pursue their commercial goals and pass through all monies earned back to them. Therefore, it is for the owners to fund the working capital needs of the pool, just as they would have to do for their ships were they to be commercially operated by them. Working capital requirements typically met by vessels entering a pool consist of voyage expenses between the time of entry in the pool until collection of the first freight. The level of working capital normally depends on the position at which the vessel is delivered to the pool i.e. how long the positioning voyage is before the vessel's first earning voyage. Contribution of working capital is typically by way of bunkers and a cash payment or withholdings from early distributions.

As to exit conditions, the first question has to do with required notice. Owners considering joining a pool for the first time typically have trepidations about being caught in a web from which they will not be able to easily extricate themselves in the event the experience does not prove successful. In fact, most pools try to relieve this tension by making exit conditions as easy as possible, limiting the notice period to 3 months, or even less in the event of serious falling out with the departing owner.

As mentioned above, orthodox pooling philosophy requires owners to commit their entire fleet of similar tonnage to a pool. Rare are the cases that owners are allowed to have a few ships in one pool, with the rest in another pool and/or the spot market. However, in some cases, pools allow owners to withdraw one or more vessels in order for them to pursue time charter employment of over a certain period threshold above which the pool would not itself pursue employment opportunities. This concession is made to accommodate owners experiencing financial difficulties or otherwise needing to fix the income of part of their fleet.

Whether all or part of an owner's fleet is withdrawn from a pool, cognizance needs to be made of the "booked" commitments (i.e. contracts of affreightment, time charters, consecutive voyages etc.) and of their variance from the market at the date of the exit of particular vessel(s). A departing owner must pay or receive, as the case may be, the present value of any deficit below or premium above the prevailing market arising from future charter or cargo commitments, such that the vessel's departure from the pool does not affect the remaining fleet.

15.10 Guiding Principles

Ship-owners are by and large very conservative and are not given to light-heartedly abdicating control of their direct customer relations and revenues without good reason and without being certain of the professionalism with which their interests will be handled. Therefore, no discussion of shipping pools can be complete without mention of certain paramount principles that must govern the management of a pool operation if owners are to entrust their assets in the hands of one or another professional pool manager. These are:

1. Customer Relations: Pool managers essentially usurp from ship-owners the responsibility of managing relationships with customers. Therefore, it is incumbent upon pool management to maintain only the highest professional standards in dealings with customers.

2. Prompt Settlement of Costs: The timely settlement of bunker and other voyage costs, of broker commissions, of charter hire on inward-chartered vessels and of other market obligations are of paramount importance in establishing the market respect a pool must command, and the commitment of participating owners on which it depends for its existence.
3. Prompt Distribution of Revenues: Monies received into a pool account are the property of participating tonnage and must be passed through to their rightful owners after payment of the above costs and the maintenance of a reasonable working capital buffer.
4. Independence of Operation: A pool manager needs to be scrupulous in maintaining a level playing field for all owners, ensuring equitable, arms-length dealings with pool participants no matter how close the relationship may be between a pool manager and some of the participating owners.
5. Transparency: Finally, transparency of operations and accounts and timely reporting to participating owners are a necessary feature of any modern pool operation, especially in the light of the information and communication technologies available today.

15.11 The Role of Shipping Pools in Marine Finance

Time and again, ship-owners have been berated for embarking on ship-building programs without first securing period employment. Period charters have been regarded as implicit proof of real demand for a given vessel. As history has shown, markets do not tend to behave according to plan. In fact, period charters have served to exacerbate over-investment in ships by introducing a totally exogenous stimulus (the balance sheet of the charterer) in an investment process that should be inspired purely by an objective assessment of demand and supply—considerations endogenous to the market itself.

Time and again, charterers have miscalculated the true need for the tonnage they have committed to and have found ways of frustrating the engagements they have entered into when the market has gone south. Moreover, owners have been left holding the bag, suffering under the yolk of investments that would never have been made in the absence of the initial backing of the charterer.

Other, wiser, observers of shipping markets have described fixed-rate time charters as arrangements under which owners accept a ceiling to their earnings without due regard to the signature underpinning the floor. As a minimum, fixed-rate period charters are a recipe for the displeasure of one of the two contracting parties and therefore an inherently unsatisfactory arrangement.

Therefore, it is not surprising that, in a market affected by unpredictable economic circumstances and characterized by volatile earnings, charter engagements are increasingly made on the basis of flexible charter payments pegged to an index or to actual earnings of the vessel chartered. The advantage of a variable-rate charter with an end-user is the security of employment. However, the disadvantages are significant:

- If the rate paid by the charterer is linked to a market index, it does not reflect the actual earnings of the ship employed in the charterer's program which invariably benefits from the type of fleet efficiencies enjoyed by pools;
- If the rate is based on the vessel's actual earnings, there is no way of protecting against the conflicts of interest inherent in the integration of this vessel in a charterer's total fleet, unless those earnings are calculated on the basis of distributions from a pool (or virtual pool) with all the charterer's other similar tonnage.
- Under the time charter, the owner is committed to take a market-related income without having the ability to opt out by withdrawing his vessel

Pools, by contrast:

- Give the owner the full benefit of fleet efficiencies derived
- Eliminate all conflicts of interest
- Allow the owner to pull out and sell or period charter his vessel if he cannot take the heat any longer

In other words, in an age when the rates paid under time charters are increasingly linked to the market, shipping pools provide an attractive alternative both for the owner and the lender.

15.12 Future Challenges

Notwithstanding the small percentage of any sector even the largest of shipping pools represent and despite their benign character in relation to the liner conference system, shipping pools continue to attract the attention of policy-makers. The eternal quest to find fault in the conduct of shipping and its respect for the economic and environmental standards of the nations whose transport needs it serves will doubtless persist for generations to come. However, hopefully, shipping pools will not fall victim to the populist agendas of governments and international agencies, and will be allowed to continue providing transport services to the trading world—services they have proven they can provide more professionally and efficiently than the fragmented industry from which they have sprung.

Chapter 16
Restructurings in Shipping

Dirk Lammerskötter

Abstract This article aims to investigate the restructuring situations that have taken place in the shipping sector over the last years. It analyzes the reasons why companies entered financial distress, takes a look at the involved stakeholders and their potential contributions to a restructuring, describes the restructuring process and lists success factors for a restructuring. It closes with a short case study on the restructuring work that took place at the Chilean liner company CSAV in 2009.

16.1 The Challenging Environment of Today's Shipping Market

The shipping industry has not escaped the turbulences caused by the economic crisis that has affected the world over the past few years. On the contrary, shipping being a cyclical business, the volatility of the sector has once again proven to be quite significant. In the booming years of 2004–2008, the foundations of the current crisis were laid: A flourishing world economy, further increase in globalization and international trade, and high demand especially in China and India for raw materials but also for machinery and infrastructure goods led to a strong demand for seaborne logistics. This caused charter rates and second-hand prices of vessels to rise significantly. These positive developments caused most players in the shipping industry to be very optimistic. This optimism, coupled with the availability of cheap and plentiful bank financing, an increase in the number of yards, and a large amount of equity entering the shipping sector, be it through public markets as in the US or through closed-end funds as in Germany ("KG system"), led to a wave of new orderings. Moreover, because of the high demand, the price of these assets was close to all-time highs.

D. Lammerskötter (✉)
HSH Nordbank AG, Gerhart-Hauptmann-Platz 50, 20095 Hamburg, Germany
e-mail: dirk.lammerskoetter@hsh-nordbank.com

O. Schinas et al. (eds.), *HSBA Handbook on Ship Finance*,
DOI 10.1007/978-3-662-43410-9_16, © Springer-Verlag Berlin Heidelberg 2015

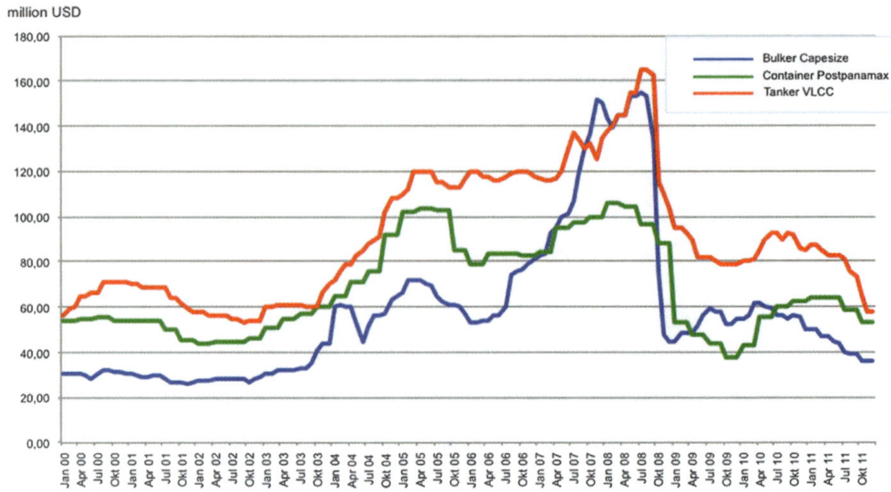

Fig. 16.1 Development of second-hand vessel prices

The optimism that prevailed in the shipping sector up until the middle of 2008 can be illustrated by the relationship between existing fleet and order book of new vessels. To give just one example by looking at container vessels bigger than 3,000 TEU in size, in the summer of 2008, there were 606 existing vessels in the water, while the order book comprised 525 vessels ignoring scrapping. This number implies that the number of vessels was to be increased by 87 %. Looking at the transport capacity, the existing fleet of vessels larger than 3,000 TEU had an overall capacity of about 4,165,000 TEU, while the order book comprised a capacity of 4,710,000 TEU, which would mean an increase of about 115 %. These numbers also show that the vessels got bigger and bigger. While the average size of a vessel in the existing fleet amounted to 6,870 TEU, the average size per vessel in the order book was 8,970 TEU, which means an increase of about 30 %.[1]

With the economic crisis, there came a significant reduction in demand for logistic services as provided for by the shipping sector in 2009. At the same time, this resulted in an increase in the supply of vessels and capacity, as ever more vessels, which had been ordered in the last boom, entered the market, causing a significant supply-demand imbalance. In consequence, companies operating in the shipping sector today face a very challenging environment, characterized by significantly reduced freight rates, charter rates, and low asset values. The graphs (Figs. 16.1 and 16.2) illustrate the development of major freight rates and second-hand asset values.

[1] All data by Clarkson Research Services.

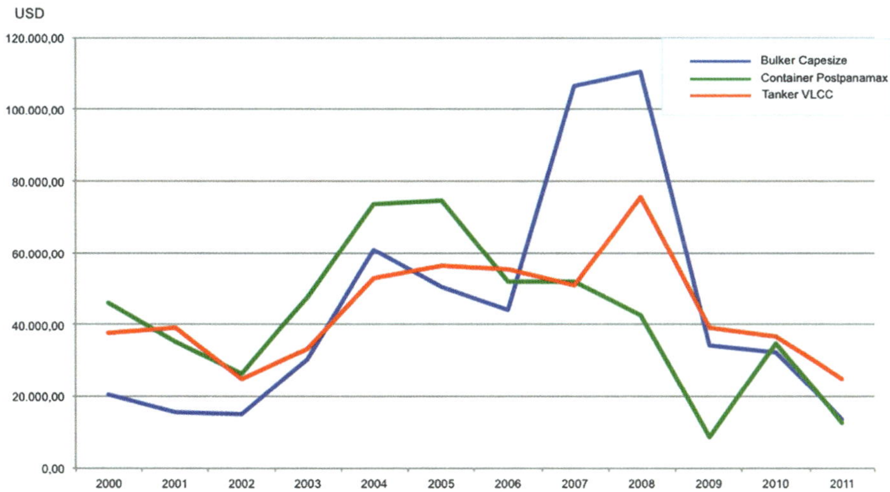

Fig. 16.2 Development of charter rates

In this distressed environment, many companies in the shipping sector do not generate enough revenues to fully cover the debt service. This problem is especially observable for vessels, which were ordered at peak prices, and had a high leverage of bank debt. In many cases the operative result of vessels barely covers their operating expenses and perhaps the interest costs to be paid to the banks, but not the repayment of the loan principal.

At the same time, the reduced asset values have led to many loan-to-value problems with the banks. With asset prices falling in some cases more than 50 %, the value of the assets dropped many times below the outstanding loan amount. This is a problem for banks, especially if the loans are only secured by the assets themselves (which is typical in the shipping sector, with the vessels being owned by single-purpose companies, with a nonrecourse status to the parent company). Figure 16.3 gives an overview of the effect on loan-to-value caused by a given decrease in asset value.

As can be imagined, the combination of these effects have caused all sectors of the shipping industry to suffer: The yards, the non-operating owners, the ship management companies, the chartering and broker companies, the liner companies, and the ship financing banks. In addition, while the shipping industry was always of a cyclical nature, the magnitude and the length of this last downturn is especially severe. The first signs of a crisis appeared in the second half of 2008, and in 2012 there was still no sign of a real recovery, with some experts still expecting further trouble to come before an eventual recovery.

In such an environment, it is essential for all stakeholders to find solutions in case of financial distress. Thus, many companies of the shipping sector needed a restructuring. Some of these restructurings could be observed in the open, the company involved being a public company. One example of this is CSAV, the

Original situation: LTV at 70%

Vessel value	Loan Amount	Loan-to-Value
100	70	**70%**

Reduction in Vessel value by 20% --> LTV rises to 88%

Vessel value	Loan Amount	Loan-to-Value
80	70	**88%**

Reduction in Vessel value by 40% --> LTV rises to 117%

Vessel value	Loan Amount	Loan-to-Value
60	70	**117%**

Reduction in Vessel value by 60% --> LTV rises to 175%

Vessel value	Loan Amount	Loan-to-Value
40	70	**175%**

Fig. 16.3 Effect of falling asset prices on loan-to-value

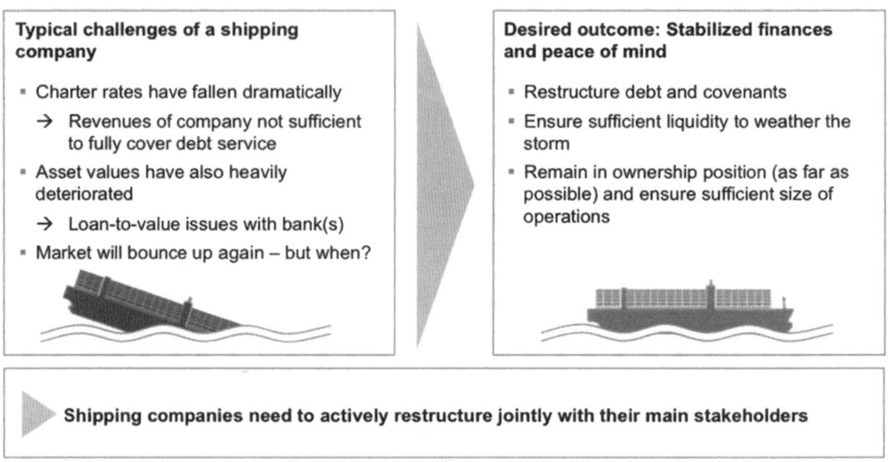

Fig. 16.4 Shipping companies face a very challenging environment

largest South-American liner operator, listed at the Santiago stock exchange, which restructured in the beginning of 2009 (see also the case study at the end of this chapter). Other companies that had to restructure encompass Danaos, Torm, General Maritime, or CMA CGM, to give some examples. However, with many shipping companies being privately held, many restructurings were done in the background, with the involvement of only a small number of stakeholders.

The chart (Fig. 16.4) summarizes why the challenging environment of the shipping sector calls for restructurings of many involved companies.

16.2 Potential Contributions of the Key Stakeholders

It is important in a restructuring process to identify the main stakeholders. Always involved are the shareholders and the banks. However, it is important to also analyze whether further stakeholders can also contribute to a restructuring.

16.2.1 Shareholders

The shareholders of a company play the most important role in a restructuring. Not only can they supply liquidity in the form of a shareholder loan or a capital increase, or give guarantees backed by their personal wealth to the banks in exchange for new loans. They can also agree to sell certain assets of a company to raise cash. In addition, if they cannot contribute with their own cash injections, they can pave the way for a third-party investor to enter the company, which would mean that existing shareholders must accept a dilution.

Moreover, the attitude of shareholders is crucial to a restructuring. Are they flexible and trying to seek solutions jointly with the other stakeholders to save the company? Can they accept with humbleness that their company is in trouble and unable to comply with its obligations? Alternatively, are they playing hardball, trying to block all solutions claiming that the problem lies with the other stakeholders? Depending on the attitude of the shareholders, restructurings with similar starting points can take on very different routes.

It is also very important that shareholders paint a true picture of the state of the company, and lay out all the facts. Transparency about the expected cash inflows and outflows is crucial. Negative surprises of matters that should have been foreseen or which were intentionally not disclosed could severely endanger a restructuring and certainly lead to the other stakeholders to revise what contributions they will carry.

16.2.2 Banks

Banks naturally play a crucial part in all restructurings. This is especially true in shipping, which is a very capital-intensive industry with high leverage, i.e. high amount of debt. Banks have various means for assisting in a restructuring. First of all, they can ease the cash-outflow of a company by accepting a full or partial moratorium on the principle payments. Interest payments can be converted into so-called "payments in kind," meaning that part of the interest payment is only due at a later stage. Loans can also be restructured to temporarily allow for a "pay-as-you-can" period in which case the company only pays to the banks if its cash flow allows for it.

Furthermore, if the banks believe in the future prospects of a company, it is also not uncommon to supply a bridge facility, i.e. a short-term cash injection to help a company through the crisis. This facility is usually highly priced (high interest, often with a payment-in-kind element), and often combined with a share pledge. This means that if the bridge facility is not repaid, then the bank shall receive (parts of) the shareholdings in the company. Thus, while such a bridge facility is in place, the banks need to give their consent if a sale of the company is intended.

Banks also can pave the way for external capital to enter a company by allowing a tranching of the loans. This usually happens if the LTV of a company is significantly above 100 %. An outside investor in this case would not enter with fresh money if their cash injection were to be fully behind the banks. Thus banks divide their loans into various tranches such as a fully senior tranche and a junior tranche. Usually, the fresh money then enters between the senior and the junior tranche. As the junior tranche has lower possibility to be repaid, it is often also referred to as a "first loss piece." As can be imagined, banks do not like this approach much, as their internal systems require the junior piece to be rated badly, with subsequent high requirements to allocate equity to this junior loan. Another way to facilitate the entry of an external investor is to take a so-called "haircut" on the loan, meaning to write-off a certain part of the loan. Naturally, this is a last resort for the banks.

Lastly, banks can also convert some of their debt into equity, thus easing the cash outflow of a company significantly. However, banks usually do not like to be in an equity position, so they seek clear exit rules for their shareholdings or already define a way to dispose of the shareholdings at a later point in time.

16.2.3 Other Stakeholders

Other stakeholders that can contribute to a restructuring are usually suppliers and customers. However, it needs to be evaluated carefully whether creating transparency to these groups is beneficial or should be avoided. Customers often have a chance to switch their suppliers on a short notice, which would lead to a reduced cash-inflow for the restructuring company. Here the relative importance of the restructuring company to the stakeholders needs to be evaluated. If the survival of the company is crucial for the suppliers or customers, then they can be asked to contribute to a restructuring. However, if suppliers or customers can switch easily or only little business is done with the restructuring company, then it might be better not to inform these stakeholders about the financial trouble the company is in, if a quick restructuring solution can be found in another way.

As an example of supplier and customer contributions in the shipping sector, vessel owners can reduce charter rates, at least for a certain period of time. Ship management and other service providers can also reduce or capitalize fees providing additional financial resources for the company. Typically, yards are also asked to contribute in a restructuring, either by way of delaying the delivery of vessels, by reducing the price of the vessels, or by giving a seller's credit.

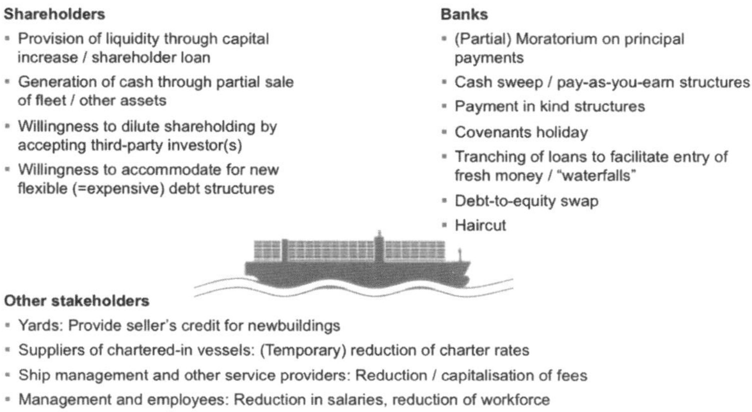

Fig. 16.5 What can the various stakeholders potentially contribute to a restructuring?

Other stakeholders could be states and government institutions. For example, Hapag Lloyd was able to secure a guarantee ultimately backed by the state of Germany when the company was in financial difficulties in 2009. Backed by these guarantees, banks were then willing to restructure their loans to the company. Management and employees are also stakeholders that often need to contribute during a restructuring. Depending on the size of the company, such contribution might only be marginal in size, but of high symbolic importance to the other contributing stakeholders.

The chart (Fig. 16.5) summarizes the main stakeholders in a shipping restructuring and their potential contributions.

16.3 The Restructuring Process

While each restructuring is somehow unique, the restructuring process can generally be divided into three phases-a preparation phase, a negotiation phase, and an implementation phase.

16.3.1 Preparation Phase

This phase is done internally within the company, and usually comprises the management, the shareholders, and advisers who assist in the restructuring. During the preparation phase, a thorough analysis of the business concept of the restructuring company has to be carried out. This includes the creation of a business plan, which lays out the value drivers of the company, its position within its industry and its unique selling points. Very importantly, a thorough and honest forecast of the liquidity situation for the next 24–36 months needs to be created, including scenarios to foresee the potential effect of certain assumptions not materializing. Such a liquidity plan should always include a "sources of funds" analysis to determine how much liquidity the company needs and at what stages, and from where it can source liquidity. Based on this analysis, the liquidity shortfall can be calculated and it can be estimated how much additional liquidity needs to be achieved through the restructuring.

It is also important in the preparation phase to identify the stakeholders who can contribute to the restructuring. The main stakeholders have been described in the previous section, but there might be others, depending on the specific case. A first plan should be created regarding who should contribute with what amount. It is also important to assess how the relationship among the main stakeholders might be. After the identification of stakeholders and their possible contributions to the restructuring process, strategy and objectives for the following negotiation phase are to be defined. The preparation phase is very important in this respect; the better prepared a company is at the time of restructuring, the more actively it can shape things to come.

16.3.2 Negotiation Phase

The second stage of the restructuring process begins with the presentation of the company, its business plan, and its liquidity requirements to the identified stakeholders. The company thus lays out that it is in financial distress, and presents a first plan how this can be healed. In most cases, it makes sense to present this to the stakeholders in a joint session, in order for them to feel that all main stakeholders are asked to contribute and that their contribution shall be equal ("fair share of the burden").

This presentation is then followed by individual and joint negotiations, and the restructuring plan is fine-tuned. To facilitate a quick solution, it is helpful if there is a certain date in the near future where a solution needs to have been found (e.g. a certain large payment to be made, e.g. for a bank loan repayment or for the delivery of a vessel). Otherwise, there is a danger if restructurings drag on-the momentum is lost. An efficient process management is thus of high importance and usually supplied for by advisers. Once the negotiations are successful and the main aspects of a restructuring plan are agreed on, it is usually important for the banks to have an independent assessment of this plan by a respected auditing firm. Such a report is usually called an "independent business review," and it testifies that with the restructuring contributions in place and under certain assumptions about the business development, the restructuring company will remain an ongoing concern.

16.3.3 Implementation Phase

This is the phase when the restructuring plan is implemented. This includes the final agreement of the restructuring plan, outlining the agreed-upon contributions

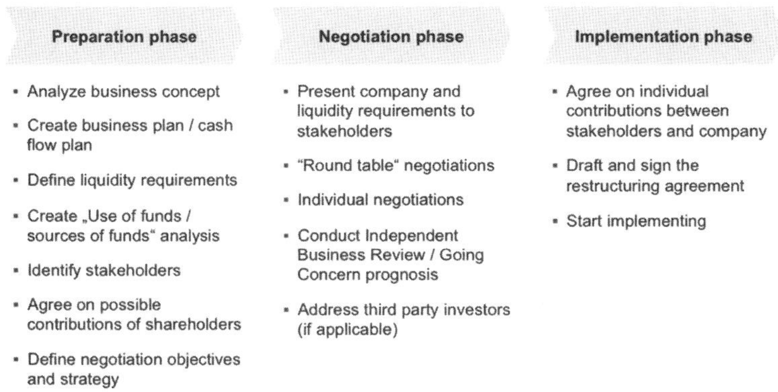

Fig. 16.6 The restructuring process is straight-forward on paper (but more difficult in reality)

by the various stakeholders, and the legal documentation of the individually agreed restructuring measures. These various contributions are then implemented according to the restructuring plan, including potential operational measures of the company. Depending on the individual situation, a communication of the successful restructuring might be advisable, in order for the company to regain the trust of its customers and suppliers.

The chart (Fig. 16.6) illustrates the restructuring process.

16.4 Excursion: The Critical Role of Access to External Capital

Unfortunately, shareholders are not always able to provide sufficient capital to support their company in a difficult financial situation. If a company is publicly listed, then it might be possible to use the capital markets to raise cash, be it through a capital increase (follow-on offering) or through the issuance of debt, e.g. via a (high-yield) bond. However, many companies are privately owned, and thus without access to capital markets. This is where private equity companies may come into play. Although private equity and the maritime industry are not natural bedfellows, the involvement of private equity firms in the shipping market is not unusual. There are a number of PE firms engaged in shipping, such as Alterna Capital Partners, Carlyle, Oaktree, Eton Park, Northern Shipping Funds, Wilbur Ross/Invesco, Triton, Apollo, Goldman Sachs, and J.P. Morgan, to name just a few. But not only American but also Arabian and Asian money is invested in the shipping sector in various ways, mostly through asset platforms operated jointly with ship-owners, but sometimes also in corporate structures.

Sometimes these private equity firms enter in a restructuring situation; sometimes they enter as normal investors to allow for further growth of a company, to enable an owner to acquire further vessels while the market going through a slowdown. The forms of investment are thus manifold, as are the investment criteria of the private equity firms (e.g. majority or minority stakes, equity only or debt plus equity, asset focus or corporate focus, distressed situation or growth situation, etc.).

Regardless of the investment focus, private equity firms as well as family offices have shown themselves to be active, highly professional, and cost-conscious investors that place great emphasis on clearly structured and detailed reporting, mostly on a monthly basis. This requires good organizational structures at the shipping companies and a high degree of transparency as far as the business figures are concerned. Based on current risk assessments, return expectations are 15 % or more per year. As a result, private equity firms also factor a rise in the value of the vessels into their budgets because it is seldom possible to generate this level of returns from ongoing revenue. In a restructuring situation, if an owner has access to such sources of liquidity as can be supplied by private equity, and is willing to accept a dilution of their shareholdings, then this can be very helpful for reaching a successful restructuring solution with all relevant stakeholders.

16.5 Lessons Learnt from Successful Restructurings

The success of a restructuring process depends on several factors. The following lessons are learnt from the successful restructurings the author could observe through his advisory work:

- Time is of essence.
  - Prioritization must take place, efforts must be concentrated on the biggest cash outflow items, and a momentum must be created and maintained.
- Transparency is of high importance.
  - Hiding information or supplying different information to different people is counterproductive.
- Treat everybody equally.
  - Partners will be willing to help but only if they feel that everybody else is treated the same way.
- Joint negotiations, no individual negotiations
  - You usually do not have the time to work individually. Besides, a joint approach ensures that parties feel treated equally (see above).
- Act decisively, but be humble.
  - You will need business partners to accept that you cannot honor contracts anymore. Make them feel that you are sorry about this but have no other choice.

- Appoint experienced advisers.
  - Use advisers (financial advisers, lawyers), who have done restructurings before and know the industry and its players.

16.6 Case Study of CSAV

As an example of an efficient and successful restructuring, the handling of a severe financial crisis at the Chilean company Compania Sudamericana de Vapores (CSAV) in the year 2009 can be analyzed.

CSAV, headquartered in Valparaiso, Chile, is the largest American liner operator, with sales of close to $5 billion in 2008. On a worldwide level, the company was at that time the 13th largest liner operator in the world. The company is listed on the Chilean stock exchange, in the stock exchange's highest market segment ("IPSA"). One peculiar fact about CSAV is that the great majority of its fleet is not owned, but chartered in from ship-owners, mainly from Germany.

Due to the severe fall in freight volumes and tariffs starting in the second half of 2008, CSAV was rapidly losing cash, and in danger of entering a very difficult financial position. It was clear that a solution needed to incorporate the ship-owners from which CSAV chartered its vessels. Charter rates were in many cases fixed for a mid- to long-term and were too high to be supported by income from trade, thus causing significant cash burn.

A corporate finance advisory company from Hamburg was officially mandated by CSAV as its exclusive adviser for the restructuring in March, and a team immediately flew to Chile to get transparency on the business plan and according liquidity requirements of the group, and to structure a possible solution.

This analysis phase lasted until the beginning of April, and a first meeting with the ship-owners and the financing banks took place shortly thereafter in Hamburg. In the course of this first meeting, various decisions were made:

- Standstill agreement between CSAV and the ship-owners was signed which allowed CSAV to reduce its charter rates temporarily while a solution was being negotiated, and
- That the ship-owners were represented in the negotiations by a group of "Spokesmen" to facilitate such negotiations.

Over the next weeks, a solution was being worked upon. The timeframe was extremely short, as CSAV had a previously committed capital increase coming up, which either needed to be confirmed or cancelled by the 29th of May. This capital increase of planned $130 million was an essential part of the envisaged restructuring package. However, as the shareholders refused to make this happen without a commitment by the ship-owners, it was clear that a solution needed to be found before the 28th of May.

CSAV as company	▪ Reduction in headcount, voluntary salary cut for top management ▪ Scaling down of services ▪ Further operational cost saving measures
CSAV shareholders	▪ Infusion of new equity ▪ Allow for dilution
Shipowners	▪ Reduction of charter ▪ Conversion of charter debt into equity
Shipowners' banks	▪ Easing of debt service for affected vessel companies
Yards	▪ Amendment of newbuilding programme to changed company strategy

Fig. 16.7 Overview of restructuring plan—contribution by the various stakeholders

After many negotiation rounds and ample speculation in the shipping publications if CSAV was to survive the structure of the deal was agreed upon between the company, the ship-owners and the financing banks, and signed literally on the last minute on the 28th of May.

The deal incorporated the following elements:

- Shareholders to supply fresh money by way of two equity increases, with a minimum amount to be raised of $350 million.
- Ship-owners to reduce their charter rates by an average of 36 % for a timeframe of maximum 24 months starting from April 2009, and converting it into equity at a pre-agreed upon share-price once the two capital increases by existing shareholders have taken place.
- Ship-owners' banks to show flexibility if reduced income on vessels caused by charter rate reduction was to affect debt service of the participating vessels.
- Overall package to be at least $710 m (actually about $770 m were raised, as the first two capital increases raised a higher amount of money than anticipated).
- Next to the restructuring package with the ship-owners and shareholders, CSAV was also able to significantly alter their newbuilding program. While this program had originally foreseen delivery of four 12,600 TEU vessels, the company was able to change this into five 8,000 TEU vessels with a high reefer capacity, which fitted better into the revised company strategy.
- In addition to the financial restructuring and the change in newbuildings, CSAV also worked on an internal efficiency-improvement program, which was being implemented on a global scale.

The graph (Fig. 16.7) summarizes the contributions by the various stakeholders.

With this package in place, the first capital increase was initiated on the May 29, 2009, and raised an amount of $145 m in July. A second capital increase was successfully conducted in December 2010, with further $270 m entering the company. Both capital increases were 100 % subscribed, which showed the

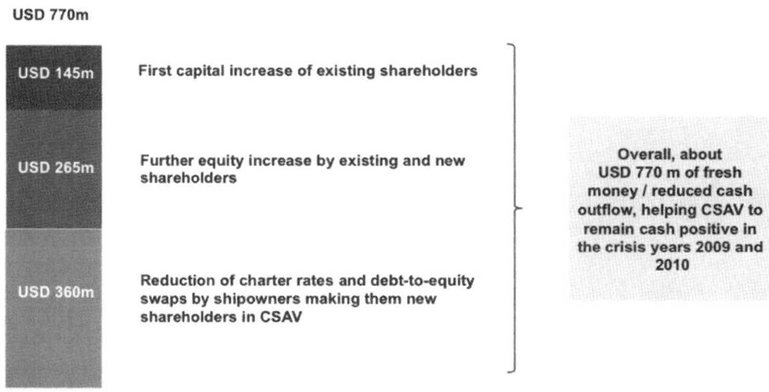

Fig. 16.8 Shareholder and shipowners contributed US$770 million to CSAV's restructuring

confidence of the shareholders that CSAV would with the restructuring package in place be among the winning survivors of the shipping crisis.

The third capital increase, i.e. the debt-to-equity swap of the charter rate reduction into shares of CSAV was conducted in April 2010. As the share price of CSAV had increased in the meantime, most of the owners who participated in the restructuring quickly sold their shares, recouping through the increased price what they originally had forfeited in the restructuring agreement through the agreed rate reductions.

The graph (Fig. 16.8) shows that the monetary effects of the three capital increases between 2009 and 2010.

With the restructuring package in place, a more suitable newbuilding profile, internal efficiency gains and proven access to the capital market, CSAV was able to sail through the crisis years of 2009 and 2010, and was even able to increase its market position, rising to be the seventh largest liner company in the world.

In retrospect, what were the factors of success?

- A company with a strong management that was willing to give transparency to its stakeholders about its actual situation and plans to overcome challenges
- Shareholders that not only supported with fresh money, but that accepted to be diluted
- A strong main shareholder that lead the way for other shareholders to follow, and that assisted in the negotiations with the stakeholders
- Access of the company to the capital market
- Ship-owners which showed goodwill and solidarity with an important client and which acted in unity
- Financing banks were able to facilitate ship-owners to make their contribution

Unfortunately, CSAV suffered a crisis again in 2011, similar to most liner companies, who had to operate in an environment of low freight rates and high bunker prices. This time, the necessary cash injections at CSAV were supplied by the capital markets in Chile, but also by the entry of a new major shareholder, the Luksic family; at the same time, the previously dominant shareholder, the Claro group of Chile, diluted their shareholdings.

16.7 Conclusions

To sum up, the high volatility of the shipping sector has caused and is continuing to cause many of its participants to restructure their respective companies. A good preparation on the side of the company and its shareholders, joint actions of all relevant stakeholders, information transparency and readiness for compromises, and sometimes access to third-party capital, are vital factors to overcome financial difficulties and for a successful restructuring, to secure the future prospects of a company.

Chapter 17
Risk Management and Applications

Kai Miller, Richard Ward, Ashley W. Craig, Elizabeth K. Lowe, Carrie A. Kroll, Tyler Hale, Edward Miller, John Cassels, Swen Schöne, and Andreas Höth

Abstract Containerisation is one of the youngest sectors in the shipping industry. It first emerged in 1955. A decade later, the container fleet stood at r.d. 2.8 m TEU, and it has continued this significant growth. As of May 2012, the total container fleet is recorded at r.d. 15.7 m TEU, an increase of 458 % in 16 years at the rate of 28.6 % per year.

This chapter aims to outline a concept of how new projects—either the acquisition of second-hand tonnage or the placement of new building orders—in the container segment could be structured and considers the limitations of the traditional models used in the container shipping industry.

The concept follows the assumption that ships earn money through the transportation of cargo. The basis of the charter rate for a ship should be connected to the income generated in the freight market. As a benchmark, one of the existing

K. Miller (✉)
HSH Nordbank AG, Gerhardt-Hauptmann-Platz 50, 20095 Hamburg, Germany
e-mail: kai.miller@t-online.de

R. Ward
Freight Investor Services, London, UK
e-mail: RichardW@freightinvestor.com

A.W. Craig • E.K. Lowe • C.A. Kroll • T. Hale
Venable LLP, 575 Seventh Street NW, Washington, DC, USA
e-mail: awcraig@venable.com; eklowe@venable.com; cakroll@venable.com

E. Miller • J. Cassels
Field Fisher Waterhouse LLP, 35 Vine Street, London EC3N 2AA, UK
e-mail: edward.miller@ffw.com; John.Cassels@ffw.com

S. Schöne
Field Fisher Waterhouse LLP, Am Sandtorkai 68, 20459 Hamburg, Germany
e-mail: swen.schoene@ffw.de

A. Höth
TPW Todt & Partner GmbH & Co. KG, Valentinskamp 88, 20355 Hamburg, Germany
e-mail: andreas.hoeth@tpw.de

O. Schinas et al. (eds.), *HSBA Handbook on Ship Finance*,
DOI 10.1007/978-3-662-43410-9_17,

container freight indices will be used. Through the use of derivatives that are settled against the same index, the remaining market risk can be transferred to a third party within the industry, or outside, to a professional risk taker.

17.1 The Freight Market

The container-shipping segment differs from other shipping markets because of the following aspects:

- Only a limited number of existing intercontinental liner services currently organise the ocean transportation of boxes.
- Ocean carriers offer to transport containers in "loops" along a certain route calling at several ports as per a published timetable. These are comparable to a London red bus service with its various fixed drop-off and pick-up points.
- Regarding the transhipment in use, containers are transported along with smaller vessels from smaller ports to central container hubs, where they are reloaded to larger vessels for the long haul trade. This is comparable to intercontinental airline services—e.g. the hub feeder system.
- Container vessels are never empty. Some containers will still be on board when arriving at the final destination of the trade lane, because most of the vessels are employed on round trips.
- With respect to an imbalance of equipment, empty boxes have to be transported to areas with higher cargo output.
- The base of BCOs (Beneficial Cargo Owners) is highly diversified as virtually anyone producing or trading goods for the international market is a potential customer.

This differs considerably from the bulk or oil markets where only a few users of coal or crude oil ship the same kind of cargo in huge lots from A to B. Commodities are commonly transported via ships on a "tramp" or "voyage" basis. This is best compared with the black cab service in London.

The container carrier market is a good example of an oligopoly: only a few major shipping lines control the majority of the market. This is especially true in key trade lanes such as Asia–Europe, Asia–USA, the US east coast and the US west coast (Transpacific). Theoretically, it allows carriers to influence directly the market where they operate either singularly or collectively.

Container cargo was commonly priced through the establishment of tariffs, where the transportation of certain goods was priced differently—i.e. the freight rate for coffee was cheaper than that of electronics or garments, as it was a more stable and high-volume business. Over several years, the tariffs were agreed upon in regular meetings. Such meetings no longer take place. This is mainly due to antitrust market regulations and competition rules. The term, "tariffs", has largely been replaced by the term, "FAK" (freight all kind). The income of ocean carriers represents a mix of earnings from contract and spot cargo. Carriers try to cover their costs—i.e.

time charter rates, staff, bunkers, etc. by long term contracts—and earn profits through spot freight rates and additional surcharges. However, in the eyes of the shipper, surcharges like the BAF (Bunker Adjustment Factor) and the FAF (Fuel Adjustment Factor), as well as location-based charges like a fog surcharge at certain international ports, are considered to be irritating additional costs.

It seems that over the long term, the majority of logistics services have been sold purely on price. It has been observed that relationships between carriers and third-party logistics providers (3PLs), as well as between carriers and BCOs, have been changing because of minimal fluctuations in the freight rate of oceangoing cargo. This is despite the set-up of additional services like—warehousing, labelling, IT solutions etc.—being costly in the initial set-up phase and requiring longer-term client relationships. Many industry participants say that service and reliability is sacrificed for the sake of minimal cost savings.

17.2 The Charter Market (Tramp Owners)

It is common practice for ocean carriers to secure their tonnage from ship owners via bareboat (b/b) or time charter (t/c) agreements with different durations.

From a carrier's perspective, a charter strategy can be implemented by building a portfolio of long and short-term tonnage. Different durations provide the opportunity to return tonnage to the tramp market to adjust the supply side and remove excess capacity from the market. The ability to use this option is becoming obsolete as ocean carriers increasingly act as ship owners themselves. Most of the larger vessels in the market or those that are currently on order are directly intended for the account of one of the main liner companies. Even when leasing structures, trusts, or other finance vehicles have been used to fund this tonnage. Lenders or investors usually back the order with long-term charters to one of the larger liner networks. Capacity adjustments become difficult for individual industry participants because they own the vessel but lack the option of returning it to the ship owner for the duration of the contract. As tonnage becomes ever larger with charter contracts extended in duration, it becomes increasingly difficult for the entire industry to adjust capacity on demand.

The market for charter tonnage, the so-called "tramp market", is dominated out of Europe, especially in Germany and Greece. A further significant fraction of container tonnage is controlled out of Asia.

Mainly small to mid-sized companies act as ship owners and provide the following services to their clients, the shipping lines:

- Arranging finance (debt and equity)
- Design/order/purchase of tonnage
- Bearing the employment risk
- Crewing
- Insurance
- Technical management

- Dry docking (maintenance)
- Voyage administration
- Commercial management of the asset (chartering)

A substantial proportion of the market comprises companies that secured loans (debt) with capital provided by private investors who contributed via KG or KS (limited partnership) structures funds arranged by so called "issuing houses" or "emission houses". These investment arrangers can be directly linked to the actual manager and/or disponent owner in many cases. KG and KS funds are legally independent special purpose vehicles (SPVs) that invest the funds in the ownership of a vessel. The regular share between EQT and debt was r.d. 50–50 pct, but in boom years, it rose to 70–30 pct.

In terms of cash flow for these financial models, a t/c or b/b agreement with a major shipping line was considered the ultimate security for both lenders and investors in the SPVs. However, after the initial charter period, the employment risk—i.e. the risk that the vessel cannot find suitable employment to earn sufficient revenue—is transferred to the investors who bear the associated risk. On the other hand, investors benefit if the employment of the vessel results in a higher financial return to the SPV.

A weakness of the model is the necessity for a long-term forecast over the assumed 25-year lifetime of the vessel. This can only be an assumption, considering the fast-changing world with respect to technology, market regulation, inflation and volatile interest and foreign exchange (FX) markets.

Even if the initial time charter was agreed to extend over a long period, thereby reducing the employment risk, the SPVs still face the problems of an imprecise financial model. Operational costs (OPEX), especially the costs of crew, lube oils, and insurance premiums, might escalate further than initially expected. In addition, interest rates on the loan and changes in exchange rates may fluctuate significantly, thereby resulting in an inaccurate initial calculation. Owners and investors face unstable costs related to the employment of the vessel while maintaining a fixed income that cannot be amended to cover potentially increasing costs.

Naturally, a vessel's t/c is finite. Once the current t/c runs out, all participants are exposed to current market conditions, which can be negative or positive for investors. If OPEX and CAPX were to increase beyond expectations, their associated costs would absorb a larger proportion of the vessel's generated income from a higher charter market. A worse situation could occur if costs go up and the t/c market weakens.

If a vessel enters employment in a bullish market and its use is always prolonged in other high markets, it will naturally turn into an outperformer. Similarly, if a vessel enters the market at a certain point and the charter agreement needs to be prolonged for the short to mid-term, it might miss certain highs and end up in a low market again; it will become an underperformer from a purely investment perspective. As indicated below, two equivalent vessels that might have been ordered at the same time may end up with completely different financial results simply because they delayed slightly before entering the market (see Fig. 17.1).

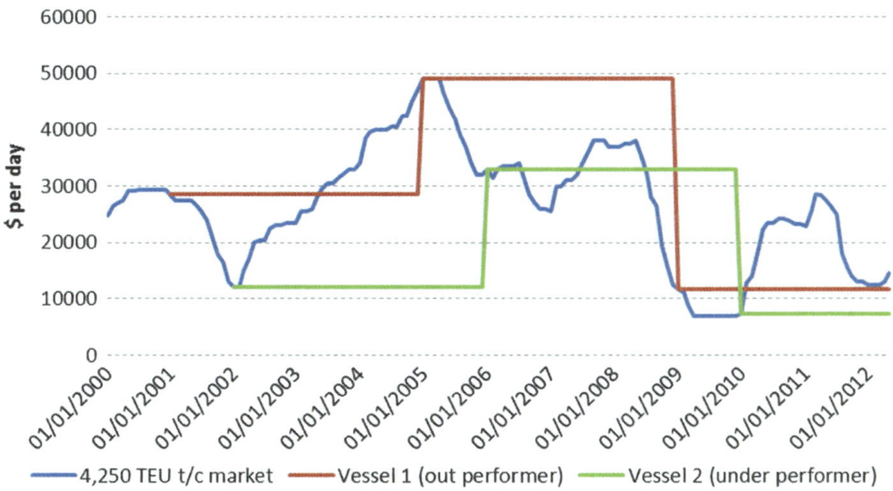

Fig. 17.1 t/c spot market 4,250 TEU. *Source*: ICAP Shipping Ltd

It appears that even with the current oversupply in the market, demand for new tonnage will emerge soon. Previous advances in vessels related to size rather than to economical engines and environmental standards—i.e. ballast water management, filters, CO_2-emissions, etc. It seems realistic that vessels will be scrapped before their maximum assumed lifetime simply because they are uneconomical. Ships will have to adhere to the stricter environmental standards that are set to be introduced. Hence, there will be a greater emphasis on efficiency to keep bunker costs low.

17.3 The Container Market: A Commodities Market

With the growing size of container vessels, more and more cargo has been containerised. By the end of the twentieth century, a larger portion of high-valued goods had been transported in boxes. For several years now, an increasing amount of low-value, high-volume cargo like soya beans, scrap metal, woodchips and waste paper is being containerised.

Commoditisation takes place when goods or services lose differentiation across their supply base. We have seen this occur in the container market with standard 20-ft. and 40-ft. dry containers on the major trade lanes being described as commodities, with carriers hardly able to differentiate their product offerings. Some carriers use the proposal of service quality—i.e. on time deliveries—as a method to differentiate their product. With cargo now being quoted on a FAK (freight all kind) basis, the underlying product—i.e. the container—is identical regardless of the provider.

The industry has seen huge losses, as well as profits over the years, as market volatility has led to large swings in container freight rates and t/c rates. It is still common practice during times of heavy losses for governments to keep companies afloat due to political or nationalistic interests. Moreover, many container divisions have been subsidised through group activities, profits, or by virtue of being state-backed businesses.

17.4 Freight Indices

Freight indices have been in existence since the beginning of the twenty-first century. A freight index is a snapshot of the actual market environment and can be used as an indicator in the physical market. It can also be used as a neutral benchmark for future settlements in the securities market.

The Shanghai Shipping Exchange (SSE) launched several container-related indices focusing on ex-Asia cargo. Other currently available indices include the WCI (World Container Index), the CCFI (China Container Freight Index), the CTS (Container Trade Statistics) and the TSA Index (Transpacific Stabilisation Agreement). Each index has a slightly different methodology, as is outlined below (see Table 17.1). This suggests that the core number may differ individually. However, there is a high correlation between the rate movements reported in each. Market players have been familiar with indexation in the stock, energy, and commodities markets for decades. Users must deem the indices to be trustworthy. This can happen only if the index reflects the market accurately and is transparent in its methodology. Participants are unlikely to use it if they do not believe that it reflects the market or if they do not understand or trust how it is calculated.

In the container industry, the Hamburg ConTex has already been used as a charter benchmark. However, this index reflects only the t/c market. The approach to index the relatively small t/c market is difficult. Although standards are clearly defined, too many differentiating factors separate individual vessels. Successful indexation of the commodity itself seems to hold more promise.

It appears that a derivatives market can be established in a much easier way in the underlying freight market. Risk can be successfully transferred to more potential risk takers.

17.5 Derivatives

Many believe that the first record of a modern futures exchange originated in seventeenth century Japan with rice futures commonly hailed as the first. Gluts and shortages of the product led to price fluctuations. Participants were able to trade in forward (future) contracts, which insulated them from adverse movements in price. This is now more commonly known as a hedge and is commonplace in other

Table 17.1 Comparison of currently existing container freight indices

	SCFI	WCI	CCFI	CTS	TSA
Data frequency	Weekly	Weekly	Weekly	Monthly	Monthly
Freight rate timing	Week of quoting	Last 2 days prior to index publication	Time of payment	Time of loading	Last day of departure
Publication delay	None	None	None	One month	One month
Measurement	TEU/FEU	FEU	Index	Index	index
No. of rate providers	30	Minimum 8	15	Unknown	12
Known panellists	Yes	No	Yes	No	No
Carrier input	Yes	No	Yes	Yes	Yes
Shipper input	Yes	Yes	No	No	No
THC included	No	US:Yes Europe:Yes, apart from Rotterdam/ Genoa imports	Yes	Yes	Yes
BAF included	Yes	Yes	Yes	Yes	No

Source: SeaIntel, Copenhagen, November 2011

Table 17.2 Specifications of derivatives

Forward	Future
Private contract between two parties	Traded on an exchange
Not standardised	Standardised contract
Usually one specified delivery date	Range of delivery dates
Settled at the end of the contract	Settled daily
Delivery or final cash settlement usually takes place	Contract is usually closed prior to maturity
Some credit risk	Virtually no credit risk

Source: ICAP Shipping Ltd

markets, such as those dealing in interest rate swaps, foreign exchange (FX), and oil, to name a few. A derivative is a financial product whose value is derived from an underlying variable. This variable may be a freight index such as the Shanghai Containerized Freight Index (SCFI). Swaps, options and forward freight agreements (FFAs) are forms of derivatives.

In particular, a forward contract is an agreement made on a specific date (X) between two parties to exchange at a fixed future date (Y) a specific quantity of an underlying asset for an amount of money that was agreed upon at the start of the contract (X). Future contracts are closely linked to forward contracts but are instead normally traded on an exchange. To make trading on an exchange possible, contracts have specific standardised features (see Table 17.2) .

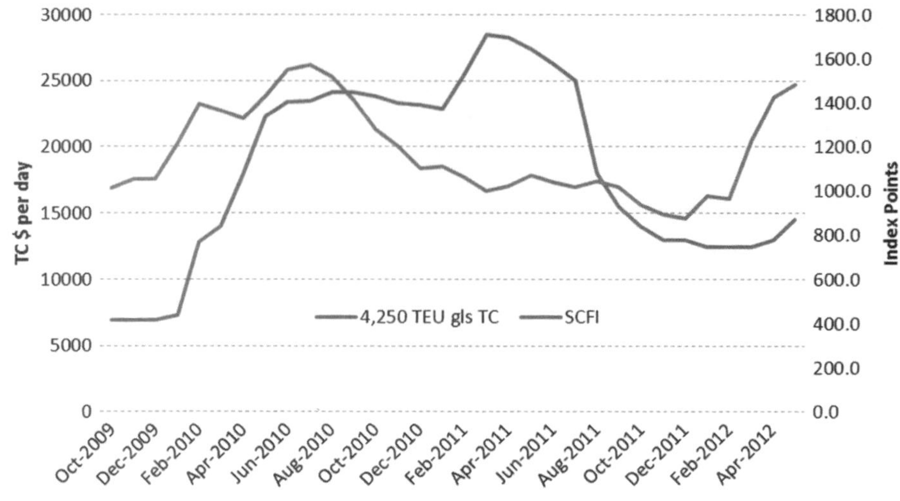

Fig. 17.2 TC rates vs. Freight rates. *Source*: ICAP Shipping Ltd

17.6 Freight Index-Linked Vessel Employment

The correlation of the two existing markets in the container industry-i.e. charter market vs. freight market-has been controversialy discussed for many years. It seems logical that also container vessels are ultimately earning money through the cargo they transport. Due to technological (e.g. rapid development of vessel size) and several artificial influences (e.g. tax exemptions, government support of the shipbuilding industry, cartels, substations, etc.) the two markets can appear to have an extensive time delay, although in the end, the markets have been following one another. Ultimately, the demand for vessels and, thus, for the t/c rate in the market is influenced by demand from operators for vessel employment. The operators, in turn, are affected by the growing demand for containerised cargo. Therefore, it is logical to suggest that when demand for cargo is high (freight rates increase), there is a greater demand for vessels (t/c rates increase) and vice versa (see Fig. 17.2). As discussed earlier, other influencing factors can affect each market individually, but due to market fundamentals over the long term, the two markets are closely correlated.

It has been common practice for many years in the wet and dry shipping markets to link charter contracts to indices. The Baltic Freight Index (for bulkers) and the Worldscale (for tankers) are commonly accepted industry standards.

To make long-term projects happen, owners and carriers must discuss how a flexible agreement can be reached. If both parties earn more in good markets and less in weak markets, both sides should be satisfied.

The current t/c model creates an artificial separation of the cargo from the tonnage market. Hence, the underlying market conditions are not connected to the asset being deployed. In reality, revenue earned through the freight market goes towards

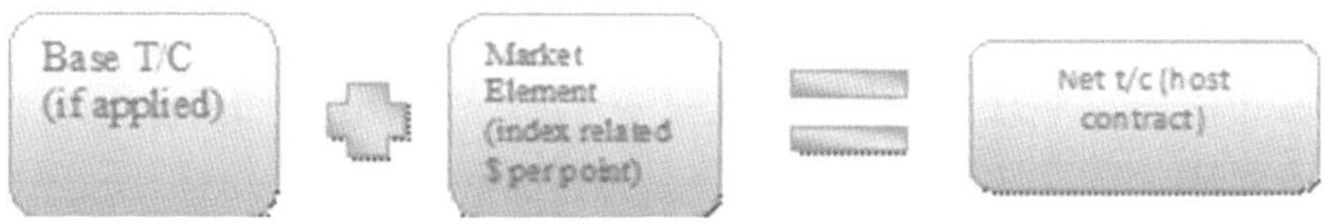

Fig. 17.3 Floating charter contract

paying for the t/c of the vessel. From an owner's point of view, an upside in the freight market should be reflected in his charter income, as presumably in a bullish economic environment his financing, crewing, and other expenses will rise.

The distortion of costs or revenues can be solved by reuniting the two markets using a freight index as a basis to calculate the charter income/costs.

A certain factor is connected to each index point; the charter rate payable is calculated by multiplying both of these factors. Besides, on creating a charter rate that always conforms to market conditions, counter-parties can benefit from the container FFA market to lock in their cash flows, as these financial tools are settled against the same index.

Procedure:

To implement an index-linked contract, a number of parameters need to be negotiated to allow owners, charterers, and brokers to continue playing the market.

Certain quality criteria of individual tonnage evolve around by what factor to apply as well as any possible base rate. Simple calculation tools can help both parties establish the possible effect on the overall t/c.

1. How to calculate the floating element of the contract
   (a) Which index to use (e.g. SCFI)
   (b) What factor to apply (the floating element)
2. If any, base t/c rate is to be applied
3. Payment terms
   (a) Weekly/fortnightly debit or credit notes
   (b) Weekly/fortnightly payment in arrears

Floating element: This would be linked to a suitable index such as the Shanghai Containerized Freight Index (SCFI) and would indicate the factor with which to multiply the index. This would establish the floating t/c element, which would fluctuate as the index increased or decreased.

Basis rate: A base t/c that is fixed for a given period may be added (see Fig. 17.3). This could be a figure that would allow the owner to cover OPEX costs.

Once these negotiations between the two parties (owner and charterer) are completed, the owner or charterer may wish to enter into an FFA position to secure their income (owner) or costs (charterer). Because FFAs are future contracts, they can be bought or sold before the actual vessel delivery.

Because Forward Freight Agreements (FFAs) are linked to the same index as the one where the floating t/c is based, they can be used to lock in future cash flows.

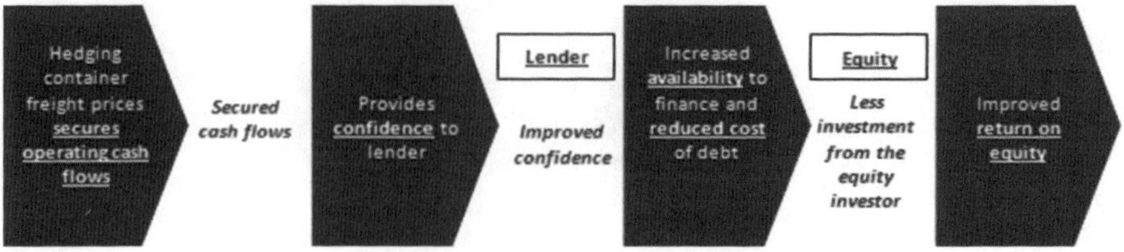

Fig. 17.4 Use of derivatives in a floating charter contract

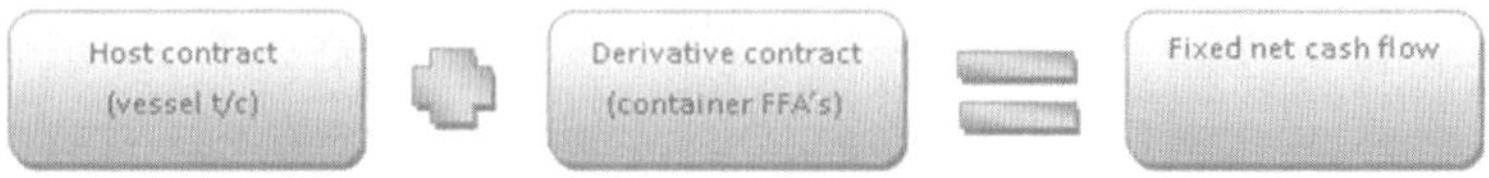

Fig. 17.5 FFAs used to provide stable cash flows

They also remain fungible, allowing either party to reverse their fixed cash flow and participate in the spot market. Another important factor is that FFAs remain flexible as they can be traded for a chosen period. This can provide parties with long-term cash flow security, which should attract lenders and investors (see Fig. 17.4).

An embedded derivative is formed when a derivative instrument, such as a container FFA, is combined with a non-derivative contract, such as a vessel employment contract (t/c), to create a single hybrid contract (see Fig. 17.5). An embedded derivative causes some or all of the cash flows generated from the host contract to be adjusted based on a specified variable, such as a freight index. The use of such derivatives enables participants to secure cash flows that would otherwise fluctuate due to changes in the host contract. The use of derivatives in this manner is commonplace in the oil markets, with companies that participate in crude derivatives being able to cover exploration costs. In the meanwhile, index-linked contracts are regularly used in the bulk and tanker markets with settlements against the BDI and BCI.

17.7 Examples

17.7.1 General Example

A vessel owner negotiates a rate with a prospective charterer using the following parameters.

Base t/c: $5,000/day

Market element: Additional $10 per index point

At the time of negotiation, the SCFI is at 1,500 points.

Therefore, the t/c for Day 1 will be $\$5{,}000 + \$15{,}000(10 * 1{,}500) = \$20{,}000$

On Day 2, the SCFI will be at 1,400 points.

Fig. 17.6 Market movements netted against FFA outcome

Therefore, the t/c for Day 2 will be $\$5{,}000 + \$14{,}000(10 * 1{,}400) = \$19{,}000$

Therefore, in good freight markets—i.e. when the charterer (carrier) is earning more through higher freight rates—the owner will receive a higher t/c and vice versa.

17.7.2 Example Using FFAs

Using the above, the t/c for Day 1 will be $\$5{,}000 + \$15{,}000(10 * 1{,}500) = \$20{,}000$

On Day 1, the owner decides to sell FFAs to lock in their income at $20,000

The owner, therefore, sells 300 FFAs (30 days per month * $10 per index point) at 1,500 points to lock in their income for the month (assuming 30 days).

On Day 2, the SCFI is at 1,400 points.

Therefore, the physical t/c for Day 2 will be $\$5{,}000 + \$14{,}000(10 * 1{,}400) = \$19{,}000$

We must now add to the physical t/c the cash flow from the container FFA, which was sold at 1,500.

Assuming that the index settles at 1,400 points, the owner will receive $100 per FFA contract (1,500–1,400).

The owner sold 300 FFAs; hence, he will receive $30,000 ($100 * 300) in cash at the end of the month.

Assuming that the month has 30 days, $30,000/30 days = $1,000 per day in cash received through the FFA.

Therefore, $19,000 t/c income + $1,000 FFA income = net t/c income of $20,000 per day.

Changes in the physical contract are equally and oppositely offset by the cash flow received through the FFA. This creates a fixed net t/c income for the owner (see Fig. 17.6).

17.8 Main Arguments for the Index-Linked Employment of Container Vessels

- There is no over-commitment from the operator.
- Tonnage will be competitive in every market environment.
- There is no under-commitment from the owner.

- The base rate should cover OPEX/CAPEX.
- Investors and owners have the chance to participate in the upside of the global freight market.
- There are no expensive repositioning or delivery procedures due to the likelihood of long-term employment with the same account.
- Flexibility is present, even in long-term projects.
- Swaps (Container FFA's) lock in minimum returns or fix convenient market levels.

17.9 Failures and Limitations of the Index-Linked Employment of Container Vessels

At present, only four to six regularly traded routes exist in the FFA market. These include Asia-NWE, Asia-Med, Asia-USWC, and Asia-USEC. This does not provide complete market coverage, but allows participants to be active in the main trade lanes. As the existing instruments reflect more than 50 % of the total market, entering a sufficient proxy hedge is possible.

As with any derivative, market liquidity begins low as participants usually enter with low volume trades before placing larger volumes. This trend is reflected in the current market with increasing participants entering and volumes gradually increasing as players become familiar with the process.

Compared to a classical time charter, an index-linked employment requires a little more administration. The accounting and finance department has to check the index and calculate the amount payable for each specific week.

17.10 Counter-Party Risk in the Derivatives Market

When trading derivatives, transacting a deal involves two options:

1. Bilateral
2. Cleared

Bilateral: Two parties agree on a contract. This is commonly a standard contract—e.g. International Swaps and Derivatives Association (ISDA). As with any business transaction, counter-party risk always exists when agreements are made between two parties. The risk is that the counter-party may default upon settlement.

Cleared deals: A clearing house assumes the function of a central risk taker. Clearing houses have substantial capital base and insure their risks. This enables them to step in should a counter-party fail. The service is comparable to PayPal in the retail industry.

This method of trading eliminates the counter-party risk associated with bilateral trading. Since the clearing house acts as the central counter-party, it also ensures anonymity for all market participants. As transactions are registered there and the clearing houses are normally regulated by the local financial authorities, they play an important role in an increasingly regulated financial market.

17.11 The Role of the Broker

Brokers gather people and organisations that possess the willingness to buy or sell. Brokers normally staff trading desks or run electronic networks to bring these buyers and sellers together, facilitating price discovery and receiving a commission when a transaction is finalised.

This helps provide price transparency and aids in establishing the best possible rate in derivative markets for their clients.

17.12 Costs

The costs of hedging are commission and clearing fees ranging from US$5 to US$15 as well as some margin and administration costs (see Table 17.3).

In theory, these can be offset because of a lower cost of capital or less invested capital (see Fig. 17.7).

In the Tables 17.4 and 17.5 selected clearing fees are presented.

17.13 Illustration of Charter Agreements and Derivatives in the Balance Sheets of Ship Owners and Charterers

Charter rates stipulated in the charter agreement are recorded in the accounts of ship owners as earnings and in the accounts of charterers as expenses. Whether it involves a time charter agreement or an index-linked contract is irrelevant because the rates will be recorded in the same area of the financial accounts. A contract whose running time causes earnings and expenses to be recorded beyond the date of the balance sheet will not normally be recorded in the balance sheets of the contractual partners. According to the realisation principle, unrealised gains must not be considered.

The situation is different in the case of an onerous contract. According to IAS 37.68, an onerous contract is a contract where the unavoidable costs of meeting the obligations under the contract exceed the economic benefits expected to be received under it. If an entity has a contract that is onerous, the present obligation under the contract shall be recognised and measured as a provision (IAS 37.66). §249 (1) HGB

Table 17.3 Broker commissions

Volume	Commission
0–99 TEU pm	$15 per TEU
100–999 TEU pm	$10 per TEU
1,000+ TEU pm	$5 per TEU

Source: ICAP Shipping

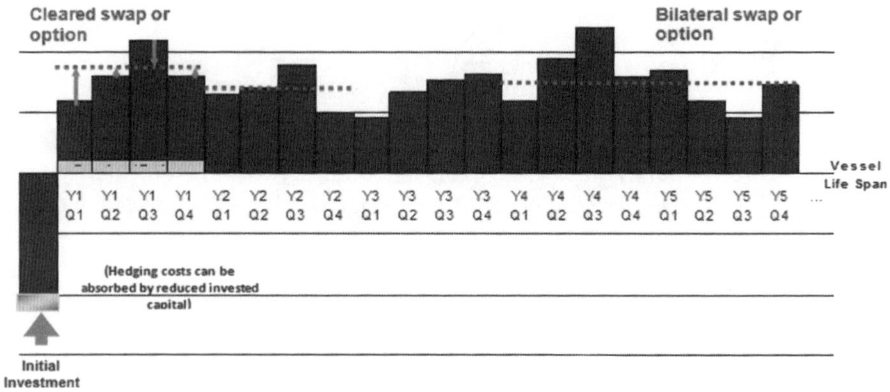

Fig. 17.7 Costs of hedging over a projects life span

Table 17.4 SGX clearing fees as per summer 2012

	Non-SGX members	SGX members
SGX clearing fee	$10 per lot	$8 per lot
Clearing member fee	$10 per lot	n/a

Lot size = ten containers
Source: SGX, Singapore

Table 17.5 LCH clearing fees as per summer 2012

	Non-LCH members	LCH members
LCH clearing fee	$3 per lot	$3 per lot
Clearing member fee	$3 per lot	n/a

Lot size = one container
Source: LCH Clearnet, London

contains the same consequence and deals with an "accrual for contingent losses". For the calculation of the provision, the full costs have to be used. For several benefits and costs, the best possible estimations have to be made and the provision has to be discounted. Difficulties concerning the estimations arise out of long-term index-linked contracts. However, in a functioning market, such contracts lead to a kind of correlation between benefits and costs, which means that no onerous contract will be in existence.

As already mentioned, the owner or charterer may wish to enter into an FFA position to secure their income (owner) or costs (charterer). If these financial products or agreements have been entered into and will be closed beyond the balance sheet date, there is again the question of accounting. According to IFRS regulations, the costs of hedging—commission, clearing fees, margin, administration costs, etc.—are recognised as assets in the balance sheet. The balance sheet will record whether future economic benefits for the business are likely and whether the asset has a cost or value that can be measured reliably (source: framework.89). Recognising the costs of hedging as an asset is a consequence of the accrual basis of accounting. In contrast to IFRS, the German HGB considers a balancing as an accrued item. An accrued item is no asset, but only a capitalisable aid. According to §250 (1) HGB, the balance sheet must record any expenditures both before and after the balance sheet date. The main difference between the IFRS and HGB regulations is that the latter requires the capitalisable aid to be shown in the balance sheet even though no future economic benefits are expected.

More significant than balancing the costs of hedging is balancing the FFA itself. Regarding the FFA, an initial forecast is necessary to see if benefits or costs are expected from the FFA in the future. The resulting transaction will not be shown in the balance sheet of a company that expects benefits. The company that expects costs will have to record this onerous contract in the provisions. If the considered company is not an owner or charterer entering into the FFA position to secure income (owner) or costs (charterer), then all aspects of balance sheet preparation are explained as mentioned above.

The situation differs, for example, when ship owner and charterer agree upon an index-linked employment, and the owner, as acceptor of a fixed charter rate and donor of the same index-linked rate agreed with the charterer, closes an FFA.

The explanations above and especially the example show that, in this case, the charter contract plus the FFA leads to a constant fixed net cash flow. For better understanding, it is assumed that this fixed net cash flow is larger than the unavoidable costs incurred by the owner. In our example, a massive decline of the charter rates and the indices leads to small benefits out of the charter agreement for the owner. If on balance sheet date the future expected unavoidable costs are higher than the benefits from the charter agreement, the present obligation under the contract shall be recognised and measured as a provision. This provision contains the amount of which costs exceed the benefits. At the same time, the owner receives benefits from the FFA. These benefits cannot be considered in the balance sheet.

The reverse is also applicable, future benefits from the charter agreement cannot be balanced, whereas a loss-making FFA has to be considered in the provisions. Both examples show that the hedging relationship of the deals is not visible in the annual financial statements. The economical view of connected deals requires an overall evaluation.

The special regulations for hedge accounting are applicable, according to IFRS, if all of the following conditions are met (source: IAS 39.88):

(a) At the inception of the hedge, there is formal designation and documentation of the hedging relationship and the entity's risk management objective and strategy for undertaking the hedge. That documentation shall include identification of the hedging instrument, the hedged transaction, the nature of the risk being hedged and how the entity will assess the hedging instrument's effectiveness in offsetting the exposure to changes in the hedged item's fair value or cash flows attributable to the hedged risk.

(b) The hedge is expected to be highly effective in achieving offsetting changes in fair value or cash flows attributable to the hedged risk, consistently with the originally documented risk management strategy for the particular hedging relationship.

(c) The effectiveness of the hedge can be reliably measured, i.e. the cash flows of the hedged item that are attributable to the hedged risk and the fair value of the hedging instrument can be reliably measured.

(d) The hedge is assessed on an ongoing basis and determined actually to have been highly effective throughout the financial reporting period for which the hedge was designated.

The example above, where the owner agrees to index-linked employment and secures its cash flows with a counter-directional FFA, is based on the same index; hence, it should easily fulfil the conditions. The initial and subsequent documentation should be easy, the probability of the compensating effect is 100 % and future expectations concerning the development of the index and the resulting values of the covering transactions can be delivered by branch services.

The index-linked employment is a binding agreement for the exchange of a specified quantity of resources at a specified price on a specified future date or dates (firm commitment, source: IAS 39.9).

If the index-linked employment, which is an unrecognised firm commitment, is designated as a hedged item, the subsequent cumulative change in the fair value of the firm's commitment attributable to the hedged risk is recognised as an asset or liability with corresponding gain or loss recognised in terms of profit or loss. The changes in the fair value of the hedging instrument are also recognised in terms of profit or loss (source: IAS 39.93).

It becomes more difficult when, for example, a charterer backs a large volume of forward agreements or hedged business with only a few covering transactions, or when multiple indices are applied. If the effectiveness of a hedge remains unfulfilled, then general accounting principles will apply for unmatched financial hedges. Generally, the company drawing up a balance sheet can choose whether to apply for hedge accounting.

In the German accounting rules, the overall evaluation is codified in §254 HGB. The German (legally uncodified) accounting principles also require the documentation of the covering intention, the quantitative proof and a continuous monitoring of the effectiveness of the hedging relationship. Proof for the existence of a hedging relationship should be easy to provide, according to IFRS. If a hedging relationship exists, the regulation according to §254 HGB for the creation of an accrual for contingent losses (§249 (1) HGB) is not applicable.

Unlike in IFRS standards, the German practice of balance sheet preparation ensures that neither the underlying transaction nor the covering transaction would be balanced. Nevertheless, new German commentaries also allow financial accounting as per IFRS.

Nevertheless, this is applicable only if the cash flow of the underlying transaction plus covering FFA transaction (fixed net result) is bigger in total than the unavoidable costs incurred in running the vessel.

17.14 Employment of Vessels: Index-Linked Employment from a Contractual Perspective

The charterer may take over a fully-equipped vessel including crew for one or more specified trips (voyage charter) or for a particular period (time charter).

Alternatively, the vessels can be placed on a bareboat charter where the charterer hires the vessel without the crew.

In contrast to, for example, tankers that are predominantly employed via voyage charters, container ships are usually chartered within the framework of time charters based on internationally accepted standard forms—such as BOXTIME or BALTIME.

Traditionally, and in line with these standard forms, English law is agreed upon between the owner and the charterer in the vast majority of cases.

In contrast, German law is almost never proposed by either party because Germany's national maritime and shipping laws have generally been considered outdated, unclear and, thus, impractical.

However, the new German maritime and shipping laws—scheduled to come into effect in December 2012 will set a considerably improved legal framework.

Therefore, in the long term, German law may constitute an alternative in the container-shipping segment and in other shipping markets.

For the first time, the law will also contain special rules on bareboat charters, in §553ff German Commercial Code (HGB), and time charters, in §557ff HGB.

In our view, the new rules will not exclude new pricing methods such as the replacement of a fixed charter rate (US$ per day) by a flexible time charter rate linked to an existing or a new trusted container freight index.

In contrast, the new §557 (2) HGB states solely that the (time) "charterer is obligated to pay the agreed time freight". For that reason, we believe—in accordance with general contract law principles—that the agreement on a flexible calculation method instead of a fixed amount would not cause significant legal problems, provided the method is based on a transparent and accurate formula.

In particular, an index-linked calculation method would not violate the standard rules in relation to general terms and conditions (§§307ff German Civil Code-BGB).

Index-linked employment is an integral part of the parties' agreement on price-determining factors. Consequently, it is subject only to the general transparency requirements of §307 (1) sentence 2 German Civil Code-BGB.

Therefore, a violation of §§307 (1) sentence 1 BGB is not possible.

An index-linked employment would also comply with the German Price Clause Act (Preisklauselgesetz) which—subject to exceptions—provides for prohibition of pricing clauses to prevent unregulated price increases with inflationary trends.

The flexible pricing terms of index-linked employment will reflect general market development in the container industry (charter market vs. freight market).

Additionally, they link to associated services (time charter and carriage of goods) that are—in view of the purpose of the Price Clause Act—sufficiently "similar or at least comparable" within the meaning of §1 (2) No. 2 to justify an exemption from the prohibitions of §1 (1) of the Price Clause Act.

In practice, the time charter parties may insert an index-linked formula into the standard time charter forms to document the hire of the time charter.

The application of a flexible, index-linked calculation method would also not raise serious legal concerns in relation to payment dates.

In this respect, the new German law in §565 (1) HGB states that in the absence of any agreement to the contrary, the time freight shall be paid semi-monthly in advance, as reflects customary international practice.

Therefore, alternative agreements such as advance payment of a higher pre-agreed base rate in connection with a 2-week balancing of accounts (via a credit note) or a weekly debit note (i.e. the payment in arrears of the difference between the base-rate and the calculated final time freight) remain legally possible.

Thus, from a contractual point of view, index-linked employment of vessels would not cause significant legal issues under German law.

The applicability of English law does not lead to a different legal assessment.

In the event that the parties agree on a trusted index within the framework of a transparent, objective, and unambiguous formula, we see no serious legal issues under English law in connection with index-linked employment of the vessels.

Consequently, the commercial concept behind index-linked employment can be considered a legally practicable alternative to a fixed charter rate (US$ per day).

17.15 Legal Overview of Container Freight Swap Agreements

Bilateral deals involving derivatives require a specific contract: an ISDA master agreement. This reflects that derivatives differ from financial products such as loans and bonds. Loans and bonds feature two parties with fixed roles—one counter-party is the debtor and the other is the creditor. Hence, cash flows are in one direction only. However, derivatives differ as the debtor and creditor can change, thereby leading to a "two-way road". For example, with container swaps, if the settlement price is above the swap price, the buyer is the creditor and the seller the debtor. If the settlement price is below the swap price, the seller is the creditor and the buyer the debtor.

The structure of an ISDA agreement is shown in the diagram below. There is a fixed, pre-printed, non-negotiable part: the master agreement. This contains no information regarding the price or quantity of the transaction. Therefore, once a master agreement has been signed between counter-parties, they are able to trade without renegotiating a contract each time. Furthermore, the master agreement allows positions to be netted. Hence, multiple transactions between the two counterparties can be reduced to one.

The agreement also allows a party to liquidate positions if the other defaults—i.e. if an event of default occurs. This covers:

- Failure to pay or deliver collateral
- Failure to provide credit support
- Misrepresentation
- Default due to financial obligations
- Bankruptcy

Positions can also be liquidated under a termination event, which can be defined as:

- Illegal changes in the law-making performance of the master agreement
- A merger that results in a decline in creditworthiness
- A merger or a change in tax law, which results in increased taxes being paid

17.16 Credit Support Annex

A credit support annex (CSA) is an optional part of an ISDA contract. This outlines the rules under which counter-parties post collateral. This is done to reduce the credit risk arising from a counter-party defaulting.

Terms of a CSA include:

- Threshold—i.e. when transfers of money should be made
- Minimum transfer amounts
- What is accepted as collateral, and the associated haircuts
- Rules for settling disputes regarding over-valued positions

17.17 Maritime Sector Regulatory Environment: EU

The maritime sector for trades to and from the EU is subject to some of the most stringent antitrust rules in the world. The scope of application of the rules prohibiting restrictive agreements is wider than in other jurisdictions and the levels of the penalties imposed for infringements more severe.

The limited safe harbour provided by the liner conference block exemption disappeared with the expiry of that exemption on 18 October 2008. There is now only a very limited block exemption regulation applicable to maritime transport: Commission Regulation (EC) No. 906/2009, the liner shipping consortia block exemption.

17.17.1 Liner Conferences

Since 18 October 2008, liner conferences for shipping lines operating on trades to and from the EU have been subject to the full application of the EU antitrust rules.

This means that liner conferences that have the purpose or effect of fixing tariffs and conditions of carriage on trades to and from the EU have been prohibited with effect from 18 October 2008. Exchange pricing, capacity, costs, and other commercially sensitive data as well as participation in discussion agreements for trades to and from the EU are likely to fall foul of the EU rules—in particular of Article 101 of the Treaty on the Functioning of the European Union—even if the exchange of information does not result in any change in behaviour. It does not matter that conferences are permitted in other jurisdictions; the fact that price fixing is permitted elsewhere does not authorise it on trades to and from the EU and would not afford an effective defence in antitrust proceedings. The EU rule change does not prevent shipping lines from participating in price-fixing and capacity-limiting conferences on non-EU trade routes.

17.17.2 Shipping Consortia

The liner shipping consortia block exemption was adopted on 29 September 2009 and came into force on 26 April 2010. It has a duration of 5 years. The block exemption applies to international liner shipping services for the carriage of cargo, excluding maritime cabotage. For the purposes of the EU antitrust rules, consortia involve the carrying out of activities in common by shipping lines for the primary purpose of rationalising costs. On that basis, they are distinguishable from conferences, which pursue the objective of coordinating tariffs.

Consortia that satisfy the requirements of the revised block exemption—in particular, those that have a market share below 30 % on all trades on which they operate and that do not involve price fixing and customer allocation—will benefit from antitrust immunity. The European Commission has clarified the method for calculating the market share: the individual market share of each consortium member in the relevant market covering all activities, whether inside or outside the consortium, should be considered when determining market share.

More types of services are covered by the definition of consortia in the revised block exemption since references to services being carried out chiefly by container have been removed: all liner shipping cargo is covered.

The list of exempted activities covers only what is indispensable for operating joint services: activities of a consortium operating within a conference, cargo, revenue or net revenue pools, joint marketing activities, and joint documentation systems are no longer covered by the block exemption. Coordination of sailing timetables, exchange or cross-chartering of slots, pooling of vessels or port installations, use of joint operations offices and port services, use of a computerised data exchange system and/or joint documentation system, and joint marketing are generally permitted because they facilitate rationalisation and economies of scale in the use of vessels and port services. Joint or coordinated capacity changes are permitted only where they are a response to fluctuations in supply and demand and are not a strategy to drive up prices.

The liner shipping consortia block exemption will not apply to agreements that include price fixing when selling liner services, limitation of capacity or sales except for permitted capacity adjustments, and market or customer allocation.

The relationship between the European Commission and many international shipping operators has not been particularly harmonious over the years. Fines for breaching the antitrust rules have been imposed in a number of cases. Even before the liner conference block exemption was repealed last year, the Commission condemned a number of shipping conferences that were found to not meet exactly the requirements of the block exemption. For example, fines totaling €273 million were imposed on 15 participants in the Trans-Atlantic Conference Agreement (TACA) in 1998. Subsequently, the Commission granted immunity to an amended version of the TACA, which included only seven participants and which placed strict limits on the nature and amount of commercially sensitive information exchanged between its members. Restrictions on the freedom of conference participants to enter into individual service contracts had also been removed.

17.17.3 Freight Indices

Freight indices and index-linked employment, in principle, do not give rise to antitrust risks in the EU. However, the maritime sector is a high-risk sector. In the past, it has been subject to antitrust investigations on numerous occasions in the EU and is currently under investigation by the European Commission. Therefore, any mechanism or development that provides transparency regarding commercially sensitive information amongst competing carriers, or which may enable carriers to coordinate their behaviour or otherwise remove a degree of uncertainty as to the operation of the market should be reviewed carefully before introduction.

17.18 Regulatory Environment: US

17.18.1 US Perspective on CFDs

For the past several years, the great unknown in US shipping regulation has been the prospect of a market for container freight derivatives (CFDs). Given the economic instability of the global market since 2007–2008, the US Federal Maritime Commission (FMC) has made modernising certain aspects of US shipping regulations a priority, among them the use of container freight rate indices. The FMC has encouraged the use of negotiated rate agreements (NRAs), for example, and as of 31 May 2012, announced its interest in creating and distributing an index of container freight rates for US agricultural exports. Given the global market where carriers exist, are CFDs the obvious next step in the US shipping market? If so, questions regarding how the US index will be populated and maintained are at the forefront for all types of players in the US market. In many ways, the creation of a futures trade for containerised cargo has been on the rise. Hedging and speculation have been used for centuries in both new ventures and well-established industries to steady markets and create profit out of uncertainty. Shippers of bulk freight are so reliant on derivatives that the Baltic Dry Index, the ruler against which forward freight agreements (FFAs) are measured, has been a key indicator of the health of the global economy. However, dry bulk accounts for only around 7 % of worldwide shipping value. Since it was pioneered in the 1960s, container freight has steadily climbed to become the dominant model for global trade. It now financially comprises around half of the international fleet—seven times more than dry bulk. Adding in the inherent uncertainty of spot-contracted voyages of container vessels, the question becomes even more compelling: how did the container freight market elude risk management until now?

17.18.2 History of CFDs

In 1975, the United States created the Commodity Futures Trading Commission (CFTC), an independent regulatory body tasked with ensuring clarity and fair dealing in futures markets. Although it dealt mostly with agricultural and industrial materials, CFTC was confronted with something entirely new when Clarkson Securities of London conceptualised the FFA in the 1990s. FFAs allow shippers and carriers of dry bulk freight to hedge against potential volatility in an inelastic market. The security of the Baltic Dry Index, now almost two centuries old , provided an added promise of legitimacy. At first, the concept was slow to take root, but in recent years, FFAs have accounted for $36 billion, 40 % of the physical activity in the dry bulk market. FFAs have proved so lucrative that many hedge and mutual funds now invest in them in lieu of the more traditional instruments.

In the aftermath of the economic collapse of 2008, trade finance began to look for a way to stabilise container rates, and container freight derivatives were an obvious choice. In 2010, Clarkson Securities executed the first type of CFD, called a container freight swap agreement (CFSA), between Morgan Stanley and carrier Delphis. A CFSA is a cash-settled, principle-to-principle arrangement.

Like FFAs, CFDs require an index of prevailing container rates by route to serve as an anchor. While the Baltic Dry Index is not restricted to Baltic routes, it is limited to dry freight. Hence, for its CFSA, Clarkson turned to the busiest container port in the world, Shanghai, and to the Shanghai Containerized Freight Index (SCFI), which is published by the Shanghai Shipping Exchange. The CFSAs allow for price speculation up to 6 months in advance and service fifteen routes, each originating in Shanghai. Other indices have been quick to found their own CFD markets. A separate Chinese index, the China Containerized Freight Index, has earned some popularity, along with the Transpacific Stabilization Agreement Index. Drewry of London offers the World Container Index as well as the Global Container Rate Index, a joint venture with Cleartrade Exchange. However, CFSAs based in Shanghai have capitalised on creating the market. Under the eye of UK's Financial Services Authority, trades of derivatives on the Shanghai–Europe route indexed by the SCFI are becoming established as financial tools for European companies.

17.18.3 Current US Shipping Climate/FMC Activities

Although routes from China to both the east and the west coasts of the United States are hotly followed on the SCFI, American shipping has been slow to adopt CFDs. First, the popular indices track only US imports despite unexpectedly surging export strength—US exports are up by 34 % since President Obama's announcement of his initiative to double exports by 2015. Only the World Container Index lists American export routes, and even then, only as backhaul. However, more importantly, US shipping is accustomed to dealing with the stringent transparency requirements of the Federal Maritime Commission.

In accordance with the Shipping Act of 1984, the FMC requires the rates for freight carriage to be published in tariffs that are made accessible to the Commission and to the public. However, in March 2011, it issued a rule exempting thousands of small non-vessel operating container carriers (NVOCCs) from such requirements, citing a duty to promote efficiency and reduce regulatory burdens on shippers through the establishment of NRAs . NRAs breathed new life into the shipping industry, encouraging stronger and better-tailored relationships between carriers and shippers.

The FMC soon turned its attention to the recent European creation of a CFD market. In May 2011, FMC Chairman Richard Lidinsky, Jr., formally announced the creation of a Container Freight Index and Derivatives Working Group. "Index-based ocean freight rates and derivatives have potential to be useful tools for shippers, intermediaries, and ocean carriers to increase rate certainty and manage risk", Lidinsky said. "It's important that market participants have flexibility in structuring rates and hedging strategies. At the same time, I want to explore whether modest, common-sense standards are needed to ensure participants have adequate information and avoid manipulation".

Lidinsky outlined a series of concerns regarding CFDs, including compliance with the Shipping Act, public accessibility and legitimacy of indices, and restrictions imposed by Dodd-Frank and other new regulations. Although no formal report was issued, the working group confirmed its endorsement of index-based NSAs in early 2012. The FMC recommitted itself to removing regulatory barriers, and as it "began to consider whether these service contracts referencing freight indices comport with its regulation, it decided to do a more fundamental assessment of whether the regulation in its current form is more restrictive than is necessary to protect the shipping public and carry out the purposes of the Shipping Act". The Commission concluded that accessibility requirements were outdated and that indices need only be available to contracting parties and the Commission itself. By mid-2012, the FMC has solicited comments from shippers regarding a proposition to create its own index of US containerised agricultural exports. Concerned that none of the existing container indices is satisfactorily neutral, the FMC is contemplating issuing an index itself. It has received "informal requests [from] several large US agricultural shippers, intermediaries, and derivative brokers" to issue an index based on data aggregated from service contracts filed with the FMC. Although it is first asking whether US export rate indices would be beneficial for US shipping at all, whether such indices should be targeted to specific commodities, whether the FMC or another party should create such an index, and whether it may draw on the data it collects via its regulatory authority, the FMC's working group appears intent to enter the CFD index market. Drewry, co-publisher of the World Container Index, has already expressed support for the FMC's plan.

17.18.4 Conclusion and Opposition from the Industry

Even with the blessings of the FMC, many industry players are sceptical about container freight derivatives. While still in the death throes of the economic collapse, stakeholders in ocean carriage have unfavourable associations with the words "derivative" and "futures", connecting them closely to the dangerous and unsound financial practices that caused a global economic shutdown. The CEO of Maersk Line famously likened them to "casinos".

Perhaps more critically, carriers foresee CFDs transforming container shipping into a commodity. Indeed, it is the freedom and alienability of commoditisation that gives derivatives their value. However, container space has traditionally been something different. Carriers develop relationships with shippers that provide for requirements beyond price and volume, including the use of containers themselves or arranging for complex inland transportation routes. Some carriers insist that these relationships provide true stability that an increasingly liquid market cannot offer. Whether these concerns can prevent a repeat of the exponential growth of the FFA market will soon be seen. If the FMC does endorse the general use of container freight derivatives in the US shipping market, all industry players would benefit from closely examining their business models to see how the changes will affect them individually. Shippers and NVOCCs may indeed find, as Chairman Lidinsky predicts, that CFDs offer an opportunity to plan for and manage turbulent economic climates beforehand. Carriers may find that prospective shippers are less interested in creating exclusive relationships than before as they swap for the lowest rates possible. Non-traditional parties may begin to take an interest in the ebb and flow of the containerised freight market. Lines dealing exclusively with containers may suddenly find themselves forced to deal with the CFTC if it finds CFDs within its jurisdiction.

Over the past 2 years, the Federal Maritime Commission has implemented the most serious set of deregulatory actions since Congress last amended the Shipping Act. Likely spurred by the US fleet's limited ability to flex with an unstable economy, the Commission has consistently removed administrative burdens on the industry and called for modernisation and innovation. Allowing for extensive use of indices in contracting would further the FMC's goals of modernisation and innovation.

Regardless of whether a stable US index rises to the fore, players in the US shipping market will see the effects of the debate ripple through to their businesses. As with all major regulatory changes, adjustments will begin with small tweaks and targeted rules as regulators attempt to balance and solidify the new market. Remaining informed is crucial to survival in the new and changing container freight derivatives market.

Chapter 18
Islamic Finance in Shipping: Dawn of a New Reality

Nijoe Joseph

Abstract In a newly released report titled, "Global Islamic Finance Jurisdictions" by KFH Research Limited, Islamic finance is seen to be rapidly expanding across the global financial system with as many as 600 financial institutions across 75 countries offering Islamic law compliant products and services. As like any other industry or sector wherein Islamic finance has permeated, the global shipping industry too has reaped the benefits of an ever increasing interest in *Shariah* compliant finance products and services. The aim of this chapter is to introduce to the reader the basic concepts of *Shariah* based lending (e.g. *riba*, *gharar*, *maysir* etc.), the popular methods of Islamic finance utilised currently by various ship owners and ship finance institutions (e.g. *ijara*, *murabaha*, *sukuk* etc.) and a brief analysis of the risks associated with each method of financing thereof. The chapter ends with a listing of certain considerations, which are unique to Islamic finance that must be borne in mind by anyone who chooses to be involved in an Islamic finance transaction.

18.1 Introduction

After a period of unprecedented economic growth and prosperity, the recent credit crisis and the consequential financial meltdown resulted in the conventional banking system's appetite for financing capital-intensive projects, in general, to become greatly satiated. The tangible slump in global trade meant that there was also a free fall in freight rates and charter hires, and with that, the value of ships

N. Joseph (✉)
Stephenson Harwood Middle East LLP, Al Fattan Currency House, Dubai International Financial Centre, P.O. Box 482017, Dubai, UAE
e-mail: nijoe.joseph@shlegal.com

O. Schinas et al. (eds.), *HSBA Handbook on Ship Finance*,
DOI 10.1007/978-3-662-43410-9_18, © Springer-Verlag Berlin Heidelberg 2015

plying in the trade had also regressed. All this generated further disinterest among the conventional banking fraternity (Measures et al. 2011). The general lack of liquidity meant that conventional ship financing institutions and banks could not provide adequate financing, which was required by liquidity-strapped ship owners to upgrade or expand their fleets to remain competitive in a difficult market.

Though it is still too early to confirm, in early 2012 there were signs that new finance facilities were becoming available to a greater extent than earlier. Traditional ship finance banks remained exceedingly cautious and circumspect about the kind of customers that they would want to lend to. This, in real terms, would mean that ship-owners, who do not find themselves in the higher end of creditworthiness of the small and medium enterprise (SME) configurations, will still find the going tough when they try to finance their businesses.

In such situations, it was but inevitable that alternative sources of finance would be sought out by those who are in real need to grow and sustain their businesses. Islamic finance is one such source, which is fast consolidating its position in the global financial industry as a key alternative to conventional banking products and facilities. However, not a new phenomenon in the international finance industry by any means, Islamic finance has nevertheless managed to quietly secure its position in the global finance scene as a reliable source of alternative funding.

Though the direct and indirect effects of the global economic crisis have equally affected the Islamic finance institutions, it is interesting to note that assets under the management of Islamic banks and financial institutions are now estimated to total well over US$1 trillion. However, over the past 10 years, Islamic finance has emerged from being a niche sector restricted to a few local players to becoming a sizable, high-growth component of mainstream finance across several countries. This growth from a modest US$150 bln worth of assets at about mid-1990s to the second half of 2013 with total assets estimated to exceed US$1.8 trillion as at end-2013, representing a more than 12.5 % increase in assets.[1] Other sources confirm that the current value of global Islamic banking assets reached US$1.8 trillion in 2013[2]; considering the figures in 2011 (US$1.3 trillion), an average annual growth of 17 % is reported in the last years of credit crunch. The growth outlook for Islamic banking continues to be very positive. Market estimations suggest that Islamic financial bodies have a market potential of at least US$5 trillion.[3] These types of growth projections show the enormous extent of the opportunities.

[1] See also http://www.bi-me.com/main.php?c=3&cg=4&t=1&id=63405.

[2] See also Ernst & Young's World Islamic Banking Competitiveness Report 2013.

[3] See also http://www.shariahfinancewatch.org/blog/2010/04/12/moodys-shariah-compliant-assets-could-reach-5-trillion/.

18.2 Basis of Islamic Finance

Islamic finance may be described as a form of ethical[4] (Ahmed 2011) commerce in which the products, facilities and services are structured so as to comply not only with the law of the contract, but also with the guiding principles of the canon law of Islam, which is referred to as the *Sharia'a*. *Sharia'a* encompasses principles pertaining to religious, ethical and legal values, and is derived from four primary sources:

1. The *Quran*, the holy book of the Muslims that is believed to be revelations from God;
2. *Sunnah*, the authenticated sayings and actions of Prophet Muhammad (PBUH);
3. *Hadith*, which refers to reports of statements or actions of Prophet Muhammad (PBUH), or of his tacit approval or criticism of something said or done in his presence;
4. *Fiqh*, collection of interpretations and rulings by various Islamic scholars (Mutahhari 2008).

As such, *Sharia'a* is not found in a single comprehensive code, text or resource, but is ascertained from all the above referenced sources. *Sharia'a* is applied by religious scholars who interpret the various Islamic laws and rules, as may be applicable to different matters, transactions or cases, and give their findings or judgements on the same.

The fundamental underlying requirements for a valid Islamic financial transaction can be said to be the following:

1. True and fair sharing of risk between the parties to a financial or commercial arrangement;
2. No exploitation of a weaker party by the other contracting party;
3. Avoidance of economically wasteful and unproductive activities;

while charitable conduct and social and economic development are encouraged (Khorshid 2009).

18.2.1 Prohibitions in Islamic Finance

As a corollary to the above mentioned fundamental rules, Islamic finance also has the following well-known prohibitions regarding its transactions:

---

[4]Quoting the source: "A business activity will be ethical if it promotes good in the society. We use the same logic to determine the ethicality of transactions and activities of Islamic banks. Specifically, activity of an Islamic bank would be ethical when it enhances welfare (*maslahah*) and morality of individuals in the society. On the contrary, any banking practice that produces adverse effects on either welfare or Islamic morals would be considered unethical".

1. *Riba* or *Usury* is excess compensation without consideration.
2. *Gharar* or *Uncertainty* is to unknowingly expose oneself or one's property to jeopardy and occurs in transactions that are not to the benefit of one of the parties. It is considered to be deceit.
3. *Maysir* or *Gambling* is to participate in games of chance. It does not apply to risks taken in life or in business activities (Lewis and Algaoud 2001).

Prohibition of interest in Islamic finance is due to the position taken by Islam that all income must be determined by the actual supply of work effort associated with the factors of production or other similarly valuable consideration or contribution made by the parties to the transaction. Money by itself is only seen as a medium of exchange, with no intrinsic value in itself. The objective underlying the prohibition of usury is to prevent the commercial exploitation by one party in a transaction of another party with a weaker negotiating power.

However, Islamic finance encourages and fosters partnerships among parties to a transaction or a business, whereby the profits and risks of the transaction or business in which the investment is made are shared by all parties. True gain in Islamic finance is "justified" only when one faces the risks associated in securing it.

18.3 Islamic Financial Instruments of Ship Finance

18.3.1 Murabaha ("Cost Plus" Finance)

Murabaha, simply stated, is the sale of a property or commodity at cost plus margin (Muhammad 2009). However, to be a valid transaction, the transaction in question must fulfil all the conditions of a valid sale. It may either be a spot sale or a deferred/credit sale. Deferred sale *Murabaha* is commonly used as a mode of trade financing by Islamic banks for short-term, low-risk investments. Deferred price becomes a debt and is dealt with as a loan transaction. The price once agreed to at the time of the sale cannot be changed subsequently due to the default of the creditor as anything above the sale price would be *Riba* or *usury*.

The *Murabaha* transaction in shipping (see Fig. 18.1) can be explained as follows:

1. The customer/borrower identifies the asset/vessel (e.g. a second-hand ship) it wishes to acquire and requests the creditor/lender to finance the asset.
2. The borrower and the lender enter into a *Murabaha* agreement wherein it is agreed that
   (a) The lender will purchase the vessel and the borrower will immediately buy back the vessel from the lender
   (b) The borrower shall pay the lender the price of the asset on a specified date or dates in the future at a specified price (the deferred price being the cost price of the vessel plus a declared "profit" margin.)

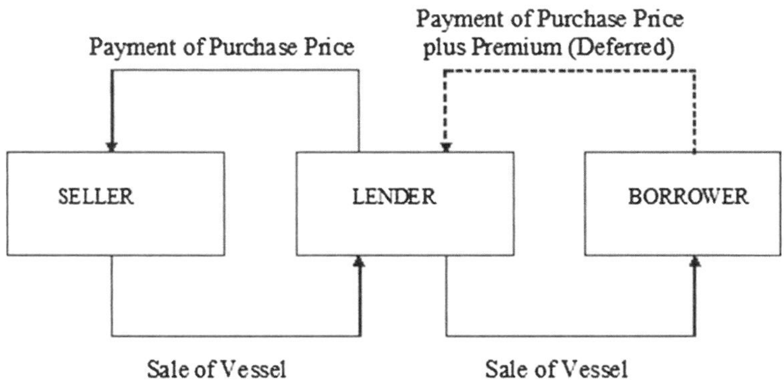

Fig. 18.1 *Murabaha* transaction

3. The lender thereafter appoints the borrower as its agent to purchase the vessel directly from the manufacturer or seller of the asset on behalf of the lender.
4. The lender then buys the vessel under a sale and purchase contract with the seller and pays the price (simple cost price of the asset) under that contract. The title to the vessel vests in the lender.
5. The lender then sells the asset to the borrower, with immediate delivery of the asset to the borrower, along with the title, which passes to the borrower. There is a deferred payment of a pre-agreed purchase price in specific instalments throughout the *Murabaha* period or in one lump sum on the last day of that period.

There is a "profit" factor that is included in the deferred pre-agreed "purchase price" between the borrower and the lender, which has taken into consideration the lenders risk in the transaction. The "profit" portion is usually benchmarked against conventional indices, such as London Interbank Offered Rate (Libor) or Euro Interbank Offered Rate (Euribor), plus a margin. Though this aspect has led many to conclude that this is akin to that of a conventional loan with interest, Islamic scholars have opined that unlike interest, the profit element in an Islamic *Murabaha* transaction does not amount to a charge for the use of the money itself (because it is prohibited as *riba*), but that it is a charge for the risk that the lender assumes in taking title to the asset.

18.3.1.1 Example of *Murabaha* Finance

In July 2011, Saudi Arabia's National Shipping Company (NSCSA) signed a US$ 219 million *Murabaha* financing agreement with Saudi British Bank (SABB) and National Commercial Bank (NCB).

Eighty per cent of the funding will be made by SABB along with NCB, which will finance the construction of two general cargo ships, while NSCSA will finance the remaining 20 %.

The deal has a 12-year tenor and will be repaid in equal quarterly instalments with a balloon repayment of approximately 30 % of the contract value at the end of the *Murabaha* period.[5]

18.3.1.2 Risk Management Tools in *Murabaha*

- **Risk No. 1—Borrower refuses to purchase the asset from the lender**
  This can be managed to a great extent by utilising a promise to purchase instrument as well as an earnest deposit, to be obtained from the borrower right at the beginning, so that it can cover the lender's risk in taking the title to the assets under the *Murabaha*.
- **Risk No. 2—Overdue and/or late payment(s) by the borrower**
  As late payment "penalties" to the lender are prohibited in Islamic finance, an undertaking from the borrower is usually obtained that he/she will give a certain amount of money to charity in case of any late payments. Though none of the parties benefits from such charity payouts, the payment is intended to act as a deterrent for breach of the contract.[6]
- **Risk No. 3—Default risk**
  This risk, which accompanies any financial transaction, can be negated to a great extent by the realisation of the securities/collateral taken from the borrower to recover the losses. *Takaful* (Islamic insurance policy) schemes may be taken up for ownership-related risks in Islamic *Murabaha* transactions as well.

18.3.2 Istisna'a (Procurement)

An *istisna'a* financing is a cash sales contract made against the promised future delivery of goods. It is similar in character to a "*Murabaha*" financing and therefore the risk management tools that is applicable in a Murabaha transaction is equally applicable in an Istisnaa and so the same are not repeated in this section. *Istisna'a* is used for funding major construction projects. A shipbuilding contract is an ideal agreement that can be financed by means of an *Istisna'a* as it includes the pre-delivery financing of a ship under construction, but bears all the requirements for a *Sharia'a*-compliant financing structure.

[5]See also http://www.nscsa.com/article-details.php?id=165&from=14&cat=11.

[6]The requirement for payment to charity stems from the fact that pecuniary penalties or "default interest" is prohibited in Sharia'a. However, to compel the borrower to adhere to the terms of the *Ijara* agreement, such mechanisms of compulsory payment(s) for charitable purposes in case of a default are greatly helpful as a deterrent.

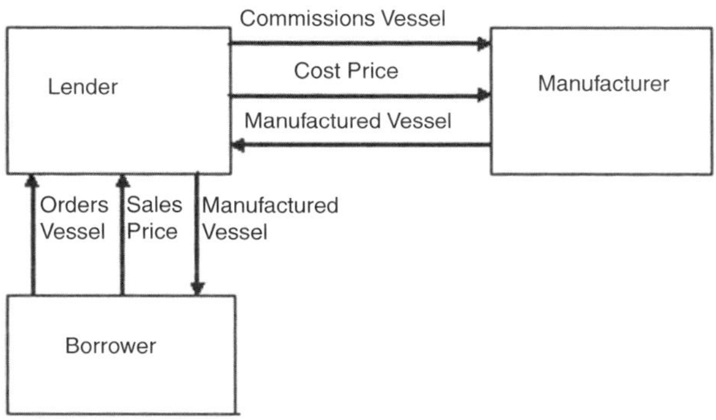

Fig. 18.2 *Istisna'a* transaction

An *Istisna'a* transaction (see Fig. 18.2) can be described as follows:

1. The borrower (i.e. the ship-owner) first negotiates and reaches a final agreement with the chosen shipyard on all the terms and conditions of the shipbuilding contract.
2. The borrower then requests the lender to finance the construction of the vessel (as contemplated by the shipbuilding contract) by entering into an independent *Istisna'a* agreement and pays an earnest deposit (*arboun*), representing the borrower's own equity share in the vessel, to the lender.
3. The *Istisna'a* agreement will essentially mirror the terms of the pre-agreed shipbuilding contract and will also contain the provisions and conditions of the credit relationship between the lender and the borrower as well.
4. The lender will then execute and enter into the pre-agreed shipbuilding contract with the shipyard on behalf of the borrower and will pay the *arboun* as the first instalment to the shipbuilder.
5. Thereafter, the instalment payments—as agreed in the shipbuilding contract and subject to the qualifications thereof—will be made by the lender to the shipyard.
6. Upon the delivery of the completed vessel under the shipbuilding contract to the lender, the vessel is immediately sold to the borrower for a pre-agreed price (which includes the cost price plus the lender's margin on the same) under the *Istisna'a* agreement.
7. The lender may alternatively also agree to refinance the borrower by taking delivery of the vessel under its own name or its SPC and then leasing the vessel to the borrower under an *Ijara wa iqtina'a* (lease with an option to purchase) structure.

18.3.2.1 Example of *Istisna'a* Transaction

The financing of Brunei Gas Carriers (BGC) through a syndicated Islamic ship financing transaction in July 2008 is a classic example of an *Istisna'a* operation in practice. The joint primary underwriter and book runner, facility agent and Islamic finance coordinator was *Saadiq* (Standard Chartered's Islamic finance department). Under an *Istisna'a/Ijara* structure (pre-delivery construction facility and forward lease), a best-in-its-class *Sharia'a*-compliant financial solution for US$505 million was made available to BGC to fund the construction and procurement of its liquefied natural gas (LNG) vessels.[7]

18.3.3 Musharaka (Partnership Financing or Profit and Loss Sharing)

Though the *Musharaka* has not been widely used in ship finance, it is a useful and flexible structure that can be adapted for assets, such as finance for sea-going vessels, as well as for assets that are of a certain type or age for which other forms of finance would be expensive and/or complex. In a *Musharaka* transaction, all parties have a share in the capital and according to this capital ratio, the profits as well as losses (if any) of the transaction/venture/project are divided between the parties. Each partner is considered an agent of the other. However, the management of the entire project may be conducted by just one party, as may be agreed in the *Musharaka* agreement. The *Musharaka* is increasingly gaining popularity as a method for financing purchases of second-hand vessels.

A *Musharaka* transaction (see Fig. 18.3) may be described as follows (Muhammad 2009):

1. The borrower and the lender first enter into a *Musharaka* or partnership agreement, wherein they agree to contribute certain predetermined amounts respectively toward the construction or the purchase and delivery of a vessel.
2. The *Musharaka* agreement prescribes that once the vessel has been delivered, it will be legally owned under the name of the borrower. This is, more importantly, for the benefit of the partnership (i.e. the *Musharaka*).
3. The *Musharaka* agreement will set out the respective profit and loss rates for the partners and these will correspond to their equity contributions to the *Musharaka*.
4. The borrower, as it would be most knowledgeable about the subject matter of the *Musharaka*, is also appointed the technical partner and acts as the trustee of the partners in the *Musharaka*.
5. Significantly, the *Musharaka* agreement will, in most cases, also reference a bareboat charter agreement between the borrower and a third party charterer or other similar agreement of employing the asset/vessel, which is the subject matter of the *Musharaka*.

---

[7]See also http://www.bt.com.bn/home_news/2009/04/02/local_industries_drawing_foreign_business_interest.

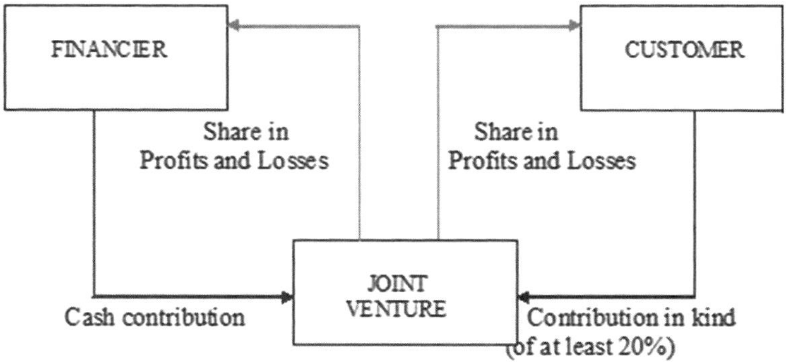

Fig. 18.3 *Musharaka* transaction

6. In accordance with a pre-agreed schedule of payments as per the construction or purchase agreement of the vessel, both the lender and the borrower make payments to the seller/manufacturer of the vessel in accordance with their pre-determined ratios.
7. Upon delivery, the vessel is then engaged into the bareboat charter with the third party charterer as referenced in the *Musharaka* agreement. The charter payments received by the borrower from the charterer are applied (whether partially or fully) to purchase an increasingly greater share in the *Musharaka* in favour of the borrower until the lenders portion of the equity is eventually bought out by the borrower.

18.3.3.1 Example of *Musharaka* Finance

The *Al Islami* Shipping Fund of the Dubai Islamic Bank (DIB) (managed by Tufton Oceanic) is utilised by the Oceanic Shipping Company Limited (which is also 100 % owned by DIB) to invest the same in selected shipping assets through *Musharaka* joint ventures with investors. The underlying investments are intended to be ocean-going vessels on bareboat charters to major shipping groups with "end-of-term" purchase obligations included in the *Musharaka*. The minimum investment amount was US$25,000, with total investment units worth US$32 million available. The tenor of the funds is 4 years and the same is extendable up to a maximum of two more years. The fund is targeting an estimated profit rate of 8.5 % per annum with a quarterly distribution of profits. The first deal under the fund was the purchase of a very large crude carrier (VLCC) from Saudi Pac Star, which was then leased back.[8]

---

[8]See also http://www.ameinfo.com/90484.html.

18.3.3.2 Risk Management Tools in *Musharaka* Finance

- **Risk No. 1—Misconduct, breach of contract, negligence by a partner in taking care of the *Musharaka* assets, and so on.**
  To counter such risks, adequate security or guarantees from the partners have to be obtained by the lender(s) at the time of entering into the *Musharaka* agreement itself. Clauses may be inserted into the *Musharaka* agreement, wherein a partner in default of his/her minimum care obligations is required to pay certain fixed amounts for charitable purposes. This can act as a deterrent as well (Lewis and Algaoud 2001).
- **Risk No. 2—Loss of capital or assets, etc.**
  Adequate *Takaful* or insurance coverage for all ownership-related risks must be taken and there must be active participation either by the lender(s) themselves or by competent managers or experts in the management of the *Musharaka* business. Alternatively, a third party (e.g. the parent entity) guarantee for capital loss, subject to *Sharia'a* conditions and qualifications, could also be extremely useful.

18.3.4 Ijara (Lease)

Another popular method of Islamic finance is the *Ijara* (lease) transaction, wherein the usufruct of an asset (e.g. a vessel) is passed to the other party (the lessee) against a periodic rent payment, with an option to buy the asset at the end of the lease period. The *Ijara* transaction is preferred by investors opting for longer term, higher yielding investments (Muhammad 2009). The fundamental conditions for a valid Ijara transaction are that the asset must have a corpus (body) and should be in existence at time of the lease. The asset in question must also not be consumable in nature (i.e. the nature of the asset is such that it should not vanish if utilised as, for example, money, food, etc.).

An important factor to bear in mind is that in an *Ijara*, all ownership rights and responsibilities incidental to ownership of the asset will remain with the lessor (i.e. lender) and he/she will bear all the risks related to ownership till the asset/vessel is transferred to the ownership of the borrower. Advantages under the *Ijara* transaction include flexibility in payment terms and other provisions for transferability as well as the possibility of a hire purchase structure. *Ijara* is very useful in buying second-hand vessels or for refinancing vessels already owned.

A simplified *Ijara* transaction (with the assumption that it is not a pre-delivery financing) in shipping (see Fig. 18.4) can be described as follows:

1. A special purpose company (SPC) is formed for the purpose of arranging the transaction and the SPC is administered by the lender or the lender's agent.
2. The SPC enters into a purchase agreement with the borrower for the purchase of existing and pre-identified vessel(s).

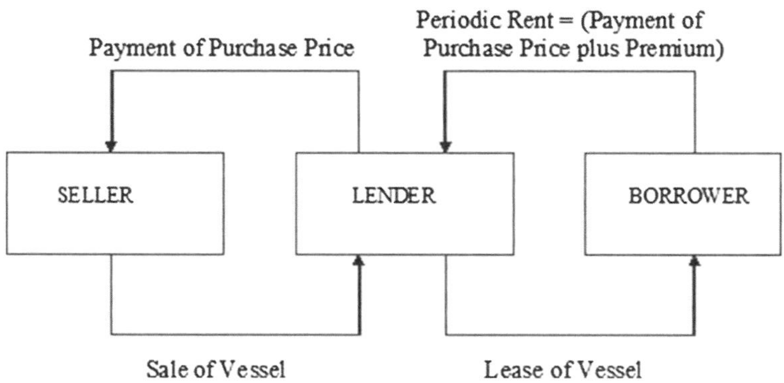

Fig. 18.4 *Ijara* transaction

3. Once purchased, the SPC (acting through the lender's agent) will enter into an *Ijara* (lease) agreement to lease the vessel(s) to the borrower for a fixed period against the payment of rental consideration.
4. The SPC thereafter enters into a servicing agency agreement with the obligor, through which it appoints the borrower as its agent responsible for major maintenance and structural repairs and the procurement of insurance on the vessel(s).
5. The borrower also provides a purchase undertaking wherein it undertakes to purchase the vessel(s) from the SPC, either at the end of the lease term or on the occurrence of an event of default.
6. The borrower makes periodic lease rental payments to the SPC during the term of the *Ijara* lease and the rental rates can be either fixed or floating rates (benchmarked to an index such as the Libor).
7. At maturity, the SPC transfers the vessel(s) back to the borrower at an agreed price or a nominal amount. The ownership of the vessel is thereby transferred to the borrower.

18.3.4.1 Example of *Ijara* Transaction

The Bank of London and Middle East (BLME) recently completed a US$50 million *Ijara* leasing facility for Al Ghadeer Marine Shipping LLC. The facility was used to fund the acquisition of the 53,000 DWT double-hulled bulk carrier, "Sara V." The transaction was structured using a Cayman Islands-based special purpose company (SPC). The SPC holds the beneficial title to the vessel. The vessel is then leased back to Al Ghadeer, which pays periodic but fixed and pre-agreed amounts as lease rentals (plus purchase premium) and finally purchases the vessel at the maturity date.[9]

[9]See also http://www.ameinfo.com/160841.html.

18.3.4.2 Risk Management Tools in *Ijara*

- **Risk No. 1—Refusal by the borrower to take the vessel on lease**
  The danger of the borrower not taking the vessel on lease after the lender has acquired it can be countered to a great extent by having the borrower enter into a written and binding promise to lease that should be obtained at the time of purchasing or reserving the vessel by the lender along with the requirement of an adequate earnest deposit, to be provided by the borrower.
- **Risk No. 2—Borrower may default in payment of due rental**
  An undertaking should be obtained from the customer to pay certain amount to charity or for charitable purposes and the usual satisfactory securities/collateral should also be realised from the borrower.
- **Risk No. 3—The risk of major destruction or of repairs being needed for the asset/vessel**
  Once again, such risks can sought to be mitigated by ensuring that adequate insurance or *Takaful* (Islamic insurance schemes) are subscribed to and maintained in full force by the borrower during the tenor of the *Ijara*.
- **Risk No. 4—Early Lease Termination Risk**
  In such a case, the bank may both take the vessel back and sell the same in the open market (in accordance with the laws thereof) or, in risky cases, have the customer give an undertaking to purchase the asset at a pre-agreed price schedule.
- **Risk No. 5—Careless use of the vessel by the lessee**
  A documentary counter to the above risk is to have the lessee issue a trust receipt wherein it is stated that the lessee shall be bound to use the vessel as a binding trust, with the lenders as the beneficiary.
- **Risk No. 6—Customer may decline to buy asset at maturity**
  Protection from this risk could be taken care of by a separate promise to purchase undertaking from the borrower.

18.3.5 Sukuk (Islamic Bonds): Al Ijara and Al Istisna'a

One of the most popular Islamic investment products that has achieved global recognition is the *Sukuk*. The concept of *Sukuk* is based on the premise that any Islamic financing contract that represents ownership in a tangible asset can be bought or sold, and hence can be securitised in the form of tradable securities (Muhammad 2009).

Sukuk is defined by the Accounting and Auditing Organization for Islamic Financial Institutions' (AAOFI's) Sharia'a standards as "Certificates of equal value representing undivided shares in ownership of tangible assets, usufruct and services or (in the ownership of) the assets of particular projects or special investment activity".[10]

[10]See also http://www.aaoifi.com/aaoifi_sb_sukuk_Feb2008_Eng.pdf.

In the light of the above definition, to term a *Sukuk* an Islamic bond is a misnomer, as the subject matter of the trade is not a loan but a share of the ownership of the asset (Agha and Grainger 2010). However, naming a Sukuk a bond may be valid because, in commercial terms, a *sukuk*—in most of its characteristics, such as trading, listing, rating, etc. resembles that of a conventional bond issuance. However, it is to be noted that this is more of a remark on the presently available avenues of listing *sukuk* in the global financial markets rather than a description of the nature of the *sukuk* itself.

Through the issuance of a *Sukuk*, greater diversification of funding from sources other than "basic" Islamic leasing (*ijara*) structure can be achieved by the borrower. *Sukuk* can provide access to larger volumes of capital and has the potential to provide liquid investments for Islamic investors.

Sukuk can be structured in a number of ways, depending on the underlying assets and the purpose of the business. While most of the *sukuk* issued have traditionally utilised *Ijara* structures based on the fact that real estate was the underlying asset, the *sukuk* issued recently have also used financial contracts as the underlying asset base. *Sukuk* typically are issued through a special purpose vehicle (SPV) which acts as the investors' trustee. The investors, by subscribing to the *Sukuk*, fund the SPV, which then on behalf of the investors enters into a set of contracts through which the SPV will earn a *Sharia'a*-compliant return for the investors.

The investor's returns are derived from legal or beneficial interest in assets rather than interest-based debt obligations. *Sukuk* rank *pari passu* with other senior obligations of the issuer and through this structure, a cash profile, which is exactly the same as a conventional bond with the same level of legal enforceability, is possible. It is for this reason that conventional investors in Europe and the Asia-Pacific are growing increasingly comfortable with a *Sukuk* issuance as they consider it more or less to be on an equal footing with a conventional bond issuance.

A couple of instances where *Sukuk* can be effectively utilised in ship finance transactions are described below.

18.3.5.1 Sukuk Al Ijara

Under the *Sukuk Al Ijara*, the lender forms an SPV to purchase the vessel(s) from the borrower. The SPV thereafter declares a trust in favour of the investors and issues *Sukuk* certificates at an agreed price. The investors fund the SPV for the amount of the *Sukuk* issuance (i.e. "purchase price"). The SPV thereafter pays the purchase price to the borrower. The borrower, upon receipt of the purchase price, then transfers the title to the underlying vessel(s) to the SPV. This is immediately followed by the SPV leasing back the same vessel(s) to the borrower against payment of periodic rental amounts. The borrower also enters into a unilateral purchase undertaking to purchase back the SPV's interest in the asset upon maturity or any interim date at the purchase price. Periodic lease rental payments made by the borrower to the SPV are utilised to make periodic distribution payments to the investors under the *Sukuk*. At maturity, the borrower buys back the SPV's interest in the assets from the SPV at the purchase price and the *Sukuk* are redeemed.

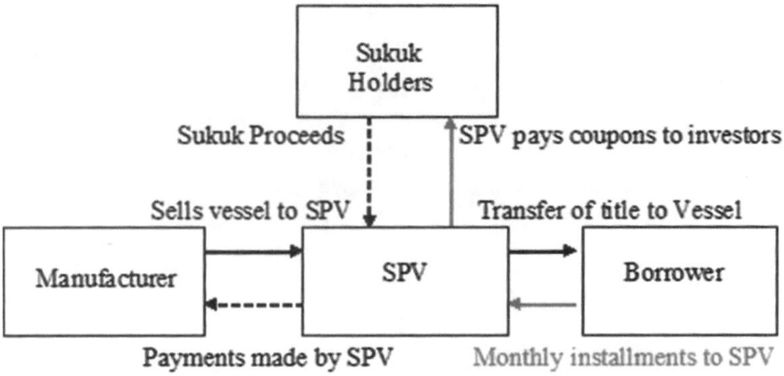

Fig. 18.5 *Sukuk Al Istisna'a*

Example of *Ijara Sukuk*

ABC International Bank, jointly with Abu Dhabi Commercial Bank, arranged, structured and jointly underwrote an Islamic ship financing transaction worth over US$26 million. Called the Al Safeena Ijara Sukuk, the *sukuk* certificates were issued through a Jersey-based issuance SPV. The leased asset was a VLCC (called "Venus Glory"), owned by Pacific Star (Pac Star) International Holding Corporation, which in turn is owned by Saudi Aramco.[11] Upon maturity of the Sukuk, the ownership of the vessel was transferred back to Saudi Aramco.

18.3.5.2 Sukuk Al Istisna'a

Sukuk Al Istisna'a (see Fig. 18.5) are ideally utilised to fund building of new vessels or for vessels already under construction. Similar to the *Sukuk Al Ijara*, a special purpose vehicle (SPV) is formed by the lender and this SPV issues *Sukuk* certificates to interested or targeted investors to raise funds for the project. The proceeds of the *Sukuk* issuance are then used to pay the contractor/manufacturer under the *Istisna'a*[12] contract to build and deliver the vessel/future asset. The title to the vessel, post construction, is then transferred to the SPV. The completed vessel is then either sold or leased to the borrower (who is the end buyer of the vessel) upon conditions of either deferred payment or periodic lease rental instalments. The returns gained from periodic payments made by the end-buyer are distributed to the *Sukuk* holders (investors) as profit. Upon maturity, the vessel is transferred to the end buyer (borrower) and the *Sukuk* is redeemed by the SPV and the lender(s).

---

[11] See also http://www.khaleejtimes.com/DisplayArticle09.asp?xfile=data/business/2005/April/business_April562.xml&section=business.

[12] See Sect. 18.3.2.

Important Considerations in an Islamic Ship Finance

Despite the wide availability and increasing popularity of Islamic financing transactions, there are certain important factors that parties to such transactions have to take into account before they embark on the project itself. Some of these considerations are unique to Islamic finance transactions to the extent that they act at times as a discouragement to traditional borrowers and institutions alike, despite the cost efficiency and the nature of shared risk of Islamic finance products. A few of the most fundamental considerations are:

18.4 Important Considerations in an Islamic Ship Finance

Despite the wide availability and increasing popularity of Islamic financing transactions, there are certain important factors that parties to such transactions have to take into account before they embark on the project itself. Some of these considerations are unique to Islamic finance transactions to the extent that they act at times as a discouragement to traditional borrowers and institutions alike, despite the cost efficiency and the nature of shared risk of Islamic finance products. A few of the most fundamental considerations are:

18.4.1 Requirement of Title to the Asset

As per *Sharia'a* requirements and processes, it is necessary for the financial institution to hold title to or at least appropriate equity in the asset/vessel that is being financed. In the light of this fundamental requirement, it is incumbent on the lenders to try and reduce their related liabilities as much as possible to offer competitively priced products to their customers. During the interim period, between delivery of the vessel and sale of the same to the borrower in a *Murabaha* transaction, the lenders are obligated by *Sharia'a* to be responsible, as owners of the vessel, for the maintenance and repairs of the asset. Even though such responsibilities may be circumvented to a great extent by using *takaful* (Islamic insurance) or other *Sharia'a*-compliant insurance policies, the same may not necessarily find favour or approval from the *Sharia'a* Board presiding over the product or the transaction. The logical and necessary approach would be to try and offset, as much as possible, tangible title-related risks of the lenders, by establishing special purpose companies in favourable jurisdictions, even though such arrangements may slightly increase the complexity and alter the cost of a product.

18.4.2 Dispute Resolution and Governing Laws

As is the case with most instruments of vessel finance, parties often choose the laws of more sophisticated jurisdictions, like London or New York, to govern the provisions of Islamic finance documents as well. This could definitely become an internalised conflict, when *Sharia'a* law would prohibit a certain action which is otherwise permissible under the chosen governing law of the contract and vice versa. The Courts of Appeal in England in 2004[13] resolved this issue in favour of English Law (being the governing law of the contract in question) and stating that *Sharia'a* was not a system of national law and it was "unusual and improbable" for a secular court to determine and apply *Sharia'a* in relation to the enforceability of contractual terms mutually agreed between the parties.

The answer to this problem could lie in the careful drafting of the contract, wherein the parties would clearly define and express which principles of *Sharia'a* would apply to what provision in the contract. This could also be coupled with waivers issued by both parties, either internalised in the contract or through external agreements, to waive any objections or any *Sharia'a*-related defences that a transaction party may have with regard to their respective obligations in the contract. There also, if *Sharia'a* courts-which are present and function in leading countries in the West Asia and also in *Sharia'a*-knowledgeable countries such as Malaysia and Indonesia-are chosen as the agreed court of jurisdiction over any disputes that may arise under the contract, then such courts may be able to effectively interpret both the substantial national law governing the contract as well as do justice to the *Sharia'a* underpinnings of the contract as well. Such careful considerations in governing law and forum for dispute resolutions can work out to be quite cost-efficient as well.

18.4.3 Sharia'a Compliance and Oversight

A financial product obtains its status as "a *Sharia'a*-compliant product" only after it has been studied, scrutinised and approved by a group of eminent Islamic scholars, chosen by the bank, who meet periodically to discuss either the operating policy of the bank or a specific transaction so as to ensure the compliance of those products with Islamic principles and teachings (Abdullah and Chee 2010). Such a group of Islamic scholars are referred to as a *Sharia'a* board or a *Sharia'a* committee. The process of approving a new product is called issuing a "fatwa" or a legal opinion (Muhammad 2009).

An important consideration for parties to an Islamic finance transaction is that there are occasions in which the particular School of Islamic Law[14] that is applied

[13]See also Shamil Bank of Bahrain v Beximco Pharmaceuticals Ltd and others (2004), www.bailii.org/ew/cases/EWCA/Civ/2004/19.html.

[14]"Within Sunni and *Shi'a* Islam, there are six main schools of Islamic law—*fiqh*:

by the *Sharia'a* committee or the treatment of the *Sharia'a* committee of a particular issue or facet of the transaction is not acceptable to the various parties involved in a transaction. Such fundamental issues of interpretation and application of *Sharia'a* will have to be sorted out right at the beginning of establishing the arrangement. There is also no certainty that the structuring of an arrangement will also be acceptable in the Islamic sense to other participants in the transaction and therefore the *Sharia'a* board presiding over the specific product or transaction will need to be influential and knowledgeable to tide over such disputes and arguments that may crop up as well. Every bank has its own supervisory *Sharia'a* board and international organisations, such as the "Accounting and Auditing Organization of Islamic Financial Institutions" (AAOIFI) located in Bahrain[15] and the Malaysia International Islamic Finance Centre in Kuala Lumpur,[16] ensure that credible standards are maintained across all Islamic finance institutions and that these are better coordinated globally as well.

18.4.4 Taxation and Capital Adequacy

As tax and tax-related considerations continue to be of great significance in every financial transaction, whether *Sharia'a*-compliant or not, without efficient and reasonable structuring, any intended benefit that could be garnered from even the most competitively priced *Sharia'a*-compliant product may be lost to the borrower. Where a tax is imposed on the generated profits or on the income derived from Islamic finance products along with value-added tax (VAT) and similar duties, or where there are costs to the banks due to mandatory capital adequacy ratios, etc., such charges will inevitably be passed on to the borrower. This would remain the case unless and until such costs or the policies related to the same are relaxed or withdrawn by the relevant countries where the Islamic finance transaction is

---

- **Sunni schools:**
  - The Hanbali School is named after Ahmad Ibn Hanbal (d. 855)
  - The Hanafi School is named after Abu Hanifa (d. 767)
  - The Shafi'i is named after al-Shafi'i (d. 819)
  - The Maliki is named after Anas bin Malik (d. 795)
- **Shi'a schools:**
  - The Zaydi School is named after Zayd Ibn Ali (d. 740)
  - The Ja'fari School is named after Ja'far al-Sadiq (d. 765)

There was a sweeping range of opinion in the first three centuries of Islamic history, and at one point, there were over 100 different schools of thought". Quoted from www.maslaha.org/untold-islam/schools-of-islamic-law-and-their-differences.

[15]See also www.aaoifi.com.

[16]See also www.mifc.com.

structured or the relevant product is ultimately marketed in. Therefore, borrowers should ideally seek out necessary legal and tax advice on proper structuring of the Islamic finance transaction in tax-neutral or tax-free countries prior to embarking in a full-fledged way on a project. Alternatively, seeking to structure finance from *Sharia'a*-friendly nations, wherein the considerations of *Sharia'a* are recognised and adjustments to the relevant domestic tax policies are made, can also be a consideration for the borrower.

18.5 Conclusion

It is undeniable that there is a sustained and increasing demand for *Sharia'a*-compliant financial and investment products the world over. Although not yet fully developed, Islamic finance has become a widely used and flexible tool in international finance as an alternative funding resource for a large number of business houses and enterprises in helping grow their businesses in a depressive fiscal environment. Devout Muslim investors, who had been locked out of many individual financial vehicles, now have an opportunity to explore and find appropriate fiscal products that are in compliance with their faith and religious beliefs. It is understood that the Islamic banking sector in 2010 had 456 *Sharia'a* institutions and 199 conventional institutions with *Sharia'a* windows spanning 54 countries across the globe, with an asset growth rate of 8.85 %.[17]

Islamic finance is also becoming increasingly popular in industry project and asset finance, with a growing number of high profile *Sharia'a*-compliant aviation and maritime financial transactions seen globally. The asset-backed nature of vessel financing makes the shipping industry naturally compliant with most *Sharia'a* principles as well. It provides a great opportunity for financial institutions, global corporations, sovereign funds and countries to develop untapped financial resources from the West Asia and North African regions, where the appetite for *Sharia'a*-compliant financing and liquidity ratios are quite high. Given the appreciation accorded to Islamic finance products in non-Muslim countries as well, the interest in and success of Islamic finance are only bound to grow further.

References

Abdullah DV, Chee K (2010) Islamic finance – why it makes sense, 1st edn. Marshall Cavendish Business, Singapore

Agha O, Grainger C (2010) Sukuk: when is a default not really a default? The Magazine for Bond Investors (January 2010)

[17]The Banker, Top 500 Islamic Financial Institutions 2011.

Ahmed H (2011) Defining ethics in Islamic finance: looking beyond legality. In: Eighth international conference on Islamic economics and finance, December 2011
Khorshid A (2009) Euromoney encyclopedia of Islamic finance. Euromoney Institutional Investor PLC, London
Lewis MK, Algaoud LM (2001) Islamic banking. Edward Elgar Publishing, Northampton
Measures P, Brown M, Marais S (2011) Sharia'a compliant methods for the financing of ships. In: Shipping finance review 2011–2012 Euromoney Yearbooks. Ince & Co International LLP
Muhammad A (2009) Understanding Islamic finance. Wiley, West Sussex
Mutahhari A (2008) Jurisprudence and its principles. Tahrike Tarsile Qur'an. http://www.al-islam.org/jurisprudence-and-its-principles-ayatullah-murtadha-mutahhari. Retrieved 26 July 2008

Part VI
Related Services

Chapter 19
Investor Relations and Their Role in Effective Corporate Communications

Nicolas Bornozis

Abstract Investor relations are a critical function for a publicly-traded company to convey the performance of the company in a clear and concise manner to its shareholders, stakeholders, and other constituents. For investor relations professionals, the most critical task is in being a conduit for information for the company, regarding its performance both operationally and financially. Their mission is to establish and manage a two way process. On the one hand, they have to ensure that the company provides a regular flow of meaningful information to the investment community and organize systematic forms of interaction with investors, analysts and the financial media; on the other hand, they have to monitor the stock market behavior of its peer group public companies in the same sector, and gather and analyze feedback from the investment community about the company itself, its sector and its peers.

19.1 What Are Investor Relations?

Investor relations are a combination of critical activities that are consistent and proactive in nature, all with the purpose of communicating the company's investment thesis and for achieving the company's proper valuation. With constant competition for capital among peer companies within a sector and industry, as well as the need for companies to have strong share trading liquidity that will help mitigate share price volatility, it is of critical importance for investor relations to be in constant communication with all key stakeholders of the company. Stakeholders will typically include the company's current investors, analysts covering the company, investors in the peer group, or similar industry/sector, along with the appropriate financial media covering the industry. In addition, the investor relations

N. Bornozis (✉)
Capital Link Inc., 230 Park Avenue, Suite 1536, New York, NY 10169, USA
e-mail: nbornozis@capitallink.com

O. Schinas et al. (eds.), *HSBA Handbook on Ship Finance*,
DOI 10.1007/978-3-662-43410-9_19, © Springer-Verlag Berlin Heidelberg 2015

professional can be considered the most direct access to the company's management while allowing the management to continue running the company.

Investor relations combine finance, strategic communications, marketing and compliance with securities and law within one department. The investor relations practitioner distributes a variety of information, both voluntarily and as required under certain financial regulations. The purpose of this is to give specific information on how the company operates, its overall performance as well as any future plans and prospects. In essence, the rationale behind the investor relations communication is to give the audience as much information to make a thoughtful decision on whether to invest in a company or not. Investor relations professionals achieve this through many different kinds of mediums, but all have the same strategic purposes. These mediums include press releases, fact sheets, annual reports, road shows, regulatory filings, conference calls, investor newsletters, media interviews, investor relations sections in the company website, and the numerous social media websites catering to the general public. The investor relations staff will utilize these mediums in an effort to distribute information on the company to as wide an audience as possible in the investment community.

Among its core responsibilities, investor relations must ensure adherence to security regulations. In the US, the Securities and Exchange Commission was formed during the Great Depression in 1934 after the stock market crash of 1929. The purpose of the SEC was to regulate the stock market and to prevent corruption in public companies during the trading of securities and to establish corporate disclosures. The SEC was given the power to license and regulate stock exchanges, the companies whose securities traded in them and the brokers and dealers who conducted the trading. In essence, the SEC was formed to be the watchdog for the retail investor community.

In 2000, the SEC put into effect Regulation Full Disclosure, which mandated that all companies' material information and announcements must be made public to all investors at the same time. Earlier, public companies would hold meetings with fund managers and make presentations at bank conferences, often disclosing non-public and material information that professional investors would use to their advantage to trade stocks. However, investors without the same access to the company would be on the other side of the trade, not privy to the same information that was disseminated. Many public companies would not make quarterly conferences open to the general public, who in turn had to rely on their stock broker for company information and analysis. In the 1990s, as retail investors became savvier in trading stocks, along with the new trend of trading stocks online, investors craved more company access and information. The SEC proposed Regulation Full Disclosure to level the playing field between the more traditional, professional investors and the retail investors.

The Sarbanes-Oxley Act of 2002 significantly increased the importance of investor relations in financial markets. The act established new requirements for corporate governance and regulatory compliance, with an increased emphasis on accuracy in auditing and public disclosure. Notable provisions of the act that apply to investor relations include enhanced financial disclosures and accuracy of financial reports, real-time disclosures, off-balance-sheet transaction disclosures, pro forma financial disclosures, management assessment of internal controls, and corporate responsibility for financial reports.

The investor relations function also includes the transmission of information relating to intangible values such as the company's policy on corporate governance or corporate social responsibility. Additionally, investors have trended toward an increasingly popular movement for data that is clear, concise, and easy to compare and manipulate, leading to management of company filings through streaming-data solutions such as Extensible Business Reporting Language (XBRL) and other forms of electronic disclosure.

19.2 A Historical Perspective on Investor Relations

Investor relations originated out of necessity for public companies looking to attract necessary capital to grow their businesses. After the Second World War, America emerged as the world's leading financial power, and with that, significant investment capital to employ. While investors in equities had suffered terribly during the years of Great Depression following the Wall Street Crash of 1929, investors domestically returned to the equities markets. This, after years of low risk and return investment in "War Bonds" or U.S. Savings bonds, saw the government raise over $180 billion to finance the war efforts in the US. While few in population, most investors at the time were largely wealthy individuals, who hired portfolio managers to invest their capital, often quietly.

Although issuers have always met investors to seek investment, the first actual investor relations department did not emerge until the 1950s as company's share rolls began to expand and the idea that communicating effectively with sources of investment capital gained credence. Back in 1953, Ralph Cordiner, the then president (later chairman and CEO) of General Electric (NYSE: GE) made the first systematic effort to formalize a corporation's relationship with its shareholders. Under his initiative, a new department was created and the term investor relations was coined. The first in-depth research was undertaken into who the shareholders were, what they perceived their needs to be and what was the best way to communicate with them and for them to communicate with the management.

As the financial world became more sophisticated and interconnected, investment trends and investor relations changed to meet the new investor land-scape. Institutional investors, armed with the backing of their investors' capital, became more prevalent and active than individuals. With growing demand for institutional investors, the impetus shifted towards financial elements of investor relations such as greater financial disclosure, heightened regulatory requirements, investor meetings with management, and the communication of the company's overall strategy. However, one drawback to this was the growing misconception of investor relations being the predominant means of making a company's stock price to go up, as the costs of investor relations budgets needed justification as a worthwhile cost center.

Despite this, the focus on financial communications was a significantly positive development for both investors and companies. The investor relations role helped cultivate the necessary two-way communication between management and investors, leading to investors making smarter, sounder decisions, while companies built the necessary credibility towards their current and prospective investors and fostering long-term relationships with them. While a company might not have taken advice from a retail investor too seriously earlier, it often befits a company to study and examine any feedback from a fund manager who represents hundreds of millions (or billions) of dollars of assets.

19.3 Investor Audience

In the development of a company's shareholder base, it is critical to identify the investors who would be most receptive to the company's investment thesis. While there are a plethora of investment styles and objectives, it is of paramount importance to match the company with the proper institutional investors at the specified point of a company's profile for the investor relations function. The following investors something is missing?

19.3.1 Growth Investors

These investors typically acquire shares of a company in its early stages, often times pre-revenue, with the hope that as the company grows, revenues will increase in turn at more rapid rates. Growth is typically compared in earnings per share and revenue growth with those of a peer group of similar size and development. A growth investor will likely liquidate his position in a company where the growth rate begins to lag as business fundamentals begin to mature.

19.3.2 Value Investors

Simply put, a value investor looks for companies that are trading at a discounted price in comparison to its peers in the same industry group. The valuation of the company is judged upon its book value, while underlying financial aspects are examined to determine if there is any financial concern fundamentally hurting the company. Typically, activist investors fall into this category as they will (individually or in organized groups) purchase large amounts of shares of the company, (sometimes in concert with obtaining seats in board of directors) to affect significant company changes.

19.3.3 Income Investors

These investors give priority to the level of dividend payments they receive from their investments. Income investors will often monitor the annual dividend yield of a specific industry and invest in the companies that offer the greatest amount. It is the visibility of the company's distributable cash flow, and assured continuous dividend payouts with potentially growing dividends that draw this potentially volatile investor. If a company chose a variable dividend payout strategy, an income investor is likely to liquidate his position completely upon any negative change in the payout.

19.3.4 Industry Specific Investors

Some investors, based upon their background or personal interest, will focus on a particular industry and keen only on investing in that area. For example, in the global shipping markets, an investor may choose to either invest in the ship-owning companies that transport specific cargoes or sell the corresponding freight derivatives short. In another example, an investor may be an expert on the macroeconomic demand for BRIC economies within many industries and choose investments based on those economic impacts. Typically, this kind of investor will invest in smaller clusters of an entire industry sector (for example, in shipping, buying dry-bulk stocks vs. container stocks), being less concerned with the profitability and outlook of any one particular company.

19.3.5 Growth and Reasonable Price Investors

Some investors prefer a blend of growth and value investing. These investors will buy shares upon a currently perceived market discount, only with the reasonable prospect of future growth. The growth and reasonable price investors (GARP) investor will likely sell the shares when a company's valuation has moved in line with the peer group average, but may continue to keep a passive position with the prospect of further revenue growth.

19.3.6 Arbitrage Investors

These investors will look towards opportunities to simultaneously buy and sell a company's shares that possess a value differential. While this kind of investor is not the focal point of the investor relations practitioner as the arbitrage investor cares little about the company at all, the merger arbitrage investor is of greater concern. The merger arbitrageur buys shares of a company that is expected to be acquired, and eventually profit from the sale price at which acquisition is completed, which is typically much higher than the levels of the original purchase. From the perspective of investor relations, this investment strategy can result in massive surges and declines in the volume of shares traded as news of the potential acquisition materializes.

19.3.7 Quantitative Investors

These types of investors base their strategies on the most sophisticated computer programs designed by highly educated scientists and all based upon statistical models that form trading algorithms. Clearly, the "quant" investor has little time for homework on the companies in his portfolio.

19.3.8 Technical Analysis Investors

Again, this type of investor will rarely need an audience with the company's management. A market technician is an investor who utilizes the historical behavior of a stock to determine the proper entry and exit points. Also referred to as "behavioural finance", these technicians will study and identify historical trends that can be exploited in a highly active trading program. These investors have only a moderate interest in a company's fundamentals because they are moving in and out of investment positions continuously.

19.4 International Investor Relations

Investor relations began as a specifically US concept emerging out of the competition for investment capital at that time. As the field grew exponentially, the National Investor Relations Institute was founded as an information resource for practitioners in 1969. With growing emphasis on international finance and institutional investment from the 1970s onwards, listed companies around the world seeking large scale investment capital also sought to ensure investors understood their direction, strategy and performance. Throughout the 1980s, public companies listed in the UK established investor relations departments in greater numbers. With the growth of perceived necessity for investor relations, these departments became stand-alone from their earlier avatar of just being a section of the finance department. As the financial services industry cut burdensome government regulations in 1986, institutional investment capital surged in the UK equities market, making the need for investor relations more critical to what had become a greater audience.

During the 1980s and 1990s, investor relations continued its necessary growth into markets where companies sought to convey their investor thesis, becoming a key component in companies across the industrialized world. Investor relations are specifically held in high esteem in Germany and it is often a common practice among larger German companies to have investor relations departments comprising at least ten individuals.

19.5 The Investor Relations Process: The IPO

Companies prepare diligently for the IPO process by going through increased and pro-longed scrutiny by their accountants, lawyers and investment bankers, not to mention the respective national securities regulators. Upon approval of a public listing, the investor relations program commences. The development of establishing the company narrative, what will eventually answer the question, "why should someone invest in this company" is critical, as it ties in all the work of the company's management, investment bankers, lawyers and accountants, in preparation for the IPO roadshow. The roadshow consists of a series of meetings with the clients of the investment bankers underwriting the IPO; these meetings are scheduled with the banks sales force as well as with large institutional investors, investment funds and high net worth individuals with the purpose of directly selling shares of the new public company.

The IPO process can take several months to prepare, and depending on the size and structure of the company, can involve hundreds of people in offices across the world. Once public, they must adhere to increased standards of transparency and financial disclosure, corporate governance, financial communications and investor relations. The market itself sets expectations and standards that in many occasions are well beyond those defined by the regulators.

Companies that do not comply with market expectations risk becoming marginalized in terms of investor attention. They may pay the price as potentially successful business endeavors will not translate into proportionate shareholder value, thereby adversely impacting their ability to raise capital in the future. Furthermore, a negative performance in the stock market may over time erode the company's corporate image with wider business implications.

Investment banks are critical for the success of the IPO and for making a company public. Once this is done, their role diminishes substantially and the company must then stand on its own feet and create its own structure, internally or externally, for investor relations.

A company starts its life as a public entity with those investors who bought into the specific IPO. However, these investors represent just a fraction of the total investment universe. Therefore, the company must reach out to the whole investment community, including both institutional and individual investors, to ensure an ongoing liquid secondary market in its shares. Company management must spend part of its time on communicating with investors, analysts and media.

The company may designate an executive as the investor relations contact. In some cases, this becomes another function of the chief financial officer. In any case, the chief financial officer, and on occasion the chief executive officer, must play an active role in the company's investor relations. The most effective mechanism is the one that combines an internal company structure with support from external specialized consultants. The investor relations function cannot and should not be outsourced in its entirety. Investors invest in the company and its management; therefore, these must maintain an active and visible role in investor relations.

19.6 The Investor Relations Process: After the IPO

Institutional investor targeting is a key component of an effective investor relations strategy. The company must reach out to those investors whose investment criteria and strategy matches the company's profile. Just reaching out to those who invest in shipping stocks may not be enough, particularly if the company positions itself as a dividend play. Furthermore, within the major investment houses, there are several portfolio managers, each one with different strategies, who however could be interested in the company's shares. Therefore, along with identifying the proper institutions, the company must also identify the proper contacts within each institution and position itself properly so that it can fit into their strategy and portfolios.

Research coverage by brokerage houses is another key factor. In the post-IPO period, the company must establish "arms-length" relationships with all major brokerage houses and ensure that its stock is included in the proper peer group and if possible analyzed in detail. It must be remembered, though, that broker research, important as it is, is only one of the many inputs in the decision making strategy of institutional investors. Most of them rely on their own internal analysts and procedures, so the company must ensure that it maintains direct contact with them and supplies them with the proper information continuously. Externally-provided research cannot make up for the lack of proper communication by the company itself.

In the US, individual investors account for about half of the daily trading volume in the exchanges. Therefore, it is vital for a company to ensure that the same message it delivers to targeted institutional investors is also made available to the investment community as a whole. Furthermore, in the US, Regulation Fair Disclosure stipulates equal treatment of all investors when it comes to the dissemination of information.

Financial media play an important role as well as they ensure that information is delivered to a wider institutional audience, including prospective investors and the community as a whole. One cannot create proper shareholder value without maximum publicity and institutions who invest in particular stocks want to know that the proper mechanism exists to externalize the company's message and alert the whole community on the company's prospects and developments. Finally, a company must monitor investor behavior in its peer group and continuously collect and analyze feedbacks from analysts and investors to formulate the proper investor relations strategy.

19.7 The Investor Relations Firm

Investor Relations firms can provide a company with material assistance in all aspects of the process, such as defining the proper message, identifying the proper target group, ensuring maximum publicity, securing analyst coverage, organizing contacts with investors with conference calls and roadshows, advising the company how to properly position itself among investor portfolios, gathering and analyzing investor feedback and maximizing the company's visibility through the proper financial media. Another key role is to address requests by investors and filter the proper ones to the company itself, thereby ensuring efficient utilization of management time and resources.

19.8 Shipping Investor Relations

The shipping industry has clearly come of age in the public capital markets, which is evident from the flurry of Initial Public Offerings (IPOs) on global stock exchanges in the US, Europe and Asia. Shipping is a capital intensive business and as the availability of bank financing decline, publicly-listed shipping companies may have a competitive advantage over their private peers in terms of access to capital. Today, publicly traded shipping companies typically enjoy significant following by analysts as well as a large institutional and retail investor base. From 2005 to 2012, over $44.9 billion of equity was raised by shipping companies globally, through public offerings with IPOs accounting for $15.8 billion. However, public shipping companies today represent only a fraction of the global fleet, indicating the future potential of shipping for the capital markets. Being a public company opens a new world of opportunities for shipping companies, but at the same time creates a new set of tasks and responsibilities, both in the US and other parts of the world.

Working with an investor relations firm, which has other clients in shipping, can be an advantage as it enables all shipping clients to benefit from the established investor penetration, the accumulated knowledge and the synergies and economies of scale. The objective is not to pit one shipping company against the other, but to help them define their positioning in a complementary manner, so that more of them can become part of an investor's portfolio. Shipping is not yet a well-known sector among US investors; therefore, an investor relations firm with a broader scope can assist both companies and help investors to make a choice based on several factual criteria such as fleet composition and profile, fleet employment, dividend payout, etc.

Investors follow a multitude of companies across many sectors and countries and therefore there is tremendous competition for their attention and time. An investor relations firm with established penetration among shipping investors can materially assist its clients by facilitating access to this investment universe.

In the earlier stages, when few shipping companies were public, investors had limited choices. Now, as more companies join the public markets, investor choices increase. In an effort to build diversified and balanced portfolios, they may well decide to include several shipping companies with different and possibly complementary (from an investment point of view) profiles and strategies.

19.9 Conclusion

Investor relations as a critical function were initially considered as a public relations function of communicating with retail shareholders. As financial markets grew in sophistication, investor audiences of the institutionalized and retail variety demanded a greater information flow that was in line with senior management of the company, ensuring accuracy and credibility. Whereas previous attributes for success in the profession was born in the finance department, usually under the guidance of the chief financial officer, today, the investor relations practitioner often possesses the financial prowess along with essential public relations and marketing skills necessary to complement and support the sophisticated investor relations of the twenty-first century. Increased transparency requirements, instantaneous communication, access to information and advent of XBRL demand continuous changes in the way investor relations are practiced. The most essential function for the investor relations professional is to ensure that the investor community has an in-depth understanding of the company. Both communication and financial skills are valued equally high for their contribution to investor relations. The goal of the function is the improved understanding of the company among investors and analysts. The communication is two-way with information travelling from the corporations to investors and back from investors to the corporation. Feedback from investors is actively sought and shareholder research is conducted. The feedback is analyzed at the highest level of the organizational hierarchy and is used in decision-making and strategic planning. CEOs expect their IROs to be actively engaged in the corporate decision-making and supply the information from shareholders and about shareholders to the management team. This focus of the synergy era on the improved understanding of the company requires investor relations to provide both positive and negative information. The goal is not high value of stock, but fair value of stock. Overvaluation can be as detrimental as undervaluation because it can lead to a sudden drop in price as well as to increased price and volume volatility when additional information becomes available.

The effect of an investor relations program can only be measured by the priorities of the company management, and what it values most. However, it is vital that all publicly-traded companies are committed to a proactive and consistent investor relations program. On judging companies with successful investor relations track records, it is seen that what ultimately pays is careful planning, transparency, consistency and persistence. Any company that adopts and implements these principles in its investor relations strategy will be clearly appreciated by investors in the long run.

Chapter 20
The Role of Newbuilding Broker

Leandros von Ruffin-Zisiadis

Abstract This article aims to outline the challenges and the role of the newbuilding brokers. In ship broking, almost every aspect of this industry comes together and a good shipbroker needs to understand all of these different aspects, to be able to add value for his clients. A crucial element for a successful shipbroker is the profound knowledge and understanding of various disciplines and professional aspects, such as world trade, economics, ship building, ship owning, ship operations and finance. A good shipbroker must possess a certain portion of Emotional Intelligence (EI) to successfully fulfill the tasks assigned by the principals and play his role among all parties involved. The emotionally intelligent person can harness emotions, even negative ones, and manage them to achieve intended goals.

20.1 The Newbuilding Broker

Over the recent years, the application of new and improved communication technologies has enabled information to flow seamlessly without significant time delays. This process had a significant impact on the broker's daily work, forcing him to be very flexible and highly responsive to occurring events and the requirements of his customers, enabling him to automate and speed up processes, reduce costs, relate more closely to customers, and offer them more convenience.

The shipbroker works in a very international environment, including all time zones that make it necessary to act, react, and to work almost day and night. Flexibility is of utmost importance. The willingness and ability of shipbrokers to respond to the dramatic changes affecting the shipping industry will determine whether their own organizations survive and prosper or go down to defeat at the hands of more agile and adaptive competitors. Shipbrokers should be aware that

L. von Ruffin-Zisiadis (✉)
W.J. Hinneberg, Ballindam 17, 20095 Hamburg, Germany
e-mail: ship@wjhinneberg.de

O. Schinas et al. (eds.), *HSBA Handbook on Ship Finance*,
DOI 10.1007/978-3-662-43410-9_20,

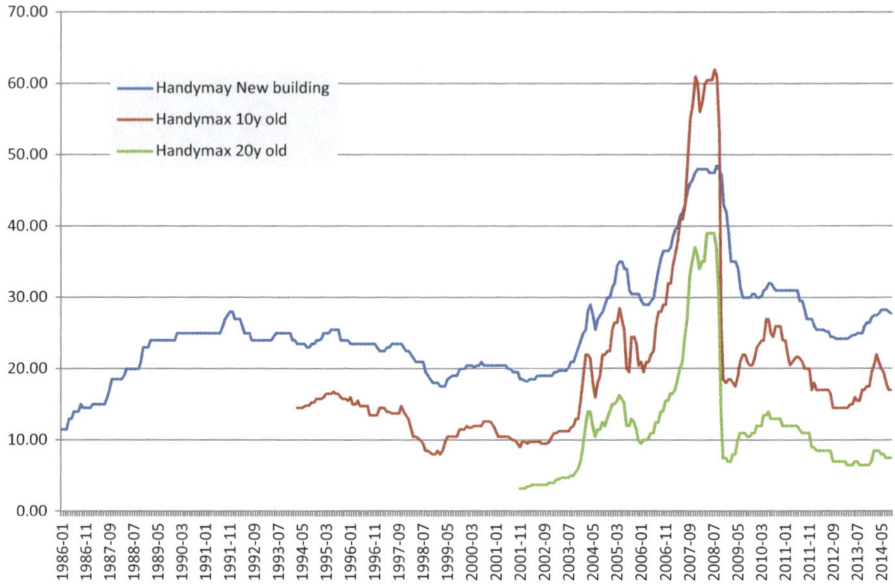

Fig. 20.1 Historical prices; newbuildings vs. secondhand handymaxes. *Source*: Clarksons' Shipping Intelligence Network

they are offering a variety of services and have to be customer service oriented. The service product must be tailored to customer needs, distributed through convenient channels and actively promoted to clients.

This paper aims to address the contribution of the broker in successful newbuilding deals. Before proceeding into the analysis, it is important to briefly remind the reader of the pros and cons of newbuilding vessels over second hand vessels.

The advantage of a newbuilding over a second hand vessel is that it often has lower operating expenses such as maintenance, insurance, fuel and staffing. It is tailor-made and can serve special trading routes in the most efficient and effective ways. A newbuilding vessel can add to the uniformity of the fleet and has a longer expected life span. However, depending on the market cycle, the fixed price is higher than for a second hand vessel. The second hand vessel is immediately available to meet the market demand, will immediately contribute to the cash flow of the company which may be important for financial investors. In addition, the second hand vessel has a history, which can be assessed and the buyer will have more security regarding the vessel's overall performance. Finally, it is important to note, that in boom markets the newbuilding price can be significantly below the second-hand value of a similar vessel because of the immediately expected cash flows (see Fig. 20.1, where in exuberant markets the ten year old vessel was more than 25% more expensive than the newbuilding).

The main goal of the newbuilding broker is to establish a shipbuilding contract between the shipbuilder and the ship owner. It is important to manage both parties' expectations from the beginning so that a successful deal can be concluded. A broker should never underestimate the role of psychology within this process. It is crucial to understand that the broker is dealing with human beings that have their specific expectations. The role of the shipbroker is to identify them and to put oneself under the skin of these two parties to manage them throughout the process. These expectations are heavily determined by the nature of the company, their history, location, financial status and background but also by the current market environment. However, there are a few things that apply to every shipyard and ship owner. A ship owner no matter if he is a genuine ship owner or a financial investor aiming to build a cheap vessel of high quality with rich specifications to be able to operate the vessel at low cost over the vessel's lifetime and to deliver quality to his clients.

An inexpensive vessel will enable the owner to generate a good return on investment and to successfully gain from peaks in the market. A shipbuilder aims to build the vessel at low costs and to timely deliver the vessel to his client with minimum defects. Therefore, a yard feels in boom-times of the shipping cycle typically more comfortable to repeat a standard type of vessel which they have built before, to diminish the costs of the design and being most quality, time and cost efficient in the overall production process.

20.1.1 Information Gathering

Information can be gathered from different sources in the industry. The broker should be well connected to the different players in the industry (e.g. ship operators, tramp owners and building facilities) to obtain relevant market information from first hand sources and to be up to date. These players are typically spread across various countries and continents. There are also other sources which are available to the shipping community such as shipping papers, websites and magazines (e.g. Lloyd's List, Tradewinds, Fairplay et al.) and the data bases of the larger ship broking houses (e.g. Clarksons et al.) which keep good track record of the relevant developments. Most of the ship broking companies also publish weekly and monthly reports where they report recent newbuilding activities and certain trends in the market. The broker needs to be up to date and well informed at all times.

For a specific newbuilding project, the following information should be well assessed before choosing or approaching a specific ship builder.

20.1.2 Owners Background

There are several types of owners around the world, located in various countries around the globe and being influenced by different cultures, jurisdictions and tax environments. Each of them has a different background. A shipbroker should be well aware of these cultural differences and able to successfully manage them and guide other parties wherever necessary. People see, interpret and evaluate the vast amount of available information in different ways. What is considered and appropriate behavior in one culture is frequently inappropriate in another one. Misunderstandings arise when we use our meanings to make sense of others' reality.

However, one can generally divide owners in to two groups:

Financial Asset Player:
: These are owners with a financial background, such as equity funds, stock listed companies, KG owners etc. These companies usually have a more project based approach and generate their profit through management and supervision fees one the one hand and possibly asset play on the other hand. The technical and commercial management of the vessels is very often outsourced to other shipping companies and service providers. In many cases, these owners are transparent companies, due to their legal nature. The broker can easily gain access to relevant information.

Traditional Owners:
: These are mostly old established companies and often family run. Traditional owners tend to keep the commercial and technical management of the vessels under one roof. These companies tend to be very experienced and have seen and survived many difficulties of the shipping markets over the time. Some of them keep the vessels in their fleet during their lifetime of approximately 20–25 years and are therefore very focused on the technical specifications of a vessel and the overall quality. Traditional owners are very often privately run. The Owners try to run their companies very secretive for several reasons. This makes it less easy and often very difficult for a shipbroker to gather information. Every company has a reputation and leaves a trace over a certain period of time. Companies are known for their business behavior, performances and non performances and a shipbroker should be well aware, before recommending a shipping company to any third party.

20.1.3 Owners Trading Areas and Patterns

It is useful to understand and to know the trading patterns of the operating owners, to assess the future demand of tonnage. It enables the broker to make assumptions and predictions, to guide clients and to be involved in their decision making process.

There are clients trading from Europe to Latin America requiring slower vessels with high intake and an extensive reefer capacity. Others are trading in the Baltic Sea requiring highest ice class. In addition, they will have to think about new propulsion systems, due to new regulations coming in to force. Therefore, such knowledge will also prove to be useful to select a suitable shipbuilding facility in line with owner's requirements.

20.1.4 Owners Motivation

Owners have different motivation to order newbuildings. It is predominantly determined by their background, available finance or equity sources and their assessment of the future market outlook, including employment opportunities for their vessels.

Sometimes operating owners like to lease[1] or charter in new tonnage from tramp owners up to a certain percentage of their overall operating fleet on a long term or short term basis, to increase the size of their total fleet without equity input from their shareholders. Such commitments often do not appear on their balance sheet, which leaves them some more room for alternative investments. It also offers them some sort of comfort and security during difficult times where they can simply redeliver excessive tonnage to the tramp owners without having to operate the vessels at a loss or in the worst case to be forced to leave them idle. Tramp owners in return benefit from more attractive finance terms, enabling them to add additional tonnage to their owned fleet and making use of the economies of scale. Naturally there are always two sides of the coin, whereas the owner may not participate in market peaks where he has fixed his vessels at a lower rate over a longer period of time or might not be able to gain from the asset play where the charter contract is not transferable to a new Buyer and the charterer might be caught with an excessive rate at the bottom of the market where he is hit by significant losses.

There are other ship owners that see future potential in a specific ship type or market segment. There may be several reasons for their assumptions such as the age profile, new technological inventions, rules and regulations where existing vessels might become inferior or obsolete, a positive future outlook for a specific ship type and trade or very low shipbuilding prices that occur at the bottom of the shipping cycle. Therefore, some ship owners place an order on a speculative basis at their own risk, without relating their order to a charter contract or serious discussions with an end user. The broker should participate in the above mentioned decision making process, trying to assist his client to derive the right conclusions for his future investment and to give valuable advice wherever he can. Of course, no one possesses a crystal ball to foresee the future but information gathering and profound knowledge can lay a solid foundation to facilitate this decision making process. The broker often serves as sparring partner for the owner in the decision-making process.

20.1.5 Yards Track Record and Background

One of the most significant tasks of a newbuilding broker is to locate a suitable shipyard according to the requirements of the owner. Not every yard can build every ship type due to lack of knowledge, experience or capacity.

[1] Chapter leasing.

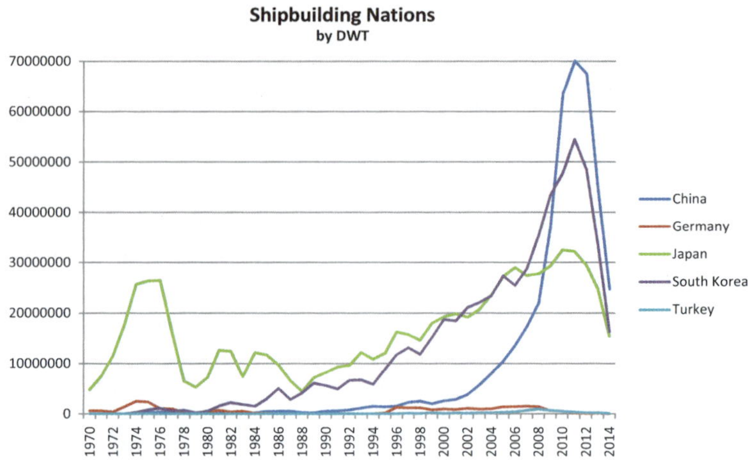

Fig. 20.2 Shipbuilding output in DWT per country. *Source*: Clarksons' Shipping Intelligence Network

The majority of the world's shipbuilding capacity is located in Korea, China and Japan (Fig. 20.2). However, there are also yards which are located in Vietnam, the Philippines, Europe, Turkey, India and many other countries in the world. However, not all services are provided in all countries and by all yards. Consider the following anecdote: a broker in early 2007, had a newbuilding project for a ship owner who trades in the Baltic with chemicals. The intention of the owner was to build a series of chemical tankers with highest ice class and the tanks had to be built out of solid stainless steel, to be able to carry high-grade chemicals. The broker contacted the major reputable shipbuilders in Asia with this promising newbuilding project but to his surprise, none of these yards was interested in a four vessel newbuilding order. The tankers were too small and too sophisticated. The broker discovered that some of these big ship yards had never built ice classed vessels before and moreover had no experience in the treatment and fabrication of stainless steel that requires special storage and workmanship. Along the way, this young broker realized that from thousand of ship yards over the world only three to four smaller and very sophisticated ship builders had enough experience and the facilities to do the job. By the time he had put one and one together, he had already lost this project to one of his competitors.

20.1.6 Yards Current Status and Conditions

Outside and inside dynamics have a significant impact on the ship builders. As outlined before, the shipbuilding industry is very volatile and naturally also the yards have to cope with constant changes. The newbuilding broker has to be aware of the shipbuilder's current status under the prevailing market circumstances, to advise the owner correctly. The following anecdote reveals the critical input of a broker towards safeguarding the interests of his principal.

A Greek ship owner once visited a ship yard in China and was impressed by the modern state of the art facilities that he inspected. On top, the yard offered him a very attractive price. When he returned back home from his trip, he was determined to place this order. By coincidence, his newbuilding broker had a telephone conversation with another client who was building a series of smaller bulk carriers at the same ship yard. Due to its nature, a bulk carrier normally is a simpler vessel to build. Therefore, the broker asked the client about his experience and if he was satisfied with the yard's performance. To his surprise, the owner was not satisfied at all with the performance. When the broker asked him for the reasons, he advised him that the majority of the experienced work force had left the shipyard and moved to other ship building facilities that offered them higher salaries. Thus, although the yard had very modern facilities and equipment, it was not able to build a quality vessel with timely delivery. Luckily, this order was never placed.

20.1.7 Yards Financial Status

Ship yards are enormous facilities that construct heavy industrial products. These facilities require the acquisition of land located at the sea or larger rivers and the construction of the shipbuilding facilities, dry docks, slip ways, heavy cranes, paint shops, etc. To construct a vessel, the builders have to purchase large amounts of steel and equipment. These operations are also very labor intensive. For example, the world's biggest ship builder Hyundai Heavy Industries in Korea employs 48,000 workers at their main yard in Ulsan alone. All these employees want to have their pay check at the end of the month.

Therefore, every shipyard has significant financial risks, which it has to manage throughout the very volatile shipping markets. This is an extremely difficult task and we have highest respect for those ship builders, which have managed to survive and to be successful throughout decades.

Because a ship owner places a significant amount of money to construct a vessel, the newbuilding broker should be in the position to accurately guide the owner in every respect, to prevent him from a loss. Of course, such losses can always be prevented through waterproof independent guarantees but a ship owner commits important financial resources to receive a ship in the end and not to have to deal with unreliable ship builders and having to claim back his investment through the guarantees with the banks.

20.1.8 The Letter of Intent

Once the initial phase of scanning the market and matching the newbuilding project with an appropriate yard, the serious deal-making phase begins. In jargon of brokers, the Letter of Intent (LoI) is considered as the beginning of the "engagement stage". One may lay fingers on the "bride" but he is not fully committed and bound to her. However, with an engagement one will have a strong moral commitment to someone and has laid a strong and solid foundation.

The LoI is the product of serious and firm negotiations between a ship owner and a shipyard after a specific builder has been selected. Both parties agree on the main terms and characteristics that lay the foundation for the shipbuilding contract itself.

The reader will find an executed LoI as an example here below, which lead to a shipbuilding contract. There is no standard format for a LoI but it should always cover at least the following points: The full style of the parties involved, type and number of the vessel(s), the vessel(s) price and the currency, the payment scheme, the delivery date of the vessel(s), subjects, jurisdiction and the validity of the LoI.

LETTER OF INTENT

This Letter of Intent is made on this 10th day of December 2012, by and between The Buying Company or its nominees (hereinafter called the "Buyer") and The Shipyard (hereinafter called the "Builder").

WHEREAS:

The Builder intends to build, launch, equip, complete and deliver firm two (2) plus optional up to two (2) units of 7,000 TEU container carrier (hereinafter called the "Vessels") as more fully specified herein below to the Buyer; and

The Buyer intends to purchase and take delivery of the Vessels from the Builder.

NOW, THEREFORE, both parties hereby intend to enter into Shipbuilding Contracts regarding the Vessels on the following terms and conditions.

1. **Type and Number of the Vessels**
   Firm two (2) plus optional up to two (2) units of 7,000TEU container carrier based on the Builder's outline specifications (Ref. No. DP07-13027TB, dated July 31, 2012).and sketched GA plan(Ref. No. DP07-12026TB, dated August 29, 2012).
2. **Price (Ex-yard and 1% commission included) per unit**
   USD65,000,000.- (United States Dollars Sixty Five Million only)
3. **Payment terms**

   - 1st Installment: Ten percent (20%) of the Price upon Contract Signing and receipt by Buyers of Refund Guarantee

(continued)

- 2nd Installment: Ten percent (20%) of the Price upon Six(6) Month after the Contract Signing and receipt by Buyers of Refund Guarantee
- 3rd Installment: Ten percent (10%) of the Price upon Keel Laying
- 4th Installment: Seventy percent (50%) of the Price upon Delivery

4. **Delivery (Ex-yard)**
   The vessel shall be delivered to the Buyer at the Builder's shipyard in "Location X" as follows:

   a. Firm two (2) vessels:

   - 1st unit within the end of September 2014
   - 2nd unit within the end of October 2014

   b. Optional two (2) vessels:

   - 1st unit within the end of December 2014
   - 2nd unit within the end of March 2015

5. **Others**

   a. The optional two (2) units shall be declared by the Buyer within three (3) months after the contract singing and receipt by Buyers of Refund Guarantee of firm two (2) units.
   b. Refund Guarantee shall be issued by the first class Korean bank acceptable to the Buyer.
   c. If the contractual buyer for the Vessels is a special purpose company who has no substance, then the Buyer shall, upon signing the Contract, provide the Builder with irrevocable and unconditional performance guarantee from "The Buying Company" for the due and faithful performance of the Buyer under the Contract.
   d. Flag: intention
   e. Subject review and agreement of full specification and makers list.
   f. Subject agreement of all other terms and conditions.

6. **Confidentiality**
   This Letter of Intent shall be kept strictly private and confidential and no details to be disclosed to any third party until the execution of firm contract.
7. **Validity**
   This Letter of Intent shall be valid on or before [Specific Date]. Should both parties not sign the shipbuilding contracts within aforementioned validity, this Letter of Intent shall be null and void without either party hereto incurring any liability to the other party.
8. **Governing Law, Jurisdiction, and Entire Agreement**
   This Letter of Intent shall be governed by the English law, shall be subject to the exclusive jurisdiction of the High Court of Justice in London,

(continued)

England, and shall constitute the only and entire agreement between the parties and unless otherwise expressly agreed between the parties, all other agreement, oral or written, made and entered into between the parties prior to the execution of this Letter of Intent shall be null and void.

IN WITNESS WHEREOF, both parties have caused this Letter of Intent to be duly executed on the day and year first above written.

For and on behalf of the Buyer	For and on behalf of the Builder
Name:	Name:
Title:	Title:

The result of the main terms will be determined by the bargaining power of each party, which heavily depends on the market cycle and the reputation, and size of the companies. Further, it will be influenced by the human beings involved, including the newbuilding broker.

It is apparent from the example above that the technical specifications, including all technical drawings, the list of suppliers, and the shipbuilding contract have to be concluded within a certain validity period that usually covers a period of around two to six weeks. Should both parties fail to agree within the validity on the technical-, contractual- or other aspects, the deal itself would become null and void. During this phase, both parties will set technical and commercial meetings to form the full technical specifications and the shipbuilding contract. It is the role of the newbuilding broker to assist both parties in every respect of this process, to establish effective communication between the various managers in charge, to coordinate and lead the meetings and negotiations, to solve occurring problems by bringing in his newbuilding experience, by handling the human aspect and by being creative and finding compromise solutions which are to the benefit of both sides.

20.1.9 Technical Specifications and List of Suppliers

The technical departments of the buyer and the ship yard together with the newbuilding broker will arrange technical meetings to form the full technical specifications including all drawings that have to be agreed and signed by both parties. The ship yard will try to keep the specifications to a certain standard that allows standardized production and the major concern is on the production phase of 18–24 months. However, the ship owner builds a vessel to operate same over a life time cycle of around 20 years and will have to anticipate the future and make sure that all recent technology improvements will be included and that all rules and regulations are met so that his vessel will be competitive in the years to come and to be best prepared to meet an uncertain future. The broker will have to be aware of these adverse interests and to negotiate best possible and practical solution and compromise for both parties.

The list of suppliers is an important document that plays a significant role for both parties in terms of quality and cost. The yard will be interested to include a variety of suppliers to be able to negotiate the prices of the different equipment in a most cost saving manner and to bring down the overall building cost. Therefore, the yard will also try to insert local and low cost equipment makers instead of highly sophisticated European equipment suppliers. Logically, the ship owner is interested to apply the highest standards to his vessel that will increase the overall safety, quality, and value of his vessel. It will also determine the performance of the vessel. Therefore, the owner is biased to certain equipment makers, often through his experience on his existing fleet, because of an existing relationship of trust and confidentiality, also and especially when technical service and support is required. A makers list that contains solid and reliable equipment manufacturers can drive the value of the vessel at a later stage once it enters the second-hand market quite significantly. It is also important to note that the value of the equipment built into the ship is more important than the hull itself. Thus, the makers list carries great importance in the course of the negotiations.

20.1.10 The Shipbuilding Contract

The shipbuilding contract consists of the negotiated main terms, the full technical specifications which have to be agreed and signed by both parties during the technical meetings and all other basic terms and conditions which will be referred to hereunder.

20.1.11 Description and Class

Under the first clause of the shipbuilding contract, the vessel has to be properly described. Special reference will be made to the full specifications, the general arrangement drawings and the makers list which form an integral part thereof and contain the main dimensions which include the deadweight at design and scantling draft, the length over all (LOA), the beam, the draft and the depth of the vessel. In addition, other crucial parameters and technical figures are described in the first clause and the full specifications such as the selected classification society, rules, and regulations that are applicable at the point of time, estimated speed and consumption, the layout of the tanks or cargo holds and the stability of the vessel among many other important items.

Furthermore, it should be stated that the shipbuilder undertakes that the quality of the design, construction, testing and trials of the vessel, the quality of the vessel and of her workmanship shall be in accordance with good and sound shipbuilding practice at major shipyards; and in accordance with the rules and regulations with the edition and amendments thereto being in force and effect as of the date of the shipbuilding contract, together with all mandatory rules and regulations and amendments thereto, which have already been ratified up to the date of contract signature and to come into force prior to the delivery date of the vessel under survey of the classification society. The exact meaning of *good and sound shipbuilding practice* will be defined at a later stage in the contract.

The ship builder will reserve his right, at his sole responsibility, but in almost all cases with prior written notice to the buyer, to subcontract a defined portion of the construction work to experienced subcontractors outside of the shipyard. Through this method, the yard may save cost and time to construct the final product.

20.1.12 Contract Price

The final shipbuilding price in the contract will most probably vary from the negotiated price under the LoI. This will depend on the chosen equipment makers and the extra items that have been added during the technical discussions at an extra cost for the buyer. In addition, the newbuilding price is a reflection of the shipping cycles. Once the orderbook has been shrinking like it was the case in the years after the beginning shipping crisis after 2008, shipyards try to attract orders through competitive pricing.

The price will include the payment for services for the inspection, tests, survey, and classification of the vessel that will be rendered by the classification society. However, it will not include the cost of the buyer's supplies which will be dealt with at later clauses.

The majority of the newbuilding prices will be fixed in United States Dollars.

20.1.13 Adjustment of the Contract Price

The ship owner may be entitled to adjust the contract price in line with this clause or to have the right to fully terminate the shipbuilding contract as a whole. In our experience, shipbuilders and ship owners have most difficulties to find an agreement on these items, because these clauses can become commercially very important to both parties. Again, it will be the current bargaining power of each party that will shape the result of this article and the type of the vessel. For example, a container carrier is competing at higher speed and consumption levels than other type of vessels. The owner has a high risk should the vessel be of insufficient speed or excessive fuel oil consumption and will therefore ask for a higher compensation should the actual figures deviate from the estimated figures in the specifications. Should a ship owner back his order with a time charter employment where the charterer is entitled to cancel the charter party after a certain period of time, he will ask the builder for a greater compensation under the terms of *delayed delivery* to ensure that the builder does everything he can to deliver the vessel without delay.

Usually under every of the following clauses the builder will be granted a certain grace under which the contract price remains unchanged. Should specific occurrences exceed the defined boundaries, the buyer will be entitled to terminate the contract.

20.1.13.1 Delayed Delivery

The normal grace period is 30 calendar days. After such due date, the contract price of the vessel shall be reduced by a certain amount under the same currency for each full day. Examples vary from US$6,000 per day to US$40,000 per day. If the delay in delivery of the vessel continues for a period of more than 150–210 days, the buyer may at his option cancel the contract.

20.1.13.2 Insufficient Speed

This case is highly influenced by the ship type. In cases where a certain minimum speed is important, the ship builder will not be granted more than (3/10) of a not grace. Thereafter the contract price shall be adjusted for each full one-tenth (1/10) of a knot in excess of the said three-tenths (3/10) of a knot of deficiency in speed. In most cases, the ship owner is entitled to cancel the shipbuilding contract if the deficiency of the actual speed exceeds one full knot.

20.1.13.3 Excessive Fuel Consumption

The grace of the excessive fuel oil consumption includes the grace of the engine maker and the grace of the builder. It varies from about 4 to 8 %. Considering today's bunker prices and the environmental awareness of today, this clause has become more and more important.

20.1.13.4 Deadweight Below Contract Requirements

The deadweight is referred to in metric tons. The grace depends on the size of vessel but we have not seen that it exceeds more than 1,800 mt.

It is clear that the events when an adjustment of the contract price is possible are totally independent from each other.

20.1.14 Inspection and Approval

Under almost all shipbuilding contracts buyers have the right to appoint one or more representative(s) to supervise the shipbuilding process and work which is carried out by the shipyard during the shipbuilding phase. The supervisor is appointed by the buyer for the purpose of determining that the vessel, her equipment and accessories are being constructed in accordance with the terms of the contract and/or the specifications. The supervisor will be present during the testing phases of the vessel, which are carried out by the builder and the classification society as an observer. This will be the model tests and the sea trials prior to the delivery of the vessel. The necessary tests and inspection by the classification society and other regulatory bodies concerned shall be recorded and all results of quality control and tests and inspections shall be communicated to the Buyer's representatives. The supervision of the buyer's representatives will be under the buyer's own cost and the article will clearly describe the level of authority and limits the representative will possess. Such supervision teams can be very expensive and the size of the team will be determined by the experience of the ship yard.

There are also ship yards in Japan that do not allow any supervision from the owner during the construction period of the vessels.

Furthermore, the buyer will have to approve the drawings and plans that will be submitted by the ship builder within a reasonable period agreed by both parties hereunder. In most cases, such approval or comments will have to be submitted within 2–3 weeks. Thereafter the reply time of the ship builder will be specified. Should the buyer or his representative fail to approve or comment on the plans and drawings within the time limit as specified hereunder, such plans and drawings shall be deemed to have been automatically approved without any comment. In the event the plans and drawings do not meet with the buyer's approval, and the ship builder does not agree with the buyer's comments, the matter may be submitted to the classification society.

20.1.15 Trials and Completion

After her completion, the vessel will conduct her trials at a specific location, date, and time. This is a very crucial event, in which the ship yard will have to prove under the presence of the classification society and the buyer's representative that the vessel complies with the shipbuilding contract and the vessel's specifications. The shipbuilding contract and the vessel's specifications will describe how the trials will be conducted and under which weather conditions they will be allowed to take place. After the trial run, the classification society and the shipbuilder will present the results to the buyer who can either approve or reject the conformity of the vessel or certain parts of the equipment. It will be decided which parts require alteration or correction within a reasonable time frame.

20.1.16 Delivery

The delivery date of the vessel will be set under this clause. Under most agreements this will be at the location of the ship yard, safely afloat after completion of satisfactory tests, trials and acceptance by the buyer, except that, in the event of delays in delivery of the vessel which under the terms of the shipbuilding contract permit extensions of the time for delivery. The delivery of the vessel is the most important event and the title and risk will be shifted from the ship builder to the buyer who will become the physical owner of the vessel.

The buyer has to pay the last installment after having received the final notice from the yard and the builder will furnish the buyer with all necessary delivery documents such as the protocol of trials, the protocol of inventory of the equipment and spare parts, the protocol of stores of consumable nature (such as all fuel oil and fresh water remaining in tanks and other relating items), finished drawings and plans including the trim and stability booklet, all certificates such as the classification certificate, the safety construction certificate, the safety equipment certificate, the safety radio certificate, the international loadline certificate and the international tonnage certificate.

The buyer has to take possession of the vessel immediately upon delivery thereof and has to remove the ship from the delivery location within a short period of time. Port dues and other charges levied by government authorities after delivery of the vessel and any other costs related to the removal have to be borne by the buyer.

Other clauses such as warranty of quality, permissible, non permissible and excessive delay of delivery, builder's and buyer's default, buyer's supplies etc will go into too much detail and will not be referred to by the authors. The aim of the clauses described and explained here and above is to outline the duties and obligations of both parties and the complexity of the shipbuilding process. The newbuilding broker will be fully involved in forming and executing this document.

20.2 The Shipbuilding Phase

The role of the newbuilding broker is to ensure that both parties fulfill their duties and obligations during the construction phase as per the shipbuilding contract. Again, his presence is required should any problem or dispute arise and therefore it is important for him to monitor and coordinate any written exchange, to keep close contact to both parties and to stay on top of everything. The main duty of the shipbuilder is to timely fulfill the key events and the main duty of the ship owner is to deliver Buyer's supply items in a timely manner, to make punctual payments according to the agreed payment scheme that is linked to those key events and to take over the vessel on delivery (Fig. 20.3).

This sounds all very easy and straight forward but in practice many problems may occur due to internal or external factors. Periods of financial distress have

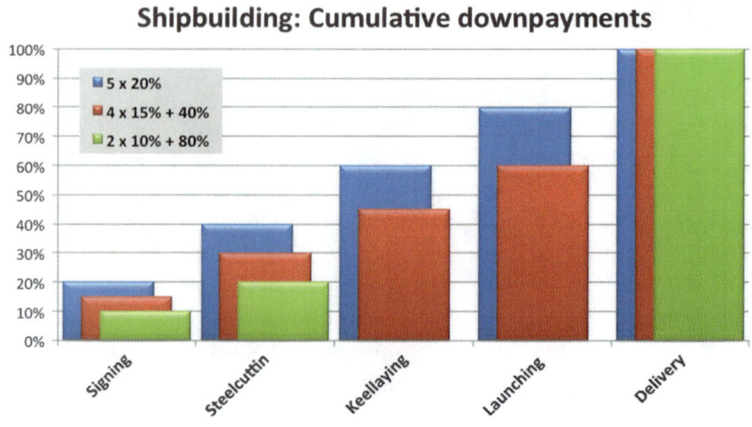

Fig. 20.3 Common cumulative downpayment schemes. *Source*: Authors' compilation

a significant impact on shipping and the liquidity crunch impacts severely the shipbuilding activity. As in the case of the post-Lehman crisis years, ship owners might be faced with lack of finance, diminishing sources of equity, decreased demand in world trade that resulted in very low charter rates for the tramp owners and significant losses for both operators and tramp owners. In almost all cases the loan agreements between the banks and the ship owners contained the so called *loan to value clause* which kicked in the event that value of the vessel fell. Most of the modern tonnage as of today was ordered pre Lehman at the peak of the market cycle where finance was available. When the market fell, the values of the assets decreased dramatically, forcing the ship owners to inject additional equity where at the time no equity or alternative finance was available. Many ship owners had no means to fulfill their payment obligation under the shipbuilding contract and we as the newbuilding broker were requested to approach the shipbuilder to find solutions such as to defer the payments to a later point of time, to ask for yard's credit or to cancel the whole newbuilding contract. Others requested us to convert the newbuildings into different ship types where the market outlook was more prosperous or to delay the whole delivery of the vessels, due to the low cargo volume in the hope that the market would recover later on. All solutions imposed a significant impact for the shipbuilders in terms of revenue, cash flow and their production schedule. In these situations, a good and experienced newbuilding broker can distinguish himself from his competitors, by finding and proposing one of the above compromises or solutions with the least pain for both parties.

20.2.1 Resale Opportunities

A shipping company does not necessarily earn most of their money from trading the vessels and transferring goods and commodities from point A to B. It is the asset play that acts a significant role for the ship owner and underlies constant changes due to volatility of the shipping market and its various segments. The completion of a vessel normally takes around 18–24 months. During this period, the value of a vessel may substantially increase or decrease. For example, during the shipping boom from 2004 to mid 2008 these values where at a constant rise (see Fig. 20.1).

The market has seen cases where during the shipbuilding process the price of a vessel rose by US$10,000,000–20,000,000, enabling the Owner to resell the shipbuilding contract to a third party. Obviously, this was a very favorable situation for these owners enabling them to generate a substantial and quick profit for only holding a contract and not even having taken delivery of the vessel. The above example is not a single case but was observed many times during these years.

The role of the newbuilding broker is to make the ship owner aware of such arising opportunities.

20.2.2 After Sales Service/Problem Solving

After successful delivery of the vessel from the ship builder to the ship owner the newbuilding broker will work to maintain a good relationship between both parties with the long term goal to establish a fresh newbuilding contract in the future.

This can take place in different ways by solving immediate problems after the delivery of the vessel, by exchanging important market information between both parties and by organizing and coordinating courtesy visits between the technical and commercial staff of both companies. He will furnish both parties with any developments that the companies may undergo during the often dramatic changes of the shipping markets.

20.3 Concluding Remarks

Considering the above analysis, it is apparent that the newbuilding broker is not only representing the interests of a yard or of an owner, but at the same time acts as buffer. One could also assume that the broker is also assisting in the financing of the newbuildings. This is in many cases true. However, it is beyond doubt that the decisions supported and the directions offered by the broker dictate at large the fate of the investment. The selection of the yard, the negotiation of the costs and of the makers' lists, determine the capital expenses of the ship and influence its financial performance. A newbuilding project is very complicated and the assistance of the broker is critical, because of his troubleshooting capabilities and the nature of his role as intermediary.

About the Editors

Orestis Schinas is the Professor of Shipping and Ship Finance and Head of the Maritime Business School of the Hamburg School of Business Administration (HSBA) since 2008. He has served in senior and top-management positions and has a vast experience in the maritime and logistics industry and has offered his services to private and public entities as well as to international organizations. His professional career includes large corporate and business development projects as well as advanced research assignments in the maritime and port sectors. He holds a Dipl.-Ing. degree in Naval Architecture and Marine Engineering (NTUA, 1994), a Masters in Shipping Management (WMU, 1998) and he was awarded the doctoral title in 2005 (NTUA) for his thesis on Ship Finance. His work is published in major business and academic journals.

Carsten Grau is German lawyer—Rechtsanwalt—and Solicitor (England and Wales). He has practiced maritime and corporate law in Bremen and Hamburg since 1998 and specializes in advising corporate entities and individuals in all areas of maritime business. At HSBA, he is module responsible for the maritime law contents in the M.B.A. Shipping programme. He holds a law degree from the University of Hamburg and a German and Liberian Master Mariner License.

Max Johns is Managing Director at VDR German Ship owners' Association in Hamburg. He is teaching ship finance at the Maritime Business School of the Hamburg School of Business Administration (HSBA) since 2008. He holds B.A. and M.A. degrees from Université Paul Valéry Montpellier III in France, an M.B.A. from KU Leuven in Belgium and was awarded the doctoral title from the University of Tübingen in Germany. He publishes frequently on maritime issues.

O. Schinas et al. (eds.), *HSBA Handbook on Ship Finance*,

DOI 10.1007/978-3-662-43410-9, © Springer-Verlag Berlin Heidelberg 2015

Index

O. Schinas et al. (eds.), *HSBA Handbook on Ship Finance*,
DOI 10.1007/978-3-662-43410-9, © Springer-Verlag Berlin Heidelberg 2015

Printed by Printforce, the Netherlands